CHILDREN'S LAW HANDBOOK

Justice Marvin A. Zuker
Randolph C. Hammond, B.A. (Hon.), LL.B.
Roderick C. Flynn, B.A. (Hon.), LLB.

THOMSON
CARSWELL

© 2005 Thomson Canada Limited

NOTICE AND DISCLAIMER: All rights reserved. No part of this publication may be reproduced, stored in a retrieval system, or transmitted, in any form or by any means, electronic, mechanical, photocopying, recording, or otherwise, without the prior written permission of the publisher (Carswell).

Carswell and all persons involved in the preparation and sale of this publication disclaim any warranty as to accuracy or currency of the publication. This publication is provided on the understanding and basis that none of Carswell, the author's or other persons involved in the creation of this publication shall be responsible for the accuracy or currency of the contents, or for the results of any action taken on the basis of the information contained in this publication, or for any errors or omissions contained herein. No one involved in this publication is attempting herein to render legal, accounting, or other professional advice.

Library and Archives Canada Cataloguing in Publication

Flynn, Roderick C. (Roderick Cavill), 1966-
   Children's law handbook / Roderick C. Flynn, Randolph C. Hammond, Marvin A. Zuker.

Includes bibliographical references and index.
ISBN 0-459-24265-2

   1. Children—Legal status, laws, etc.—Canada. 2. Youth—Legal status, laws, etc.—Canada. I. Zuker, Marvin A. II. Hammond, Randolph C. III. Title.

KF512.F59 2005   346.7101'35   C2005-906029-8

KF479.F59 2005

Composition: Computer Composition of Canada Inc.

One Corporate Plaza, 2075 Kennedy Road, Toronto, Ontario M1T 3V4
Customer Relations:
Toronto 1-416-609-3800
Elsewhere in Canada/U.S. 1-800-387-5164   www.carswell.com
Fax 1-416-298-5082   carswell.orders@thomson.com

A THOUGHT, OR MAYBE A FOREWORD

In a perfect world, every baby born in this country will be loved by knowledgeable adults because some learned to be good parents from the adults who raised them, and because everyone, well-loved or not, received compulsory parenting education in schools. Every baby will be nourished and protected. Babies will be encouraged to play and, in play, those small persons will be excited by their rapidly expanding skills. People will sing to babies, read to babies, cuddle babies. Regulated early children education facilities will be available for all toddlers, on the same government-financed basis as high schools are available to teenagers—as a right with proven benefits.

Every child will go to school well fed, emotionally secure, and eager and ready to learn. Poverty may not be eradicated, not completely, but housing will be affordable for all so that family life can be stabilized. With secure housing, children's schooling will be anchored. Because they have consistency in their lives, children will be able to form deep and lasting friendships.

Developers and city planners will be required to provide play spaces for children and recreational facilities for teens, much as they now are obliged to provide parking spaces for cars.

Everyone in the full-time work force will be paid salaries and benefits sufficient to maintain themselves above the poverty line.

When all that happens, and the good news is that it has started, the country will be transformed. Most adults will be able to function at their best and appreciate one another. Experts say crime, addiction, mental illness and suicide would be greatly reduced. If better lives for children could become a worldwide reality, it is not outrageous to believe that wars and genocide would end. It *could* happen, if only humans cared about their young half as much as the rest of the animal kingdom does about its progeny.

Judge Marvin Zuker's superb report on children and the law is an important part of what is changing in this country, as we progress in the development of a holistic approach to safeguarding children. It is reminiscent of another judge, Thomas Berger of British Columbia, who, in the 1970s, created a prophetic bill of rights for children that was pointed in the same direction. It was viewed then as wildly impractical and unrealistic, except by those who also understood the needs of children. Wherever the Berger document is now, dust might be deep upon it, though it was saturated in wisdom and insight. One notable observation Berger made was that every child is entitled to a "receivable education". That is a powerful concept, yet to be realized.

Judge Zuker strikes out on the same path, using as his tool the weapon of matchless research. He has collected in his fine book all the laws relating to children. *Children's Law Handbook*, not incidentally, also shows the failure of existing legal approaches to guarantee children even basic necessities. This makes it not only an essential handbook for today's families and for professionals who deal with children, but also a useful resource for lawmakers and program developers who are now vigorously engaged in making changes on behalf of children.

Canada only recently became serious about legislation and programs aimed at helping children thrive, and the movement now in progress can learn much from this overview of what is happening now. I am very grateful to Marvin Zuker for his comprehensive and solidly researched status report. The journey this nation has begun, after a century of patchwork, underfunded and botched exercises, is desperately in need of information of this quality.

In a generation, or maybe two, Canadian newborns will be off to the infinite blessing of a good start. If that happens, they are very likely to unfold as very fine, flourishing adults. What better gift could we give our young, or our country? Thanks, Marvin.

June Callwood

PREFACE

Educators (and others working with children) who find themselves in court are there because they did not know the relevant law or did not practice sound management based on an understanding of existing court decisions. This book will help them better understand various legal principles and will give them a stronger foundation for their interaction with young persons.

We designed this book to be a desk reference where those who work with children can quickly find and identify important legal points to consider during decision-making processes when such decisions may have legal consequences. To further assist in that process, as far as possible, we have used straightforward, non-technical language and followed a standard format in presenting pertinent information. This book and the statements of the authors represent an attempt to respond to the professional needs of the reader. The case law interpretation is not designed as statements of final authority. Only a court of law, guided by individual case facts, can be considered as an authority on a specific issue. An issue may be treated differently from court to court, province to province.

This book serves a purpose for the education profession and other professionals who work with children. It should not be considered a forecaster of impending or future litigation. It should also be noted that any guidelines suggested should be treated with caution in light of the specific subject matter examined and the expected level of personal involvement. There are those administrative and teaching responsibilities that transcend the norm, requiring a higher degree of duty and care, supervision, instruction, and maintenance. This book is designed to provide accurate and authoritative information with regard to the subject matter covered. In publishing this book, neither the authors nor the publisher is engaged in rendering legal service. If legal advice or assistance is required, the services of a competent lawyer should be sought.

John Milton foresaw students' cries long ago when he stated: "Give me the liberty to know, to utter, and to argue freely according to conscience, above all liberties."

Moreover, youths are demanding the liberty to be and to become themselves.

John Stuart Mill made the distinction between formal freedom and effective freedom. He tells that formal freedom entailed the removal of legal and authoritative barriers in exercising one's rights and that effective freedom required that the individual be protected from repressive social customs and private retribution for exercising his or her rights such as supporting an unpopular cause.

Laws reflect the society that develops them. Similarly, judges operate within a social context that influences the outcome of litigation concerning particular issues. Consequently, laws and judicial decisions reflect the political trends, philosophical attitudes, ethical viewpoints, and even the tendency toward compassion that prevail when legislatures enact them and courts interpret them.

Children and teenagers mature cognitively and emotionally through their life experiences, education, and guidance from adults. They, however, do not acquire knowledge, reason, and wisdom without trial and tribulation. It is incumbent on adults to aid children in their growth and through this often difficult process by articulating expectations, by instructing children when they err, by establishing reasonable responses to undesirable behaviour, and by helping them to develop better problem-solving and social skills.

A goal of this book is to provide comprehensive and practical knowledge of relevant and contemporary issues that affect children. Practicing and prospective educational leaders, students of educational leadership, teachers, prospective teachers, policy-makers at all educational levels and other professionals will hopefully gain knowledge that will help them effectively perform their professional duties having regard to the information provided.

This book is organized and written in a style that facilitates ease of reading even for those individuals who have little or no legal background. Significant court cases that address the issues most relevant to effective practice have been carefully selected. The text begins with an in-depth focused discussion of major legal issues followed by relevant constitutional issues, statutory considerations, and case law. Legal citations are used to support and enhance the discussion of these issues. Legal references, where indicated, are found on each page supporting the topics under discussion, thus enabling the reader to easily ascertain the legal sources of authority related to those particular topics.

Chapter 1 offers the background to facilitate a better understanding of succeeding chapters. This includes a discussion of who is a child and an overview of provincial and federal legislation that impacts a "child", depending on his or her age, be it the federal *Youth Criminal Justice Act* dealing with children over the age of 12 or the Ontario *Child and Family Services Act*, which deals with apprehending and protecting children under the age of 12 who may have been involved in what otherwise might well be serious criminal behaviour.

Chapter 2 examines the extent and authority of the state/ province to deal with children in need of protection, the laws of child abuse, mandatory reporting of child abuse, and of course the role of Children's Aid Societies in our child protection legislation.

Chapter 3 deals with the evidence of children both from a common law and statutory perspective, such as the difficulties inherent in a child actually giving evidence in a courtroom, what is required of them, the uniqueness attached to being a child, issues of necessity and reliability, understanding what it means to tell the truth, and simply a child's ability to communicate, to tell his or her story.

The repatriation of our Constitution, on April 17, 1982, and in particular the *Canadian Charter of Rights and Freedoms*, Part 1 of the *Constitution Act, 1982*, is the focus of Chapter 4. The application of the *Charter* to the "family" as we have known it and the concept of "the best interest of the child", from a *Charter* perspective are thoroughly discussed.

Custody and access of children is dealt with in Chapter 5. These terms, of course, have evolved over the passage of time, as has the "family" changed over the last century. Perhaps family law is the area of the law that most mirrors changes in our society. At the beginning of the 20th century, children were treated as property and "owned" by their fathers, then became presumptively better off with their mothers. Now of course, the Ontario *Children's Law Reform Act* makes it clear that both parents are equally entitled to the custody of the child. Then came "joint" custody" with its variety of meanings as reflected in the back of a particular case, and more laterally we have the concept of parallel parenting. In any event, the best interests of the child must be the court's paramount consideration.

The *Youth Criminal Justice Act*, discussed in Chapter 6, goes beyond the previous *Young Offenders Act* of 1984, itself having replaced the *Juvenile Delinquents Act*, which was introduced in 1908 as Canada's first legislation to govern young persons in conflict with the law. The *Youth Criminal Justice Act* clearly expresses some new ideas with respect to youth justice as well as the best practices learned from history. The principles in the *Youth Criminal Justice Act* are clearer and have been inserted in the applicable sections throughout the Act rather than lumped altogether as they were in the *Young Offenders Act*. Protection of society is a key goal of this Act, and this is achieved by preventing crime, applying meaningful consequences for youth crime, and rehabilitating and reintegrating youth. There is greater emphasis on victim participation and repair to the victim and the community.

The definitions in this legislation have been expanded and include new definitions, such as extra-judicial measures, serious violent offences, and expanded presumptive offences. Extra-judicial measures also introduce the ability to establish police and Crown caution programs. Extra-judicial sanctions replace the alternative measures program under the *Young Offenders Act* and mark the beginning of a youth record that may later be used in court. Conferences can be convened to assist at various stages in the informal and formal proceedings, and the judiciary may cause a conference to be convened to give advice on sentencing.

Chapter 7 of the book deals with the use of force to "correct" a child's behavior if it is "reasonable", as set out in section 43 of Canada's *Criminal Code*. The Canadian Foundation for Children, Youth, and the Law (otherwise known as Justice for Children and Youth), challenged section 43 based on the constitutional argument that it infringes on child's equality rights under section 15 of the *Charter*. The case was originally commenced in the Ontario Court (General Division), now the Superior Court, in 1998. Justice McCombs ruled that section 43 was constitutional and dismissed the application. On January 15, 2002 the Ontario Court of Appeal dismissed the appeal and again upheld the constitutionality of this section stating that the objective of the section is to permit ". . .parents or persons standing in the place of parents '...to apply strictly limited corrective force to children without criminal sanctions so that they can carry out their important responsibilities to train and nurture children without the harm that such sanctions would bring to them, to their tasks and to the families concerned'". The decision of the Ontario Court of Appeal was upheld by the Supreme Court of Canada in January 2004.

Chapter 8 deals with children and education, with an overview as to how Ontario's *Education Act*, its regulations, and other provincial statutes and common law principles impact on children.

Chapter 9 deals with the obligation to pay child support, an area of concurrent jurisdiction between the Federal, Provincial and Territorial governments. The procedure necessary to obtain an order for child support therefore depends on the legislation and rules of practice governing the particular court. We discuss the implications in determining child support with the advent of the Federal Child Support Guidelines on May 1, 1997. We have provided an overview in an attempt to safely interpret the words of the regulations and the relationship between these regulators and the relevant legislation.

Chapter 10 provides a brief overview dealing with issues of information disclosure, assessments, and the Office of the Children's Lawyer. A person charged with an offence has a constitutional right to disclosure, enshrined in section 7 of the *Canadian Charter of Rights and Freedoms*, as a component of the right to make full answer and defence. Third parties can be ordered to produce relevant materials, pursuant to the O'Connor decision, which we address in this chapter. Disclosure, of course, may be subject to privacy rights.

The provisions of the *Evidence Act* of Ontario or Canada's *Evidence Act* and the common law apply to evidence at trial.

Under section 30 of the CLRA, a court has the authority to appoint an assessor to report to the court on the needs of the child and the ability and willingness of the parents, or either one of them, to satisfy those needs.

An assessment report is an expert report for trial. It is evidence and therefore subject to the rigors of cross-examination at trial. The assessment report will provide the judge with the child's views and preferences and that child's best interests through the eyes of an independent professional.

In Ontario, the Office of the Children's Lawyer is a separate office within the Ministry of the Attorney General, which is responsible for advocating on behalf of children under the age of majority.

Once the Children's Lawyer agrees to represent the child, it has the authority to carry out a variety of functions. The Children's Lawyer may request the assistance of a social worker. A social worker may perform a variety of functions. He or she may prepare a report comparable to a section 30 assessment on the needs of the child.

Appendices provide additional information enabling the reader to gain a broader perspective. We thought it most important to include the most relevant sections of the laws that impact on our children, as referred to in the book. This should prove invaluable to the reader who does not have access to a law library or a friendly lawyer. Certainly readers are encouraged to read the entire court decisions and statutes where they have a particular interest. Cases are cited to facilitate this goal.

The book's purpose is to provide those involved with children with a knowledge base for making sound decisions within our legal framework. Having such knowledge may reduce the tendency to act on the basis of what the law should be rather than what it is. In that sense, this book stresses the descriptive, and not the prescriptive. This book does not serve as a substitute for competent legal advice should such counsel be required. However, an understanding of the material in this book should help foster a more fruitful exchange with any solicitor when that is necessary.

In completing this book, we are truly indebted to many persons, too numerous to list, who provided us with indispensable support.

At Thomson Carswell, our very special thanks go to Julia Gulej, Fred Glady and Todd Pinsky. Particular recognition should go to Ainsley Davison of Thomson Carswell; a terrific editor who gently but meticulously shaped our manuscript into this final product. Kudos as well to Ken Mathies for his fine work regarding the cover design. Thanks too should go to Andrew Lawetz for his help with marketing and promotion.

Roderick C. Flynn would like to thank his family for their support and understanding during the currency of this project. Recognition should go as well to my law partners, Eric J. Bundgard and Richard Evenson, and to my secretary, Jennifer Short. I would like to dedicate my part of this book to the memory of my late mother, Florence Cavill Flynn, who committed her life to her work with children, both in the classroom and at home.

Randy Hammond would like to thank his colleague and friend, Tamra Mann, Robinson Mann and his parents, Claire and Catherine Hammond, as well as his nephews Nicholas Knechtel and Carter Huxley.

Marvin Zuker would like to thank June Callwood for her incredibly thoughtful remarks in the Foreword, keeping in mind, however, that if it were not for the co-authors, this project would never have been completed.

Marvin A. Zuker
Randolph C. Hammond
Roderick C. Flynn
October 2005

TABLE OF CONTENTS

Foreword iii
Preface vii
Table of Cases xxiii

1 — WHO IS THE CHILD? 1
AGE 7 AND OVER 2
UNDER AGE 10 2
AGE 12 AND UNDER 3
OVER THE AGE OF 12 3
OVER THE AGE OF 14 5
AGE 15 6
AGE 16 6
OVER 17 8
AGE 18 8
AGE 19 9
UNDER 21 10

2 — AN INTRODUCTION TO THE *CHILD AND FAMILY SERVICES ACT* 13
WHAT IS CHILD PROTECTION LEGISLATION? 14
WHEN IS A CHILD IN NEED OF PROTECTION? 17
THE *CHILD AND FAMILY SERVICES ACT* 24
DIFFERENT JURISDICTIONS 26
CHILD PROTECTION DIFFERS FROM CUSTODY 26
STATUTORY PATHWAY 28
ROLE OF THE STATE IN THE PRIVATE SPHERE 31
BEST INTERESTS 32
NOT A CRIMINAL MATTER 33
DEFINITION OF A CHILD 34
LIMITED TO PROTECTING FROM PERSONS IN CHARGE 35
HOW DOES A SOCIETY ANALYZE A REPORT OF ABUSE? .. 37
VOLUNTARY INTERVENTION – PART II OF THE CFSA 37
INVOLUNTARY INTERVENTION – PART III OF THE
    CFSA 39
PLAN OF CARE 45
TIMELINES 46
DUTY TO REPORT 48

IMPORTANCE OF THE DUTY TO REPORT AND
CONSEQUENCES OF NOT REPORTING 52

3 — THE EVIDENCE OF CHILDREN 57
RULES OF EVIDENCE 57
EVIDENCE IN FAMILY LAW 58
THE GENERAL APPROACH OF THE LAW TO CHILDREN'S
   EVIDENCE 59
RULES OF EVIDENCE IN FAMILY LAW 60
EVIDENCE STATUTES 61
PROCESSING A CHILD'S EVIDENCE 62
   (a) An Inquiry 62
   (b) Assessing Competency to Take an Oath or Affirmation
       64
   (c) Ability to Communicate: Testimonial Competence 64
   (d) Promise to Tell the Truth: Unsworn Testimony 65
   (e) The Role of the Trial Judge 67
   (f) Court Assessment of Children's Evidence 67
ADMISSION OF HEARSAY EVIDENCE OF A CHILD 69
WEIGHT OF OUT-OF-COURT STATEMENT – CHILD NOT
   TESTIFYING 72
   (a) Was the Statement Made? 73
   (b) The Need for Caution 73
CHILDREN'S VIDEOTAPED EVIDENCE 74
VOIR DIRE 77
CROSS-EXAMINATION 79
CREDIBILITY OF CHILDREN 81
CHILDREN'S WISHES 82

4 — THE *CHARTER*, CIVIL RIGHTS AND CHILDREN 85
THE FAMILY 87
THE FAMILY AND THE *CHARTER* 88
CHILD PROTECTION 95
CHILD ABUSE 99
   (a) Sexual Abuse of Children 100
   (b) Allegations of Sexual Assault and Schools 102
   (c) Offence 103
RIGHTS OF UNBORN CHILDREN 104

5 — AN INTRODUCTION TO CUSTODY AND ACCESS 109

HOW CUSTODY AND ACCESS DIFFERS FROM CHILD PROTECTION	114
"BEST INTERESTS TEST"	117
DEVELOPMENT OF BEST INTERESTS AS PRIMARY TEST	117
CUSTODY AND ACCESS LEGISLATION	121
(a) The *Divorce Act*	122
(b) The *Children's Law Reform Act*	122
(c) Applying the *Divorce Act* and the CLRA to Custody/Access Matters	122
WHO MAY APPLY FOR CUSTODY OR ACCESS?	124
BEST INTERESTS TEST UNDER THE TWO ACTS	124
(a) The Meaning of the "Best Interests" Test	126
PAST CONDUCT	127
DEFINING CUSTODY AND ACCESS	129
WHAT IS CUSTODY?	131
JOINT CUSTODY VERSUS SOLE CUSTODY	132
PARALLEL PARENTING	134
INCIDENTS OF CUSTODY	136
DETERMINING CUSTODY: APPROACHES TO "THE BEST INTERESTS OF THE CHILD"	137
(a) The Traditional Approach	137
(b) The "Primary Parent" Model or "Status Quo"	137
(c) The "Status Quo" in Legislation	139
(d) Determining the "Status Quo" for the Purposes of Child Custody Awards	142
OTHERS MAY APPLY FOR CUSTODY	143
DE FACTO CUSTODY, INTERIM CUSTODY, FINAL CUSTODY	145
(a) *De Facto* Custody	145
(b) Formal Custody Arrangements: Separation Agreements and Orders	146
(i) SEPARATION AGREEMENTS	146
(ii) INTERIM ORDERS CONCERNING CUSTODY	146
(iii) FINAL ORDERS CONCERNING CUSTODY	147
MATERIAL CHANGE IN CIRCUMSTANCES	148
WHAT DOES ACCESS MEAN?	149
TIME-SHARING	153
DECISION-MAKING DURING ACCESS	154
"SUPERVISED ACCESS" AND "SUPERVISED ACCESS CENTRE"	155

HAGUE CONVENTION ON THE CIVIL ASPECTS OF
INTERNATIONAL CHILD ABDUCTION 156
PREVENTION 157
PARENTAL ABDUCTION 158
EXTRADITION 159
CONCLUSIONS 160

6 — *YOUTH CRIMINAL JUSTICE ACT* 161
HISTORY 161
APPLICATION OF THE YCJA 162
APPLICATION OF THE *CRIMINAL CODE* 162
DIFFERENCES BETWEEN THE YCJA AND YOA 162
GUIDING PRINCIPLES 165
ORGANIZATION OF THE YCJA 166
EXTRAJUDICIAL MEASURES 167
  (a) Extrajudicial Measures Defined 167
  (b) When to Use Extrajudicial Measures 168
  (c) The Aim of Extrajudicial Measures 168
  (d) Who Considers Extrajudicial Measures? 169
  (e) Extrajudicial Sanctions Defined 170
  (f) Using Extrajudicial Sanctions 170
  (g) Admissions for Purposes of Extrajudicial Sanctions as Evidence 171
  (h) Extrajudicial Sanctions and Criminal Charges 171
  (i) Success with Extrajudicial Programs 172
  (j) The Role of Extrajudicial Measures in Youth Criminal Justice 172
COMMITTEES AND CONFERENCES 172
  (a) Youth Justice Committees 172
  (b) Conferences 174
YOUTH COURT 174
  (a) Youth Court and Adult Court Differences 174
  (b) Youth Court Jurisdiction and Powers 175
  (c) Youth's Age Unknown at Time of Offence 176
  (d) Enactments to Youth Court Proceedings 176
  (e) Involving a Justice of the Peace in Youth Court 177
  (f) The Role of the Court Clerk in Youth Court 178
JUDICIAL MEASURES 178
  (a) A Young Person's Right to Counsel 179
  (b) Specific Procedural Protections for Young People 179
  (c) Privacy Protections for Young People 180

PRE-TRIAL DETENTION	181
COURT APPEARANCES	182
(a) First Appearance	182
(b) "Presumptive Offence"	183
(c) Pleading Guilty	183
(d) Release from Custody	184
(e) Medical or Psychological Evaluation	185
(f) Assessing a Young Person	186
(g) Custody for the Purposes of Assessment	186
(h) The Assessment Report	187
(i) Involving Children's Aid or Child Welfare Agencies in the Youth Court Process	188
(j) Proceeding to Trial	188
(k) Mode of Trial	188
(l) Rules for Trial Conduct	189
SENTENCING UNDER THE YCJA	190
(a) Youth Sentencing	191
(b) Purpose	191
(c) General Principles	192
(d) Factors to Consider	192
(e) Outside Help on Sentencing	193
(f) Pre-Sentence Report	194
(g) Other Sentencing Recommendations	195
(h) Custodial Sentences	196
(i) Determining a "Reasonable Alternative to Custody"	198
(j) Records and Documents for Sentencing	198
(k) Length of Custody	199
(l) Alternatives to Youth Sentencing	200
ADULT SENTENCING	203
(a) Imposing an "Adult Sentence"	204
(b) Adult Sentencing Process	205
(i) MURDER, ATTEMPTED MURDER, MANSLAUGHTER AND AGGRAVATED SEXUAL ASSAULT	205
(ii) "SERIOUS VIOLENT OFFENCE"	205
(c) Adult Sentences for "Non-Presumptive Offences"	206
(d) Determining Which Sentence to Impose	206
(e) Factors to Review in Determining an Adult or Youth Sentence	207
(f) Sentencing Length	208
(g) Youth Identification in Adult Sentencing	208

CUSTODY	208
INFORMATION AND PRIVACY	209
7 — DEALING WITH CHILDREN AND THE BOUNDARIES OF USING FORCE	**215**
SECTION 43 OF CANADA'S *CRIMINAL CODE*	216
HISTORY OF SECTION 43	218
THE CURRENT APPROACH: THE *CANADIAN FOUNDATION CHARTER* CHALLENGE	223
PERMISSIBLE "CORRECTION" AFTER THE SECTION 43 CHALLENGE	230
8 — CHILDREN AT SCHOOL	**235**
LAWS GOVERNING SCHOOLS	236
CHARTER APPLICATION TO SCHOOLS	238
HUMAN RIGHTS LEGISLATION APPLICATION TO SCHOOLS	240
MANDATORY SCHOOL ATTENDANCE	242
A CHILD'S RIGHT TO ATTEND SCHOOL	242
ENFORCING ATTENDANCE	244
ENTITIES PROVIDING PUBLIC EDUCATION SERVICES	245
WHAT IS A SCHOOL BOARD IN LAW?	247
THE SCHOOL BOARD'S DUTIES WITH RESPECT TO INSTRUCTION	248
THE SCHOOL BOARD'S DUTIES WITH RESPECT TO SPECIAL EDUCATION	249
SCHOOL BOARD ADMINSTRATION	252
SPECIFIC STATUTORY DUTIES OF SCHOOL BOARD EMPLOYEES	253
SCHOOL BOARDS' STATUTORY DUTIES WITH RESPECT TO CHILD PROTECTION	254
STATUTORY DUTIES CONCERNING STUDENT RECORDS	258
SCHOOL BOARDS DUTIES TO CHILDREN BEYOND THOSE STATED IN THE STATUTE	261
A SCHOOL BOARD'S DUTY OF CARE TOWARD A STUDENT	262
THE COMMON LAW DUTY OF CARE BEYOND THE CLASSROOM (AND SCHOOL-RELATED ACTIVITIES)	264

THE SCHOOL BOARD'S LEGAL RESPONSIBILITY FOR
STUDENT ABUSE BY A TEACHER OR OTHER
EMPLOYEE 267
SCHOOL BOARD RESPONSIBILITY AND HEALTH AND
SAFETY 269
SCHOOL BOARD POWERS 270
SUSPENSION AND EXPULSION 271
THE ISSUE OF BULLYING IN SCHOOLS 277
SCHOOL AUTHORITIES' POWER TO PREVENT
TRESPASSING 281
RIGHTS OF PARENTS 284
WHAT ELSE? 285

9 — AN INTRODUCTION TO CHILD SUPPORT 287
BACKGROUND 290
WHO IS ENTITLED TO CHILD SUPPORT? 292
DETERMINING THE AMOUNT OF SUPPORT 294
ADULT CHILDREN 295
DISCRETION REGARDING HIGH INCOME 296
HARDSHIP 297
ADD-ONS / EXTRAORDINARY BENEFITS 299
DISCLOSURE 301
SPLIT CUSTODY 302
SHARED CUSTODY 303
PREDICTABILITY? 304
TAX CONSEQUENCE CHANGES 304
ENFORCEMENT 304
CONCLUSION 306

10 — INFORMATION AND DISCLOSURE /
ASSESSMENTS / CHILDREN'S LAWYER 307
SUBPOENA OR SUMMONS TO ATTEND AT TRIAL 308
O'CONNOR APPLICATION (CRIMINAL) 311
PRE-TRIAL MOTION FOR DOCUMENTS 317
ASSESSMENT REPORTS 320
LEGAL REPRESENTATION OF CHILDREN 327
CONCLUSIONS 332

APPENDICES 333

ONTARIO 335

Child and Family Services Act, sections 1-3; 15; 27; 37; 38; 72; and 79 335

Children's Law Reform Act, sections 1-10; 20-24; 30; 35; and 36 365

Education Act, sections 170-171; 264; 265; and 300-316 385

    Ontario Regulation 298 – Operation of Schools, General 443

Family Law Act, sections 1; 29; 30-34; and 46 473

    Child Support Guidelines, sections 1-21 487

FEDERAL

Canadian Charter of Rights and Freedoms, sections 1-34; and 52 503

Divorce Act, sections 1; 2; 8; 15; and 16 517

Youth Criminal Justice Act, sections 1-13; and 125 525

INDEX 541

TABLE OF CASES

A., Re (1990), 1990 CarswellOnt 287, 72 D.L.R. (4th) 722, 75 O.R. (2d) 82, 28 R.F.L. (3d) 288 (Ont. U.F.C.) 35

Adler v. Ontario, 1996 CarswellOnt 3989, 1996 CarswellOnt 3990, 30 O.R. (3d) 642 (note), 204 N.R. 81, [1996] 3 S.C.R. 609, 95 O.A.C. 1, 140 D.L.R. (4th) 385, 40 C.R.R. (2d) 1 (S.C.C.) 238

Alexander v. Etobicoke Board of Education (1981), 1981 CarswellOnt 482, 34 O.R. (2d) 76, 17 M.P.L.R. 18, 131 D.L.R. (3d) 36 (Ont. H.C.) 247

Attis v. New Brunswick District No. 15 Board of Education, 1996 CarswellNB 125, 1996 CarswellNB 125F, [1996] S.C.J. No. 40, (*sub nom. Ross v. New Brunswick School District No. 15*) 133 D.L.R. (4th) 1, 195 N.R. 81, 37 Admin. L.R. (2d) 131, (*sub nom. Ross v. New Brunswick School District No. 15*) [1996] 1 S.C.R. 825, (*sub nom. Ross v. New Brunswick School District No. 15*) 25 C.H.R.R. D/175, (*sub nom. Attis v. Board of School Trustees, District No. 15*) 35 C.R.R. (2d) 1, 437 A.P.R. 321, (*sub nom. Attis v. Board of School Trustees, District No. 15*) 96 C.L.L.C. 230-020, 171 N.B.R. (2d) 321 (S.C.C.) 235, 239, 265

Auton (Guardian ad litem of) v. British Columbia (Attorney General) (2004), [2004] S.C.J. No. 71, 2004 CarswellBC 2675, 2004 CarswellBC 2676, 245 D.L.R. (4th) 1, 34 B.C.L.R. (4th) 24, [2005] 2 W.W.R. 189, (*sub nom. Auton v. British Columbia (Minister of Health)*) 327 N.R. 1, [2004] 3 S.C.R. 657, 206 B.C.A.C. 1, 338 W.A.C. 1, 124 C.R.R. (2d) 135, 2004 SCC 78 (S.C.C.)   239, 241, 252

Auton v. British Columbia (Minister of Health) — see *Auton (Guardian ad litem of) v. British Columbia (Attorney General)*.

B. (K.L.) v. British Columbia, (*sub nom. K.L.B. v. British Columbia*) [2003] S.C.J. No. 51, 2003 CarswellBC 2405, 2003 CarswellBC 2406, 18 B.C.L.R. (4th) 1, 19 C.C.L.T. (3d) 66, 230 D.L.R. (4th) 513, [2003] 11 W.W.R. 203, 309 N.R. 306, [2003] 2 S.C.R. 403, [2003] R.R.A. 1065, 44 R.F.L. (5th) 245, 187 B.C.A.C. 42, 307 W.A.C. 42, 38 C.P.C. (5th) 199, 2003 SCC 51, 2004 C.L.L.C. 210-014 (S.C.C.) 263

B. (R.) v. Children's Aid Society of Metropolitan Toronto, 1995 CarswellOnt 105, 1995 CarswellOnt 515, [1994] S.C.J. No. 24, 9 R.F.L. (4th) 157, 21 O.R. (3d) 479 (note), 122 D.L.R. (4th) 1, [1995] 1 S.C.R. 315, 26 C.R.R. (2d) 202, (*sub nom. Sheena B., Re*) 176 N.R. 161, (*sub nom. Sheena B., Re*) 78 O.A.C. 1 (S.C.C.) 89, 92, 93, 94

Baker v. Baker (1979), 1979 CarswellOnt 367, 23 O.R. (2d) 391, 2 Fam. L. Rev. 69, 8 R.F.L. (2d) 236, 95 D.L.R. (3d) 529 (Ont. C.A.) 132

Balo v. Motlagh, 2004 CarswellOnt 3565, 10 R.F.L. (6th) 243, 2004 ONCJ 166, [2004] O.J. No. 3611 (Ont. C.J.) 287

Bater v. Alessandro (October 28, 2002), Doc. 02-FA-011287, 2002 CarswellOnt 3573 (Ont. S.C.J.) 138, 141

Bell v. Bell, 1955 CarswellOnt 165, [1955] O.W.N. 341 (Ont. C.A.) 120

Boer v. Cairns (2003), [2003] O.J. No. 2750, 2003 CarswellOnt 2524, (*sub nom. B. (V.) v. Cairns*) 65 O.R. (3d) 343, 17 C.C.L.T. (3d) 34 (Ont. S.C.J.) 54

Brown v. Board of Ed. of Topeka, Shawnee County, Kan. 347 U.S. 483, 74 S.Ct. 686, 98 L.Ed. 873, 38 A.L.R.2d 1180, U.S. 1954 236

Brown, Re (1975), 1975 CarswellOnt 182, 9 O.R. (2d) 185, 21 R.F.L. 315 (Ont. Co. Ct.) 30

Canadian Foundation for Children v. Canada — see *Canadian Foundation for Children, Youth & the Law v. Canada (Attorney General)*.

Canadian Foundation for Children, Youth & the Law v. Canada (Attorney General), 2004 CarswellOnt 252, 2004 CarswellOnt 253, [2004] S.C.J. No. 6, 2004 SCC 4, 70 O.R. (3d) 94 (note), 115 C.R.R. (2d) 88, (*sub nom. Canadian Foundation for Children v. Canada*) [2004] 1 S.C.R. 76, 16 C.R. (6th) 203, 46 R.F.L. (5th) 1, 183 O.A.C. 1, 234 D.L.R. (4th) 257, 180 C.C.C. (3d) 353, 315 N.R. 201 (S.C.C.) 21, 215, 223, 224, 225, 226, 227, 232, 271

Carter v. Brooks (1990), 1990 CarswellOnt 317, [1990] O.J. No. 2182, 41 O.A.C. 389, 2 O.R. (3d) 321, 77 D.L.R. (4th) 45, 30 R.F.L. (3d) 53 (Ont. C.A.)   141

Catholic Children's Aid Society of Toronto v. M.R., [2003] 2003 CarswellOnt 4505, [2003] 2003 CarswellOnt 4542, [2003] O.J. No. 4385 (Ont. C.J.) ... 20

Catholic Children's Aid Society of Hamilton-Wentworth v. L. (C.), (November 4, 2002), Doc. C-370/95, 2002 CarswellOnt 3713, [2002] O.J. No. 4255 (Ont. S.C.J.) 20

Catholic Children's Aid Society of Metropolitan Toronto v. M. (C.) (1994), 1994 CarswellOnt 376, 1994 CarswellOnt 1157, [1994] S.C.J. No. 37, 2 R.F.L. (4th) 313, [1994] 2 S.C.R. 165, 165 N.R. 161, 71 O.A.C. 81, 113 D.L.R. (4th) 321, 18 O.R. (3d) 160 (note) (S.C.C.) 31, 91

Chamberlain v. Surrey School District No. 36, [2002] S.C.J. No. 87, 2002 CarswellBC 3021, 2002 CarswellBC 3022, [2002] 4 S.C.R. 710, 2002 SCC 86, 221 D.L.R. (4th) 156, (*sub nom.*

Chamberlain v. Board of Education of School District No. 36 (Surrey)) 299 N.R. 1, 46 Admin. L.R. (3d) 1, 100 C.R.R. (2d) 288, 175 B.C.A.C. 161, 289 W.A.C. 161 (S.C.C.) 238, 249

Children and Family Services for York Region v. S.D. [2003] O.J. No. 4330 (Ont. S.C.) 20

Children's Aid Society of Hamilton-Wentworth v. T. (S.) (October 11, 1996), 1996 CarswellOnt 3748, [1996] O.J. No. 3578 (Ont. Gen. Div.) 320

Children's Aid Society of Ottawa v. S. (N.) (2005), 2005 CarswellOnt 1084, [2005] O.J. 1070 (Ont. S.C.J.) 259

Children's Aid Society of Peel (Region) v. L. (Y.C.) (October 5, 2001), Doc. Brampton 1591/98, 2001 CarswellOnt 3793 (Ont. C.J.) 34

TABLE OF CASES ♦ xxv

Children's Aid Society of Toronto v. M. (A.) (2002), 2002 CarswellOnt 1051, [2002] O.J. No. 1432, 26 R.F.L. (5th) 265 (Ont. C.J.) 23
Children's Aid Society of Waterloo (Regional Municipality) v. L. (T.) (June 4, 1990), Doc. Kitchener 65/90, 1990 CarswellOnt 3196, [1990] O.J. No. 1174 (Ont. Fam. Ct.) 259
Chou v. Chou (2005), 2005 CarswellOnt 1390, [2005] O.J. 1374, 253 D.L.R. (4th) 548 (Ont. S.C.J.)
Chou v. Chou, [2005] O.J. No. 1374 (Ont. S.C.J.) 243
Contino v. Leonelli-Contino (2004), [2003] S.C.C.A. No. 557, 2004 CarswellOnt 1319, 2004 CarswellOnt 1320, 329 N.R. 396 (note) (S.C.C.), allowing leave to appeal (2003), 2003 CarswellOnt 4099, [2003] O.J. No. 4128, 42 R.F.L. (5th) 295, 178 O.A.C. 281, 232 D.L.R. (4th) 654, 67 O.R. (3d) 703 (Ont. C.A.) 303
D. v. North York (City) Board of Education (1980), 1980 CarswellOnt 496, 13 M.P.L.R. 1 (Ont. H.C.) 244
Daigle v. Tremblay — see *Tremblay c. Daigle*.
Dobson (Litigation Guardian of) v. Dobson, 1999 CarswellNB 248, [1999] S.C.J. No. 41, 1999 CarswellNB 249, 174 D.L.R. (4th) 1, 44 M.V.R. (3d) 1, (*sub nom. Dobson v. Dobson*) 242 N.R. 201, 45 C.C.L.T. (2d) 217, 33 C.P.C. (4th) 217, [1999] 2 S.C.R. 753, (*sub nom. Dobson v. Dobson*) 214 N.B.R. (2d) 201, (*sub nom. Dobson v. Dobson*) 547 A.P.R. 201 (S.C.C.) 104
Droit de la famille - 1150, 1993 CarswellQue 64, 1993 CarswellQue 163, (*sub nom. P. (D.) v. S. (C.)*) [1993] S.C.J. No. 111, 49 R.F.L. (3d) 317, (*sub nom. P. (D.) v. S. (C.)*) 58 Q.A.C. 1, (*sub nom. P. (D.) v. S. (C.)*) 18 C.R.R. (2d) 1, (*sub nom. P. (D.) v. S. (C.)*) [1993] R.D.F. 712, (*sub nom. P. (D.) v. S. (C.)*) 159 N.R. 241, 108 D.L.R. (4th) 287, [1993] 4 S.C.R. 141 (S.C.C.) 89, 90, 91
Eaton v. Board of Education of Brant County — see *Eaton v. Brant (County) Board of Education*.
Eaton v. Brant (County) Board of Education (1996), 1996 CarswellOnt 5035, 1996 CarswellOnt 5036, [1996] S.C.J. No. 98, 31 O.R. (3d) 574 (note), 41 C.R.R. (2d) 240, 142 D.L.R. (4th) 385, (*sub nom. Eaton v. Board of Education of Brant County*) 207 N.R. 171, (*sub nom. Eaton v. Board of Education of Brant County*) 97 O.A.C. 161, [1997] 1 S.C.R. 241 (S.C.C.) 238, 249
Eddington v. Kent (County) Board of Education (1986), 1986 CarswellOnt 1176, 56 O.R. (2d) 403 (Ont. Dist. Ct.) 247
Essex (County) Roman Catholic Separate School Board v. Porter (1978), 1978 CarswellOnt 1271, 21 O.R. (2d) 255, 89 D.L.R. (3d) 445 (Ont. C.A.) ... 241
Essex (County) Roman Catholic Separate School Board v. Tremblay-Webster (1983), 1983 CarswellOnt 1301, 83 C.L.L.C. 14,029, 142 D.L.R. (3d) 479 (Ont. Div. Ct.), affirmed (1984), 1984 CarswellOnt 1250, 45 O.R. (2d) 83, 84 C.L.L.C. 14,030, 5 D.L.R. (4th) 665, 2 O.A.C. 74 (Ont. C.A.) 241

Etobicoke (Borough) Board of Education v. O.S.S.T.F., District 12 (1981), 2 L.A.C. (3d) 265 (Ont. Arb. Bd.) 258

Francis v. Baker, [1999] S.C.J. No. 52, 1999 CarswellOnt 2734, 1999 CarswellOnt 2948, [1999] 3 S.C.R. 250, 44 O.R. (3d) 736 (headnote only), 177 D.L.R. (4th) 1, 246 N.R. 45, 50 R.F.L. (4th) 228, 125 O.A.C. 201 (S.C.C.) 296

G. (E.D.) v. Hammer, [2003] S.C.J. No. 52, 2003 CarswellBC 2407, 2003 CarswellBC 2408, 18 B.C.L.R. (4th) 42, 19 C.C.L.T. (3d) 38, 230 D.L.R. (4th) 554, [2003] 11 W.W.R. 244, [2003] R.R.A. 1069, [2003] 2 S.C.R. 459, 187 B.C.A.C. 193, 307 W.A.C. 193, 310 N.R. 1, 2004 C.L.L.C. 210-011, 2003 SCC 52 (S.C.C.) 267

G.T.-J. v. Griffiths — see *Jacobi v. Griffiths*.

Gordon v. Goertz (1996), 1996 CarswellSask 199, [1996] S.C.J. No. 52, 1996 CarswellSask 199F, [1996] 5 W.W.R. 457, 19 R.F.L. (4th) 177, 196 N.R. 321, 134 D.L.R. (4th) 321, 141 Sask. R. 241, 114 W.A.C. 241, [1996] 2 S.C.R. 27, (*sub nom. Goertz c. Gordon*) [1996] R.D.F. 209 (S.C.C.) 91, 148

Gosselin c. Québec (Procureur général), 2005 CarswellQue 763, 2005 CarswellQue 764, 2005 SCC 15, (*sub nom. Gosselin v. Quebec (Attorney General)*) 250 D.L.R. (4th) 483 (S.C.C.) 238

Gubody v. Gubody, 1955 CarswellOnt 231, [1955] O.W.N. 548, [1955] 4 D.L.R. 693 (Ont. H.C.) 150

H. (S.G.) v. Gorsline (2004), 2004 CarswellAlta 688, 354 A.R. 46, 329 W.A.C. 46, [2005] 2 W.W.R. 716, 29 Alta. L.R. (4th) 203, 2004 ABCA 186, 23 C.C.L.T. (3d) 65 (Alta. C.A.), leave to appeal refused (January 20, 2005), Doc. 30493, 2005 CarswellAlta 62, 2005 CarswellAlta 63 (S.C.C.) 267

Halpern v. Canada (Attorney General) — see *Halpern v. Toronto (City)*.

Halpern v. Toronto (City) (2003), 2003 CarswellOnt 2159, (*sub nom. Halpern v. Canada (Attorney General)*) [2003] O.J. No. 2268, 65 O.R. (3d) 161, 65 O.R. (3d) 201, (*sub nom. Halpern v. Canada (Attorney General)*) 106 C.R.R. (2d) 329, (*sub nom. Halpern v. Canada (Attorney General)*) 172 O.A.C. 276, 36 R.F.L. (5th) 127, 225 D.L.R. (4th) 529 (Ont. C.A.) 111

Hatch v. London (City) Board of Education (1979), 1979 CarswellOnt 583, 25 O.R. (2d) 481, 9 M.P.L.R. 278, 104 D.L.R. (3d) 153 (Ont. H.C.) 244

Hentze (Guardian ad litem of) v. Campbell River School District No. 72 (1994), 1994 CarswellBC 1047, [1994] B.C.J. No. 1876, (*sub nom. Hentze v. Board of Education of School District No. 72*) 49 B.C.A.C. 241, (*sub nom. Hentze v. Board of Education of School District No. 72*) 80 W.A.C. 241 (B.C. C.A.) 279

Hicks v. Etobicoke (City) Board of Education (November 23, 1988), Doc. 306622/87, [1988] O.J. No. 1900 (Ont. Dist. Ct.) 249

Hildinger v. Carroll (2004), 2004 CarswellOnt 444, [2004] O.J. No. 291, 2 R.F.L. (6th) 331 (Ont. C.A.) 135

TABLE OF CASES ♦ xxvii

Hockey v. Hockey (1989), 1989 CarswellOnt 256, [1989] O.J. No. 1036, 21 R.F.L.
(3d) 105, 69 O.R. (2d) 338, 60 D.L.R. (4th) 765, 35 O.A.C. 257 (Ont. Div.
Ct.) 154
Jacobi v. Griffiths, 1999 CarswellBC 1262, 1999 CarswellBC 1263, [1999] S.C.J.
No. 36, (*sub nom. J. v. Griffiths*) 99 C.L.L.C. 210-034, (*sub nom. G.T.-J. v.
Griffiths*) 241 N.R. 201, 174 D.L.R. (4th) 71, 124 B.C.A.C. 161, 203 W.A.C.
161, 63 B.C.L.R. (3d) 1, [1999] L.V.I. 3046-2, [1999] 9 W.W.R. 1, 46 C.C.L.T.
(2d) 49, 44 C.C.E.L. (2d) 169, [1999] 2 S.C.R. 570 (S.C.C.) 263, 267
Jane Doe v. Metropolitan Toronto (Municipality) Commissioners of Police (1989),
[1989] O.J. No. 471, 1989 CarswellOnt 684, (*sub nom. Jane Doe v. Police Bd.
of Commissioners (Metropolitan Toronto)*) 48 C.C.L.T. 105, (*sub nom. Doe v.
Metropolitan Toronto (Municipality) Commissioners of Police*) 58 D.L.R. (4th)
396 (Ont. H.C.), affirmed (1990), 1990 CarswellOnt 442, (*sub nom. Jane
Doe v. Board of Police Commissioners of Metropolitan Toronto*) 40 O.A.C. 161,
5 C.C.L.T. (2d) 77, (*sub nom. Doe v. Metropolitan Toronto (Municipality)
Commissioners of Police*) 74 O.R. (2d) 225, 50 C.P.C. (2d) 92, (*sub nom. Doe
v. Metropolitan Toronto (Municipality) Commissioners of Police*) 1 C.R.R. (2d)
211, (*sub nom. Doe v. Metropolitan Toronto (Municipality) Commissioners of
Police*) 72 D.L.R. (4th) 580 (Ont. Div. Ct.), leave to appeal refused (1991),
1991 CarswellOnt 1009, (*sub nom. Doe v. Metropolitan Toronto
(Municipality) Commissioners of Police*) 1 O.R. (3d) 416 (note)
(Ont. C.A.) 55
John Doe v. Avalon East School Board, 2004 CarswellNfld 378, 37 C.C.E.L. (3d)
279, 244 Nfld. & P.E.I.R. 153, 726 A.P.R. 153, 28 C.C.L.T. (3d) 88, 2004
NLTD 239 (N.L. T.D.) 267
Jubran v. North Vancouver School District No. 44 — see *North Vancouver School
District No. 44 v. Jubran*.
K.L.B. v. British Columbia — see *B. (K.L.) v. British Columbia*.
Kaplanis v. Kaplanis (2005), 2005 CarswellOnt 266, [2005] O.J. No. 275, 249
D.L.R. (4th) 620, 194 O.A.C. 106, 10 R.F.L. (6th) 373 (Ont. C.A.) 136
Kenora-Patricia Child & Family Services v. G. (J.) (2001), [2001] O.J. No. 2290,
2001 CarswellOnt 2100, 21 R.F.L. (5th) 80 (Ont. C.J.) 40
Knight v. Indian Head School Division No. 19, 1990 CarswellSask 146, 1990
CarswellSask 408, [1990] S.C.J. No. 26, [1990] 1 S.C.R. 653, 69 D.L.R. (4th)
489, [1990] 3 W.W.R. 289, 30 C.C.E.L. 237, 90 C.L.L.C. 14,010, 43 Admin.
L.R. 157, 83 Sask. R. 81, 106 N.R. 17 (S.C.C.) 239
Kruger v. Kruger (1979), 1979 CarswellOnt 299, 25 O.R. (2d) 673, 11 R.F.L. (2d)
52, 2 Fam. L. Rev. 197, 104 D.L.R. (3d) 481 (Ont. C.A.) 132
L. (R.) v. Children's Aid Society of Niagara Region (2002), 2002 CarswellOnt
4262, [2002] O.J. No. 4793, 167 O.A.C. 105, 16 O.F.L.R. 127, 34 R.F.L. (5th)
44 (Ont. C.A.) 30, 43, 45, 47

xxviii ♦ CHILDREN'S LAW HANDBOOK

Lambton (County) Board of Education v. Beauchamp (1979), 1979 CarswellOnt
293, 10 R.F.L. (2d) 354 (Ont. Prov. Ct.) 244

M v. H, 1999 CarswellOnt 1348, 1999 CarswellOnt 1349, [1999] S.C.J. No. 23,
(*sub nom. M. v. H.*) 171 D.L.R. (4th) 577, (*sub nom. M. v. H.*) 238 N.R. 179,
(*sub nom. M. v. H.*) 43 O.R. (3d) 254 (headnote only), (*sub nom. M. v. H.*) 62
C.R.R. (2d) 1, (*sub nom. M. v. H.*) 121 O.A.C. 1, 46 R.F.L. (4th) 32, (*sub nom.
Attorney General for Ontario v. M. & H.*) C.E.B. & P.G.R. 8354 (headnote
only), (*sub nom. M. v. H.*) [1999] 2 S.C.R. 3, 7 B.H.R.C. 489 (S.C.C.),
reconsideration refused (May 25, 2000), Doc. 25838, 2000 CarswellOnt
1913, 2000 CarswellOnt 1914 (S.C.C.) 88

MacDonald v. Lambton County Board of Education (1982), 1982 CarswellOnt 803,
37 O.R. (2d) 221 (Ont. H.C.) 247

Mainville v. Ottawa (Board of Education) (1990), 1990 CarswellOnt 2719, 75 O.R.
(2d) 315 (Ont. Prov. Ct.) 279

McInroy v. R. — see *R. v. Rouse*.

McMaster v. Smith (1971), 1971 CarswellOnt 138, [1972] 1 O.R. 416, 6 R.F.L.
143, 23 D.L.R. (3d) 264 (Ont. H.C.) 120

Miron v. Trudel, 1995 CarswellOnt 93, 1995 CarswellOnt 526, [1995] S.C.J. No.
44, 10 M.V.R. (3d) 151, 23 O.R. (3d) 160 (note), [1995] I.L.R. 1-3185, 13
R.F.L. (4th) 1, C.E.B. & P.G.R. 8217, 181 N.R. 253, 124 D.L.R. (4th) 693, 81
O.A.C. 253, [1995] 2 S.C.R. 418, 29 C.R.R. (2d) 189 (S.C.C.) 89

Moddejonge v. Huron (County) Board of Education, 1972 CarswellOnt 476, [1972]
2 O.R. 437, 25 D.L.R. (3d) 661 (Ont. H.C.) 263

Moge v. Moge (1992), [1992] S.C.J. No. 107, 1992 CarswellMan 143, 1992
CarswellMan 222, [1993] 1 W.W.R. 481, 99 D.L.R. (4th) 456, [1992] 3
S.C.R. 813, 81 Man. R. (2d) 161, 30 W.A.C. 161, 43 R.F.L. (3d) 345, 145
N.R. 1, [1993] R.D.F. 168 (S.C.C.) 88

Montreal Tramways Co. v. Léveillé, 1933 CarswellQue 36, [1933] S.C.R. 456, 41
C.R.C. 291, [1933] 4 D.L.R. 337 (S.C.C.) 106

Morra v. Metropolitan (Separate School Board) (1981), 3 C.H.R.R. D/1034 (Ont.
Bd. of Inquiry) 241

Myers v. Peel (County) Board of Education, 1981 CarswellOnt 579, 1981
CarswellOnt 612, [1981] 2 S.C.R. 21, 123 D.L.R. (3d) 1, 17 C.C.L.T. 269, 37
N.R. 227 (S.C.C.) 262

N. (F.), Re, 2000 CarswellNfld 213, 2000 CarswellNfld 214, [2000] S.C.J. No.
34, 2000 SCC 35, 146 C.C.C. (3d) 1, 188 D.L.R. (4th) 1, 35 C.R. (5th) 1,
[2000] 1 S.C.R. 880, 191 Nfld. & P.E.I.R. 181, 577 A.P.R. 181
(S.C.C.) 211, 212

New Brunswick (Minister of Health & Community Services) v. G. (J.), 1999
CarswellNB 305, 1999 CarswellNB 306, [1999] S.C.J. No. 47, 26 C.R. (5th)
203, 244 N.R. 276, 177 D.L.R. (4th) 124, 50 R.F.L. (4th) 63, 66 C.R.R. (2d)

TABLE OF CASES ♦ xxix

267, 216 N.B.R. (2d) 25, 552 A.P.R. 25, [1999] 3 S.C.R. 46, 7 B.H.R.C. 615 (S.C.C.) 32, 92, 94, 95, 99
Nielsen v. Kamloops (City) (1984), 1984 CarswellBC 476, 1984 CarswellBC 821, [1984] 5 W.W.R. 1, [1984] 2 S.C.R. 2, 10 D.L.R. (4th) 641, 54 N.R. 1, 11 Admin. L.R. 1, 29 C.C.L.T. 97, 8 C.L.R. 1, 26 M.P.L.R. 81, 66 B.C.L.R. 273 (S.C.C.) 106
North Vancouver School District No. 44 v. Jubran, (sub nom. Jubran v. North Vancouver School District No. 44) [2002] B.C.H.R.T.D. No. 10, 2002 CarswellBC 3345, 2002 BCHRT 10, 42 C.H.R.R. D/273 (B.C. Human Rights Trib.), reversed 2003 CarswellBC 11, [2003] B.C.J. No. 10, 2003 BCSC 6, [2003] 3 W.W.R. 288, 9 B.C.L.R. (4th) 338, 45 C.H.R.R. D/249 (B.C. S.C.), reversed 2005 CarswellBC 788, 2005 BCCA 201, 39 B.C.L.R. (4th) 153 (B.C. C.A.) 241, 279, 280
Nurmi v. Nurmi (1988), 1988 CarswellOnt 283, [1988] O.J. No. 1288, 16 R.F.L. (3d) 201 (Ont. U.F.C.) 133
O.E.C.T.A. v. Ontario (Attorney General), 2001 CarswellOnt 580, 2001 CarswellOnt 581, 2001 SCC 15, (sub nom. Ontario English Catholic Teachers' Assn. v. Ontario (Attorney General)) 196 D.L.R. (4th) 577, (sub nom. Ontario English Catholic Teachers' Assn. v. Ontario (Attorney General)) [2001] 1 S.C.R. 470, 267 N.R. 10, (sub nom. Ontario English Catholic Teachers' Assn. v. Ontario (Attorney General)) 53 O.R. (3d) 263 (headnote only), (sub nom. Ontario English Catholic Teachers' Assn. v. Ontario (Attorney General)) 144 O.A.C. 1 (S.C.C.) 237, 238
O'Malley v. Simpsons-Sears Ltd., 1985 CarswellOnt 887, 1985 CarswellOnt 946, (sub nom. Ontario Human Rights Commission v. Simpsons-Sears Ltd.) [1985] S.C.J. No. 74, (sub nom. Ontario Human Rights Commission v. Simpsons-Sears Ltd.) [1985] 2 S.C.R. 536, 23 D.L.R. (4th) 321, 64 N.R. 161, 12 O.A.C. 241, 17 Admin. L.R. 89, (sub nom. Ontario (Human Rights Commission) v. Simpsons-Sears Ltd.) 9 C.C.E.L. 185, 86 C.L.L.C. 17,002, 7 C.H.R.R. D/3102, [1986] D.L.Q. 89 (note), 52 O.R. (2d) 799 (note) (S.C.C.) 240
Ontario (Police Complaints Commissioner) v. Dunlop (1995), 1995 CarswellOnt 1741, 26 O.R. (3d) 582, 88 O.A.C. 115 (Ont. Div. Ct.) 52, 53
Ontario English Catholic Teachers' Assn. v. Ontario (Attorney General) — see O.E.C.T.A. v. Ontario (Attorney General).
Ontario Human Rights Commission v. Simpsons-Sears Ltd. — see O'Malley v. Simpsons-Sears Ltd.
P. (D.) v. S. (C.) — see Droit de la famille – 1150.
Pelletier v. Pelletier (2003), 2003 CarswellOnt 422, [2003] O.J. No. 417 (Ont. S.C.J.) 128
Pierce v. Pierce, 1977 CarswellBC 410, [1977] 5 W.W.R. 572 (B.C. S.C.) 150
Powers v. Powers, 2004 CarswellOnt 4738, 11 R.F.L. (6th) 373, 2004 ONCJ 281 (Ont. C.J.) 136

xxx ♦ CHILDREN'S LAW HANDBOOK

Quebec Assn. of Protestant School Boards v. Quebec (Attorney General) (No. 2),
1984 CarswellQue 100, 1984 CarswellQue 100F, [1984] 2 S.C.R. 66, 10
D.L.R. (4th) 321, 54 N.R. 196, 9 C.R.R. 133 (S.C.C.) 238

R. (C.) v. Children's Aid Society of Hamilton (2004), [2004] O.J. No. 1251, 2004
CarswellOnt 2268, 4 R.F.L. (6th) 98 (Ont. S.C.J.) 329

R. c. Audet, [1996] S.C.J. No. 61, 1996 CarswellNB 259, 1996 CarswellNB 260,
48 C.R. (4th) 1, 197 N.R. 172, 106 C.C.C. (3d) 481, 135 D.L.R. (4th) 20, 175
N.B.R. (2d) 81, 446 A.P.R. 81, [1996] 2 S.C.R. 171 (S.C.C.) ... 238, 240, 264,
265

R. v. A. (K.) (1999), 1999 CarswellOnt 2118, [1999] O.J. No. 2640, 123 O.A.C.
161, 137 C.C.C. (3d) 554 (Ont. C.A.) 66

R. v. A. (S.) (1992), 1992 CarswellOnt 116, [1992] O.J. No. 2160, 17 C.R. (4th)
233, 76 C.C.C. (3d) 522, 11 O.R. (3d) 16, 59 O.A.C. 234 (Ont. C.A.) 72

R. v. Antoine, 1949 CarswellBC 18, 7 C.R. 412, 94 C.C.C. 106, [1949] 1 W.W.R.
701 (B.C. C.A.) 76

R. v. Atikian (1990), 1990 CarswellOnt 70, 1 O.R. (3d) 263, 3 C.R. (4th) 77, 42
O.A.C. 214, 62 C.C.C. (3d) 357 (Ont. C.A.) 77

R. v. B. (G.), 1990 CarswellSask 20, 1990 CarswellSask 410, [1990] S.C.J. No.
58, 56 C.C.C. (3d) 200, [1990] 2 S.C.R. 30, (*sub nom. R. v. B. (G.) (No. 2)*)
111 N.R. 31, (*sub nom. R. v. B. (G.) (No. 2)*) 86 Sask. R. 111, 77 C.R. (3d) 347
(S.C.C.) 59, 67, 79, 81

R. v. B. (K.G.), 1993 CarswellOnt 76, 1993 CarswellOnt 975, [1993] S.C.J. No.
22, 19 C.R. (4th) 1, [1993] 1 S.C.R. 740, 61 O.A.C. 1, 148 N.R. 241, 79
C.C.C. (3d) 257 (S.C.C.) 80

R. v. Bannerman, 1966 CarswellMan 53, 50 C.R. 76, 57 W.W.R. 736, [1966]
S.C.R. v (S.C.C.) 64

R. v. Baptiste (1980), 1980 CarswellOnt 1436, 61 C.C.C. (2d) 438 (Ont. Prov.
Ct.) 221

R. v. Bickford (1989), 1989 CarswellOnt 990, [1989] O.J. No. 835, 34 O.A.C. 34,
48 C.R.R. 194, 51 C.C.C. (3d) 181 (Ont. C.A.) 69

R. v. Bond, [1997] O.J. No. 3420 (Ont. C.A.) 64

R. v. Boyd, 2004 CarswellAlta 920, 2004 ABPC 125 (Alta. Prov. Ct.) 231

R. v. Breckenridge, [1997] O.J. No. 2262 (Ont. C.A.) 66

R. v. C. (D.L.) 2003 CanLII 32877 (N.L. P.C.) 197, 199

R. v. C. (K.L.), 2004 CarswellSask 580, 252 Sask. R. 254, 2004 SKPC 98 (Sask.
Prov. Ct.) 201, 202

R. v. Caron (1994), 1994 CarswellOnt 866, [1994] O.J. No. 1591, 19 O.R. (3d)
323, 72 O.A.C. 287, 94 C.C.C. (3d) 466 (Ont. C.A.) 65

R. v. D. (D.), 2000 CarswellOnt 3255, 2000 CarswellOnt 3256, [2000] S.C.J. No.
44, 2000 SCC 43, 36 C.R. (5th) 261, 148 C.C.C. (3d) 41, 191 D.L.R. (4th) 60,
259 N.R. 156, 136 O.A.C. 201, [2000] 2 S.C.R. 275 (S.C.C.) 101

TABLE OF CASES ♦ xxxi

R. v. D. (W.A.L.) (1), [2004] S.J. No. 120, 2004 CarswellSask 140, 245 Sask. R. 98, 2004 SKPC 40 (Sask. Prov. Ct.) 201

R. v. Dupperon (1984), 1984 CarswellSask 198, [1985] 2 W.W.R. 369, 37 Sask. R. 84, 43 C.R. (3d) 70, 16 C.C.C. (3d) 453 (Sask. C.A.) 221, 222, 225

R. v. E. (A.W.), 1993 CarswellAlta 77, 1993 CarswellAlta 565, 12 Alta. L.R. (3d) 1, 156 N.R. 321, 23 C.R. (4th) 357, 83 C.C.C. (3d) 462, 141 A.R. 353, 46 W.A.C. 353, [1993] 3 S.C.R. 155 (S.C.C.) 81

R. v. F. (C.) (1996), [1996] O.J. No. 379, 1996 CarswellOnt 323, 88 O.A.C. 397 (Ont. C.A.), leave to appeal allowed (1996), (*sub nom. R. v. C.C.F.*) 96 O.A.C. 399 (note), (*sub nom. R. v. C.C.F.*) 206 N.R. 73 (note) (S.C.C.), reversed (October 16, 1997), Doc. 25198, 1997 CarswellOnt 4465, 1997 CarswellOnt 4466 (S.C.C.), additional reasons at 1997 CarswellOnt 4448, 1997 CarswellOnt 4449, (*sub nom. R. v. C.C.F.*) [1997] S.C.J. No. 89, (*sub nom. R. v. C.C.F.*) 220 N.R. 362, (*sub nom. R. v. F. (C.C.)*) 154 D.L.R. (4th) 13, (*sub nom. R. v. F. (C.C.)*) 120 C.C.C. (3d) 225, 11 C.R. (5th) 209, (*sub nom. R. v. F. (C.C.)*) [1997] 3 S.C.R. 1183, (*sub nom. R. v. C.C.F.*) 104 O.A.C. 321 (S.C.C.) 67, 82

R. v. F. (W.J.), 1999 CarswellSask 625, 1999 CarswellSask 626, [1999] S.C.J. No. 61, [1999] 3 S.C.R. 569, 138 C.C.C. (3d) 1, 178 D.L.R. (4th) 53, 27 C.R. (5th) 169, 247 N.R. 62, [1999] 12 W.W.R. 587, 180 Sask. R. 161, 205 W.A.C. 161 (S.C.C.) 69

R. v. Farley (1995), 1995 CarswellOnt 119, [1995] O.J. No. 1278, 40 C.R. (4th) 190, 23 O.R. (3d) 445, 80 O.A.C. 337, 99 C.C.C. (3d) 76 (Ont. C.A.) 66

R. v. Fletcher (1982), 1982 CarswellOnt 1229, 1 C.C.C. (3d) 370 (Ont. C.A.), leave to appeal refused (1983), 48 N.R. 319 (S.C.C.) 64

R. v. Fong (1994), 1994 CarswellAlta 697, 92 C.C.C. (3d) 171, 157 A.R. 73, 77 W.A.C. 73 (Alta. C.A.), leave to appeal refused (1995), 94 C.C.C. (3d) vii (note), 188 N.R. 236 (note), 174 A.R. 398 (note), 102 W.A.C. 398 (note) (S.C.C.) 63

R. v. Gagnon (2000), 2000 CarswellOnt 3317, [2000] O.J. No. 3410, 147 C.C.C. (3d) 193, 136 O.A.C. 116 (Ont. C.A.) 58

R. v. Gaul (1904), 1904 CarswellNS 11, 36 N.S.R. 504, 24 C.L.T. 135, 8 C.C.C. 178 (N.S. C.A.) 219

R. v. Haberstock (1970), 1 C.C.C. (2d) 433 (Sask. C.A.) 220

R. v. Harrer, 1995 CarswellBC 651, 1995 CarswellBC 1144, [1995] S.C.J. No. 81, 42 C.R. (4th) 269, 101 C.C.C. (3d) 193, 128 D.L.R. (4th) 98, 186 N.R. 329, 64 B.C.A.C. 161, 105 W.A.C. 161, 32 C.R.R. (2d) 273, [1995] 3 S.C.R. 562 (S.C.C.) 58

R. v. Jones, 1986 CarswellAlta 181, 1986 CarswellAlta 716, 69 N.R. 241, [1986] 2 S.C.R. 284, (*sub nom. Jones v. R.*) 31 D.L.R. (4th) 569, [1986] 6 W.W.R. 577, 47 Alta. L.R. (2d) 97, 73 A.R. 133, 28 C.C.C. (3d) 513, (*sub nom. Jones v. R.*) 25 C.R.R. 63 (S.C.C.) 245, 249

R. v. K. (A.J.) (1995), 1995 CarswellOnt 852, 23 O.R. (3d) 582 (Ont. Gen. Div.) 260
R. v. K. (F.) (1990), 1990 CarswellOnt 751, 73 O.R. (2d) 480, 39 O.A.C. 57, 56 C.C.C. (3d) 555 (Ont. C.A.) 62
R. v. Keegstra, 1990 CarswellAlta 192, 1990 CarswellAlta 661, 1 C.R. (4th) 129, [1990] 3 S.C.R. 697, 77 Alta. L.R. (2d) 193, 117 N.R. 1, [1991] 2 W.W.R. 1, 114 A.R. 81, 61 C.C.C. (3d) 1, 3 C.R.R. (2d) 193 (S.C.C.) 239
R. v. Khan, 1990 CarswellOnt 108, 1990 CarswellOnt 1001, [1990] S.C.J. No. 81, 113 N.R. 53, 79 C.R. (3d) 1, 41 O.A.C. 353, [1990] 2 S.C.R. 531, 59 C.C.C. (3d) 92 (S.C.C.) 65, 72, 83
R. v. Kotelmach (1989), 1989 CarswellSask 179, 76 Sask. R. 116 (Sask. Q.B.) 245
R. v. L. (D.O.), 1993 CarswellMan 348, 1993 CarswellMan 24, [1993] S.C.J. No. 72, 25 C.R. (4th) 285, 161 N.R. 1, 85 C.C.C. (3d) 289, 88 Man. R. (2d) 241, 51 W.A.C. 241, [1993] 4 S.C.R. 419, 18 C.R.R. (2d) 257 (S.C.C.) 67
R. v. L. (D.O.), 1993 CarswellMan 348, 1993 CarswellMan 24, [1993] S.C.J. No. 72, 25 C.R. (4th) 285, 161 N.R. 1, 85 C.C.C. (3d) 289, 88 Man. R. (2d) 241, 51 W.A.C. 241, [1993] 4 S.C.R. 419, 18 C.R.R. (2d) 257 (S.C.C.) 75, 79
R. v. L. (J.) (1990), 1990 CarswellOnt 895, 54 C.C.C. (3d) 225, 37 O.A.C. 269 (Ont. C.A.) 64
R. v. M. (B.), [2003] S.J. No. 377, 2003 CarswellSask 385, 234 Sask. R. 244, 2003 SKPC 83, [2003] 3 C.N.L.R. 277 (Sask. Prov. Ct.), additional reasons at (2003), 2003 CarswellSask 643, 2003 SKPC 133 (Sask. Prov. Ct.), varied (2003), 2003 CarswellSask 923, [2003] S.J. No. 870, 2003 SKCA 135, 241 Sask. R. 135, 313 W.A.C. 135 (Sask. C.A.) 194
R. v. M. (M.A.), 2001 CarswellBC 19, [2001] B.C.J. No. 18, 2001 BCCA 6, 151 C.C.C. (3d) 22, 40 C.R. (5th) 66, 149 B.C.A.C. 89, 244 W.A.C. 89 (B.C. C.A.), leave to appeal refused (2001), 2001 CarswellBC 3245, 2001 CarswellBC 3246, 271 N.R. 195 (note), 157 B.C.A.C. 160 (note), 256 W.A.C. 160 (note) (S.C.C.) 63
R. v. M. (M.R.), 1998 CarswellNS 346, [1998] S.C.J. No. 83, 1998 CarswellNS 347, 166 D.L.R. (4th) 261, 129 C.C.C. (3d) 361, 233 N.R. 1, 20 C.R. (5th) 197, 171 N.S.R. (2d) 125, 519 A.P.R. 125, [1998] 3 S.C.R. 393, 57 C.R.R. (2d) 189, 5 B.H.R.C. 474 (S.C.C.) 238, 239
R. v. M. (W.H.), 1992 CarswellPEI 110F, 1992 CarswellPEI 110, [1992] 1 S.C.R. 984, 98 Nfld. & P.E.I.R. 359, 311 A.P.R. 359, 139 N.R. 321 (S.C.C.) 82
R. v. Marquard, 1993 CarswellOnt 127, 1993 CarswellOnt 995, [1993] S.C.J. No. 119, 25 C.R. (4th) 1, 85 C.C.C. (3d) 193, [1993] 4 S.C.R. 223, 108 D.L.R. (4th) 47, 159 N.R. 81, 66 O.A.C. 161 (S.C.C.) 65, 67
R. v. McMaster (1998), 1998 CarswellOnt 23, 122 C.C.C. (3d) 371, 37 O.R. (3d) 543, 106 O.A.C. 236 (Ont. C.A.), leave to appeal refused (1999), 125 O.A.C. 399 (note), 248 N.R. 406 (note) (S.C.C.) 70

TABLE OF CASES ♦ xxxiii

R. v. *Metcalfe*, 1927 CarswellSask 84, [1927] 3 W.W.R. 194, 49 C.C.C. 260 (Sask. Dist. Ct.) 216, 220
R. v. *Mohan*, 1994 CarswellOnt 66, 1994 CarswellOnt 1155, [1994] S.C.J. No. 36, 29 C.R. (4th) 243, 71 O.A.C. 241, 166 N.R. 245, 89 C.C.C. (3d) 402, 114 D.L.R. (4th) 419, [1994] 2 S.C.R. 9, 18 O.R. (3d) 160 (note) (S.C.C.) 70
R. v. *Morgentaler* (1993), 1993 CarswellNS 19, 1993 CarswellNS 272, [1993] S.C.J. No. 95, 157 N.R. 97, 125 N.S.R. (2d) 81, 349 A.P.R. 81, [1993] 3 S.C.R. 463, 107 D.L.R. (4th) 537, 85 C.C.C. (3d) 118, 25 C.R. (4th) 179 (S.C.C.) 104
R. v. *Nikolovski*, 1996 CarswellOnt 4425, 1996 CarswellOnt 4426, [1996] S.C.J. No. 122, 111 C.C.C. (3d) 403, 31 O.R. (3d) 480 (headnote only), 141 D.L.R. (4th) 647, 3 C.R. (5th) 362, 96 O.A.C. 1, [1996] 3 S.C.R. 1197, 204 N.R. 333 (S.C.C.) 78
R. v. *O'Connor* (1995), 1995 CarswellBC 1098, 1995 CarswellBC 1151, [1995] S.C.J. No. 98, [1996] 2 W.W.R. 153, [1995] 4 S.C.R. 411, 44 C.R. (4th) 1, 103 C.C.C. (3d) 1, 130 D.L.R. (4th) 235, 191 N.R. 1, 68 B.C.A.C. 1, 112 W.A.C. 1, 33 C.R.R. (2d) 1 (S.C.C.) 260, 311
R. v. *Ogg-Moss*, 1984 CarswellOnt 804, 1984 CarswellOnt 64, [1984] 2 S.C.R. 173, 41 C.R. (3d) 297, 14 C.C.C. (3d) 116, 11 D.L.R. (4th) 549, 6 C.H.R.R. D/2498, 5 O.A.C. 81, 54 N.R. 81 (S.C.C.) 221
R. v. *Parrott*, 2001 CarswellNfld 13, 2001 CarswellNfld 14, [2001] S.C.J. No. 4, 2001 SCC 3, 150 C.C.C. (3d) 449, 194 D.L.R. (4th) 427, 39 C.R. (5th) 255, 265 N.R. 304, 198 Nfld. & P.E.I.R. 260, 595 A.P.R. 260, [2001] 1 S.C.R. 178 (S.C.C.) 63, 70, 74
R. v. *Peterson* (1996), 1996 CarswellOnt 628, 47 C.R. (4th) 161, 89 O.A.C. 60, 27 O.R. (3d) 739, 106 C.C.C. (3d) 64 (Ont. C.A.), leave to appeal refused 109 C.C.C. (3d) vi, 96 O.A.C. 79 (note), [1996] 3 S.C.R. xii, 206 N.R. 233 (note) (S.C.C.) 63, 66
R. v. *Prentice* (October 19, 1984), Doc. Oshawa 101/84, 1984 CarswellOnt 1685, 14 W.C.B. 39 (Ont. Fam. Ct.) 244
R. v. *R. (D.)*, 1996 CarswellSask 448, 1996 CarswellSask 449, [1996] S.C.J. No. 8, 197 N.R. 321, 107 C.C.C. (3d) 289, 136 D.L.R. (4th) 525, [1996] 2 S.C.R. 291, 48 C.R. (4th) 368, 144 Sask. R. 81, 124 W.A.C. 81 (S.C.C.) 71
R. v. *Robinson* (1899), 7 C.C.C. 52 (N.S. Co. Ct.) 218
R. v. *Rouse* (1978), 1978 CarswellBC 508, 1978 CarswellBC 561, (*sub nom.* McInroy v. R.) [1979] 1 S.C.R. 588, 5 C.R. (3d) 125, [1978] 6 W.W.R. 585, 42 C.C.C. (2d) 481, 23 N.R. 589, 89 D.L.R. (3d) 609 (S.C.C.) 76
R. v. *S. (W.)* (1994), 1994 CarswellOnt 63, [1994] O.J. No. 811, 29 C.R. (4th) 143, 18 O.R. (3d) 509, 90 C.C.C. (3d) 242, 70 O.A.C. 370 (Ont. C.A.), leave to appeal refused 35 C.R. (4th) 402 (note), 20 O.R. (3d) xv (note), 93 C.C.C. (3d) vi (note), 185 N.R. 398 (note), 86 O.A.C. 78 (note), [1994] 2 S.C.R. x (S.C.C.) 69, 81

R. v. Smith (1985), 1985 CarswellAlta 370, 66 A.R. 195 (Alta. C.A.) 77
R. v. Smith, 1992 CarswellOnt 103, [1992] S.C.J. No. 74, 1992 CarswellOnt 997, 15 C.R. (4th) 133, 75 C.C.C. (3d) 257, [1992] 2 S.C.R. 915, 55 O.A.C. 321, 139 N.R. 323, 94 D.L.R. (4th) 590 (S.C.C.) 69, 70, 71
R. v. Starr, 2000 CarswellMan 449, 2000 CarswellMan 450, [2000] S.C.J. No. 40, [1998] S.C.C.A. No. 141, 2000 SCC 40, 36 C.R. (5th) 1, 147 C.C.C. (3d) 449, 190 D.L.R. (4th) 591, [2000] 11 W.W.R. 1, 148 Man. R. (2d) 161, 224 W.A.C. 161, 258 N.R. 250, [2000] 2 S.C.R. 144 (S.C.C.) 74
R. v. Terry, 1996 CarswellBC 2299, 1996 CarswellBC 2300, 197 N.R. 105, 106 C.C.C. (3d) 508, 48 C.R. (4th) 137, 135 D.L.R. (4th) 214, 76 B.C.A.C. 25, 125 W.A.C. 25, 36 C.R.R. (2d) 21, [1996] 2 S.C.R. 207 (S.C.C.) 58
R. v. U. (F.J.), 1995 CarswellOnt 555, 1995 CarswellOnt 1175, 42 C.R. (4th) 133, 101 C.C.C. (3d) 97, 128 D.L.R. (4th) 121, 186 N.R. 365, 85 O.A.C. 321, [1995] 3 S.C.R. 764 (S.C.C.) 80
R. v. Vetrovec, 1982 CarswellBC 663, 1982 CarswellBC 682, [1982] 1 S.C.R. 811, *(sub nom. R. v. Gaja)* 67 C.C.C. (2d) 1, [1983] 1 W.W.R. 193, 27 C.R. (3d) 304, 136 D.L.R. (3d) 89, 41 N.R. 606 (S.C.C.) 79
R. v. W. (R.), 1992 CarswellOnt 90, 1992 CarswellOnt 991, [1992] S.C.J. No. 56, 13 C.R. (4th) 257, 137 N.R. 214, *(sub nom. R. c. W.)* [1992] 2 S.C.R. 122, 54 O.A.C. 164, 74 C.C.C. (3d) 134 (S.C.C.), reconsideration refused (November 18, 1992), Doc. 21820 (S.C.C.) 59, 68, 80
R. v. Watson (1996), 1996 CarswellOnt 2884, [1996] O.J. No. 2695, 108 C.C.C. (3d) 310, 50 C.R. (4th) 245, 92 O.A.C. 131, 30 O.R. (3d) 161 (Ont. C.A.) 58
Reference re Bill 30, an Act to amend the Education Act — see *Reference re Roman Catholic Separate High Schools Funding*.
Reference re Roman Catholic Separate High Schools Funding, 1987 CarswellOnt 1049, 1987 CarswellOnt 1049F, 77 N.R. 241, *(sub nom. Reference re Bill 30, an Act to amend the Education Act)* [1987] 1 S.C.R. 1148, *(sub nom. Reference re Act to Amend the Education Act (Ont.))* 40 D.L.R. (4th) 18, 22 O.A.C. 321, *(sub nom. Reference re Act to Amend the Education Act (Ont.))* 36 C.R.R. 305 (S.C.C.) 238
Robertson v. Niagara South Board of Education (1973), 1973 CarswellOnt 287, 1 O.R. (2d) 548, 41 D.L.R. (3d) 57 (Ont. Div. Ct.) 244
Ross v. New Brunswick School District No. 15 — see *Attis v. New Brunswick District No. 15 Board of Education*.
S. (B.), Re (1996), 1996 CarswellOnt 4811, [1996] O.J. No. 4428, 21 O.T.C. 308 (Ont. Gen. Div.) 36
S. (J.M.) v. M. (F.J.) (2004), 2004 CarswellOnt 3712, [2004] O.J. No. 3768, 244 D.L.R. (4th) 495, 6 R.F.L. (6th) 191 (Ont. S.C.J.) 287
S. (P.) v. Batth (1997), 1997 CarswellOnt 4216, [1997] O.J. No. 4089, 40 O.T.C. 236 (Ont. Gen. Div.) 53, 54

Seabrook v. Major (2005), 2005 CarswellOnt 3168, [2005] O.J. No. 3085 (Ont. Div. Ct.) 287
Solski c. Québec (Procureure générale), 2005 CarswellQue 762, 2005 SCC 14, *(sub nom. Solski (Tutor of) v. Quebec (Attorney General))* 250 D.L.R. (4th) 421 (S.C.C.) 238
South v. Tichelaar (2001), 2001 CarswellOnt 2447, [2001] O.J. No. 2823, 20 R.F.L. (5th) 175 (Ont. S.C.J.) 135
Strobridge v. Strobridge (1994), 1994 CarswellOnt 400, [1994] O.J. No. 1247, 18 O.R. (3d) 753, 115 D.L.R. (4th) 489, 4 R.F.L. (4th) 169, 72 O.A.C. 379 (Ont. C.A.) 328
Sudeyko v. Sudeyko (1974), 1974 CarswellBC 47, 18 R.F.L. 273 (B.C. S.C.) .. 150
Symes v. Canada — see *Symes v. R.*
Symes v. R., 1993 CarswellNat 1178, 1993 CarswellNat 1387, [1993] S.C.J. No. 131, 94 D.T.C. 6001, *(sub nom. Symes v. Canada)* [1993] 4 S.C.R. 695, *(sub nom. Symes v. Canada)* 19 C.R.R. (2d) 1, *(sub nom. Symes v. Canada)* [1994] 1 C.T.C. 40, *(sub nom. Symes v. Canada)* 110 D.L.R. (4th) 470, *(sub nom. Symes v. Minister of National Revenue)* 161 N.R. 243 (S.C.C.) 89
Thibaudeau v. Canada — see *Thibaudeau v. R.*
Thibaudeau v. R., 1995 CarswellNat 281, 1995 CarswellNat 704, [1995] S.C.J. No. 42, *(sub nom. R. v. Thibaudeau)* 95 D.T.C. 5273, 12 R.F.L. (4th) 1, *(sub nom. Thibaudeau v. Canada)* [1995] 1 C.T.C. 382, *(sub nom. Thibaudeau v. Canada)* 124 D.L.R. (4th) 449, *(sub nom. Thibaudeau v. Canada)* [1995] 2 S.C.R. 627, *(sub nom. Thibaudeau v. Minister of National Revenue)* 182 N.R. 1, *(sub nom. Thibaudeau v. Canada)* 29 C.R.R. (2d) 1 (S.C.C.) 89
Toronto (City) Board of Education v. Higgs (1959), 1959 CarswellOnt 91, [1960] S.C.R. 174, 22 D.L.R. (2d) 49 (S.C.C.) 279
Toronto (City) Board of Education v. O.S.S.T.F., District 15, [1997] S.C.J. No. 27, 1997 CarswellOnt 244, 1997 CarswellOnt 245, 25 C.C.E.L. (2d) 153, 144 D.L.R. (4th) 385, *(sub nom. Board of Education of Toronto v. Ontario Secondary School Teachers' Federation District 15)* 98 O.A.C. 241, [1997] 1 S.C.R. 487, 44 Admin. L.R. (2d) 1, 97 C.L.L.C. 220-018, *(sub nom. Board of Education of Toronto v. Ontario Secondary School Teachers' Federation District 15)* 208 N.R. 245, [1997] L.V.I. 2831-1 (S.C.C.) 266
Tremblay c. Daigle (1989), 1989 CarswellQue 124, 1989 CarswellQue 124F, [1989] S.C.J. No. 79, [1989] 2 S.C.R. 530, 62 D.L.R. (4th) 634, 102 N.R. 81, *(sub nom. Daigle v. Tremblay)* 11 C.H.R.R. D/165, *(sub nom. Daigle v. Tremblay)* 27 Q.A.C. 81 (S.C.C.) 88, 104, 105
Winnipeg Child & Family Services (Central Area) v. W. (K.L.), 2000 CarswellMan 469, 2000 CarswellMan 470, [2000] S.C.J. No. 48, 2000 SCC 48, 191 D.L.R. (4th) 1, [2001] 1 W.W.R. 1, 260 N.R. 203, 10 R.F.L. (5th) 122, 78 C.R.R. (2d) 1, [2000] 2 S.C.R. 519, 150 Man. R. (2d) 161, 230 W.A.C. 161 (S.C.C.) .. 40, 98, 99

Winnipeg Child & Family Services (Northwest Area) v. G. (D.F.) (1997), 1997 CarswellMan 475, 1997 CarswellMan 476, 152 D.L.R. (4th) 193, 31 R.F.L. (4th) 165, (*sub nom. Child & Family Services of Winnipeg Northwest v. D.F.G.*) 219 N.R. 241, 121 Man. R. (2d) 241, 158 W.A.C. 241, [1998] 1 W.W.R. 1, 39 C.C.L.T. (2d) 203 (Fr.), [1997] 3 S.C.R. 925, 39 C.C.L.T. (2d) 155 (Eng.), 3 B.H.R.C. 611 (S.C.C.) 104, 106, 108

Wynberg v. Ontario (2005), 2005 CarswellOnt 1242, [2005] O.J. No. 1228, 252 D.L.R. (4th) 10 (Ont. S.C.J.) 241, 252

Young v. Young, [1993] S.C.J. No. 112, 1993 CarswellBC 264, 1993 CarswellBC 1269, [1993] 8 W.W.R. 513, 108 D.L.R. (4th) 193, 18 C.R.R. (2d) 41, [1993] 4 S.C.R. 3, 84 B.C.L.R. (2d) 1, 160 N.R. 1, 49 R.F.L. (3d) 117, 34 B.C.A.C. 161, 56 W.A.C. 161, [1993] R.D.F. 703 (S.C.C.) 89, 109, 116, 117, 119, 121, 141, 143

Zylberberg v. Sudbury (Board of Education) (1988), 1988 CarswellOnt 1093, 29 O.A.C. 23, 34 C.R.R. 1, 65 O.R. (2d) 641, 52 D.L.R. (4th) 577 (Ont. C.A.) 238

1
WHO IS THE CHILD?

> Unless the investment in children is made, all of humanity's most fundamental long-term problems will remain fundamental long-term problems.
> *UNICEF, "The State of the World's Children" (1995)*

> Lawyers, I suppose, were children once.
> *Charles Lamb (1775 - 1834)*

The aim of this book is to provide some guidance on the law as it relates to children. But, before that somewhat daunting task is attempted, a more fundamental issue arises. Who is the child?

The answer to this question is perhaps more complex than one might anticipate. In fact, the tangle of legal regulations defining, delineating or impacting "the child" sets no one standard by which this junior status is consistently defined. Age of Majority and Accountability legislation pegs the graduation date from youth at the somewhat advanced standard of 18. Liquor laws commonly demand that no sales be made to individuals under the age of 19. Still other legal regimes (such as Ontario's *Child and Family Services Act*) accord rights to individuals as young as 7 years old (e.g., for the purposes of consenting to adoption). Still other sources of law consider the issue apart from the matter of chronological standing and on the basis of capacity.

The simple answer to this difficult question is that there is no one legal definition of "the child". Rather, there are a multitude of standards and definitions of "the child" for the purposes of the law in Ontario and in Canada, which makes understanding the many areas of the law that impinge upon the lives of young persons all that more challenging.

Simply put, the definition of "the child" for the purposes of the law (and by inference the ascension to adulthood or license for the purposes of various legal standards) varies, and must be viewed and applied in the context (and frequently within the statutory or regulatory authority) in which it arises. While no complete catalogue of definitions of the term "child" is possible, the following is a necessarily incomplete survey of some of the statutory authority in Ontario and Canada that set the benchmarks for "child".[1]

AGE 7 AND OVER

Pursuant to subsection 137(6) of the *Child and Family Services Act*,[2] an order for the adoption of a "person" over the age of 7 years cannot be made without that person's written consent. Even at the young age of 7, in small measure, a person acquires some legal recognition as an individual capable of views and choices.

UNDER AGE 10

Pursuant to the *Day Nurseries Act*,[3] to receive temporary care in a facility governed by that statute, including private home daycare (which is independent of a school), one has to be under the age of 10 years (except for a day nursery for children with developmental disabilities where the threshold is 18 years old).

---
[1] "Legal Milestones" *Justice for Children and Youth*, 2000.
[2] R.S.O. 1990, c. C.11 (as amended) [hereinafter "CFSA"].
[3] R.S.O. 1990, c. D.2.

AGE 12 AND UNDER

Under the CFSA, clauses 37(2)(j) and 37(2)(k), a "child" under the age of 12 years can be apprehended as "in need of protection" for engaging in serious criminal behaviour (e.g., having killed or seriously injured another person, or caused serious damage to another's property). Further, subsection 117(2) of the CFSA requires the Minister of Community and Social Services to provide consent if a child younger than 12 is to be the subject of a "secure treatment order" in a "secure treatment program" (a program for the treatment of children with mental disorders, in which continuous restrictions are imposed on their liberty).

A person "apparently under twelve years of age" who is not accompanied by a person of "apparently sixteen years or more of age" is not permitted to buy a ticket or be admitted to a movie theatre after 7:30 p.m. on any day, pursuant to the *Theatres Act*. Such an individual is also constrained from buying a movie ticket during the school year, except during school holidays between the hours of 9:30 and 7:30 p.m., and during regular school days between the post-dismissal hours of 3:30 and 7:30.

OVER THE AGE OF 12

Section 94 of the *Provincial Offences Act*[4] limits the ability of a Provincial Offences Court to convict anyone for the breach of such an enactment that was committed before the individual attained 12 years of age. This makes such a young person vulnerable to conviction for such offences as truancy as provided in subsection 30(5) of the *Education Act*. Similarly, attaining the age of 12 is also the benchmark for the *Youth Criminal Justice Act*.[5]

---

[4] R.S.O. 1990, c. P.33 [hereinafter "POA"].
[5] S.C. 2002, c. 1.

Numerous aspects of Ontario's primary child protection legislation, the CFSA, are also engaged after age 12. Under this legislation, a child over 12 can:

- consent to counselling provided by a "service provider" as defined in the statute (section 28);
- consent to a voluntary care arrangement by a children's aid society (section 29);
- consent to a voluntary child protection proceeding (subsection 37(2)(l));
- apply for a review of his/her status of being in care (society supervision, society wardship or Crown wardship) (subsection 64(4)(a)); and
- be committed to a "secure treatment program" (a program for treatment of children with mental disorders with continuous restrictions on their liberty) (subsection 117(2)).

A child between over the age of 12 and under the age of 16 who has been an informal patient in a psychiatric facility is conferred the right to apply to the Consent and Capacity Review Board for a hearing to determine whether he or she needs care in a psychiatric facility pursuant to the *Mental Health Act*.[6]

A child over the age of 12 may also consent to an application made by a person with custody of that younger person to a change of name made pursuant to the *Change of Name Act*.[7]

A person over 12 also enjoys miscellaneous privileges as a matter of law. For example, an Ontario resident who is over 12 may be issued an "Apprentice Hunter Safety Card" (with parental consent) after successfully completing a "hunter education course", pursuant to the regulations made under the *Fish and Wildlife Conservation Act, 1997*.[8]

---

[6] S.O. 1997, c. M.7.
[7] R.S.O. 1990, c. C.7.
[8] S.O. 1997, c. 41.

OVER THE AGE OF 14

A person over the age of 14 attains a number of diverse benchmarks for the purpose of legal status. A regulation made under the *Occupational Health and Safety Act*[9] requires that as a matter of safety, all workers in "industrial establishments" (other than a factory) must be at least 14 years of age.[10] For the purposes of the *Theatres Act*, an individual over the age of 14 may attend movies rated "14A" without adult accompaniment.

A parent of a child of 14 years or older of compulsory school age may apply, pursuant to Ontario Regulation 308,[11] for their child to be admitted to a "supervised alternative learning program" offered by a school board pursuant to that regulation.

Canada's *Criminal Code* sets the age of 14 as the threshold under which certain acts toward or involving such a person constitute an offence, including the abduction of an individual under that threshold, in certain circumstances. A person over the age of 14 can also consent to sexual conduct, provided that his or her partner is not in a position of trust or authority in respect to them, as might constitute the offences of sexual interference or sexual exploitation contrary to sections 151 and 153, respectively, of that statute.

Under the *Youth Criminal Justice Act*, the former practice of transfer to adult court has been succeeded by clothing the Youth Court with the power to impose adult sentences. Under the statute, the age where it is presumed that adult sentences are appropriate dispositions for the most serious of criminal offences is 14 (with some latitude given to the Provinces concerning the age at which the presumption will apply in their respective jurisdictions).

---

[9] R.R.O. 1990, Reg. 851, amended to O. Reg. 280/05.
[10] *Ibid.* at s. 4(1)(e).
[11] R.R.O. 1990, pursuant to the *Education Act*.

AGE 15

An individual's passage of this seldom-used, 'in-between' age standard very occasionally accords rights to an individual as a matter of law, including the right to get certain types of licences so long as there is parental consent.[12] Regarding employment, a worker must be 15 to work in a factory (but not in a logging operation).[13]

AGE 16

The age of 16 is the benchmark for children's aid legislation in Ontario, with individuals under that age being subject to protection as a matter of law from the categories of mistreatment and misbehaviour set out in Part III of the *Child and Family Services Act*.

Similarly, after reaching 16, a child can withdraw from parental control pursuant to the *Child and Family Services Act* (section 65); in which case a parent's obligation to provide support under the *Family Law Act*, subsection 31(2) is ended. The age of 16 also brings an end to the obligation of mandatory school attendance in Ontario (under section 21 of the *Education Act*), although at this writing, a review of this standard is being considered. Relatedly, an individual of 16 years of age or more can make an agreement to enter an apprenticeship program to learn a trade or skill set, pursuant to the *Apprenticeship and Certification Act, 1998*.[14]

An individual of 16 years of age or over is enfranchised pursuant to a number of provincial enactments in Ontario. For

---

[12] See, for example, Reg. 665/98 made pursuant to the *Fish and Wildlife Conservation Act, 1997* in which a 15 year old may be granted a licence tag to hunt a variety of listed animals when parental consent is given.
[13] *Supra* note 9 at s. 4(1)(d).
[14] S.O. 1998, c. 22.

example, rights are given under provincial privacy legislation, with both the *Freedom of Information and Protection of Privacy Act* (subsection 66(c)) and its municipal counterpart, the *Municipal Freedom of Information and Protection of Privacy Act* (subsection 54(c)), allowing a person who has passed that threshold to assert and defend their individual privacy and access to information rights. A 16 year old also has the power pursuant to the *Change of Name Act* to apply to amend his or her surname, given name or both.[15] The power to make fairly serious and substantial life decisions in part comes to an individual of 16 years of age or greater, with a legal presumption being made under Ontario legislation that a person of that age has capacity to make decisions as to personal care.[16] Similarly, this age is also the threshold for status in resepect to express wishes in regard to medical treatment pursuant to the *Health Care Consent Act, 1996*.[17] Getting to age 16 also allows one to be put on the road to licensing as a driver, under *the Highway Traffic Act*.[18]

Greater power and involvement in one's own affairs is also correlated with a greater ability at the same time to get involved with matters of public concern: an individual over 16 years of age can be involved as a scrutineer in a campaign held pursuant to the *Elections Act*, and with the permission of the Chief Elections Officer can be pressed into service as a scrutineer.[19]

Greater individual involvement in the working world is also made possible at this age, with the ability to apprentice in a trade given after a person's 16th birthday.[20] This age is also

---

[15] R.S.O. 1990, c. C.7, s. 4(1).
[16] *Substitute Decisions Act, 1992*, S.O. 1992, c. 30, s. 2(2).
[17] S.O. 1996, c. 2, Sched. A. See, for example, ss.1(c), 21, 35 and 36.
[18] R.S.O. 1990, c. H.8, as amended. See, for example, s. 34.
[19] See *Elections Act*, R.S.O. 1990, c. E.6, ss. 18(3.3) and 32(1).
[20] See *Trades Qualification and Apprenticeship Act*, R.S.O. 1990, c. T.17, s. 1 and also Reg. 1055, R.R.O. 1990 made under this statute, including s. 3(a).

the gatekeeper, for safety reasons, for various types and categories of employment.[21]

OVER 17

Like age 15, there are few rights or limitations applying to individuals who attain the odd number of 17. One permission accorded at this age level is the ability to apprentice in the "certified trade" of iron-working.[22]

AGE 18

This year attainment marks a traditionally recognized entry point into adulthood: the right to vote.[23] Indeed, at least one piece of provincial legislation decrees that one leaves behind one's status as a "minor" or "infant" upon attaining this "age of majority".[24] Making the "age of majority" clothes an individual with a presumed capacity to enter into a contract.[25]

Coincident with gaining this fundamental right of citizenship, is the ability to play a prominent role in some of society's

---

[21] See, for example, Reg. 851, R.R.O. 1990 made under the *Occupational Health and Safety Act*, which requires an individual to be at least 15 to work in a factory or 16 to work in a logging operation. See also O. Reg. 213/91, which sets this standard for construction works. See also Reg. 565, R.R.O. 1990 made pursuant to the *Health Protection and Promotion Act*, s. 17, which limits lifeguard duties to individuals over 16.
[22] Ontario Reg. 1065, R.R.O. 1990, made pursuant to the *Trades Qualification and Apprenticeship Act*, s. 5.
[23] See, for example, the *Elections Act*, R.S.O. 1990, c. E.6, s. 15(1)(a) and *Canada Elections Act*, S.C. 2000, c. 9, s. 3.
[24] *Age of Majority and Accountability Act*, R.S.O. 1990, c. A.7.
[25] See *Substitute Decisions Act, 1992*, S.O. 1992, c. 30, s. 2(2).

organizations, including the recognized capacity to incorporate a company, and to serve on its board of directors.[26]

An 18 year old also becomes able to pursue or attain registration in a number of diverse professions and career pursuits that set their entry bar at this age standard.[27] Some other occupational enterprises demand a minimum age of 18 for the purposes of entry as a matter of health and safety regulations.[28]

Being 18 also lets an individual in on some perhaps more capricious aspects of modern adult life, including the ability to see a "restricted" or "18A" classification movie,[29] or to indulge in the simple (or perhaps foolish) pleasure of the purchase a lottery ticket.[30]

AGE 19

Despite the apparent assurances of uniform departure from the world of the "infant" or "minor" contained in the *Age of Majority and Accountability Act*, full access to the activities of the adult world (and perhaps, by inference, complete departure from the world and status of "the child") is not granted at a person's 18th birthday. Still other powers and abilities are

---

[26] See *Business Corporations Act*, R.S.O. 1990, c. B.16, ss. 4(2)(a) and 118(1) and also the *Corporations Act*, R.S.O. 1990, c. C.38, ss. 4(1) and 286(4). The comparable age threshold also applies in the *Condominium Act*, S.O. 1998, c. 19 (see s. 29(1)(a)) and the *Cooperative Corporations Act*, R.S.O. 1990, c. C.35.

[27] See, for example, the *Architects Act*, R.S.O. 1990, c. A.26, s. 13(1); see also Reg. 278, R.R.O. 1990 made under the *Drugless Practitioners Act*; Reg. 26/05 made under the *Travel Industry Act*, 2002, s. 5; see also the *Police Services Act*, R.S.O. 1990, c. P.15, s. 43(1)(b).

[28] See Regs. 854 and 859, R.R.O. 1990, made pursuant to the *Occupational Health and Safety Act*.

[29] See O. Reg. 1031, R.R.O. 1990, s. 2(5).

[30] See *Ontario Lottery and Gaming Corporation Act, 1999*, S.O. 1999, c. 12, Sched. L, s. 13(1).

reserved to the age of 19, including the right to: purchase and consume alcoholic beverages;[31] purchase tobacco products;[32] and attend at, and partake in, the offerings of "gaming premises".[33] In this latter realm, those licensed to provide games of chance are prohibited from directing their advertisements to encourage the participation of those who are under 19 years of age in "games of chance".[34]

Admission to community colleges is generally restricted to applicants 19 years of age or older pursuant to a regulation made under the *Ontario Colleges of Applied Arts and Technology Act, 2002*.[35]

UNDER 21

While rare, the upper limit of childhood does not entirely end at age 19 either, with a handful of public enactments conferring some aspect of "child" recognition (for limited purposes mainly in connection with benefits to dependent "children") to individuals bumping the final threshold of being under the age of 21.[36]

What does this seeming morass of apparently contradictory and independent laws and regulations mean in terms of meaningfully defining "the child" for the purpose of understanding how to deal with these individuals on a day-to-day basis? Simply, it means that in any situation, the answer to the question "who is the child" is incredibly context-specific, with def-

---

[31] *Liquor Licence Act*, R.S.O. 1990, c. L.19, s. 30(1).
[32] *Tobacco Control Act, 1994*, S.O. 1994, c. 10, s. 3(1).
[33] *Ontario Lottery and Gaming Corporation Act*, S.O. 1999, c. 12, Sched. L, s. 13(3). See also O. Reg. 385/99 made pursuant to the *Gaming Control Act*, s. 32.
[34] See O. Reg. 385/99 made under the *Gaming Control Act*, s. 31(1)(c).
[35] S.O. 2002, c. 8, Sched. F. See O. Reg. 34/03, s. 11(1).
[36] See, for example, the *Family Benefits Act*, R.S.O. 1990, c. F.2, s. 1 and Reg. 977, R.R.O. 1990, made under the *Public Service Act*, s. 74(4).

initions and applications of the term being variable and changing even in attempts to apply one statute and its regulations. At the same time, this does not mean that the assimilation and understanding of the law pertaining to the "child" (despite the term's shifting definitions) is wholly and frustratingly impossible. Rather, it serves as a reminder that anyone who deals with children should be very conscious and attuned to the context (both as a matter of practical application and law) in which this contact occurs.

In the succeeding chapters, we attempt to visit some of these contexts and explain, in what we hope is a straightforward and meaningful way, the law as it applies to many of the common contexts and concerns involving this now mysterious character called "the child". While no one publication, including this one, can completely treat and conquer all of these many situations, it is our sincere hope that we captured ones that have resonance and meaning for the reader, as both matters of interest and occupational life.

2
AN INTRODUCTION TO THE *CHILD AND FAMILY SERVICES ACT*

A famous African proverb notes for us "it takes a village to raise a child". It is unclear whether Canadian society fully subscribes to that premise in laws pertaining to children. However, it does seem certain that Canadian society agrees that it takes a "village" to protect a child.

In this regard, one of the key components of child protection law throughout Canada (and certainly within the Province of Ontario) is the notion that ordinary citizens and especially professionals have a duty to report suspected child abuse to local child protection agencies.

While one would hope that all citizens would automatically report crimes (and especially crimes involving physical injury or harm) to the proper authorities, this is not always the case. With respect to most crimes, the legal reality has been for the most part that reporting of occurrences is a voluntary action that a citizen can take or not take on his or her own initiative. This is usually accepted as being within the realm of the right of citizens to have some control over "private matters".[1]

---

[1] For a review of some of the considerations between the "right of privacy"

However, in the case of suspected child abuse or neglect, our society has decided that the welfare of children and their protection is of such importance that the entire "village" is obligated, by law, to report even the suspicion of the commission of such an offence to the local child protection agency.

Accordingly, while anyone involved in caring for children in some capacity will want to have some general knowledge of child protection laws given their importance, because of the mandatory duty to report in many jurisdictions, it is especially important that one is aware of the laws in one's own area regarding the obligation to report suspected child abuse. A failure to report can potentially result in serious consequences for an individual and/or his or her organization.

Before examining the reporting requirements concerning child abuse and neglect, it may be appropriate to provide a general overview of child protection legislation and how it differs from other legislation regarding children.

WHAT IS CHILD PROTECTION LEGISLATION?

In simplest terms, child protection legislation is a law intended to protect children. However, there is a great difference of opinion—from area to area and culture to culture—concerning from *what* children need to be protected, from *whom* they are to be protected; and *who is* charged with *doing the protecting*.

In Canada, the provinces (and territories) have responsibility under the Constitution for children and each has established its' own legislation with its own system to protect children. In Ontario, the legislation intended to protect children is entitled the *Child and Family Services Act* (the "CFSA").

---

and the mandatory obligation to report child abuse with reference to the Alberta Act, see Wayne N. Renke's article, "The Mandatory Reporting of Child Abuse Under the Child Welfare Act" (1999) 7 Health L.J. 91-140.

The CFSA was amended substantially in 1999. One of the major amendments to the CFSA at that time was to "beef up" the obligations to report suspected child abuse for the general population and especially the duties of professionals.

Prior to the 1999 amendments, the Act was unclear as to what consequences would be imposed for failing to report child abuse to the Ontario welfare authorities. The revised Act not only makes it mandatory for professionals to report suspicions of abuse, but for the first time makes it an offence to fail to report the abuse that comes to the attention of a professional while performing his or her professional duties. A professional who fails in this obligation faces a fine of up to $1,000.[2]

It remains unclear whether or not these new provisions will have the desired effect of protecting more children. There is no doubt that since the amendments, there has been (and continues to be) an increase in the families who come into contact with Ontario child protection agencies. However, there is debate as to whether or not this is because of an increase in reporting or because of other factors.

Some have attributed the increase to various other factors that are not solely related to the increased obligation to report.[3] Other reasons for increased contact include the reductions that have occurred in social assistance and other services that are available to parents living in or close to poverty. Parents with marginal incomes find it increasingly difficult to provide basic necessities for their children, let alone pay for the additional services their children may need. At the same time that resources of the parents are being cut back, Children's Aid Societies have had their resources and mandate increased. As a

---

[2] Section 72 of the *Child and Family Services Act*, R.S.O. 1990, c. C.11, as amended [hereinafter "CFSA"].

[3] See, for example, Professors Karen J. Swift and Henry Parada, "Child Welfare Reform: Protecting Children or Policing the Poor" (Article prepared for the Journal of Law and Social Policy) [accepted for publication].

result, more and more scrutiny is being placed on these families.

Unfortunately other protections in place for the families have also been decreased. For example, it is generally agreed that difficulties in accessing funding assistance has led to decreased willingness on the part of legal counsel to take child protection matters on behalf of parents. A consequence of that is some cases with self-represented parents "linger" in the system longer than they should. Of course these cases take up time and resources that the courts might be better using on other, perhaps more urgent, matters.

Other factors for increased contact will be specific to the particular population being examined.[4]

Historically, it has been and continues to be extremely difficult to track whether or not mandatory reporting of child abuse results in increased protection for children. It is difficult to determine in hindsight whether or not something should have been reported at the time it occurred. In this respect, each professional may differ on whether or not there are reasonable grounds to believe a child is being abused and "in need of protection". There are a number of factors that contribute to a professional's decision-making and whether or not something is "reportable".[5]

---

[4] See, for example, the University of Western Ontario's study released in October 2003, entitled Protecting Children is Everybody's Business: Investigating the Increasing Demand for Service at the Children's Aid Society of London and Middlesex, by Leschied, Whitehead, Hurley and Chiodo.

[5] For a review of a "study" on the factors that go into the reporting of child abuse and whether or not it is under reported please see Ronda Bessner's article, "The Duty to Report Child Abuse" (1999-2000) 17 C.F.L.Q. 277.

WHEN IS A CHILD IN NEED OF PROTECTION?

Being "in need of protection" is a broad term, with many categories. Essentially, the use of this term denotes that a child's circumstances have been such that they fall under one of the enumerated headings for a finding under section 37 of the CFSA. These categories of circumstances for a child range from physical abuse and neglect (and the risk of abuse and neglect) to a situation where the family consents to the child coming into care.

It can be very difficult to determine when a child is in need of protection. All of us have subjective values about how children should be raised and what would be "permissible" given our own backgrounds and personal beliefs.

The new amendments on reporting specifically outline the legislative sections that are used by the court to find a child is in need of protection. It is hoped that this will assist a professional who can use his or her particular expertise to assess whether the particular matter in front of him or her qualifies as something that should be reported. They can be grouped, generally as physical abuse, sexual abuse and emotional abuse; however, the actual sections are much more detailed, namely section 37(2) of the CFSA:

> 37(2) A child is in need of protection where,
>
> > (a) the child has suffered physical harm, inflicted by the person having charge of the child or caused by or resulting from that person's,
> >
> > > (i) failure to adequately care for, provide for, supervise or protect the child, or
> > >
> > > (ii) pattern of neglect in caring for, providing for, supervising or protecting the child;
> >
> > (b) there is a risk that the child is likely to suffer physical harm inflicted by the person having charge of the child or caused by or resulting from that person's,

(i) failure to adequately care for, provide for, supervise or protect the child, or

(ii) pattern of neglect in caring for, providing for, supervising or protecting the child;

(c) the child has been sexually molested or sexually exploited, by the person having charge of the child or by another person where the person having charge of the child knows or should know of the possibility of sexual molestation or sexual exploitation and fails to protect the child;

(d) there is a risk that the child is likely to be sexually molested or sexually exploited as described in clause (c);

(e) the child requires medical treatment to cure, prevent or alleviate physical harm or suffering and the child's parent or the person having charge of the child does not provide, or refuses or is unavailable or unable to consent to, the treatment;

(f) the child has suffered emotional harm, demonstrated by serious,

(i) anxiety,

(ii) depression,

(iii) withdrawal,

(iv) self-destructive or aggressive behaviour, or

(v) delayed development,

and there are reasonable grounds to believe that the emotional harm suffered by the child results from the actions, failure to act or pattern of neglect on the part of the child's parent or the person having charge of the child;

(f.1) the child has suffered emotional harm of the kind described in subclause (f) (i), (ii), (iii), (iv) or (v) and the child's parent or the person having charge of the child does not provide, or refuses or is unavailable or unable to consent to, services or treatment to remedy or alleviate the harm;

(g) there is a risk that the child is likely to suffer emotional harm of the kind described in subclause (f) (i), (ii), (iii), (iv) or (v) resulting from the actions, failure to act or pattern of neglect on the part of the child's parent or the person having charge of the child;

(g.1) there is a risk that the child is likely to suffer emotional harm of the kind described in subclause (f) (i), (ii), (iii), (iv) or (v) and that the child's parent or the person having charge of the child

INTRODUCTION TO THE CFSA ♦ 19

does not provide, or refuses or is unavailable or unable to consent to, services or treatment to prevent the harm;

(h) the child suffers from a mental, emotional or developmental condition that, if not remedied, could seriously impair the child's development and the child's parent or the person having charge of the child does not provide, or refuses or is unavailable or unable to consent to, treatment to remedy or alleviate the condition;

(i) the child has been abandoned, the child's parent has died or is unavailable to exercise his or her custodial rights over the child and has not made adequate provision for the child's care and custody, or the child is in a residential placement and the parent refuses or is unable or unwilling to resume the child's care and custody;

(j) the child is less than twelve years old and has killed or seriously injured another person or caused serious damage to another person's property, services or treatment are necessary to prevent a recurrence and the child's parent or the person having charge of the child does not provide, or refuses or is unavailable or unable to consent to, those services or treatment;

(k) the child is less than twelve years old and has on more than one occasion injured another person or caused loss or damage to another person's property, with the encouragement of the person having charge of the child or because of that person's failure or inability to supervise the child adequately; or

(l) the child's parent is unable to care for the child and the child is brought before the court with the parent's consent and, where the child is twelve years of age or older, with the child's consent, to be dealt with under this Part.

Unfortunately, while a reading of the enumerated protection grounds in the statute make them seem concrete and easily determined, in practice, different opinions can be formed with respect to the same facts: the reality is that personal judgments and an individual's personal values enter into determining when a child is in need of protection.

For example, the statute lists "physical harm" as grounds on which a child may be in need of protection. "Physical harm", as a matter of law, seems self-evident and easily definable.

However, it becomes not quite so clear in a world with differing individual and cultural foundations. There are many examples where "physical harm" of a child occurs, but its occurrence goes unaddressed, for cultural, religious or other reason with little comment from the court or from child protection agencies. Activities ranging from piercing ears to circumcision all cause "physical harm". Yet it is doubtful that anyone would expect a professional daycare provider, nurse or teacher to report these "harms" to the child protection authorities.

Given this "flexibility" in the practical application of child protection statutes, it is understandable that confusion arises amongst people dealing with children. If concrete situations of the physical harm can result in different reactions, then it is no less surprising that there is even greater confusion where the existence of abuse is less obvious; e.g., situations in which the question is whether a child is suffering from, or at risk to suffer, "emotional harm",[6] a far less tangible form of abuse.

The confusion makes "what to report" and "when to report" a challenge for all those involved with children in their daily professional lives.

As well, just as child-rearing practices and child care preferences change from time to time, so too, does our understanding of the nature of "child abuse" change from time to time. These changes in viewpoint and opinion can sometimes occur quickly. They can also happen prior to, or significantly after, a general consensus in society as to whether such a concern needs to be addressed through changes to child protection legislation. These "value differences" can and often do cause

---

[6] Although it can be determined, and recent cases have assisted in outlining what the court will accept to be "emotional harm." See: *Catholic Children's Aid Society of Hamilton-Wentworth v. L. (C.)* [2002] O.J. No. 4255 (Ont. S.C.J.); *Catholic Children's Aid Society of Toronto v. M.R.* [2003] O.J. No. 4385 (Ont. C.J.); *Children and Family Services for York Region v. S.D.* [2003] O.J. No. 4330 (Ont. S.C.).

friction between the various stakeholders in the child protection arena as different groups and individuals disagree on the "science" of whether a child needs protecting. Even if there is an agreement reached on whether a child needs protection, there can be significant differences among experts as to how the child can be protected and ultimately what is in the best interests of each child. This is true in Ontario as much as any other jurisdiction.[7]

If a child is not found to be "in need of protection" under one or more of the categories in section 37(2), then there is no role for the child protection agencies. If, for example, a child has been removed or "apprehended" from the home in the course of an investigation, and the court finds that there was no need for protection at the time of Society intervention, then the child is sent home.

For example, we recently have seen a debate on the boundaries of physical discipline of children at the highest court level.[8] Although it was a challenge to the legality of a section of Canada's *Criminal Code* (and not, *per se*, a child protection matter), the fact that each of level of Court struggled with the different opinions of various experts on the boundaries of permissible intervention with children reveals the difficulty in arriving at a societal standard or consensus for defining child "abuse" or clarifying what steps are needed to protect children. For some professionals, seeing a child being struck by an adult is an "abuse" regardless of the reason or reasonableness of the action or the context in which the incident occurs. For some people, such an event constitutes a "reportable" matter. For others, it is simply an acceptable technique for child rearing.

---

[7] See, for example, the concerns raised by Professor Nicholas Bala in his article entitled, "Reforming Ontario's *Child and Family Services Act*: Is the Pendulum Swinging Back Too Far?" (1999) 17 C.F.L.Q. 121.

[8] *Canadian Foundation for Children, Youth & the Law v. Canada (Attorney General)* 2004 SCC 4 (S.C.C.).

There will always be these differences but one must comply with as to what is or what is not reportable, what is child abuse, and which are applicable in one's own area—whether that "area" is defined by region or profession. One may disagree with the standards, but one needs to follow the law. Only the passage of time will determine whether the system in place was one that met the objectives of all of those concerned: to ensure that children have a warm, nurturing and safe home environment. Even such tests as the "best interests of the child" (which is the governing standard in Ontario for deciding legal questions concerning children) can come under criticism where it is used as simply a means to use personal experience and feelings as a method to decide matters that have an irrevocable impact on a child's life.[9]

As a result of all of these uncertainties, you will not find in this book (or perhaps in any other book) a definitive answer regarding when or when not to report your suspicions that a child is being abused or in need of protection. The most that can be said is that if you have a reasonable suspicion that a child is in need of protection then you must report it to local child protection authorities. Whether you are correct or not correct in your assessment is ultimately a question for the court to decide. It is the court that ultimately determines the matter on a case-by-case basis in the context of the particular laws and concerns in your specific jurisdiction.

While there can be no definitive answers as to what and when to report your suspicions regarding whether a child is abused, this chapter is intended to provide you with an overview of the child protection law in Ontario. Hopefully, it will provide some insight and foundation for analyzing when, if and how

---

[9] For an example of an analysis of the "best interests" test please see "'Best Interests' in Child Protection Proceedings: Implications and Alternatives" (1994-1995) 12 C.J.F.L. 367 by Bernd Walter, Janine Alison Isenegger and Nicholas Bala.

you should make a report to the child welfare agencies in your area.

However, always keep in mind that the child protection agency is governed by the laws regarding children in their jurisdiction. There may be limits on what a child protection agency can do to intervene in the situation with which you are faced. Sometimes these limits can be frustrating. But, these legal boundaries ensure that there are safeguards against unjust use of what can be a very powerful statutory body. As one justice has put it, "The society's powers, substantial as they are, are not unbridled. Those powers are limited to those articulated in the legislation."[10]

Regardless of how the information is reported to a Society, the Society is mandated to investigate the allegations or evidence and evaluate whether a child is in need of protection as defined under the CFSA.[11] To evaluate these aspects, a number of steps and tools are used to attempt to quantify the risk to the child based on the known facts.

Again the implementation of these tools and steps in any investigation vary from area to area. In Ontario, three assessment tools are used: 1) the Eligibility Spectrum; 2) the Child Welfare Well-Being Scales; and 3) the Ontario Risk Assessment Model 2000. They are utilized by the Society to determine whether, from its perspective, the child is in need of protection.

While the tools are of assistance to the Society for reporting purposes, the criteria for determining whether or not a child is in need of protection are outlined in the CFSA.

---

[10] *Children's Aid Society of Toronto v. M. (A.)* [2002] O.J. No. 1432 (Ont. C.J.) at para. 63.
[11] See s. 15(3) of the CFSA for details on the functions of a Children's Aid Society.

THE *CHILD AND FAMILY SERVICES ACT*

The CFSA is the legislation that establishes a complete code and framework for protecting children in Ontario. It is "invoked" when it is alleged that a child has been abused or otherwise has been cared for in a way that falls below minimally acceptable standards for our community.

It must be emphasized that the CFSA is an Ontario Act and only applies to child protection matters in Ontario. Other provinces and other countries will have their own specific pieces of legislation to protect children and they will have their own specific reporting obligations and responsibilities. You should check more formally with your own legal resources in your area for specific information as to the laws and procedures with respect to protecting children in your region.

The CFSA has as its' paramount purpose ". . .to promote the best interests, protection and well being of children."[12] Within that paramount purpose, there are other purposes of the Act that factor into any decision making that is made under the CFSA. These additional purposes of the CFSA are applied so long as they are consistent with the best interests, protection and well being of children. They include the following:

. . .

> 1. To recognize that while parents may need help in caring for their children, that help should give support to the autonomy and integrity of the family unit and, wherever possible, be provided on the basis of mutual consent.
>
> 2. To recognize that the least disruptive course of action that is available and is appropriate in a particular case to help a child should be considered.
>
> 3. To recognize that children's services should be provided in a manner that,

---

[12] Section 1(1) of the CFSA.

i. respects children's needs for continuity of care and for stable family relationships, and

ii. takes into account physical and mental developmental differences among children.

4. To recognize that, wherever possible, services to children and their families should be provided in a manner that respects cultural, religious and regional differences.

5. To recognize that Indian and native people should be entitled to provide, wherever possible, their own child and family services, and that all services to Indian and native children and families should be provided in a manner that recognizes their culture, heritage and traditions and the concept of the extended family.[13]

To fulfill these purposes, the CFSA authorizes the establishment of agencies in specific jurisdictions to carry out the task of protecting children.[14] These agencies (which can have a variety of names) have a number of functions enunciated for them under the CFSA. These include the following:

. . .

(a) investigate allegations or evidence that children who are under the age of sixteen years or are in the society's care or under its supervision may be in need of protection;

(b) protect, where necessary, children who are under the age of sixteen years or are in the society's care or under its supervision;

(c) provide guidance, counselling and other services to families for protecting children or for the prevention of circumstances requiring the protection of children;

(d) provide care for children assigned or committed to its care under this Act;

(e) supervise children assigned to its supervision under this Act;

(f) place children for adoption under Part VII; and

(g) perform any other duties given to it by this or any other Act.[15]

---

[13] *Ibid.* at s. 1(2).
[14] Section 15.
[15] Section 15(3) of the CFSA.

DIFFERENT JURISDICTIONS

As noted above, while the CFSA applies to the entire province, the task of child protection is divided amongst some 53 different non-profit corporations—all of which are deemed under the CFSA to be children's aid societies. (For ease of discussion, we refer to all of the child protection agencies as "Children's Aid Societies" or the "Society" even though in reality they often have different names.)

A Society can only protect children within its own jurisdiction and must report to a court in its specific jurisdiction.[16] This fact, along with the fact that there are individual court jurisdictions within the Province of Ontario, can make for strikingly different experiences in dealing with Children's Aid Societies or courts in different parts of Ontario. However, despite these differences, there are certain "common themes" that apply to all Children's Aid Societies. Hopefully, an appreciation of these common themes will allow you to ask and address specific concerns that may arise in your own jurisdiction that may have its own particular procedures and protocols.

As with many things, it is sometimes easier to understand a concept by defining it by exclusion: ascertaining what something is by referring to what it is not. In this regard, the CFSA is different than a custody matter.

CHILD PROTECTION DIFFERS FROM CUSTODY

There is another, no less important, piece of legislation in Ontario that is concerned with the welfare of children, namely the *Children's Law Reform Act*.[17]

---

[16] Section 48 of the CFSA.
[17] R.S.O. 1990, c. C.12 [hereinafter "CLRA"].

While we will examine custody and access in Chapter 5 of this book, it is important to make some mention of the CLRA here, as "custody and access" under the CLRA is very different from child protection under the CFSA.

Unfortunately, the differences are not always apparent on the surface as both involve the best interests of children. However, while they may often involve the same parents and the same children, the area of child protection and child custody are different in both form and substance.

The CLRA is the "law" applied to determine "custody and access" (usually) between two or more individuals. In most cases, the two individuals are a male and a female parent of the child. However, as will be seen in Chapter 5, any person can claim custody of a child under the CLRA. Regardless of the relationship with the child of the person seeking custody, the court hearing a CLRA matter can grant custody of a child to any person if that is deemed to be in the child's best interests. The "best interests of the child" is the first and only test for determinations under the CLRA, the content of which is a matter to be determined based upon the facts in each case. This is the first and most important difference between the "custody and access" matters that are determined under the CLRA and the "protection" world of the CFSA.

While the CFSA is ultimately primarily concerned with the best interests of the children, as will be seen below, there is a statutory pathway of specific findings that the court must make before the issue of "the best interests of the child" is considered. Most importantly, under the CFSA, the court must consider whether the child is in need of protection before it can consider what placement and what relationships are in his or her best interest.

STATUTORY PATHWAY

Even if a child is in need of protection, before a child will be removed from the parents (or whomever had charge of the child), the court must consider a number of preliminary matters and options before the child will be placed with "strangers" in a foster care setting.

The court must consider, among other things, whether services have been provided to the child prior to intervention; whether or not the child could be placed with a family member or other community member; and, in the case of a First Nations child, whether or not another native home is available. These "hurdles" under section 57 of the CFSA are known as the Statutory Pathway and failure to follow the pathway can be an error in law for the court. In particular, section 57 confirms that before a child can be placed in the care of the Society, the court shall consider the following:

. . .

(2) Court to inquire — In determining which order to make under subsection (1), the court shall ask the parties what efforts the society or another agency or person made to assist the child before intervention under this Part. R.S.O. 1990, c. C.11, s. 57 (1, 2).

(3) Less disruptive alternatives preferred — The court shall not make an order removing the child from the care of the person who had charge of him or her immediately before intervention under this Part unless the court is satisfied that alternatives that are less disruptive to the child, including non-residential services and the assistance referred to in subsection (2), would be inadequate to protect the child. 1999, c. 2, s. 15 (1).

(4) Community placement to be considered — Where the court decides that it is necessary to remove the child from the care of the person who had charge of him or her immediately before intervention under this Part, the court shall, before making an order for society or Crown wardship under paragraph 2 or 3 of subsection (1), consider whether it is possible to place the child with a relative, neighbour or other member of the child's community or extended family under paragraph 1 of subsection (1) with the consent of the relative or other person.

(5) Idem: where child an Indian or a native person — Where the child referred to in subsection (4) is an Indian or a native person, unless there is a substantial reason for placing the child elsewhere, the court shall place the child with,

    (a) a member of the child's extended family;

    (b) a member of the child's band or native community; or

    (c) another Indian or native family.

. . .

During a court's consideration of matters along each step of the CFSA's "statutory pathway", it must look at the evidence presented and the orders that can be made in accordance with the child's best interests. Unlike a custody matter in which the applicable test is the "best interests of the child", each step in child protection proceedings is guided by a "statutory pathway" contained in the CFSA (i.e., a series of statutory provisions that are successively applicable) rather than one predominant test.

Unlike child custody, child protection is not initially a matter of securing the best interests of a child; engaging the child protection regime must be triggered by a real world event (or omission) before the court has jurisdiction to intervene and then it is within the parameters and limits of the "statutory pathway" that the question of the "best interests of the child" is addressed. It is only later, once a child protection proceeding is ongoing, that the process engaged begins to address the "best interests of the child" at various subsequent stages.

Child protection is not an exercise in the proactive service of a child's best interests but a reactive series of steps where basic needs of a child are not served. For example, a child may be removed from a situation of poverty and placed in a wealthier foster home setting. Having many more financial advantages (in care) would presumably be in the child's best interests. However, unless the child was found to be in need of protection, this analysis would not occur. Child protection is not, at least initially, a contest of best interests as it is in a custody case.

This point is illustrated by a 1975 decision that pointed out that child protection is, at first instance, not about improving children's standards but more about securing them above certain minimum thresholds of appropriate care:

> ...the community ought not to interfere merely because our institutions may be able to offer a greater opportunity to the children to achieve their potential. Society's interference in the natural family is only justified when the level of care of the children falls below that which no child in this country should be subjected to. In deciding on such intervention the Court must consider the best interests of the children in respect of their biological, social, emotional, cultural and intellectual development....[18]

Almost 30 years later, the Ontario Court of Appeal basically confirmed the same sentiment, namely, that intervention in a family is, initially, an issue of protection rather than simply a test of best interests:

> ... prior to the initial hearing foster parents are meant to provide temporary care for children pending their return to their family or transfer to a more permanent placement. They are not intended to provide a comparative basis for the determination of the child's best interests from the outset. A best interests comparison between the foster home and the original family at this stage would run contrary to the entire scheme of state intervention in cases where there is reason to believe that a child is in need of protection....[19]

However, once a child is determined to be in need of protection, then, subject to the "statutory pathway" steps noted above, the child's best interests test is the sole governing criteria.

---

[18] *Brown, Re* (1975), 21 R.F.L. 315 (Ont. Co. Ct.) at para. 24.
[19] *L. (R.) v. Children's Aid Society of Niagara Region*, [2002] O.J. No. 4793 (Ont. C.A.) at para. 38.

By the time a child is a Ward of the Society (i.e., a child has been found to be "in need of protection" and the least disruptive available order to protect him or her is to keep the child in the care of a Children's Aid Society), then "best interests of the child" becomes the primary test for the future of the child. It is the only test the court considers although there is a "...careful balancing of [the] *paramount objective of the best interests of the child with the value of maintaining the family unit and minimizing State intervention....*"[20]

The content of the CFSA, in and of itself, does not determine custody. It is used to protect children from abuse. Sometimes, the protection from abuse results in a placement with a person other than the custodial parent. However, if for some reason the CFSA order no longer applies, then custody reverts to the situation that was in place before a Society intervened.

This distinction between the regime of child custody and child protection is subtle and confusing for laypersons, professional social workers, and, on occasion, lawyers, alike.

ROLE OF THE STATE IN THE PRIVATE SPHERE

Child protection is a public law concern that involves public supervision and (sometimes) intervention in the private lives of citizens. Nonetheless, child protection legislation provides certain safeguards to ensure that the rights of parents to privacy and to make decisions concerning their child are not overly interfered with by the state.

Unlike custody matters (in which it is hoped that both parties are interested in the child's long-term best interests), protection proceedings involve the state, suggesting that a parent has failed to parent appropriately. The state is the Applicant

---

[20] *Catholic Children's Aid Society of Metropolitan Toronto v. M. (C.)* (1994), 2 R.F.L. (4th) 313 (S.C.C.) [emphasis added].

in all proceedings under the CFSA. Even though the Children's Aid Societies are private, not-for-profit corporations, they are agents of the state for the purposes of child protection matters. In that child protection involves state action toward individuals, the Supreme Court of Canada has confirmed that when a child is being removed from the home in a child protection matter, such intervention invokes *Charter* issues on behalf of both the child and the parents.

> ...Wardship proceedings, in my view, implicate these fundamental liberty interests of parents. The result of the proceeding may be that the parent is deprived of the right to make decisions on behalf of children and guide their upbringing, which is protected by s. 7. Though the state may intervene when necessary, liberty interests are engaged of which the parent can only be deprived in accordance with the principles of fundamental justice. Interpreting the interests here as protected under s. 7 also reflects the equality values set out above.[21]

This is not to mean that "parental rights" are such that they trump the best interests of the child as a primary concern. However, it means that child protection is different from a CLRA custody case. In the course of a child protection matter, certain specific concerns such as a parent's right to counsel, a right to a hearing, and issues of fundamental justice are scrutinized and considered by the court alongside the overriding question of what is in the child's best interests.

BEST INTERESTS

The best interests standard is not ignored under the CFSA. Instead, the question of what is in child's best interests is taken into account through a series of considerations that are applied in each child protection proceeding. These include:

---

[21] *New Brunswick (Minister of Health & Community Services) v. G. (J.)*, [1999] 3 S.C.R. 46 (S.C.C.) at para. 118.

. . .

1. The child's physical, mental and emotional needs, and the appropriate care or treatment to meet those needs.

2. The child's physical, mental and emotional level of development.

3. The child's cultural background.

4. The religious faith, if any, in which the child is being raised.

5. The importance for the child's development of a positive relationship with a parent and a secure place as a member of a family.

6. The child's relationships by blood or through an adoption order.

7. The importance of continuity in the child's care and the possible effect on the child of disruption of that continuity.

8. The merits of a plan for the child's care proposed by a society, including a proposal that the child be placed for adoption or adopted, compared with the merits of the child remaining with or returning to a parent.

9. The child's views and wishes, if they can be reasonably ascertained.

10. The effects on the child of delay in the disposition of the case.

11. The risk that the child may suffer harm through being removed from, kept away from, returned to or allowed to remain in the care of a parent.

12. The degree of risk, if any, that justified the finding that the child is in need of protection.

13. Any other relevant circumstance.[22]

Some of these considerations will carry more or less weight with the Society and the court depending on several factors including the age of the child, their cultural background, etc.

NOT A CRIMINAL MATTER

Just as a child protection matter under the CFSA is not a custody case, it is also not a criminal case. The facts that lead a

---

[22] Section 37(3) of the CFSA.

child to have been found "in need of protection" may or may not lead to criminal charges. Similarly, a criminal charge may not automatically result in a child protection proceeding being commenced.

There are a number of factors that are considered in child protection matters and criminal proceedings that are specific to their own particular role and tests. Therefore, a child protection proceeding and a criminal charge arising from the same facts may not yield the same or similar results. For example, while a person may be acquitted in a criminal trial arising from an allegation that he or she abused a child, under the CFSA, a finding of child abuse may be upheld due to the fact that the CFSA's civil standard of "balance of probabilities" is lower than the criminal standard for a conviction of "beyond a reasonable doubt".[23]

As well, unlike criminal proceedings, which may deal with transgressions against people of any age, child protection proceedings apply only to those who meet the definition of "child" under the CFSA.

DEFINITION OF A CHILD

As seen in Chapter 1, there are a number of pieces of legislation that deal with children and each of them is specific as to how it defines the term "child".

The CFSA can be confusing with respect to how it defines the term "child" and whom a children's aid society can assist given this definition. The Act defines the "child" as one who is under 16 unless they are already subject to a protection order under the CFSA.[24]

---

[23] For example, see *Children's Aid Society of Peel (Region) v. L. (Y.C.)* (2001), 2001 CarswellOnt 3793.

[24] Section 37(1).

There is no minimum age with respect to when a child may need protection. Once a child is born, the Society has jurisdiction to become involved in his or her protection. Societies do not have jurisdiction over children who have not been born: efforts to assist (or force) pregnant mothers to protect the unborn child have not been successful.[25]

With respect to the maximum age at which a Society may seek to protect "a child", as seen above, the answer to this question really depends on what has occurred prior to the child turning first 16 and then 18. If a report comes to a Children's Aid Society that a child is in need of protection after a child has turned 16 (and there have been no previous orders for protection of the child), then the Children's Aid Society cannot become involved other than on a voluntary basis. If the child over the age of 16 is already subject to a court order for protection, then ordinarily the Order would simply terminate on the child turning 18 years of age.[26] However, if the child is a "Crown Ward" (which will be discussed in greater detail below), then, on occasion the individual may continue to receive further assistance from the Society after his or her 18th birthday. In this regard, if the local Children's Aid Society is agreeable, an "extended care and maintenance" agreement may be reached for the Crown Ward to assist with costs of being out on their own as a young adult.[27] Again, this would depend on the individual jurisdiction and the individual Children's Aid Society.

LIMITED TO PROTECTING FROM PERSONS IN CHARGE

It is also important to note that, just as the CFSA does not apply to children of all ages (i.e., most children over 16), the

---

[25] See, for example, *A., Re* (1990), 75 O.R. (2d) 82 (Ont. U.F.C.).
[26] Section 71(1)(a) of the CFSA.
[27] Section 71(2) of the CFSA.

statute does not cover all situations where a child is harmed. In this regard, the CFSA is concerned with situations where a child is harmed (or at risk of harm) as defined within one or more of the enumerated categories in the Act. These enumerated categories, as will be noted in greater detail below, refer to a person who has "charge" of the child.

It can become a very confusing matter as to who had the charge at the time an injury or involvement of the Society occurred.[28]

Basically, not every injury and not every harm occasioned to a child will result in protection proceedings being commenced. For example, if a child has been assaulted by someone not in charge of the child, or who will no longer have contact with the child, it may be a case for criminal sanctions rather than child protection proceedings. However, even though a person may not have "charge" of the assaulted child whose harm first triggered an investigation, that person may be in charge of, or have contact with, other children. As a result, the Society may become involved in the protection of these other children even in the absence of any harm done directly to them at all. This selection of investigation by a Society, of where and when it is appropriate to be involved, can create a great deal of confusion, both for the families that the child protection agencies try to serve, as well as for those who are involved with the children on a day-to-day basis.

Ultimately, if there is concern for the safety or well being of a child, then it should be reported to a Society within your jurisdiction. From that report, the Society (and ultimately a court) can determine whether or not it believes the CFSA would apply. If it believes that the CFSA applies, then the Society (and ultimately a court) may have to decide whether or not the child is a child in need of protection.

---

[28] See, for example, Justice Wallace's decision in *S. (B.), Re*, [1996] O.J. No. 4428 (Ont. Gen. Div.).

HOW DOES A SOCIETY ANALYZE A REPORT OF ABUSE?

As noted above, there are a number of specific tools and assessments that the Society employs to determine the level of its involvement from a social work or "clinicial" perspective.

Then, for the purposes of the court, a Society must make a two-part legal determination upon receiving an initial referral. The first is a question of whether or not this is a child who would be found in need of protection by a court under the CFSA. Second, a Society tries to determine the least disruptive step it can be take to protect the child.

If the risk to the safety of the child is such that the child can be protected without the need of going to court, then the CFSA mandates that Society intervention should begin with "voluntary services".

VOLUNTARY INTERVENTION – PART II OF THE CFSA

The CFSA has an overriding paramount purpose, namely that it is an Act to promote "...the best interests, protection and well being of children".[29]

As well, the Society is obligated to ensure in its role as a service provider to families that:

> (a) that children and their parents have an opportunity where appropriate to be heard and represented when decisions affecting their interests are made and to be heard when they have concerns about the services they are receiving; and

---

[29] Section 1 of the CFSA.

(b) that decisions affecting the interests and rights of children and their parents are made according to clear, consistent criteria and are subject to procedural safeguards.[30]

The combination of these and other sections give rise to the concept that if the child can be safely protected within the home, then the first consideration for the Society should be whether or not protective services and assistance can be provided voluntarily to the family, i.e., "voluntary services". With voluntary services, a Society does not remove a child from the family, but works with the family and the child in its own context to implement steps to protect the child from further risk and the matter would never go before a court.

It is mandatory for a Society to attempt voluntary intervention prior to seeking involuntary intervention by means of a court order. The CFSA makes it clear that prior to the Society going to court under the involuntary section of the CFSA that they try to engage a family voluntarily and provide support and assistance prior to removing a child from a home or seeking to be involved through a court order.

As can be seen under section 57, the court must enquire under the "statutory pathway" whether services have been provided to the child prior to involuntary intervention. The court must enquire as to what services have been provided and whether any less disruptive services could be provided that would be adequate to protect the child.[31] If the Society has failed to provide adequate services then an Application to keep a child in care may be unsuccessful before the court.

Again, regional differences will affect what services are available. As a result, what efforts in this regard are considered appropriate will vary from jurisdiction to jurisdiction.

---

[30] Section 2(2) of the CFSA.
[31] See ss. 57(2) and 57(3) of the CFSA.

INVOLUNTARY INTERVENTION – PART III OF THE CFSA

If voluntary services are not appropriate, or if they have been tried unsuccessfully, then there is no alternative for the Society than to proceed to the court to take steps to protect a child by means of a "Child Protection Application".

A Child Protection Application is simply a form that the Society completes and serves on the parents and other interested parties. It outlines the case the Society hopes to make as to why it believes a child is in need of protection and what order it believes is necessary to protect the child. Whether an Application is commenced and when it is commenced is related to how urgent the Society believes the risk to the child is.

As noted, if the Society deems that providing services voluntarily is not safe for a child, then it must proceed to Part III of the CFSA and try to protect the child and provide services through involuntary means (i.e., without the cooperation of the child's family).

If the matter is one where the child can be protected in the home, but voluntary services are not appropriate, then the Society can commence an Application to ask the court to find that a child is "in need of protection" as defined under the CFSA. This originating document is called the Protection Application.

In the case of neglect, for an example, the child may not have any immediate risks to his or her health or safety. However, over the long term, the child's development may be seriously jeopardized by the parent's neglect. In that case, voluntary services such as referring a parent to a parent education course might be offered. If the parent refuses the offer, then a Protection Application might be commenced to force the issue by way of a term in a Supervision Order. The child is not removed from the parent, but the Application is still commenced.

However, often the risk to a child's health and/or safety is such that the Society assesses that the child cannot safely remain in the home. In those cases, the Society has the power to remove ("apprehend") a child.

If time allows, the CFSA mandates that apprehending a child should occur only after a warrant has been obtained by a justice of the peace. The warrant authorizes that a dramatic step such as removing a child from the care of the parent is necessary. If there is not enough time to allow a warrant to be obtained, then an apprehension can occur without a warrant.[32]

Whether an apprehension occurs with or without a warrant, a corresponding Protection Application to have the child declared a child in need of protection must be brought before the court with within five days.[33]

Different jurisdictions treat the "first appearance" of the Protection Application differently. In some jurisdictions, it is expected that most (if not all) of the evidence that the Society has available to find the child in need of protection will be brought before the court at the first appearance. In other jurisdictions, at the initial appearance, the materials presented to the court are a brief outline of what led the Society to take the step of apprehending the child.

---

[32] Section 40(4) and 40(7) of the CFSA. The Supreme Court of Canada has said in *Winnipeg Child & Family Services (Central Area) v. W. (K.L.)*, [2000] 2 S.C.R. 519 (S.C.C.), that apprehending without a warrant is not a violation of a parent's fundamental justice right given that the safety of a child is at stake.

[33] Section 46(1) of the CFSA. It should be noted that the "five-day rule" is calendar days and not business days. See *Kenora-Patricia Child & Family Services v. G. (J.)*, [2001] O.J. No. 2290 (Ont. C.J.).

A person who reports child abuse to a Society may have a great deal of immediate contact with a Society or very little. This will depend on the Society's decision with respect to how to proceed and, more importantly, how much information the court requires in their particular jurisdiction to satisfy the court. As such, it can be quite disconcerting for the person who reports child abuse, as they may not know what is happening with the matter for some time after their referral. All one can do is try and remain in contact with the Society in their area and hope that they can provide some guidance on what role they anticipate they will play should and if the matter goes to court.

Whether the Society is required to put a little or a lot of information and evidence before the court on the first appearance, invariably, one of the parties will require the matter to be adjourned to another date to prepare materials, retain lawyers or simply have a chance to review the plethora of Society documents that can be served at court on the first appearance of the Protection Application.

The Protection Application starts the child protection case and it then will proceed through the court until a court determines whether or not the child is in need of protection and, if so, what Order should be made to protect the child.[34]

A hearing cannot be adjourned for more than 30 days without the consent of all parties and of the person caring for the children.[35] Each time a hearing of the Protection Application is adjourned, the court must make a temporary order for the care and custody of the child.[36] The court has four choices in making such an order, namely:

---

[34] Under s. 47 of the Act the court must hold a hearing.
[35] Section 51(1) of the CFSA.
[36] Section 51(2) of the CFSA.

(a) remain in or be returned to the care and custody of the person who had charge of the child immediately before intervention under this Part;

(b) remain in or be returned to the care and custody of the person referred to in clause (a), subject to the society's supervision and on such reasonable terms and conditions relating to the child's supervision as the court considers appropriate;

(c) be placed in the care and custody of a person other than the person referred to in clause (a), with the consent of that other person, subject to the society's supervision and on such reasonable terms and conditions relating to the child's supervision as the court considers appropriate; or

(d) remain or be placed in the care and custody of the society, but not be placed in,

(i) a place of secure custody as defined in Part IV (Young Offenders), or

(ii) a place of open temporary detention as defined in that Part that has not been designated as a place of safety.[37]

Given the importance of a child's right to know and be with his or her biological family, the court will always try to balance the need to protect the child with concerns that the Society's assessment of the risk could be in error. The court balances these concerns with using the least disruptive order that is available and that will still protect the child.

The parties may disagree about which of the four choices is the least disruptive order that can safely protect the child. As a consequence, one or more "interim care hearings" or "show cause hearings" may be held to determine where the child should reside prior to the hearing to determine whether or not the child is in need of protection. These are usually conducted as "motions" with affidavit evidence (i.e., written evidence that is "sworn" on paper by a witness), rather than as a "trial" where witnesses will testify.

---

[37] R.S.O. 1990, c. C.11, s. 51(2).

If the hearing to find a child in need of protection has not been scheduled within three months, the court is obligated to schedule one.[38] However, for many reasons, despite this legislated requirement, this timeline is seldom met.[39] Eventually, however, the hearing to determine whether a child is in need of protection must be scheduled, as the court is obligated to conduct a hearing.[40]

When a protection hearing is held, and a court makes a finding that a child is in need of protection, the court will make an Order in the child's best interests pursuant to section 57 of the CFSA.

A child protection hearing may take many forms. Often the facts are disputed and the court will need to weigh and measure the testimony of each witness and apply it to the objective criteria set out in the Act and the statutory pathway. However, there is also a subjective element to the hearing, as each judge will see the facts through the lens of their own experience and viewpoint. In that regard, child protection law is often less predictable than other areas of law. This can make the area of child protection both very interesting and very frustrating for those concerned with law in the area.

Where the court finds that a child is in need of protection, but it is not satisfied that a court order is necessary to protect the child in the future, the court must order that the child remain with, or be returned to, the person who had charge of the child immediately before intervention under Part III of the CFSA.[41]

In the alternative, the court must make one of the following orders, in the child's best interests: a supervision order; a So-

---

[38] Section 52 of the CFSA.
[39] See *L. (R.), supra* note 19, where children were in care for over two years with no trial having been set.
[40] Section 47 of the CFSA.
[41] Section 57(9) of the CFSA.

ciety wardship order; a Crown wardship order; or a combination of a Society wardship/supervisions order. These orders are detailed under section 57(1) of the CFSA. The nature of these orders, respectively, is as follows.

Supervision order

1. That the child be placed with or returned to a parent or another person, subject to the supervision of the society, for a specified period of at least three and not more than twelve months.

Society wardship

2. That the child be made a ward of the society and be placed in its care and custody for a specified period not exceeding twelve months.

Crown wardship

3. That the child be made a ward of the Crown, until the wardship is terminated under section 65 or expires under subsection 71(1), and be placed in the care of the society.

Consecutive orders of society wardship and supervision

4. That the child be made a ward of the society under paragraph 2 for a specified period and then be returned to a parent or another person under paragraph 1, for a period or periods not exceeding an aggregate of twelve months.

As noted above, prior to making any Order under section 57 of the CFSA, the court must consider first whether services were provided and alternative options detailed above as the statutory pathway. If the Society has not made efforts to assist the child with services before involuntary intervention, then a Society Application to keep a child in care should not succeed.[42]

Similarly, the court has a positive obligation to consider whether it is possible to place the child with a relative, neigh-

---

[42] Sections 57(2) and (3) of the CFSA.

bour or other member of the child's community or extended family under the supervision of the Society before making an order for society or Crown wardship:[43]

> ...[T]he Act envisages that, if it is not possible to return a child to his or her parent, the possibility of placement with a member of the child's extended family will be explored expeditiously and determined prior to any hearing at which society or Crown wardship is sought. The Act does not envisage a contest between members of a child's family and a foster parent at a hearing to declare whether the child should be declared to be a society or Crown ward....[44]

In short, the family and community options should be attempted first if this can be safely done. Foster care is a last resort when other options have been tried and failed.

As well, special provisions are included for children with a First Nations heritage. Where the child is native, the CFSA mandates:

> Where the child referred to in subsection (4) is an Indian or a native person, unless there is a substantial reason for placing the child elsewhere, the court shall place the child with,
>
> (a) a member of the child's extended family;
>
> (b) a member of the child's band or native community; or
>
> (c) another Indian or native family.[45]

PLAN OF CARE

In addition to the section 57 "statutory pathway" requirements, the court must obtain and consider the Society's plan for the child's care. This Plan is prepared in writing by the Society and must include information of when they feel that

---

[43] Section 57(4) of the CFSA.
[44] *Supra* note 19 at para. 9.
[45] Section 57(5).

they will be able to return the child to his or her biological family.[46] Specifically, the plan is to include:

- a statement of the criteria by which the Society will determine when its supervision or wardship is no longer required; and
- an estimate of the time required to achieve the purpose of the Society's intervention.

TIMELINES

It is sometimes the case that the intervention of the Society will not "achieve the purpose of the Society's intervention". There are times when the parents are unwilling or unable to change the alleged behaviours that have caused the child to be in need of protection.

In this regard, the Act has set up timelines. Although there is some flexibility to them, once the timelines have been reached the court must make an Order to return the child to a parent, family or community member or make the child a Ward of the Crown.

With every order that is made (other than a Crown wardship), there must be a time limit to the Order. During the duration of the Order, the hope is that the purposes for intervention will have been achieved.

Prior to expiry of the Order for supervision or society wardship, the Society is required to apply to the court for a review of the child's status.[47] In essence, this is a "check back" for the court to see what has happened over the course of the original Order.

---

[46] Section 56 of the CFSA.
[47] Section 64(2)(b) of the CFSA.

A Status Review Application is an application much like a Protection Application. It can lead to a hearing that is almost identical to the original. At that hearing a court may make a further order or orders under section 57.

If there has been little progress over the course of the original Order and the child remains in the care of the Society, then the court may determine that an order of Crown wardship is in the child's best interests.

Crown wardship is a very significant and important Order that the court can make. As the Court of Appeal once noted:

> It is only once a child has been made a Crown ward that the Act states the Crown has the rights and responsibilities of a parent for the purpose of the child's care, custody and control: s.63(1). Until that time, the Act recognizes that children continue to be the responsibility of their parents by making provision in s. 60 for a parent to be ordered to pay support for a child. The Act also contains a presumption that access with "the person who had charge of the child immediately before intervention under this Part" is in the best interests of the child unless the court is satisfied that this would not be in the child's best interests: s. 59(1). Therefore, until an order of Crown wardship is made, the parents of a child retain a presumptive right of access. Once an order for Crown wardship is made the presumption respecting access is reversed.[48]

Under the CFSA, the child's best interests is an overriding backdrop to a statutory regime that presupposes that the child should be returned to the person who had charge of him or her at the time of Society intervention. If that return cannot be safely accomplished, then a determination must be made as to whether or not the child can safely live within a home of a member of his or her biological family or community. If there is no such placement that is in the child's best interests, then the court must consider whether the state needs to provide for the child. If it is in the child's best interests, then an Order is made to permanently place the child in the care of the State as

---

[48] *Supra* note 19 at para. 7.

a Crown ward. Once a child is a Crown ward, the role of the court ends and the Society has an obligation to take reasonable efforts to secure an adoptive home for all of its Crown wards.[49]

This is, of course, a brief overview of the CFSA. Hopefully, it provides some background to what steps may be taken once a report is received that a child may be in need of protection.

DUTY TO REPORT

As noted throughout section 72 of the CFSA, there is a positive duty on all persons (and especially professionals dealing with children) to report suspicions that a child may be in need of protection. One of the key changes to the CFSA in the 1999 amendments was "beefing up" the duty to report. As has been noted, a "penalty" section has been added to the section.

Also of importance is that the duty to report is personal to the person who has suspicions that a child is being abused. The duty is a personal duty to the child and our society at large and one that cannot be delegated. In the past, many professionals advised their supervisor, e.g., a principal, who made the report as their proxy to a Children's Aid Society. This resulted in delay and miscommunication. The amended sections clearly sets out that a delegation is no longer permissible and the report should be made directly by the source of the information.

Somewhat related to this is that a professional has an on-going duty to report as new concerns occur. Previously, there may have been some assumptions that because one report had been made that the Society would know about the family. Subsequent matters would then not be followed up due to incorrect assumptions. The new amendment makes clear that the duty to report is an on-going one.

---

[49] Section 140 of the CFSA.

The section of the CFSA dealing with the duty to report is as follows:

72(1) Duty to report child in need of protection — Despite the provisions of any other Act, if a person, including a person who performs professional or official duties with respect to children, has reasonable grounds to suspect one of the following, the person shall forthwith report the suspicion and the information on which it is based to a society:

> 1. The child has suffered physical harm, inflicted by the person having charge of the child or caused by or resulting from that person's,
>
>> i. failure to adequately care for, provide for, supervise or protect the child, or
>>
>> ii. pattern of neglect in caring for, providing for, supervising or protecting the child.
>
> 2. There is a risk that the child is likely to suffer physical harm inflicted by the person having charge of the child or caused by or resulting from that person's,
>
>> i. failure to adequately care for, provide for, supervise or protect the child, or
>>
>> ii. pattern of neglect in caring for, providing for, supervising or protecting the child.
>
> 3. The child has been sexually molested or sexually exploited, by the person having charge of the child or by another person where the person having charge of the child knows or should know of the possibility of sexual molestation or sexual exploitation and fails to protect the child.
>
> 4. There is a risk that the child is likely to be sexually molested or sexually exploited as described in paragraph 3.
>
> 5. The child requires medical treatment to cure, prevent or alleviate physical harm or suffering and the child's parent or the person having charge of the child does not provide, or refuses or is unavailable or unable to consent to, the treatment.
>
> 6. The child has suffered emotional harm, demonstrated by serious,

i. anxiety,
ii. depression,
iii. withdrawal,
iv. self-destructive or aggressive behaviour, or
v. delayed development,

and there are reasonable grounds to believe that the emotional harm suffered by the child results from the actions, failure to act or pattern of neglect on the part of the child's parent or the person having charge of the child.

7. The child has suffered emotional harm of the kind described in subparagraph i, ii, iii, iv or v of paragraph 6 and the child's parent or the person having charge of the child does not provide, or refuses or is unavailable or unable to consent to, services or treatment to remedy or alleviate the harm.

8. There is a risk that the child is likely to suffer emotional harm of the kind described in subparagraph i, ii, iii, iv or v of paragraph 6 resulting from the actions, failure to act or pattern of neglect on the part of the child's parent or the person having charge of the child.

9. There is a risk that the child is likely to suffer emotional harm of the kind described in subparagraph i, ii, iii, iv or v of paragraph 6 and that the child's parent or the person having charge of the child does not provide, or refuses or is unavailable or unable to consent to, services or treatment to prevent the harm.

10. The child suffers from a mental, emotional or developmental condition that, if not remedied, could seriously impair the child's development and the child's parent or the person having charge of the child does not provide, or refuses or is unavailable or unable to consent to, treatment to remedy or alleviate the condition.

11. The child has been abandoned, the child's parent has died or is unavailable to exercise his or her custodial rights over the child and has not made adequate provision for the child's care and custody, or the child is in a residential placement and the parent refuses or is unable or unwilling to resume the child's care and custody.

12. The child is less than 12 years old and has killed or seriously injured another person or caused serious damage to another person's property, services or treatment are necessary to prevent a recurrence and the child's parent or the person having charge of the child does not provide, or refuses or is unavailable or unable to consent to, those services or treatment.

13. The child is less than 12 years old and has on more than one occasion injured another person or caused loss or damage to another person's property, with the encouragement of the person having charge of the child or because of that person's failure or inability to supervise the child adequately.

(2) Ongoing duty to report — A person who has additional reasonable grounds to suspect one of the matters set out in subsection (1) shall make a further report under subsection (1) even if he or she has made previous reports with respect to the same child.

(3) Person must report directly — A person who has a duty to report a matter under subsection (1) or (2) shall make the report directly to the society and shall not rely on any other person to report on his or her behalf.

(4) Offence — A person referred to in subsection (5) is guilty of an offence if,

(a) he or she contravenes subsection (1) or (2) by not reporting a suspicion; and
(b) the information on which it was based was obtained in the course of his or her professional or official duties.

(5) Same — Subsection (4) applies to every person who performs professional or official duties with respect to children including,

(a) a health care professional, including a physician, nurse, dentist, pharmacist and psychologist;
(b) a teacher, school principal, social worker, family counsellor, priest, rabbi, member of the clergy, operator or employee of a day nursery and youth and recreation worker;
(c) a peace officer and a coroner;
(d) a solicitor; and
(e) a service provider and an employee of a service provider.

(6) Same — In clause (5)(b),

"youth and recreation worker" does not include a volunteer.

(6.1) Same — A director, officer or employee of a corporation who authorizes, permits or concurs in a contravention of an offence under subsection (4) by an employee of the corporation is guilty of an offence.

(6.2) Same — A person convicted of an offence under subsection (4) or (6.1) is liable to a fine of not more than $1,000.

(7) Section overrides privilege — This section applies although the information reported may be confidential or privileged, and no action for making the report shall be instituted against a person who acts in accordance with this section unless the person acts maliciously or without reasonable grounds for the suspicion.

(8) Exception: solicitor client privilege — Nothing in this section abrogates any privilege that may exist between a solicitor and his or her client.

IMPORTANCE OF THE DUTY TO REPORT AND CONSEQUENCES OF NOT REPORTING

As stated above, there were significant amendments to the CFSA in 1999 enlarging the duty to report under the statute and adding a specific offence provision. Given these specific amendments to the CFSA, there is little doubt that the legislature continues to believe the obligation to report child abuse is an important one and that professionals have a key role to play in the prevention of child abuse.

The Courts have also confirmed the importance of this obligation. In the case of *Ontario (Police Complaints Commissioner) v. Dunlop*,[50] a police officer learned that criminal proceedings against an individual were not proceeding despite the police officer's belief that an assault on a child had occurred. The officer became concerned that other children might be at risk given these circumstances. Contrary to the direct order of a

---

[50] (1995), 26 O.R. (3d) 582 (Ont. Div. Ct.).

superior officer, information regarding the accused was forwarded to the local Society. As a consequence, the officer who forwarded the information was subjected to a Board of Inquiry under the *Police Services Act*. The Board of Inquiry found that he has disobeyed orders and breached his duties. The officer's defence was that he had an obligation to report under the CFSA. On an appeal of that decision of the Police Services Board, the Divisional Court agreed with the officer that his obligation under the CFSA superseded the order of his superior officer. The Court stated:

> I am of the view that the duty imposed by s. 72 is paramount. Subsection (3) begins "Despite the provisions of any other Act ..." To treat the duty of disclosure as subject to orders of a superior officer would be contrary to the intention of s-s. (7) and would defeat the paramount purpose of the *Child and Family Services Act*.[51]

This case was decided in 1995 and prior to the more recent amendments. No doubt the statutory amendments make the duty to report even more binding on professionals involved with children.

Similarly, in the case of *S. (P.) v. Batth*,[52] a psychiatrist was completing an assessment as part of a custody and access proceeding. During the course of interviewing the daughter of the family, information was disclosed leading the doctor to believe she needed to report the information to the local Society. She did make that report and for some time the father of the child lost access to his daughter. Many years later, the father sued the reporting doctor, alleging that she had made false and misleading statements about him and was negligent. The case was dismissed because of the expiry of a statutory limitation period. However, in its reasons for decision, the Court found that the duty to report would have been protection for the doctor in any event of the limitations defence. In

---

[51] *Ibid.* at para. 26.
[52] [1997] O.J. No. 4089 (Ont. Gen. Div.).

this regard, the Court found that the doctor was correct in reporting and that was the end of her obligation. Specifically, the Court said:

> ...she had a positive duty to report her suspicions to the Childrens' Aid Society. She does not have an obligation to conduct a full investigation before making such a report and she is not negligent for failing to make such an investigation. Her actions in reporting the matter to the Childrens' Aid Society are protected by s. 77 of the Act. The reporting of suspected abuse of children must be encouraged, not discouraged. If proper investigations are then not conducted after reports are made this is a different matter, but the initial report must be protected. There is no cause of action against Dr. Batth arising from the report which she made to the Childrens' Aid Society....[53]

The court will certainly recognize and respect the person who reports child abuse. It is less clear what the consequences will be for the person that fails to report. The CFSA contains an offence provision in section 72, which subjects a person to prosecution for failure to report child abuse. It is too early to tell whether or not those who fail to report will be prosecuted under the CFSA and fined in accordance with the new penalty provisions. Traditionally, very few people have been prosecuted for failure to report. However, many of these cases pre-date the specific section in the amended CFSA.[54]

For professionals, the possibility of a fine under the CFSA for breach of the duty to report may be of less concern to them than the increasing willingness of persons who have been subjected to abuse to commence civil actions seeking compensation for harms that have been caused to them as children.

In the 2003 case of *Boer v. Cairns*,[55] a woman of the Jehovah's Witness faith alleged that she had been sexually abused by her

---

[53] *Ibid.* at para. 9.
[54] See examples in the Bessner article, *supra* note 5.
[55] *Boer v. Cairns* (2003), [2003] O.J. No. 2750, (*sub nom. B. (V.) v. Cairns*) 65 O.R. (3d) 343 (Ont. S.C.J.).

father. Further, she claimed that when she had reported this information to three elders of her church, they advised her not to tell the Society and that they themselves failed to report the matter to the Society. As a result, the plaintiff alleged that the three elders to whom the report was made (as well as the governing body of the Jehovah's Witnesses in Canada) were negligent and in breach of their fiduciary duty to her. The Court found as a fact that the elders had not told the plaintiff not to tell the Society and that the individual defendants had not failed in their duty to report the abuse. This finding was made on the basis that the three elders had advised the plaintiff to speak to a psychiatrist who would, in turn (they believed) report the matter to the Society.

With the new amendments to the CFSA and the duty of a person to report the suspicion of child abuse to a Society directly (not through a designate), it is unlikely that this sort of "delegation" as described in the *Cairns* case above, would provide a defence if a similar situation arose today under the current duty to report.

It has been established, in other areas, that there may be civil liability for failing to warn of abuse to children even in the absence of an explicit statutory obligation to report.[56]

As a practical matter, in considering situations in which the obligation to report may be triggered, in addition to matters of law and conscience, the professional must be mindful that it is not inconceivable that if there is a failure to report, at some future time, an abused child will try to redress this failure through legal means, either through a lawsuit or a complaint to a professional organization.

---

[56] See, for example, *Jane Doe v. Metropolitan Toronto (Municipality) Commissioners of Police* (1989), [1989] O.J. No. 471 (Ont. H.C.), affirmed (1990), 74 O.R. (2d) 225 (Ont. Div. Ct.), leave to appeal refused (1991), 1991 CarswellOnt 1009, 1 O.R. (3d) 416 (note) (Ont. C.A.).

In all of the circumstances, the more appropriate approach is to become familiar with the reporting requirements under the CFSA and how they are interpreted and applied in your community. If you have reasonable grounds to report suspected child abuse, then to do so as soon as possible. While it may seem like a lot of trouble at the time, you may be saving yourself from more troubles down the road.

More important than that, of course, is that your concern and your call may end up saving a child.

3
THE EVIDENCE OF CHILDREN

RULES OF EVIDENCE

In Canada, unlike in the United States or England, the law of evidence is mostly judge-made. That means that the rules of what evidence is admissible in court are not codified in a statute or a set of rules, but are derived from previous decisions made by the courts as to what the rules of evidence should be. In the United States, there are federal and state statutes that prescribe the rules of evidence. Similarly, civil and criminal evidence statutes have shaped how matters are proved in English law. In Canada, in the absence of legislative action, the Supreme Court of Canada undertook a program of judicial reform of evidence law starting in the early 1980s. This process was largely forced by *Charter* challenges to traditional evidence rules. The *Charter*, literally from 1982 onwards, resulted in the court extending on a case-by-case basis much of the common law of evidence.

Jeremy Bentham, the 19th-century reformer, thought there should be only one rule of evidence: "all relevant evidence is admissible". The common law evidence (i.e., the judge-made rules of evidence) starts from his approach and adds on a series of somewhat more complicated exclusionary rules. During the last two centuries, many exclusionary rules of evidence law have been streamlined and those that remain have become more flexible.

As stated by Jeremy Bentham, the basic common law rule of evidence is that all relevant evidence is admissible, unless it is the subject of a specific exclusionary rule or its probative value is outweighed by its prejudicial effect. Relevance must be determined in the context of the entire case. A fact becomes relevant when it directly or indirectly increases the probability of a material fact in issue. The degree of probative value is not an issue in determining relevance. It is only an issue in determining whether it should be excluded because of possible prejudice.[1]

A trial judge has a general discretion to exclude evidence on the basis of the duty, now enshrined in section 11(d) of the *Charter*, to ensure a fair trial.[2] Unfairness can flow from two sources:

1. the manner in which the evidence was obtained (despite not involving a *Charter* violation), or
2. the prejudicial effect of its admissions.[3]

EVIDENCE IN FAMILY LAW

Generally, rules of evidence are applied less strictly in family law, less than perhaps other civil matters. In family law, the application of the "rules of evidence" is complicated by the wide range of subject matter that is litigated. These include: child protection; adoption; custody and access; division of property; child support; and spousal support. Virtually all orders made in family court are subject to variation or review.

---

[1] See *R. v. Watson* (1996), 108 C.C.C. (3d) 310 (Ont. C.A.); *R. v. Terry* (1996), 106 C.C.C. (3d) 508 (S.C.C.) at 518-19.
[2] See *R. v. Harrer* (1995), 101 C.C.C. (3d) 193 (S.C.C.).
[3] See *R. v. Harrer, ibid.* and *R. v. Gagnon* (2000), 147 C.C.C. (3d) 193 (Ont. C.A.).

In family court, interim orders (i.e., orders made prior to a full trial of a matter) on substantive issues are more common than civil or criminal proceedings.

THE GENERAL APPROACH OF THE LAW TO CHILDREN'S EVIDENCE

In several cases, the Supreme Court of Canada has addressed the issue of assessing the evidence of child witnesses.[4] As a result of these top Court decisions, traditional approaches to children's evidence have been changed. These include:

- removing the presumption that the evidence of children is inherently unreliable and, therefore, should be treated with special caution; and
- a new appreciation that it may be wrong to apply adult tests for credibility to children's evidence. In this respect, a "common sense approach" has been urged when dealing with the testimony of young children. Such an approach involves not approaching the evidence of children from the perspective of rigid stereotypes, but instead taking into account the strengths and weaknesses of the evidence in a particular case by carefully assessing its credibility.

We must assess witnesses of tender years for what they are: children and not adults. We should not expect them to perform in the same manner as adults. This does not mean, however, that courts should subject the testimony of children to a lower level of scrutiny for reliability than we would for adults. The changes to the evidentiary rules pertaining to the evidence of children are intended to make child evidence more readily available to the court by removing the restraints on its use that existed previously.

---

[4] See, for example, *R. v. B. (G.)* (1990), 56 C.C.C. (3d) 200 (S.C.C.) and *R. v. W. (R.)* (1992), 74 C.C.C. (3d) 134 (S.C.C.).

No matter what rules of evidence are applied to the evidence of children, however strict, in order to be admissible, evidence must be "relevant" to a fact in issue. "Irrelevant evidence" should not be admitted. Within the broad rubric of the concept of "relevance" are three separate concepts:

(a) logical relevance;
(b) materiality; and
(c) "pragmatic relevance" or the judicial discretion to exclude evidence.

The fact sought to be proved must be a "material" fact, a "fact in issue", or a fact "of consequence to the determination of the action". The question of whether a fact is "material" in any particular case is determined by the substantive law, the pleadings (i.e., the court filings in a particular matter), and any formal admissions or agreements by the parties. To decide whether evidence is "material" or "immaterial", we have to know what the issues are in a particular case.

RULES OF EVIDENCE IN FAMILY LAW

In family law cases, many of the "core" rules of evidence apply with only minor modifications. However, the application of certain fundamental rules of evidence is significantly altered. These aspects include admitting opinion evidence (i.e., the court generally admits into evidence opinions where such testimony is given by qualified experts) and hearsay evidence (i.e., a witness must have personal knowledge of the evidence given and not provide information received from a third party), which tend to operate in a more relaxed fashion in family proceedings than in other areas of law. There are no juries in family law. Rules can easily be characterized as "technical" rules that do not often fit within the practical setting of a family court. The rules have moved from "rules of exclusion" to "rules of preference".

EVIDENCE STATUTES

While most of the law of evidence applicable to children's evidence is governed by the common law, both federal and provincial jurisdictions have statutes that set out rules on matters of evidence. The *Canada Evidence Act* applies to trials of offences under the *Criminal Code* and other federal statutes. Provincial Evidence Acts apply to trials under provincial legislation and to trials under federal legislation where the *Canada Evidence Act* is not contradictory. The *Canada Evidence Act* contains provisions concerning the evidence of children. Section 16 of the *Canada Evidence Act* reads:

16(1) Where a proposed witness is a person under fourteen years of age or a person whose mental capacity is challenged, the court shall, before permitting the person to give evidence, conduct an inquiry to determine

(a) whether the person understands the nature of an oath or a solemn affirmation; and

(b) whether the person is able to communicate the evidence

(2) A person referred to in subsection (1) who understands the nature of an oath or a solemn affirmation and is able to communicate the evidence shall testify under oath or solemn affirmation.

(3) A person referred to in subsection (1) who does not understand the nature of an oath or a solemn affirmation but is able to communicate the evidence may, notwithstanding any provision of any Act requiring an oath or solemn affirmation, testify on promising to tell the truth.

(4) A person referred to in subsection (1) who neither understands the nature of an oath or a solemn affirmation nor is able to communicate the evidence shall not testify.

(5) A party who challenges the mental capacity of a proposed witness of fourteen years of age or more has the burden of satisfying the court that there is an issue as to the capacity of the proposed witness to testify under an oath or a solemn affirmation.

PROCESSING A CHILD'S EVIDENCE

The question arises: how does a child end up giving evidence in court? A child may end up on the stand as a function of being called as a witness in a proceeding or by way of receiving a subpoena or summons to appear. A judge has the power to vacate or set aside a subpoena to a child witness, or refuse to issue a subpoena in the first place. It is very rare for a child to testify in family court.

After a child gets to court, he or she may give evidence upon satisfying one of three conditions:

1. swearing the oath;
2. taking a solemn affirmation; or
3. promising to tell the truth.

(a) An Inquiry

However, prior to allowing a child to proceed with one of the three formal conditions for giving evidence, an inquiry must be held to determine whether the witness understands the nature of an oath (or solemn affirmation), and to see if he or she is able to communicate the evidence she or he is to give. If both these tests are satisfied, the witness will be permitted to testify under oath or solemn affirmation. If the young person is unable to understand the nature of an oath or affirmation, but the child is able to communicate his or her evidence, the child may testify on promising to tell the truth.

An inquiry of this nature is required under section 16 of the *Canada Evidence Act* for witnesses under the age of 14. The inquiry under section 16 is mandatory for witnesses under 14, even if the child had previously given sworn evidence at the preliminary inquiry.[5] A trial judge may permit a child to be

---

[5] See *R. v. K. (F.)* (1990), 56 C.C.C. (3d) 555 (Ont. C.A.).

sworn without an inquiry if opposing counsel concedes the child's competency to give evidence and allows him or her to be sworn.[6] An inquiry is usually conducted by the court (i.e., the presiding judge) asking questions of a child, but in certain circumstances a judge may permit lawyers to pose the questions on an inquiry, as directed by the court.[7] While section 16 requires the court to conduct the inquiry as to the admissibility of the child's testimony, there is no reason why counsel cannot assist in framing the kinds of questions to be put to the child. Where the child is so young as to be capable of only very limited verbal expression, non-verbal methods of communication may be used to allow the child to express his or her evidence such as pointing to, or manipulating dolls. Section 16(1) applies to witnesses over the age of 14 whose mental capacity is challenged. Section 16(5) states that the burden of satisfying the court that there is an issue as to the capacity of the proposed witness to testify under oath or solemn affirmation is on the challenger.

However, the assessment of whether the child is competent to testify is to be made by the court and it is not to be based upon the opinions of others[8] except where it is determined that a witness is likely to be traumatized by an inquiry in which case the determination may be made on the basis of the input of third parties.[9]

---

[6] See *R. v. Fong* (1994), 92 C.C.C. (3d) 171 (Alta. C.A.), leave to appeal refused (1995), 94 C.C.C. (3d) vii (note) (S.C.C.).
[7] See *R. v. Peterson* (1996), 106 C.C.C. (3d) 64 (Ont. C.A.), leave to appeal refused 109 C.C.C. (3d) vi (S.C.C.).
[8] See *R. v. Parrott* (2001), 150 C.C.C. (3d) 449 (S.C.C.) and *R. v. M. (M.A.)* (2001), 151 C.C.C. (3d) 22 (B.C. C.A.), leave to appeal refused (2001), 271 N.R. 195 (note) (S.C.C.).
[9] *R. v. Parrott, ibid.*

(b) Assessing Competency to Take an Oath or Affirmation

In order to allow a child to swear an oath or affirm, the court must be satisfied that the witness understands the moral obligation of telling the truth. This includes:

1. an appreciation of the solemnity of the occasion;
2. an understanding of the added responsibility to tell the truth over and above the duty to tell the truth as part of the ordinary duty of normal social conduct;
3. an understanding of what it means to tell the truth in court; and
4. an appreciation of what happens, in both a practical and moral sense, when a lie is told in court.[10]

The child does not need to understand the spiritual consequences of an oath or believe in a Supreme Being in order to be sworn. As with an adult, it is sufficient that a child understand that the oath involves a moral obligation to tell the truth.[11] One of the topics that may be raised on such an inquiry in criminal matters is the potential consequences to the accused in the proceedings.[12]

(c) Ability to Communicate: Testimonial Competence

The ability to communicate the evidence, section 16(1)(b), has three components:

1. the capacity to observe (including interpretation);
2. the capacity to recollect; and
3. the capacity to communicate,

---

[10] *R. v. L. (J.)* (1990), 54 C.C.C. (3d) 225 (Ont. C.A.).
[11] *R. v. Bannerman* (1966), 50 C.R. 76 (S.C.C.); *R. v. Fletcher* (1982), 1 C.C.C. (3d) 370 (Ont. C.A.), leave to appeal refused (1983), 48 N.R. 319 (S.C.C.).
[12] See *R. v. Bond*, [1997] O.J. No. 3420 (Ont. C.A.).

The issue of competence concerns only capacity to perform these functions, not whether the witness observed, recollects and can communicate events relevant to the trial. Any defect in performing these functions by the witness is to be explored during the giving of the evidence and goes to the weight the evidence is to be given, rather than bear upon its admissibility.[13]

The issue is whether the child can both comprehend the types of questions to be asked and communicate the answers to the questions effectively. In making such an assessment, a court is not to over-emphasize the aspect of a child's age, as the *Canada Evidence Act* makes no distinction between children of different ages and to do so would raise the danger that offences against very young children could not be prosecuted.[14]

In order to be permitted to give evidence, a child must show some independent ability to express contentious parts of his or her evidence, not merely the aptitude to respond to leading questions from counsel. To allow a child to testify, a court must find some indication that the child has the capacity and willingness to relate the essence of what happened.[15]

(d) Promise to Tell the Truth: Unsworn Testimony

Under section 16(3) of the *Canada Evidence Act*, a child may be permitted to give unsworn testimony under certain circumstances. These are as follows:

- the child must understand the duty to speak the truth in terms of everyday social conduct; and
- the child must be able to distinguish between telling the truth and telling a lie. The child need not understand the

---

[13] *R. v. Marquard* (1993), 85 C.C.C. (3d) 193 (S.C.C.) at 219.
[14] *R. v. Khan* (1990), 59 C.C.C. (3d) 92 (S.C.C.).
[15] See *R. v. Caron* (1994), 94 C.C.C. (3d) 466 (Ont. C.A.).

consequences of telling a lie or even understand the added duty imposed when testifying in court.[16]

Direct questioning on the issue of the difference between telling the truth and lying is not necessary. The judge can infer a child's understanding of the questions posed from truthful answers to other questions.[17]

The ability to communicate the evidence refers to cognitive and communicative capacity. The components of section 16(3) set a relatively low threshold for testimonial competence. The capacity to perceive includes not only an ability to perceive the events as they occur, but also an ability to distinguish between what is actually being perceived and what is imagined or told by others. Once the capacity to perceive, remember, and recount is established, any deficiencies in a particular witness's perception, recollection or narration go to the weight the evidence and not to competence. Understanding the duty to speak the truth in terms of everyday social conduct includes an appreciation of the duty to answer all questions in accordance with his/her recollection of what actually happened.[18] A child must explicitly promise to tell the truth, although there is no specific form for this promise. The failure to elicit the promise is a procedural error.[19]

Two requirements must be met to establish testimonial competence under section 16(3) of the *Canada Evidence Act*: the ability to communicate the evidence and the ability to promise to tell the truth.[20] The phrase to "communicate the evidence" in section 16(1)(b) indicates more than mere verbal ability. In

---

[16] See *R. v. A. (K.)* (1999), 137 C.C.C. (3d) 554 (Ont. C.A.).
[17] See *R. v. Breckenridge*, [1997] O.J. No. 2262 (Ont. C.A.).
[18] See *R. v. Farley* (1995), 99 C.C.C. (3d) 76 (Ont. C.A.) and *A. (K.) supra* note 16.
[19] See *R. v. Peterson* (1996), 106 C.C.C. (3d) 64 (Ont. C.A.), leave to appeal refused (1996), 109 C.C.C. (3d) vi (S.C.C.).
[20] See *R. v. Farley, supra* note 18.

order to establish ability to communicate, "[i]t is necessary to explore in a general way whether the witness is capable of perceiving events, remember events and communicating events to the court."[21]

While it was previously a requirement (under section 16(2) of the *Canada Evidence Act*) that corroboration be provided of a child's unsworn testimony, this section was repealed in 1988. There is therefore little distinction between the three forms of testimony: oath, affirmation, or promising to tell the truth.

(e) The Role of the Trial Judge

With fragile witnesses such as children, the trial judge must ensure that the witness understands the questions and that the evidence given by the child is clear and unambiguous. The judge may have to clarify and rephrase questions and ask subsequent questions to clarify the witness's responses. The judge should provide the proper atmosphere to enable the child to feel relaxed and calm.[22] The court has discretion to permit a child witness to testify from the lap of a trusted adult.[23]

(f) Court Assessment of Children's Evidence

The factors that should be taken into account in assessing the credibility of child witnesses was one of the issues on appeal before the Supreme Court of Canada in the case of *R. v. B. (G.)*.[24] At paragraph 56, Wilson J. stated:

---

[21] *R. v. Marquard*, [1993] 4 S.C.R. 223 (S.C.C.) at 236.
[22] See *R. v. L. (D.O.)* (1993), 85 C.C.C. (3d) 289 (S.C.C.).
[23] See *R. v. F. (C.)* (1996), 88 O.A.C. 397 (Ont. C.A.), leave to appeal allowed (1996), 96 O.A.C. 399 (note) (S.C.C.), reversed (1997), 1997 CarswellOnt 4465 (S.C.C.), additional reasons at (1997), 120 C.C.C. (3d) 225 (S.C.C.).
[24] *Supra* note 4.

...While children may not be able to recount precise details and communicate the when and where of an event with exactitude, this does not mean that they have misconceived what happened to them and who did it. In recent years we have adopted a much more benign attitude to children's evidence, lessening the strict standards of oath-taking and corroboration, and I believe that this is a desirable development. The credibility of every witness who testifies before the courts must, of course, be carefully assessed, but the standard of the "reasonable adult" is not necessarily appropriate in assessing the credibility of young children.

In *R. v. W. (R.)*,[25] McLachlin J. (as she then was) addressed the way in which the evidence of children ought to be approached by a court. She commented at page 133:

...One finds emerging a new sensitivity to the peculiar perspectives of children. Since children may experience the world differently from adults, it is hardly surprising that details important to adults, like time and place, may be missing from their recollection.

And at page 134 she said:

As Wilson J. emphasized in *B. (G.)*, these changes in the way the courts look at the evidence of children do not mean that the evidence of children should not be subject to the same standard of proof as the evidence of adult witnesses in criminal cases. Protecting the liberty of the accused and guarding against the injustice of the conviction of an innocent person require a solid foundation for a verdict of guilt, whether the complainant be an adult or a child. What the changes do mean is that we approach the evidence of children not from the perspective of rigid stereotypes, but on what Wilson J. called a "common sense" basis, taking into account the strengths and weaknesses which characterize the evidence offered in the particular case.

The evidence of children was formerly treated as inherently unreliable both at common law and by statute. Repeal of provisions in the *Criminal Code*, the *Canada Evidence Act* and the *Young Offenders Act* requiring corroboration of children's evi-

---

[25] [1992] 2 S.C.R. 122 (S.C.C.), reconsideration refused (November 18, 1992), Doc. 21820 (S.C.C.).

dence removed this notion from statute law. This evidentiary change was retroactive and applied to trials of all federal offences whether they were alleged to have been committed before or after the change.[26] The testimony of children is not to be subjected to a lower level of scrutiny than that of adults.[27]

ADMISSION OF HEARSAY EVIDENCE OF A CHILD

In certain exceptional circumstances, a child may not have to be called as a witness at all. Instead, where it is shown that the receipt of hearsay is necessary and the material tendered is "reliable", the court can receive the information available from young people by way of hearsay evidence.

The "necessity" of hearsay evidence has been interpreted to mean "reasonably necessary" to prove a fact in issue based upon the facts of each case. A number of different grounds can create "necessity", even in criminal cases:

1. "normal" unavailability, e.g., illness, absent from Canada, refuses to be sworn of to testify;
2. not competent to testify;
3. trauma or harm to the child, proved by expert evidence;
4. unable to give meaningful evidence, as when the child "freezes";
5. unable to give a full, frank and accurate account;
6. the child recants on the stand.[28]

In 1999, in *R. v. F. (W.J.)*,[29] the Supreme Court ruled that "necessity" for hearsay purposes could be inferred when a child froze on the stand, without need for extrinsic evidence. The Supreme Court of Canada has said that necessity is to . . ."be

---

[26] See *R. v. Bickford* (1989), 51 C.C.C. (3d) 181 (Ont. C.A.).
[27] See *R. v. S. (W.)* (1994), 90 C.C.C. (3d) 242 (Ont. C.A.), leave to appeal refused (1994), 93 C.C.C. (3d) vi (note) (S.C.C.).
[28] *R. v. Smith* [1992] 2 S.C.R. 915 (S.C.C.).
[29] [1999] 3 S.C.R. 569 (S.C.C.).

given a flexible definition, capable of encompassing diverse situations".[30]

An important case on the issue of the necessity to admit hearsay evidence of a witness with diminished capacity was decided by the Supreme Court in 2001. *R. v. Parrott*[31] was a sexual assault case, involving a woman with the mental capacity of a 3- to 4-year-old-child. The Crown did not call the mentally disabled complainant as a witness, but sought to introduce her hearsay statements to doctors and police officers, in a judge-alone trial. A 4-3 majority of the Court held that the complainant was available to testify and should have been called as a witness for the trial judge to assess her competence. There was no evidence of likely "trauma or adverse effects" to the complainant, as the majority repeatedly stressed, only expert evidence of her mental capacity. Even though the complainant's statements might be reliable, said Binnie J., there was no basis for finding there was "necessity" so as to compel the admission of hearsay evidence in lieu of an appearance by the witness herself. The testimonial competence of a witness is ". . .the very meat and potatoes of a trial court's existence", a matter that can be determined by the judge questioning and observing the witness. It was ruled by the Court that only *after* the judge had heard the complainant, could the judge then decide the "necessity" for some expert assistance on the young person's competence to testify.[32]

The second element of reliability is assessed in the circumstances of the child[33] and the particular case. It involves con-

---

[30] *R. v. Smith, supra* note 28 at para. 37.
[31] *Supra* note 8.
[32] The Supreme Court in *R. v. Mohan*, [1994] 2 S.C.R. 9 (S.C.C.) set out the criteria for the admissibility of expert evidence: (a) relevance; (b) necessity of the expert evidence to assist the trier of fact; (c) the absence of any rule of exclusion; and (d) an expert who is properly qualified.
[33] If the witness who received the alleged statement is not reliable, the issue of threshold reliability may not be met. See *R. v. McMaster* (1998),

sidering the reliability of both the statement maker and the witness relating the statement to the court. Also, the statement must be admissible if its maker were to give it as testimony in court. For example, the prior statement may itself contain hearsay or might have been obtained through a violation of the *Charter*. Often an assessment of reliability is based upon:

- the timing of the statement;
- the personality of the child;
- the intelligence and understanding of the child; and
- the absence of any reason to expect fabrication in the statement made.[34]

The Supreme Court has affirmed that reliability of hearsay is a function of the circumstances under which a statement was made. As stated by the Court:

> ...If a statement sought to be adduced by way of hearsay evidence is made under circumstances which substantially negate the possibility that the declarant was untruthful or mistaken, the hearsay evidence may be said to be "reliable", i.e., a circumstantial guarantee of trustworthiness is established.[35]

If the statement evidence is equally consistent with a hypothesis other than the one for which it is introduced, reliability sufficient for admissibility has not been established.[36] Reliability must be decided solely on the basis of the evidence introduced on the *voir dire* (i.e., a separate hearing during a trial to deal with the admissibility of evidence), without reference to the rest of the evidence in the trial proper. Depending on the circumstances, other factors that might enhance or detract

---

122 C.C.C. (3d) 371 (Ont. C.A.), leave to appeal refused (1999), 125 O.A.C. 399 (note) (S.C.C.).
[34] *R. v. Smith, supra* note 28 at para. 31.
[35] *Ibid.* at para. 34.
[36] See *R. v. Smith, supra* note 28 and *R. v. R. (D.)* (1996), 107 C.C.C. (3d) 289 (S.C.C.).

from the reliability of the child's statement include, but are not limited to:

1. the age and immaturity of the child;
2. the language used in the statement;
3. the relative spontaneity of the statement;
4. the passage of time between the statement and the alleged assaults (or other offence); and
5. the absence of any details in the statement referable to the time, place or circumstances in which the assault occurred.[37]

The admission of out-of-court statements by children is the exception rather than the norm. As Madam Justice McLachlin concluded in one case: "[The admission of hearsay evidence in lieu of a child's testimony] does not make out-of-court statements by children generally admissible. . .".[38]

A trial judge on an application to admit hearsay evidence must consider and rule on whether the requirements of necessity and reliability are met. Where a trial judge neglects to make a finding that is essential to determining the admissibility of a crucial piece of evidence, this may amount to an error of law.

WEIGHT OF OUT-OF-COURT STATEMENT – CHILD NOT TESTIFYING

The assessment of the weight to be given to an out-of-court statement made by a child who does not testify involves three concerns:

1. Was the statement made?
2. If satisfied that it was, what weight, if any, should it be given? Because of the absence of traditional means of testing

---

[37] See *R. v. A. (S.)* (1992), 76 C.C.C. (3d) 522 (Ont. C.A.).
[38] *R. v. Khan, supra* note 14 at para. 35.

the reliability of the statement itself, caution must be used when assessing weight.
3. Is there anything in the rest of the evidence that tends to support or undermine the reliability of the statement?

(a) Was the Statement Made?

Determining whether the statement was, in fact, made and, if it was, determining the content of the statement requires a consideration of the credibility of the witness or witnesses who testify to making the statement. In some cases, the witness may have reason to fabricate evidence against the accused. Even where no such motive exists, the witness may be mistaken as to what was said, or may be inadvertently providing interpretation of what was said rather than an actual narrative.

If a judge is not satisfied that the statement was made, it must not be admitted against the accused.

(b) The Need for Caution

Even if the judge as the trier of fact is satisfied that the out-of-court statement was made, that statement is not the same as a statement made by a witness who actually testifies. Out-of-court statements of persons who do not testify, offered for the truth of their contents, are subject to frailties that warrant a cautious approach. These include:

1. The statement was not made under oath, affirmation or a promise to tell the truth;
2. The trier of fact did not have the opportunity to see and hear the child testify; and
3. The maker of the statement was not subject to cross-examination, which not only would give an accused an opportunity to test the reliability of inculpatory evidence, but also provides a means of adducing evidence favourable to the accused.

As with all evidence, a child's out-of-court statement cannot be considered in isolation. The weight to be given to it will be affected by other evidence. For example, medical evidence or expert psychiatric evidence, if accepted, may offer direct confirmation of the allegation in the statement that the child had been sexually assaulted. In some cases, hearsay evidence is simply rejected, sometimes for lack of reliability[39] and in other cases on the grounds of lack of necessity.[40] In such instances, the concern of the court is typically fairness to the accused, in view of the lack of an opportunity to the hearsay opponent to cross-examine or test the out-of-court declarant on his or her perception, memory, narration (use of language) or sincerity. Other concerns about hearsay evidence include the danger of misreport or fabrication by the in-court witness reporting the hearsay statement; the danger of unfair surprise; the fear of unbridled discretion to admit hearsay on the part of trial judges; and the potential for abuse of police or governmental power.

CHILDREN'S VIDEOTAPED EVIDENCE

In the context of alleged sexual offences against children, Canada's *Criminal Code* has been amended to allow testimony given by way of videotape to be admissible in court, if the videotape was done within a "reasonable time" after the alleged offence and the contents of the recording are later adopted by the child. Section 715.1 of the *Criminal Code* reads:

> 715.1 In any proceeding relating to an offence under section 151, 152, 153, 155 or 159, subsection 160(2) or (3), or section 163.1, 170, 171, 172, 173, 210, 211, 212, 213, 266, 267, 268, 271, 272 or 273, in which the complainant or other witness was under the age of eighteen years at the time the offence is alleged to have been committed, a videotape made within a reasonable time after the alleged offence, in which the complainant or witness describes the acts complained of, is admissible in

---

[39] See, for example, *R. v. Starr* [2000] 2 S.C.R. 144 (S.C.C.).
[40] See, for example, *R. v. Parrott, supra* note 8.

evidence if the complainant or witness, while testifying, adopts the contents of the videotape.

Section 715.1 was unanimously held to be constitutionally valid in the context of a challenge under the *Charter* in 1993 in the case of *R. v. L. (D.O.)*.[41] In that case, Chief Justice Lamer, writing for six members of the Court, made this comment upon the aim and purpose of the section at page 429:

> ...By allowing for the videotaping of evidence under certain express conditions, s. 715.1 not only makes participation in the criminal justice system less stressful and traumatic for child and adolescent complainants, but also aids in the preservation of evidence and the discovery of truth.

It is commonly accepted that anyone, particularly children, have a better recollection of events closer to their occurrence than he or she will later on. See, e.g., Rhona Flin and J.R. Spencer, "Do Children Forget Faster?" (1991) Crim. L.R. 189, at 190. It follows that a videotape made within a reasonable time after an alleged offence that describes the act will almost inevitably reflect a more accurate recollection of events than will testimony given later at trial. Thus, the section in the Code enhances the ability of the court to find the truth by preserving a very recent recollection of the event in question.

The primary goal of videotaping permitted by section 715.1 is to create a record of what is probably the best recollection of the event to assist the court in ascertaining the truth. The video record may well be the only means of presenting a child's evidence. For example, a child assaulted at the age of 3 or 4 years may have very little real recollection of the events a year or two later when the child is attempting to testify at trial. Justice L'Heureux-Dubé, dissenting in *L. (D.O.)*,[42] noted the

---

[41] [1993] 4 S.C.R. 419 (S.C.C.).
[42] *Ibid.*

fundamental importance of having a videotape before the court. At page 450 she stated:

> Section 715.1 ensures that the child's story will be brought before the court regardless of whether the young victim is able to accomplish this unenviable task.

The idea underlying section 715.1 is to prevent or reduce materially the likelihood of inflicting further injury upon a child as a result of participating in court proceedings. This may be accomplished by reducing the number of interviews the child must undergo thereby reducing the stress occasioned to a child by repeated questioning on a painful incident. Videotaping often takes place in surroundings much less overwhelming child that in a courtroom. As Nicholas Bala and Hilary McCormack have commented:[43]

> One of the main purposes of this provision is to ensure that the courts have access to the best description possible of the events, as a child is more likely to have an accurate and complete memory of the events when the videotape is made, than several months later at the time of trial. Children are also more likely to fully remember and relate often painful memories in a relatively relaxed interview than in the strange, stressful, and formal court environment.

Section 715.1 however, does not simply allow a child to make a statement on videotape. To be admissible as evidence, a child is also required later to adopt the "prior consistent statement" that has been made on videotape in court. The issue of when an out-of-court statement is "adopted" has been widely discussed in case law. In *R. v. Antoine*,[44] it was held that adoption occurs when the witness admits the truth of the statement under oath. Later this was accepted by the Supreme Court of Canada, per Estey J. in *McInroy v. R.*[45] The Court held, at page

---

[43] See "Accommodating the Criminal Process to Child Witnesses: *L. (D.O.)* and *Levogiannis*" (1994) 25 C.R. (4th) 341 at 343.
[44] [1949] 1 W.W.R. 701 (B.C. C.A.).
[45] [1979] 1 S.C.R. 588 (S.C.C.).

608 of the judgment, that the question to be resolved was whether the witness had "...adopted it in the witness box as being the truth as she now sees it." In *R. v. Smith*,[46] the Alberta Court of Appeal held that a previous inconsistent statement is adopted if the witness accepts it as being true at the moment she is testifying. Lieberman J.A. stated that it was insufficient for the witness to affirm that when she gave the statement she was being candid. The Ontario Court of Appeal applied a similar approach to the adoption of prior inconsistent statements in *R. v. Atikian*,[47] stating at page 364:

> The jury had to understand that before they could find that the witness had adopted the statement, and that they could use what was said in the statement as proof of the truth of the facts stated in it, they had to be satisfied that she acknowledged that she made the statement, and that it was true, or, of course, that she made part of the statement and that part of it was true. And so, she adopted it as part of her testimony under oath at the trial.

There are several factors present in section 715.1 that address the requisite reliability of the videotaped statement. They include: (a) the requirement that the statement be made within a reasonable time; (b) the trier of fact can watch the entire interview, which provides an opportunity to observe the demeanour, and assess the personality and intelligence of the child; (c) the requirement that the child attest that she was attempting to be truthful at the time that the statement was made.

VOIR DIRE

A *voir dire* may take place before admitting a videotape: both as to the statutory grounds of admissibility and whether the risk of prejudice outweighs its probative value. Of primary concern is whether statements in it conform to the general rules

---

[46] (1985), 66 A.R. 195 (Alta. C.A.).
[47] (1990), 62 C.C.C. (3d) 357 (Ont. C.A.).

of evidence. Other issues relevant to the prejudice/probative consideration are:

1. The form of questions used by any other person appearing in the videotaped statement;
2. Any interest of anyone participating in the making of the statement;
3. The quality of the video and audio reproduction;
4. The presence or absence of inadmissible evidence in the statement;
5. The ability to eliminate inappropriate material by editing the tape;
6. Whether other out-of-court statements by the complainant have been entered;
7. Whether any visual information in the statement might tend to prejudice the accused (for example, unrelated injuries visible on the victim);
8. Whether the prosecution has been allowed to use any other method to facilitate the giving of evidence by the complainant;
9. Whether the trial is by judge alone or with a jury; and
10. The length of time since the tape was made and the present ability of the witness to effectively relate to the events described.

Videotapes may accurately and fairly represent the information they purport to convey[48] and the accused's reasonable expectation of privacy is not violated. The rights of the child may well take precedence over the accused's right to privacy.

The court's test is whether a particular videotape meets the threshold degree of reliability required to admit it in evidence as proof of the truth of its contents. Adopting the videotape renders the evidence admissible pursuant to section 715.1. Once a trial judge rules that the statement has been adopted, the video becomes the evidence of the events described as if

---
[48] See *R. v. Nikolovski* (1996), 111 C.C.C. (3d) 403 (S.C.C.).

the child were giving the statements on the videotape in open court.[49] An adopted videotaped statement should, together with the *viva voce* evidence given at trial, comprise the whole of the evidence-in-chief of the complainant.

CROSS-EXAMINATION

An opposing party must be given a full opportunity to cross-examine a child witness about any statement he/she has made, and wherever made, including videotaped statements. A child can be cross-examined at trial as to whether he or she was actually being truthful when the statement was made. These *indicia* provide enough guarantees of reliability to compensate for the inability to cross-examine as to the forgotten events. Where a complainant has no independent memory of the events, there is the necessity for the videotaped evidence. In such circumstances, the trier of fact should be given a special warning[50] of the dangers of convicting based on the videotape alone. If, in the course of cross-examination of a witness who has given videotaped testimony, defence counsel elicits evidence that contradicts any part of the video, this does not render those parts inadmissible. A contradicted videotape may well be given less weight, but this does not necessarily mean that the video is unreliable. The trial judge may conclude that the inconsistencies evoked by cross-examination *are insignificant and find the video more reliable than the evidence elicited at trial*. In *R. v. B. (G.)*,[51] at page 55, Wilson J. noted the fact that inconsistencies in a child's testimony are not necessarily fatal to its credibility:

---

[49] *R. v. L. (D.O), supra* note 41 at 458.
[50] Similar to *R. v. Vetrovec*, [1982] 1 S.C.R. 811 (S.C.C.). In that case, the top Court held that a trial judge has discretion, and not the duty, to give a clear warning to a jury concerning the credibility of certain witnesses based upon the Court's appreciation of all the circumstances.
[51] *Supra* note 4.

...[A] flaw, such as a contradiction, in a child's testimony should not be given the same effect as a similar flaw in the testimony of an adult...While children may not be able to recount precise details and communicate the when and where of an event with exactitude, this does not mean that they have misconceived what happened to them and who did it.

Wilson J. concluded that, although each witness's credibility must be assessed, the standard that would be applied to an adult's evidence is not always appropriate in assessing the credibility of young children. This approach to the evidence of children was reiterated in *R. v. W. (R.)*.[52] In that case, McLachlin J. acknowledged that the peculiar perspectives of children can affect their recollection of events and that the presence of inconsistencies, especially those related to peripheral matters, should be assessed in context. A skilful cross-examination is almost certain to confuse a child, even if he or she is telling the truth. That confusion can lead to inconsistencies in the testimony. Although the trier of fact must be wary of any evidence that has been contradicted, this is a matter that goes to the weight that should be attached to the videotape and not to its admissibility. Where there is a substantial degree of reliability, the judge will weigh both statements in light of the witness's explanation of the change.[53] Reliability can be established without anything comparable to an oath, warning or presence. The similarity and unique nature of statements by an accused and a recanting complainant, the absence of an opportunity for collusion, and a finding that the accused was not influenced by police officers may well establish reliability.[54]

---

[52] *Supra* note 25 at 132-34.
[53] See *R. v. B. (K.G.)* (1993), 79 C.C.C. (3d) 257 (S.C.C.).
[54] See *R. v. U. (F.J.)* (1995) 101 C.C.C. (3d) 97 (S.C.C.).

CREDIBILITY OF CHILDREN

The old rule that the testimony of children suffers from inherent frailties is no longer the law either in statute or at common law. A witness's testimony is not suspect merely because the witness is a child. The same standard of proof applies and, just as with adults, a judge may treat a child's evidence with the caution where the circumstances of the particular case indicate caution is appropriate. However, the phrase "...the problems that may arise from the testimony of youthful witnesses" was used in the majority judgment of the Supreme Court of Canada in the context of a 13-year-old complainant testifying about events that occurred when he was 5. These "problems" were adequately addressed by the charge to the jury, which highlighted four areas of concern about a young witness:

1. capacity to observe things at age 5 and relate them at 13;
2. capacity to recollect things at age 5 and capacity to relate them at 13 and to recollect them and bring them back;
3. ability to understand questions and give intelligent answers; and
4. moral responsibility as a child of 13 talking about events that occurred when he was 5.[55]

Credibility of children should not be assessed on the same basis as that of adults. Children experience the world differently from adults. Details such as time, place, and clothing that might be expected to be fixed in an adult's mind may well have been unnoticed by a child. These aspects do not necessarily denote that children cannot accurately grasp what is happening to them and who is doing it.[56]

However, the testimony of children should not be subject to a lower level of scrutiny than that of adults.[57] Where a video-

---

[55] See R. v. E. (A.W.) (1993), 83 C.C.C. (3d) 462 (S.C.C.) at para. 16.
[56] See R. v. B. (G), supra note 4.
[57] See R. v. S. (W.), supra note 27.

taped statement has been adopted per section 715.1 of the *Criminal Code*, contradictions of the statement elicited in cross-examination go only to weight, not admissibility. A skilful cross-examination is almost certain to confuse even a truthful child and elicit inconsistencies.[58]

Although corroboration is no longer required for conviction on a child's evidence (except perjury where corroboration is required for an adult as well), there is nothing wrong with a trial judge pointing out whether any evidence supports that of the child when determining the weight to be given the child's testimony. The same exercise would be appropriate for an adult witness.[59]

CHILDREN'S WISHES

In the context of a family law proceeding, a child's wish to live with one or the other parent (or neither) is hearsay. However, in the context of family court, such a statement may be admissible under a traditional exception to the hearsay rule, which allows statements about one's physical, mental or emotional state to be admitted into evidence. To be admissible, the child must be stating his or her contemporaneous "state of mind". This allows the recipient of the statement to both test the veracity of statement (by observing the accompanying behaviour and demeanour of the child) and to relay that information to the court. The "necessity" underpinning this exception is not unavailability, but simply the fact that it is not known how someone else feels. The "reliability" of such evidence flows from its contemporaneity of the statement to the feeling. Also, many such statements are spontaneous. Often, statements are made to health professionals in order to obtain treatment.

---

[58] See *R. v. F. (C.)* (1997), 120 C.C.C. (3d) 225 (S.C.C.).
[59] See *R. v. M. (W.H.)*, [1992] 1 S.C.R. 984 (S.C.C.).

In the *Khan*[60] case, the classic decision on admitting a child's out-of-court statements into evidence, Justice McLachlin limited her specific ruling to "hearsay evidence of a child's statement on crimes committed against the child". For the most part, the *Khan* exception has been used to introduce evidence of sexual or physical abuse. Under the *Khan* approach, the party putting forward the child abuse hearsay must prove both necessity and reliability, on a *voir dire*, for the hearsay to be admissible.

In most cases, proof of "necessity" is not difficult. For young children, counsel often concede the issue of necessity, based on age and likely trauma. Expert evidence of trauma or cognitive impairment is easy to obtain. In some cases, the test for necessity is relaxed, although the court may go through the *voir dire* steps.

Family law judges often suggest a "relaxed" approach to assessing evidence by children. What seems to distinguish family law from criminal approaches to the issue of the necessity of admitting children's out-of-court statements into evidence is the willingness of our family law judges to accept generalized statements of "likely harm" to the child. To many judges, no prospect of "harm" to a child by testifying is acceptable, not even the transitory "harm" or stress experienced by an adult witness.

---

[60] *R. v. Khan*, *supra* note 14.

4
THE *CHARTER*, CIVIL RIGHTS AND CHILDREN

The patriation of Canada's Constitution, on April 17, 1982, was a watershed event, putting in place the *Charter* as Part I of the *Constitution Act, 1982*. The constitutional changes made in 1982 were profound. The changes have changed the way Canadians understand themselves as individuals.

The *Charter* is a reflection of the vision championed by Prime Minister Pierre Elliott Trudeau, with its spotlight on the importance of the individual and individual rights. The *Charter* was also conceived as a unifying force for Canadians, establishing a common set of constitutionally protected rights that apply to each and every Canadian. Much debate took place as the *Charter* was constructed, both in its detail and as to the desirability of entrenching a *Charter* at all. Perhaps one of the most remarkable observations about the *Charter* is the extent to which it has become a symbol of pride and a source of identification for Canadians, thus becoming a unifying force as had been hoped.

The *Charter* has had an enormous impact on governments. Some *Charter* critics would claim that far too much power has been shifted from the legislatures and governments to the courts. Some point to the added impediments to governmental action and decision-making that come with the need to take those new rights into account. Some worry that the legislatures and governments are actually being prevented from achieving important goals or are being diverted by rights activists from social and economic reforms that are more important than the issues of the day brought by pressure groups. Some claim that the rights culture is having an effect that goes right to the root of our social structure and is damaging the very cohesion of our society.

Within Canada itself, the move towards the *Charter* was a gradual one. In 1960, the *Canadian Bill of Rights* was enacted by Parliament, but it was a simple statute and, with few exceptions, was not given pre-eminent force. During the period leading up to the entrenchment of the *Charter*, human rights codes were developing in Canada at both the federal and provincial levels.

Canada is the first country to include in its fundamental law on rights a provision contemplating the limitation of those rights. Section 1 sets out the general guarantee of the rights and freedoms in the *Charter*, and then allows for the rights and freedoms to be superseded by public interest considerations if their limitation can be "demonstrably justified". This provision, notably placed at the beginning of the *Charter*, carries with it the message that rights and freedoms are not absolutes. Rights and freedoms can be limited by law so long as the limits are justified in accordance with section 1.

There are several sections of the *Charter* that carry within themselves balancing mechanisms that limit the scope of rights even before resort is to be made to section 1. For example, section 8 refers to "*unreasonable* search and seizure" and section 9 refers to "the right not to be *arbitrarily* detained or imprisoned". Here most of the balancing takes place with the rights section itself.

The *Charter* has created a new relationship between federal, provincial and territorial governments in Canada and their citizens. It has established a direct right for any Canadian to take governments in Canada to court in relation to the infringement of any of the rights guaranteed by the *Charter*, whether by actions of a government or by statute. Canadian governments have always been answerable for failure to adhere to general principles of natural justice or for failure to meet human rights standards they have set in their own legislation, but the *Charter* has opened up a multitude of new grounds for complaint. Section 15, the equality section, is particularly fruitful in this regard. It makes governmental programs and social policy decisions vulnerable to reassessment by the courts on grounds of discrimination. The remedies for a successful challenge have, on occasion, resulted in adjustments to government programs that have expanded them beyond their original scope and have sometimes resulted in significant additional expenditures.

THE FAMILY

In the years since the *Charter* was put in place, the concept of "the family" in Canadian society has evolved. The traditional nuclear family is increasingly an exception. There are large numbers of financially beleaguered single-parent families. In those families with two parents, often both are working. Family law has moved from a central preoccupation with preserving marriages to a concern with preserving parent-child relationships and the concern with protecting the vulnerable members of family units. The family is understood more in terms of a basic relationship of interdependency that may or may not involve marriage, children, same-sex partners, heterosexual partners or even sexual affiliation at all.

The Advisory Committee on Children's Services (1990) in the Report entitled "Children First" stated the following:

> The traditional family unit – mother at home caring for children full-time and father in workforce – is no longer the norm. Most women,

including mothers of young children, have jobs, and their participation in the workforce is a necessary contribution to the financial stability of their families and to the viability of the Ontario economy. The new family arrangements of the 1990s also include a substantial increase in the number of one-parent families and blended families, with children from different marriages living in the same household.

In the last few decades, family law in Canada has risen remarkably in profile. The Supreme Court cases on family law, such as *M. v. H.*,[1] *Moge v. Moge*,[2] and *Tremblay c. Daigle*[3] have attracted great public interest. The family has become a great subject of public discourse whose very nature, function and definition are seen as very important issues. While the notion of the family unit as one that deserves respect remains vital, the family is also seen increasingly as a social unit upon which the state depends, and which it therefore should play a role in supporting. Legislation has played an increasing role in family law, from child protection to family property. In this sense, it may be as much public as private.

THE FAMILY AND THE *CHARTER*

By 1988, the family, starting with the pregnant woman, was seen as the focus of important social and legal issues that involved issues of rights. The Supreme Court was no longer merely "settling a dispute"; it was the final arbiter in light of the fact that social and political consensus on the issue has been impossible, leaving a legislative void. As Justice Wilson stated in a 1985 speech,

> ...the conclusion is inescapable that the scope of judicial review of legislative and executive acts has been vastly expanded under the *Char-*

---

[1] [1999] 2 S.C.R. 3 (S.C.C.), reconsideration refused (May 25, 2000), 2000 CarswellOnt 1913 (S.C.C.).
[2] [1992] 3 S.C.R. 813 (S.C.C.).
[3] [1989] 2 S.C.R. 530 (S.C.C.).

ter and [. . .] the courts have become the mediators between the state and the individual.[4]

In connection with the *Charter*, our courts have been cautious about the application of an individualistic rights discourse in family law and, apart from the "family definition" cases, only a few *Charter* challenges have been ultimately successful.[5] While the number of *Charter* challenges that have been successful have perhaps been few in number, the cases that have been decided have been both significant in the attention they have received and their impact on the development of the law.

Young v Young[6] was a case that attracted a great deal of public attention because it was a family law case concerning the application of the *Charter*. Mrs. Young was the sole custodian of the children of the marriage. One of the contribution factors to the marriage breakdown had been Mr. Young's adoption of the Jehovah Witness faith. The trial judge had imposed significant limits on his access, which included not speaking about his faith to the child, not taking them to Church, and not involving them in canvassing and proselytizing activities. There was evidence that indicated that the children had disliked their father's religious instructions, that it was damaging their relationship with him and contributing to the stress they were experiencing in their relation to their parents' separation. The central legal issue was whether sections 16(8) and 17(5) of the *Divorce Act* relating to custody and custody variation orders respectively violated sections 2(a), (b), (d) or 15(1) of the

---

[4] "Decision-Making in the Supreme Court" (David B. Goodman Memorial Lecture delivered at the University of Toronto, November 26 and 27, 1985, as published in (1986) 36 U.T.L.J. 227 at 238 to 239).

[5] See *Miron v. Trudel* (1995), 13 R.F.L. (4th) 1 (S.C.C.); *M. v .H.*, *supra* note 1; *Young v. Young*, [1993] 4 S.C.R. 3 (S.C.C.); *P. (D.) v. S. (C.)*, [1993] 4 S. C.R. 141 (S.C.C.); *Thibaudeau v. Canada*, [1995] 2 S.C.R 627 (S.C.C.); *Symes v. Canada*, [1993] 4 S.C.R. 695 (S.C.C.); and *B. (R.) v. Children's Aid Society of Metropolitan Toronto*, [1995] 1 S.C.R. 315 (S.C.C.).

[6] *Ibid.*

Charter. Both subsections state that in making an order, ". . .the court shall take into consideration only the best interest of the child."

None of the judgments given by the Supreme Court in *Young v. Young* expressed any enthusiasm for the direct application of the *Charter* to matters involving custody or access. McLachlin J. held that where a limitation is placed on access to a child including one made in the context of the exercise of religious expression, it should be based on evidence of harm to the child. This is predicated on the premise there is a legal presumption that maximizing the access a parent has to a child is generally a good thing, which is in the interests of the children. Therefore, in order to rebut the presumption that granting access is positive, evidence must be tendered to establish harm. McLachlin J. was of the view that harm had not been established in this case. Sopinka J. expressed general agreement with McLachlin J., but stated that while he agreed with her that the ultimate determination in deciding issues of custody and access is the "best interests of the child" test, he went on to say that this test must be reconciled with the *Charter* and that it should be overridden ". . .only it its exercise would occasion consequences that involve more than inconvenience, upset or disruption to the child and incidentally to the custodial parent". Gonthier and La Forest JJ. agreed with L'Heureux-Dubé J., who went furthest in holding that the trial judge's order was not subject to the *Charter*. Cory and Iacobucci JJ. refused to express a view on this issue as it was not necessary, in their view, to the case at bar.

The Court heard and decided another very similar case, *P. (D.) v. S. (C.)*,[7] at the same time as *Young*. In that case, the facts again raised matters of freedom of religion. The mother was the custodial parent and Roman Catholic. The father was a Jehovah Witness. The case differed from *Young*. The trial

---

[7] *Supra* note 5.

judge's order was less intrusive. While it specified that the father could not "indoctrinate" his daughter, it had also specified that he could teach his faith to her.[8] As the parents had not married, this case did not invoke the *Divorce Act*, but rather the best interests standard as articulated in the *Civil Code of Québec*.[9] In *P. (D.) v. S. (C.)*, the Supreme Court ruled that a trial judge's exercise of discretion to protect the "best interests of the child" (as expressed in the Quebec *Civil Code*) was not unconstitutionally vague or contrary to a religious parent's rights of freedom of religion, expression, association or equality pursuant to the *Charter*. Instead, a majority of the Court ruled (as it had in *Young v. Young*) that the *Charter* does not apply to private disputes in a family context.

Charter rights do not appear to pre-empt the best interests test. It is interesting to note that *Gordon v. Goertz*,[10] a case that involved, "relocation" of a custodial parent to Australia, decided in 1996, did not raise the issue of "mobility rights". This had been one of the issues discussed extensively in the academic literature in the early 1990s as potentially undermining the complex nature of families by applying unsophisticated and individualistic notions of rights. By the time *Goertz* was decided, the question of relocation was framed as an issue of parental rights. The driving concept is one of "the best interest of the child" rather than parental rights.

The reticence about direct application of the *Charter* to family law matters that was evident in *Young* and *P. (D.)* was also evident in a less publicized case decided the same year. That case was the *Catholic Children's Aid Society of Metropolitan Toronto v. M. (C.)*.[11]

---

[8] See *P. (D.) v. S. (C.)*, *supra* note 5 at 152.
[9] *Civil Code of Lower Canada*, Article 30: In every decision concerning a child, the child's interest and the respect of his rights must be the determining factors.
[10] [1996] 2 S.C.R. 27 (S.C.C.).
[11] [1994] 2 S.C.R. 165 (S.C.C.).

The 1999 Supreme Court of Canada decisions in *M. v. H.* and *New Brunswick (Minister of Health & Community Services) v. G. (J.)*[12] marked a dramatic change in judicial approach. The Supreme Court has recognized that familial relationships are of fundamental importance and worthy of constitutional recognition and protection. In *New Brunswick v. G. (J.)*, the Supreme Court recognized that child protection proceedings pose a fundamental threat to the "security of the person" of parents and their children, and hence must be conducted in accordance with "the principles of fundamental justice". This decision dealt with the right of indigent parents to a lawyer paid by the state, but is significant for a range of issues in child protection and adoption proceedings.

The 1995 decision in *B. (R.) v. Children's Aid Society of Metropolitan Toronto*[13] revealed a Supreme Court that was deeply split over whether, in principle, parents (or children) should enjoy any constitutional rights in litigation with a child protection agency. *B. (R.)* arose out of a case where Jehovah's Witness parents were refusing, on religious grounds, a blood transfusion for their newborn child who was suffering infantile glaucoma. Doctors believed that surgery, which would require a blood transfusion, was necessary to save the child's life. A court order was sought by the child protection agency to have the child made a temporary ward of the agency. The trial judge made the order, and the agency consented to the operation and transfusion. Although the operation was performed and the child returned to parental custody, the parents appealed the original decision on the ground that it had violated their constitutional rights. After a lengthy appeal process, the Supreme Court of Canada upheld the original order and the constitutional validity of the child protection legislation in question. However, the Supreme Court divided sharply over the broader question of whether there were any circumstances

---

[12] [1999] 3 S.C.R. 46 (S.C.C.).
[13] *Supra* note 5.

in which the *Charter* might apply to a child protection case. Justice La Forest, writing for four of the nine justices, recognized that parents have a constitutionally protected right to enjoy their relationship with their children, though recognizing their rights must be balanced against a state interest in promoting children's welfare. While he was prepared to uphold the constitutional validity of the legislation in question, he accepted that the concepts of "liberty and security of the person" include a parental right to enjoy a relationship with a child. Accordingly, state action to restrict parental autonomy must accord with the "principles of fundamental justice". Justice La Forest stated:

> ...[O]ur society is far from having repudiated the privileged role parents exercise in the upbringing of their children. This role translates into a protected sphere of parental decision making which is rooted in the presumption that parents should make important decisions affecting their children both because parents are more likely to appreciate the best interests of their children and because the state is ill-equipped to make such decisions itself. Moreover, individuals have a deep personal interest as parents in fostering the growth of their own children. This is not to say that the state cannot intervene when it considers it necessary to safeguard the child's autonomy or health. But such intervention must be justified. In other words, parental decision making must receive the protection of the *Charter* in order for state interference to be properly monitored by the courts, and be permitted only when it conforms to the values underlying the *Charter*.[14]

While La Forest J., with three other judges concurring, took a broad view of parental rights, four other judges of the Supreme Court appeared to dismiss the idea that parents could have any *constitutional* rights in the context of child protection proceedings. Chief Justice Lamer wrote that:

> ...the liberty interest protected by s. 7...includes neither the right of parents to choose (or refuse) medical treatment for their children nor, more generally, the right to bring up or educate their children without

---

[14] *B. (R.) v. Children's Aid Society of Metropolitan Toronto, supra* note 5 at para. 85.

undue interference by the state. . . . [T]he autonomy or integrity of the family unit. . .does not fall within the ambit of s. 7.[15]

Justices Iacobucci and Major expressed a concern that ". . .the family is often a very dangerous place for children" and felt that any concern about parental "liberty" must be balanced against the *child's* constitutionally protected rights to "security of the person". The difficulty with this analysis is that the child often lacks the capacity to articulate any views, and this type of argument suggests that a state agency can purport to use the child's constitutional rights to limit parental rights.

The ninth judge, Sopinka J., did not express an opinion on whether section 7 of the *Charter*, with its protection of "liberty and security of the person", includes parental rights, but he did conclude that the parents in this particular case were entitled to some constitutional protection for their religious freedom, an interest protected by section 2 of the *Charter*. The four judges who took the broader view of section 7, as including parental rights, agreed that parental religious freedom was infringed in a child protection proceeding if religious beliefs are the basis for resistance to state interference with the child.

In its 1999 decision in *New Brunswick (Minister of Health & Community Services) v. G. (J.)*,[16] the Supreme Court of Canada sent a strong message that parents have a vital interest in their relationship with their children, an interest that is entitled to protection under section 7 of the *Charter* as an aspect of "security of the person". The Court concluded that, pursuant to the section 7 of the *Charter*, an indigent mother whose children had been apprehended by a child welfare agency had the constitutional right to be represented by counsel paid for by the government to ensure that the temporary wardship proceedings were ". . .in accordance with the principles of fundamental justice".

---

[15] *Ibid.* at para. 1.
[16] *Supra* note 12.

Although the *Charter* arguments were not addressed in the child protection context in *M. (C.)*, they were central in *B. (R.)*, a case decided the following year. Again, though, the reasons are not easy to reconcile with one another; this case, read as a whole, does not champion the notion of parental rights in an individual and oppositional sense. Equality interests were implicated because, as L'Heureux-Dubé J. stated, ". . .women, and especially single mothers, are disproportionately and particularly affected by child protection proceedings".[17] In noting that liberty interests were also implicated, she cited La Forest J. from *B. (G.)* in support of this point.

It is now accepted that the "liberty and security of the person" of both children and parents are threatened in child welfare proceedings, and that there is the potential for both to seek constitutional protections under section 7 of the *Charter*. There may be situations in which their rights conflict and must in some way be balanced against each other. However, in most child protection situations, it is submitted that the *constitutional rights* of children and parents are not in conflict with one another, and can be *independently asserted against the state.*

CHILD PROTECTION

The protection of parental rights is based, in part, on a belief that parents will act to promote their child's interests, and hence a protection of these rights will promote a child's welfare. As parents in our society have primary responsibility for their children's care, this necessitates giving parents a very significant set of rights in regard to their children. It is also recognized that even well-intentioned state involvement in a child's life may not be beneficial. The resources of the state to care for and to control children are inevitably limited. Accordingly, it is presumed to be best to leave a child with his or her

---

[17] *New Brunswick (Minister of Health & Community Services) v. G. (J.), supra* note 12 at para. 113.

family, particularly since any change is bound to have a disruptive effect upon a child. Perhaps most fundamentally, parental rights are viewed as "natural rights". It is accepted as a basic tenet of our culture and way of life that parents have a "right" to control and care for their children; this right is inextricably related to the view of a society based on the primacy of the individual, and the protection of "liberty and security of the person".

The state has a clear interest in protecting children from harm and promoting their welfare. The protection of children will inevitably involve some infringement or curtailment of parental rights. However, if such intervention is done in an appropriate fashion, this may be action done "in accordance with the principles of fundamental justice" and hence be consistent with section 7 of the *Charter*. In other cases, the state's infringement of parental rights may be justified under section 1 of the *Charter* as a "reasonable limit. . .demonstrably justified in a free and democratic society".

In particular, the amendments made to the *Child and Family Services Act*[18] in 1999 made promoting a child's best interests, protection and well-being "paramount" and seem particularly consonant with *Charter* values. Prior to these changes, these goals for a child reflected "*a* paramount objective" (along with other objectives) whereas the amendments make these "*the* paramount purpose" and list other objectives or purposes with the proviso ". . .so long as they are consistent with the best interests, protection and well being of children".

The major focus of judicial concern about the constitutional rights of children has been on the protection of their procedural rights, and in some contexts, the right to have a decision made that is in their best interests. There has, however, been a real reluctance to allow the *Charter* to be invoked in the child wel-

---

[18] R.S.O. 1990, c. C.11 (as amended).

fare context by *children*, to give them the substantive right to make decisions that a court considers will be harmful to them. For example, most decisions dealing with the medical treatment of adolescents have tended to order treatment regarded as medically necessary, even if the adolescent is expressing religiously based views rejecting the treatment.

A child has a particular legal "status". In recognizing the child's limited development, there are certain legal obligations, privileges and capacities ascribed to this status by operation of law. The common law and legislation provide that children are legally incapable of making various decisions that affect their lives, although children who are older may have certain rights denied to younger children. In general, parents have a presumptive right to exercise a broad degree of control over their children, making decisions regarding such matters as place of residence, health care, discipline, education, religious training and even marriage. As outlined above, at least in regard to some of these matters, parents have a constitutionally protected "security interest" and may exercise rights in regard to their children subject to state intervention only "in accordance with the principles of fundamental justice".

In Ontario, the *Child and Family Services Act* provides that in certain circumstances, children are given rights to notice and of participation in a protection hearing. In a number of other Canadian jurisdictions, however, such rights are not statutorily recognized. There is a strong argument that a child who has the capacity and desire to participate in a protection proceeding, but who under legislation is denied the right to notice and participation, might be able to claim a right of participation, claiming that the proceedings threaten the child's "liberty and security of the person" under section 7 of the *Charter*. Although in some situations parents may be viewed as "natural guardians" who protect the rights of their children from the state, in many proceedings the parents may lack the inclination or ability to protect their child's rights; their views or interests may be antithetical to those of their child. Children with capacity should be able to participate in the proceedings in their *own* right. Arguments in this regard under section 7 of the *Charter* may be reinforced by reference to section 15 of the *Charter*.

In its 2000 decision in *Winnipeg Child & Family Services (Central Area) v. W. (K.L.)*,[19] the Supreme Court considered a case challenging the constitutional validity of Manitoba child welfare legislation, which permits the warrantless apprehension of a child believed to be in need of protection in non-emergency situations. By a five to two margin, the Court upheld the legislation. Writing for the majority, L'Heureux-Dubé J. concluded that a parent's right to "security of the person" is infringed by the legislation, but held that the statute accords with the principles of fundamental justice because procedural fairness is satisfied by requiring a post-apprehension judicial review. When balancing the various interests at stake in the child protection context, she placed pre-eminent importance on society's interest in protecting children from the possibility of abuse or neglect, emphasizing the difficulty and risk of distinguishing, in her view, between emergency and non-emergency apprehension situations in child protection cases.

Children's lives and health override parental rights to freedom from state intervention. The state is not required to wait until a child had been seriously harmed before intervening. An emergency threshold for apprehending a child without prior judicial authorization was inappropriate, given the seriousness of the interests at stake and the difficulty in distinguishing emergency from non-emergency child protection situations. Serious harm, or risk of serious harm, was held to be the appropriate threshold. While parents' and children's rights and responsibilities must be balanced together with children's right to life and health and the state's responsibility to protect

---

[19] [2000] 2 S.C.R. 519 (S.C.C.).

children, the underlying philosophy and policy of legislation must be kept in mind when interpreting it and determining its constitutional validity.[20]

CHILD ABUSE

There are certainly passages in the Supreme Court of Canada judgments on the *Charter* and child welfare that suggest that it is one of the "principles of fundamental justice" that decisions about children must be made according to the "best interests" of the child. For example, in *G. (J.)*, Lamer C.J. wrote:

> ...Thus, the principles of fundamental justice in child protection proceedings are both substantive and procedural. The state may only relieve a parent of custody when it is necessary to protect the best interests of the child, provided that there is a fair procedure for making this determination.[21]

In *W. (K.L.)*, Arbour J. (in dissent) observed:

> I would suggest, therefore, that to *satisfy the substantive content of the principles of fundamental justice in the child protection context, the apprehension of a child by a state agency requires an evaluation of the best interests of the child...*[22]

Notwithstanding these general statements, it is clear that the *Charter* does not require that in every situation the courts or state act to promote the best interests of children. It is clear that the *Charter* does not require that parents establish that their decisions and care are always intended to promote the best interests of their children. To the contrary, the *Charter* recognizes a substantial area of parental autonomy. A mother who smokes in the house does not risk loss of custody of her children to child welfare authorities (in the absence of special

---

[20] See *Winnipeg Child & Family Services (Central Area) v. W. (K.L.)*, ibid.
[21] *Supra* note 12 at para. 70.
[22] *Supra* note 19 at para. 9 [emphasis added].

health concerns), even though this type of parental conduct is clearly not in the best interests of her child. It is only if there is a clear and substantial risk of harm that the state can justify removing a child from parental care.

It seems unlikely that a court will order a state agency to incur the expense to undertake a course of action that will do *the most*, in the court's view, to promote the interests of a child. The situations where courts have been invoking the *Charter* to promote a child's best interests are ones in which a legislation or agency policy appear to *preclude* a court from making a decision that will promote the child's best interests. In some of these situations, courts may be prepared to find that the principles of fundamental justice require that a court be able to consider alternatives that promote a child's best interests without imposing unreasonable burdens on the state agency. The *Charter* may require judicial action if legislation precludes consideration of a reasonable alternative that would promote the interests of a child, but it does not require every decision must do the most that is conceivably possible to promote the interests of the child before the court.

(a) Sexual Abuse of Children

The sexual abuse of children is a problem that is not unique to our society let alone our schools. In recent years, sex abuse scandals have struck schools everywhere as well as churches, mentoring organizations, and daycare centres: in short, in all categories of organizations that provide services for children. These organizations, with long traditions of providing essential services to children, have understandably been shaken when child sexual abuse emerged in their ranks. Reactions have ranged from full disclosure to denial to cover-up, but rarely has there been a proactive, comprehensive effort to *prevent sexual abuse* or to prepare an effective response *before* abuse occurs. This is now changing thanks to amendments to, for example, the *College of Teachers Act, 1996*, criminal record checks, etc., and generally more vigilance by all.

After a child has disclosed an incident of sexual abuse, he or she is surprised to learn that the details must be repeated numerous times to various strangers. Victims of child sexual abuse are often subjected to multiple interviews by investigators, medical personnel, social workers, and lawyers. Thus, in the course of the investigation, the child victim is traumatized a second time—by the very individuals who are trying to help. In some cases, a child will become so confused or grow so tired of the questions that he or she will change the details, which decreases the chance that offenders will be caught and/or punished. It is vital for children that if a child reports an allegation of abuse to anyone in the school, that person is at least prepared to bring the child to someone who can provide the help and support the child is seeking.

As the Supreme Court of Canada found in the case of *R. v. D. (D.)*,[23] it is no longer a principle of law in Canada that an adverse inference should be drawn when a person alleging a sexual assaults fails to make a timely complaint. The Court held that this previous requirement of "recent complaint" was based upon rejected stereotypical assumptions of how persons react to sexual abuse. There is no inviolable rule how people who are victims of trauma like a sexual assault will behave. In this case, the complainant alleged that she was sexually assaulted when she was 5 to 6 years old. She told no one for two and a half years. She was cross-examined about delay and fabrications. The evidence of a child psychologist was found to be neither relevant nor necessary.

---

[23] [2000] 2 S.C.R. 275

(b) Allegations of Sexual Assault and Schools

As the chief administrators in their schools, principals have the ability as well as the responsibility to set the tone in their schools on a number of issues. Their efforts are critical to creating an environment in the school community where everyone knows that allegations of sexual harassment and abuse will be handled very seriously. The leaders of the local school districts must work together to send a strong message that sexual harassment and abuse of students will absolutely not be tolerated.

Section 79(2) of the *Child and Family Services Act*[24] makes it an offence for someone *having charge of a child* to inflict *abuse* on that child, by failing to care and provide for or supervise and protect the child adequately, to permit the child to suffer abuse. Abuse herein means ". . .a state or condition of being physically harmed, sexually molested or sexually exploited". A person who contravenes section 79(2), and a director, officer or employee of a corporation who authorizes, permits or concurs in such a contravention by the corporation, is guilty of an offence and on conviction is liable to a fine or not more than $2,000 or to imprisonment for a term of not more than two years, or to both. For the purposes of this enactment, a child is defined as a person under the age of 16 years.

If found to have had *charge* of the child at the material time, a teacher who sexually abuses his or her student has committed a section 79(2) offence. The obligation of educators to report suspected abuse by fellow teachers raises significant issues.

Section 72 imposes a statutory duty on *every person* to report certain suspicions of child abuse, and the information upon which those suspicions are based, to a children's aid society.

---

[24] R.S.O. 1990, c. C.11.

Also, section 72 makes it an offence for *certain professionals* to fail to so report.

Section 72(1) creates the statutory duty to report. It reads in part:

> (1) Despite the provisions of any other Act, if a person, including a person who performs professional or official duties with respect to children, has reasonable grounds to suspect one of the following, the person shall forthwith report the suspicion and the information on which it is based to a society...

Section 72, prior to recent amendments, imposed a duty upon any person to report. However, the threshold test involved a *belief*, on reasonable grounds. The lower threshold of reasonable grounds to *suspect* applied to professionals only. The legislation, as amended, continues to impose liability on professionals only, but imposes the same threshold test for everyone. The duty to report is ongoing:

> (2) A person who has additional reasonable grounds to suspect one of the matters set out in subsection (1) shall make a further report under subsection (1) even if he or she has made previous reports with respect to the same child.

The person who has a duty to report must do so *directly* to a children's aid society:

> (3) A person who has a duty to report a matter under subsection (1) or (2) shall make the report directly to the society and shall not rely on any other person to report on his or her behalf.

(c) Offence

Information that a party would otherwise keep in confidence, such as the content of sessions with a guidance counselor, must nonetheless be reported:

(7) This section applies although the information reported may be confidential or privileged, and no action for making the report shall be instituted against a person who acts in accordance with this section unless the person acts maliciously or without reasonable grounds for the suspicion.

RIGHTS OF UNBORN CHILDREN

One aspect of *Charter* jurisprudence that affects children's law are cases that involve the issue of defining the beginning of personhood or childhood. It has been established in Canadian law that a fetus is not a human being. Our courts have consistently upheld the right of a pregnant woman to have control over her body in preference to intervening to protect the interests of the fetus that she is carrying. Decisions as to the use of present and future technologies are likely to be made by individuals, not governments, perhaps raising the question as to whether the *Charter* would apply in these circumstances. Can the application of new technologies, for example, be said to constitute an infringement of the section 7 right to security of the person?

Both the juridical nature of the fetus and the protection afforded it in law have, as indicated, been canvassed in several Supreme Court cases: see, *inter alia, R. v. Morgentaler*,[25] *Tremblay c. Daigle*,[26] *Winnipeg Child & Family Services (Northwest Area) v. G. (D.F.)*[27] and *Dobson (Litigation Guardian of) v. Dobson*.[28]

The *Morgentaler* decision, of course, struck down the abortion provisions of the *Criminal Code*. The individual judgments were not primarily framed as discussions about the fetus, but rather about the impact of the impugned sections on the *Char-*

---

[25] [1993] 3 S.C.R. 463 (S.C.C.).
[26] *Supra* note 3.
[27] [1997] 3 S.C.R. 925 (S.C.C.).
[28] [1999] 2 S.C.R. 753 (S.C.C.).

ter rights of the pregnant woman. The abortion provisions were struck down as infringing on the woman's section 7 right to life, liberty and security of the person. The Court concluded that the right to liberty includes a degree of personal autonomy over important decisions affecting a woman's personal life, and the right to choose an abortion is such a decision. Further, the provisions were found to be arbitrary in their application and to engender delays, both of which exposed pregnant women to real risks to their physical health.

A thorough review of the status of the fetus in Canadian law is found in the Supreme Court decision of *Tremblay c. Daigle*. The appellant, Daigle, sought an abortion of the fetus conceived with the respondent, who sought and obtained an injunction before the Superior Court of Quebec. The injunction was upheld by the majority of the Court of Appeal on the basis that the fetus was a human being and entitled to the protection of Quebec's *Charter of Human Rights*, specifically the section 1 "right to life". In allowing the appeal, the Supreme Court of Canada had the following to say about the nature of legal inquiry into the meaning of "human being":

> The Court is not required to enter the philosophical and theological debates about whether or not a foetus is a person, but, rather, to answer the legal question of whether the Quebec legislature has accorded the foetus personhood. Metaphysical arguments may be relevant but they are not the primary focus of inquiry. Nor are scientific arguments about the biological status of a foetus determinative in our inquiry. The task of properly classifying a foetus in law and in science are different pursuits. Ascribing personhood to a foetus in law is a fundamentally normative task. It results in the recognition of rights and duties—a matter which falls outside the concerns of scientific classification. In short, this Court's task is a legal one. Decisions based upon broad social, political, moral and economic choices are more appropriately left to the legislature.[29]

---

[29] *Supra* note 3 at para. 38.

At the time of *Daigle*, the status of the fetus under provincial child welfare law was the subject of contradictory judgments, but this was addressed in *Winnipeg Child & Family Services (Northwest Area) v. G. (D.F.)*, including the issue of *parens patriae* jurisdiction to a fetus. The Manitoba Court of Queen's Bench had ordered that the respondent, then five months pregnant, be placed in the custody of the Director of Child and Family Services and detained at the Health Sciences Centre until the child's birth. The order had been made on application of the Winnipeg Child and Family Services (the agency) as a means of protecting the fetus from the effects of the mother's addiction to glue sniffing. The order was subsequently set aside by the Court of Appeal, and the agency appealed to the Supreme Court. In dismissing the appeal, McLachlin J., writing for the majority, stated, ". . .[A]n order detaining a pregnant woman for the purpose of protecting her fetus would require changes to the law which cannot properly be made by the courts and should be left to the legislature."[30]

While *Montreal Tramways*[31] addressed the right of a born child to sue a third party for injuries sustained while a fetus (a child had suffered birth defects after her pregnant mother was injured departing from a tram car), *Dobson* raised for the first time in Canadian law the question of whether a child could sue his or her own mother for harm arising from alleged negligence while the child was a fetus. The child in this case sued, through his Litigation Guardian, for injuries sustained while *en ventre sa mere*, arising from a car accident caused by the alleged negligence of his mother. The majority answered in the question in the negative, for a variety of reasons.

Cory J., for the majority, reviewed the two-step test in *Nielsen v. Kamloops (City)*[32] for the imposition of a duty of care. The

---

[30] *Supra* note 27 at para. 4.
[31] *Montreal Tramways Co. v. Léveillé*, [1933] S.C.R. 456 (S.C.C.).
[32] [1984] 2 S.C.R. 2 (S.C.C.).

first element of the test is that there is a sufficiently close relationship between the parties to give rise to a duty of care. While arguably this element of the test could not be met in light of the legal unity of the mother and the fetus, Cory J. preferred to base his judgment on the difficulties of meeting the second element, arguing that there are strong public policy considerations for not recognizing such a duty of care. For reasons similar to those in *Daigle* and *Winnipeg Child & Family Services*, the Court concluded that granting the right to sue in these circumstances would impose "...unacceptable intrusions into the bodily integrity, privacy and autonomy rights of women". Further, the Court referred to other unacceptable consequences, including the damage to the mother and child relationship. In the normal course of events (that is, in the absence of automobile insurance), such a right to sue would not achieve the objectives of tort law, of compensation to the injured and deterrence to the tortfeasor. Finally, Cory J. pointed to the difficulties of articulating a standard of conduct for pregnant women as a further reason for denying the application of tort law in these circumstances.

In *Morgentaler* and *Winnipeg Child & Family Services*, the Court recognized the validity of a state interest in protecting the fetus. The appropriate limits of this interest were not explored to any significant degree in view of the primacy given by the Court to protecting the *Charter* rights of the mother.

It is well known that a court may intervene in parental decisions that could harm their born child, invoking either its inherent *parens patriae* power or authority under child protection legislation. To what extent can this be said to imply a similar authority with respect to the *in vitro* embryo? McLachlin J., in the *Winnipeg* decision stated:

> The *parens patriae* power over born children permits the courts to override the liberty of the parents to make decisions on behalf of their children where a parental choice may result in harm to a child: *B. (R.) v.*

Children's Aid Society of Metropolitan Toronto, [1995] 1 S.C.R. 315 (S.C.C.). The only liberty interest affected is the parent's interest in making decisions for *his or her child*.[33]

Is any greater parental liberty interest affected in the case of the *in vitro* embryo? It is well established that the *Charter* may be invoked with respect to state action and not with respect to the actions between private parties.

Can the *Canadian Charter of Rights and Freedoms* address the ethical issues raised by the application of present biotechnologies? If the answer is yes, then this may suggest that the *Charter* will be applied as a means of setting limits on the use of future technologies on *in vitro* embryos where the intention is that the embryo will develop to a born child.

---

[33] *Supra* note 27 at para. 56.

5
AN INTRODUCTION TO CUSTODY AND ACCESS

> Custody and access decisions are pre-eminently exercises in discretion. Case by case consideration of the unique circumstances of each child is the hallmark of this process. This Court recognized in *Moge v. Moge*, *supra*, in the context of spousal support decisions, that the discretion vested in the trial judge is essential to effect the very purposes outlined in the Act. The wide latitude under the best interests test permits courts to respond to the spectrum of factors which can both positively and negatively affect a child. Such discretion also permits the judge to focus on the needs of the particular child before him or her, recognizing that what may constitute stressful or damaging circumstances for one child may not necessarily have the same effect on another.
> *Justice L'Heureux-Dubé,* Young v. Young[1]

> A child is like a precious stone, but also a heavy burden.
> *Swahili proverb*

The Swahili proverb quoted above notes that a child is a heavy burden. The heavy burden is, of course, not the child so much as the responsibility for a child. In having a child, a person undertakes to ensure that the "preciousness" of each child is recognized and fostered in order for the child to be safely and successfully guided to the ultimate destination of adulthood.

---

[1] [1993] 4 S.C.R. 3 (S.C.C.) at para. 164.

Children are, initially at least, vulnerable and dependent members of our society and always require one or many people to help them with their physical and emotional needs to ensure they grow into healthy, happy, productive adults.

However, just as each society may have its own definition of a "healthy, happy, productive, adult", there are also variations between and within societies as to how best to raise children in order to accomplish that goal. From time to time, there may even be disagreement within society as to which groups and individuals are capable of raising a child.[2]

Traditionally, in our society, the child's biological parents have undertaken the "heavy burden" of raising the child. As well, until fairly recently, the biological child would, more often than not, be raised by a "traditional family unit", comprising a man and a woman who were married to each other in a ceremony recognized to be legally binding on both parties. By being born to a married couple, the child would have certain legal and social rights, such as the right to inherit property from his or her parents.

Today, the distinction between biological children born to a married couple and other children has disappeared: now, every child has rights as a child whether they were born within or outside of a traditional marriage.[3]

Similarly, the unit that we call the "family" has changed. Our legal recognition of various relationships has been broadened along with the laws we use to label and recognize the impor-

---

[2] See, for example, discussion raised by Susan B. Boyd in "Lesbian (and Gay) Custody Claims: What Difference Does Difference Make?" (1998) 15 Can. J. Fam. L. 131.

[3] See s. 1 of the *Children's Law Reform Act*, R.S.O. 1990, c. C.12 as an example.

tance of the relationships.[4] It is important to always remember that the change to our concepts of family and marriage is a fairly recent development in society and in law. For much of our legal history, traditional marriage was the mainstay of the "family unit"; socially and legally it was a complicated matter to break up this cornerstone of society.

It was not too long ago that one had to apply to the Canadian Senate for a divorce; Canadian courts initially were not given the authority to deal with something as important as the breakdown of a marriage. It was not until 1930 that the Parliament of Canada conferred jurisdiction for divorces in Ontario on the Supreme Court of Ontario. Even then, Quebec and Newfoundland courts had no jurisdiction over divorces: the Senate continued to have the sole legal authority in this area for these two Provinces until a new *Divorce Act* came into being in 1968. The changes to divorce in 1968 gave authority for granting divorces to the courts in all provinces and territories. The Senate handled its last divorce case on November 26, 1969.[5] Under the new *Divorce Act*, it became significantly easier to get a divorce, the social impact of which should not be underestimated.[6]

Today, matters have changed significantly. The "family unit" can be found in its "traditional form" but it also exists in a number of different forms and titles. Given the recent recog-

---

[4] See the Ontario Court of Appeal decision of *Halpern v. Canada (Attorney General)* (2003), 36 R.F.L. (5th) 127 (Ont. C.A.) for a statement on the Court's definition of marriage in the Province of Ontario at that time.

[5] For further information on the role and history of the Senate, see "The Senate of Canada: A Legislative and Historical Overview of the Senate of Canada" from the Parliament of Canada website: http://www.parl.gc.ca/information/about/process/senate/legisfocus/legislative-e.htm.

[6] See, for example, the Canadian Broadcast Company archives on the Internet. In its report from July 2, 1968, it describes people lining up to obtain divorces given the changes that occurred in the legislation: http://archives.cbc.ca/IDC-1-69-760-4655/life_society/divorce/clip2.

nition of same-sex marriage, it is unclear how far recognizing inter-personal relationships will go as our legal and societal recognition of significant relationships continues to change.[7]

Not only have our concepts of "marriage" and "family" (and their various forms) changed, the forms and the frequency of the breakdown of these relationships has changed as well. Breakdown of a relationship may be through a "formal divorce", a formal separation agreement or simply a physical separation. Various formulas, processes and language have developed for each of these situations in various jurisdictions.

Regardless of what the conclusion of a partnership is called or how it is arrived at, it is arguable that ending a marriage or a relationship has become less complicated legally and more socially acceptable. However, throughout this changing landscape, something has not changed. Regardless of the nature of the family unit, what this grouping is called or how it ends, "break-ups" often involve children. Children can be, and often are, greatly affected by the changes that happen in their lives when their parents separate.[8]

As we know, there is a possibility that almost every aspect of a child's world will change after a divorce or other "break-up".

As a society, we turn to the adults involved to ensure that the children's needs are met throughout this often difficult time. The break-up of the family unit, whether "traditional" or not, invariably requires the adults involved to take steps to ensure the children's needs are met and the "heavy burden" of raising

---

[7] For an interesting review of how far this process may go see Brenda Cossman and Bruce Dyer's article "What is Marriage-like Like? The Irrelevance of Conjugality" (2001) 18 Can. J. Fam. L. 269.
[8] For further information, see *The Effects of Divorce on Children, A Selected Literature Review* from the Research and Statistics Division of the Department of Justice (Canada, 1997).

AN INTRODUCTION TO CUSTODY AND ACCESS ♦ 113

the child of the family is ensured. In a perfect world, the adults who are involved in a break-up (and who ostensibly love the children) would, upon family breakdown, discuss and agree on: how the child should be raised; how the responsibilities for child rearing are going to be divided; and then simply how to proceed to carry out their agreement. In some cases, this kind of accord actually does occur. In those cases, teachers, daycare providers and others involved in day-to-day interactions with the child will not necessarily note any issues with the child during this transition period. Those same teachers, daycare providers, etc., will avoid becoming involved in any litigation that may occur between the parents and/or other family members.

Unfortunately, in many, many cases, the break-up of the family results in a lack of agreement among the adults about the children. For both legitimate and less than legitimate reasons, the adults involved in the break-up of the relationship are unable or unwilling to agree on how the children's needs should be "best" met. In these situations, a court may have to decide what is best for the children. As teachers, daycare workers and others, you may become involved in the court process as a witness (or in some other fashion) as a court attempts to determine what is best for this child under the particular circumstances that he or she faces.

This chapter provides a brief overview of the court processes that occur when adults separate and the family unit breaks down, with a particular focus on the rights and determinations affecting children.

The person who has the right to make decisions about the child is the person that we say has "custody". A person who has a right to know about the child and possibly visit with the child is the person we say has "access". These roles may evolve through the mutual consent and agreement of the parents and other adults involved with the children or the roles, rights and obligations may be imposed by court order.

If the court becomes involved, the test used to determine custody and access will be the "best interests of the child". The test is a global examination of the child and his or her family and what is best for that child given the family dynamic. Given that the matter involves the family as a whole, it is often referred to globally as "family law".

However, as you saw in Chapter 2, there is another key aspect of "family law" that affects children called child protection law. This chapter is about custody and access; it not about child protection. For simplicity, the branch of family law that is discussed in this chapter is referred to as "custody and access" law. Custody and access is the family law "system" our society has put in place to ensure that the children of a relationship will continue to be protected and provided for following the breakdown of a family unit.

HOW CUSTODY AND ACCESS DIFFERS FROM CHILD PROTECTION

As reviewed in Chapter 2, an important piece of legislation in Ontario concerned with the welfare of children is the *Child and Family Services Act*.[9] The CFSA is the law that enables the state to ensure that all children are kept safe to a minimally acceptable societal standard. If the child is safe with a caregiver (who may or may not be a parent) then the child is likely not "in need of protection" for the purposes of the CFSA and the child protection regime of this statute will not be engaged.

As will be discussed in greater detail below, custody is the label that we usually give to someone who has the right to make important decisions about the child. The "custodial par-

---

[9] R.S.O. 1990, c. C.11 [hereinafter the "CFSA"].

ent" would usually be the one to determine where the child lives, what their religion would be, etc. Usually, but not always, the child would also spend the most time with the custodial parent.

Access, on the other hand, is the label that we give to someone who has the right to (usually) see the child and obtain information about him or her, but does not make the important decisions for the child (unless the court orders otherwise). Usually, but not always, the child will spend less time (albeit very important time) with the access parent.

Custody and access proceedings are different from child protection proceedings. While child protection proceedings involve the state intervening in the lives of private individuals to shield a child from harm or neglect, custody and access proceedings are litigation between private individuals. Custody and access proceedings are usually initiated by parents or family members of a child, rather than by the state.

In a custody and access matter, the court must determine what is in the "best interests of the child" by choosing among competing "plans" proposed (usually) by members of the child's "family"[10] concerning how and where a child will live and who will have the opportunity to see him or her and under what circumstances.

As we know, in a child protection matter, the government, through a child protection agency, brings the proceedings to the court. In child protection, frequently one of the dispositions proposed to the court is that the children be placed in a non-family/foster home setting.

---

[10] As will be noted further below, in Ontario, technically any person can initiate the proceedings; see ss. 21 and 24 of the *Children's Law Reform Act*, R.S.O. 1990, c. C.12, as amended.

This is a major step in the course of the child's life. There is a basic belief that a child has a right to know his or her family, history and heritage. Given the importance of the interest at stake (losing connection with one's biological family), an initial threshold test is included in child protection proceedings. The state must show that a child is in need of protection (from harm, from the family) before any consideration can be given as to whether children should be placed outside the family if this is in his or her best interests.

There is no threshold test in determining a child's best interests in custody and access matters.

A custody and access matter typically involves an application and motion being made by a private person to a court for a finding concerning what is in the child's best interests. Unlike a child protection matter, in which the primary issue is protecting the child from harm, in a custody and access matter, the risk of harm to the child is not a primary consideration. As stated by the Supreme Court of Canada (per Madame Justice L'Heureux-Dubé), in custody and access matters, considering the best interests of the child goes beyond determining the risk of harm to an assessment by the court of what is the most favourable situation for a child's future: "'Best interests' is not simply the right to be free of demonstrable harm. It is the positive right to the best possible arrangements in the parties' circumstances."[11]

As noted in Chapter 2, the difference between the areas of child protection and custody and access can at times be difficult to determine. At times, the subtle distinctions between these two subjects can be challenging. Both systems are concerned about the best interests of the child and the two regimes do overlap.

---

[11] *Young v. Young*, [1993] 4 S.C.R. 3 (S.C.C.).

However, as noted, in custody and access "best interests of the child" is the sole criterion governing a court's disposition. Accordingly, a consideration of this legal standard is the obvious place to begin in looking at custody and access matters.

"BEST INTERESTS TEST"

In child protection law, the court must make an initial determination of whether or not a child needs protecting to embark upon an inquiry of what is in the child's best interests. In custody and access matters, there is no such preliminary "threshold" enquiry. Custody and access litigation does not involve the state as a party to the proceedings. Instead, private citizens may initiate custody and access proceedings basically at any time. In so doing, they will describe and argue in support of a plan for a child's future that they have and feel is best in the best interests of the child.

The "best interests of the child" is the first and only test on which a court must rule in order to determine a custody and access matter. However, it should be noted that while the "best interests" test is the legal standard used in Ontario to determine custody of children (and this same test is used in many jurisdictions), this has not always been the case.

DEVELOPMENT OF BEST INTERESTS AS PRIMARY TEST

In the leading Supreme Court of Canada decision in the case of *Young v. Young*,[12] Madame Justice L'Heureux-Dubé reviewed the history of the "best interests" test and its development. She noted that the test in a custody and access determination had evolved—starting from a "paternal" viewpoint and moving to a "maternal" approach, and finally to the con-

---

[12] *Ibid.*

sideration of "best interests" of the child as a whole, as the legal standard.

In determining the best interests of a child now, the court will examine the particular circumstances of each child that is involved. Ideally a "customized" custody and access regime is ordered that best meets the needs of each child. What may be in the best interests of one child may not be in the best interests of the next. In contrast, the historical models made certain assumptions about child care and what was best for the child without looking at whether or not the presumption was true for that particular child. With the "paternal" view, there was a presumption that it was in every child's best interests to be with their father, regardless of the individual needs of the individual child before the court. Similarly, with the "maternal" view, there was a presumption that it was in every child's best interests to be with their mother, regardless of the individual needs of the individual child before the court.

As Her Honour observed:

> The express rule that matters of custody and access should be resolved in accordance with the "best interests of the child" is of relatively recent origin. Under the common law regime of the eighteenth and nineteenth centuries the governing principle in a custody dispute was the rule of near-absolute paternal preference: see *R. v. De Manneville* (1804), 5 East. 221, 102 E.R. 1054; *Re Taylor* (1876), 4 Ch. D. 157. The rule was defended on pragmatic grounds, including what was thought to be the general interest of children: see *Re Agar-Ellis; Agar-Ellis v. Lascelles* (1883), 24 Ch. D. 317 (C.A.). In truth, the rule probably had more to do with the acceptance of the father's dominant right in all family matters, which in turn found its roots in the notion of the inherent superiority of men over women.
>
> The rule of paternal preference was displaced by a rule establishing in the mother a primary right to custody of a child of tender years: see, for instance, *An Act to amend the Law relating to the custody of Infants*, S. Prov. Can. 1855, c. 126, s. 1. Later still there arose a presumption, in many foreign jurisdictions and to a more limited extent in Canada, of maternal preference: *Talsky v. Talsky*, [1976] 2 S.C.R. 292, *Kades v. Kades* (1961), 35

A.L.J.R. 251 (Aust. H.C.); see also Susan Maidment, *Child Custody and Divorce*, Robert H. Mnookin, "Child-Custody Adjudication: Judicial Functions in the Face of Indeterminacy" (1975), 39 L. & Contemporary Problems 226, and Roth, "The Tender Years Presumption in Child Custody Disputes" (1976–77), 15 J. of Fam. Law 423. This presumption, like the paternal preference rule, was justified on pragmatic grounds; the welfare of the child was the often cited reason for the presumption. So justified, the presumption carried the seeds of its own demise. Courts increasingly looked behind the preference to focus directly upon what was in the child's interest, which was sometimes found to conflict with a maternal preference.[13]

As Madam Justice L'Heureux-Dubé of the Supreme Court describes in the passage above, the maternal and paternal preferences were not made in total isolation of the child. It is obvious that orders were made as the Court (and likely the society as a whole at that time) truly believed that a child's best interests were best met by being with a father or a mother. As such, the preferences were interwoven into a consideration of the welfare of the child.

No doubt it was often the case that being placed with the father or the mother was in the best interests of the child. However, it is often difficult to determine that, as the "presumption" takes a more universal approach to what is in the best interests of a child rather than an individual and personal look.

Even in fairly recent cases it is startling to see how the individual child can get lost in the "preference" for one parent or the other. Although the decision will be characterized as a consideration of the best interests of the child, in hindsight we realize we never hear much about the child before the court. We do hear about what is believed to be best for all children.

For example, while the "paternal preference" should have faded into the sands of history by the early 1970s, in at least one case from that decade, the presiding Justice made the

---

[13] *Ibid.* at paras. 11-12.

comment "...that the potential presence of a man in the home was an important factor to consider".[14] In this case, the maternal grandmother had solely cared for the child for a couple of years and was competing with the mother to care for the child on a permanent basis. The mother had a new partner named "Scott" and the Judge confirmed that: "The boy will soon require the discipline of a man in the home and it is certainly the plan of Mrs. Smith that Scott should continue to live with her." While the facts of this particular case may have disclosed that the best interests of the child would be best served by an order for custody being awarded to the mother, undoubtedly many today would be shocked to hear that the "discipline of a man" would be a factor in determining what is best for a child. Most today would also want to know what the impact on the child would be of being separated from the grandmother who had cared for him. However, different times meant different issues were important for the child and therefore the court.

Similarly, a statement by a court of a "maternal preference" can be quite surprising in a decision. Such a preference is apparent in Justice Roach's somewhat famous passage in consideration of a case contesting the custody of a 4-year-old girl:

> No father, no matter how well-intentioned or how solicitous for the welfare of such a child, can take the full place of the mother. Instinctively, a little child, particularly a little girl, turns to her mother in her troubles, her doubts and her fears. In that respect nature seems to assert itself. The feminine touch means so much to a little girl; the frills and the flounces and the ribbons in the matter of dress; the whispered consultations and confidences on matters which to the child's mind should only be discussed with Mother; the tender care, the soothing voice; all these things have a tremendous effect on the emotions of the child. This is nothing new; it is as old as human nature and has been recognized time after time in the decisions of our Courts.[15]

---

[14] *McMaster v. Smith*, [1972] 1 O.R. 416 (Ont. H.C.) *per* Grant J.
[15] *Bell v. Bell*, [1955] O.W.N. 341 (Ont. C.A.) at para. 18.

Slowly perhaps, but eventually, the courts' focus on an applicant's gender became less important than a concern about a litigant's ability to parent. There are some commentators who argue that implicit gender preferences and prejudices continue to exist. While it is important that any concerns continue to be raised (to ensure equality before and under the law), the prevailing legal test at present is the "best interests of the child", irrespective of any consideration of gender. This approach to the law accords with a number of western countries that, effective in the 1970s, accorded statutory recognition to a "best interests" or "welfare of the child" test.[16]

However, while the "best interests of the child" is the test governing custody and access matters in most jurisdictions, the particulars of the laws of each province and rules of procedure should always be consulted.

CUSTODY AND ACCESS LEGISLATION

In Ontario, the court is specifically directed, in the governing legislation, to use the "best interests of the child" in determining applications for custody and access of a child.[17]

In Ontario, the *Divorce Act*[18] (a statute of Canada) and the *Children's Law Reform Act*[19] (a statute of Province of Ontario) both deal with custody and access matters.

Each applies to different children depending on whether or not the child's parents are married or not. Because of our two-tiered "federalist" system of government and the fact that we

---

[16] Madame L'Heureux-Dubé, *Young v. Young, supra* note 11.
[17] See s. 24(1) of the *Children's Law Reform Act*, R.S.O. 1990, c. C.12, as amended, and s. 16(8) of the *Divorce Act*, R.S.C. 1985, c. 3 (2nd Supp.) as amended.
[18] *Divorce Act, ibid.*
[19] R.S.O. 1990, c. C.12, as amended [hereinafter "CLRA"].

have some overlap of jurisdictions between the federal government and the provincial governments when it comes to family breakdown, the question of whether the *Divorce Act* or the CLRA will apply depends upon the relationship of the adults in the matter.

(a) The *Divorce Act*

The *Divorce Act* is a federal statute and is the mechanism for obtaining a divorce in Canada. It applies to all married couples in Canada when a divorce is sought. If custody and access of a child has been requested as part of an Application for Divorce, then the provisions in the *Divorce Act* regarding custody and access apply to those children to the exclusion of any provincial act, including the CLRA.

(b) The *Children's Law Reform Act*

The *Children's Law Reform Act* is an Ontario provincial statute that applies to custody and access proceedings where there is no application for a divorce.

Obviously, if the adults "fighting" for custody and access of children are not married, then a divorce is not a possibility and the *Divorce Act* will not apply. In Ontario, where the *Divorce Act* does not apply to a situation, any custody and access issue will be decided under the *Children's Law Reform Act*. When adults are not married, custody and access matters are fairly straightforward: custody and access issues are determined under the *Children's Law Reform Act*.

(c) Applying the *Divorce Act* and the CLRA to Custody/Access Matters

Technically, in Ontario, married parents who are divorcing may apply to resolve issues concerning custody of their children under either the *Children's Law Reform Act* or the *Divorce Act*.

However, once a matter is commenced under the *Divorce Act*, the regime for custody and access under this federal legislation will supersede any order made under the *Children's Law Reform Act*. Given this fact, most married couples who are divorcing simply ask for custody and access matters to be determined through the divorce proceedings rather than use time and resources to determine this issue under the CLRA, only to have this order displaced when a divorce application is heard. Technically, though there is a choice for parents and their children.[20]

For these couples with a choice, the question of "which court?" will depend on a number of circumstances including the urgency of seeking custody upon marriage breakdown. If the parties amicably separated and everyone agreed that a divorce would be sought then an application under the CLRA is less likely. On the other hand, if the relationship ended suddenly and there was concern about the safety of one of the parties or a child then it might be more convenient and timely to seek a temporary custody order at least under the CLRA and worry about the divorce application later. However, there are a number of factors that might affect which court is "better" including the availability of court time in the particular jurisdiction, costs, and other factors unique to the particular circumstances of the family. Accordingly, as always, anyone who is concerned about custody or access issues should seek independent legal advice, as even something as "simple" as choosing the proper court can be quite complex.

---

[20] See s. 27 of the *Children's Law Reform Act*, confirming that when divorce proceedings are commenced, the *Children's Law Reform Act* application is stayed.

WHO MAY APPLY FOR CUSTODY OR ACCESS?

It is also important to note that in Ontario, any person can apply for custody or access to any child. This legal opportunity does not mean that any person who applies for custody or access will be successful on an application or that a right will be given to see the child. In every case, a court is called upon to assess the case on its facts and to determine what is in the child's best interests. It would be very unusual for the court to order custody or access rights for a complete stranger. However, theoretically at least, everyone has the right to apply to a court for custody of any child, no matter how tenuous that person's relationship to the child may be. Such an application would obviously be under the *Children's Law Reform Act* rather than under the *Divorce Act*.

The legal ability of any adult to have standing to apply for custody of a child is an important fact for many grandparents, members of a child's extended family, and others who may love and care for a child who would be willing to step into a situation to assist, but do not believe there are any "right" to do so. While such applicants have no "automatic" right to custody, as stated above, a court will order custody based upon the "best interests" of the child. On this test, it is not inconceivable that a person other than a parent (such as a grandparent or other member of a child's extended family) may propose a plan that a court accepts as being the best option to serve a child's best interests.

BEST INTERESTS TEST UNDER THE TWO ACTS

Other than the fact that only children of a marriage are covered by the *Divorce Act*, in Ontario, the key differences between the *Divorce Act* and the CLRA are more procedural than substantive. The substantive test for custody under both regimes is the same: determining the best interests of the child. However, the Ontario Act does give more specific guidance to the court than the federal Act as to what the legislature intended by "best interests".

Section 16(8) of the *Divorce Act* confirms the best interests test and asks the court to consider the "condition, means, needs and other circumstances of the child":

> In making an order under this section, the court shall take into consideration only the best interests of the child of the marriage as determined by reference to the condition, means, needs and other circumstances of the child.

Section 24(1) of the *Children's Law Reform Act* confirms the best interest test for the provincial statute. In the CLRA, however, there is greater detail provided as to what factors should be included in determining a child's best interests:

> 24(1) Merits of application for custody or access — The merits of an application under this Part in respect of custody of or access to a child shall be determined on the basis of the best interests of the child.
>
> (2) Best interests of child — In determining the best interests of a child for the purposes of an application under this Part in respect of custody of or access to a child, a court shall consider all the needs and circumstances of the child including,
>
>> (a) the love, affection and emotional ties between the child and,
>>
>>> (i) each person entitled to or claiming custody of or access to the child,
>>> (ii) other members of the child's family who reside with the child, and
>>> (iii) persons involved in the care and upbringing of the child;
>>
>> (b) the views and preferences of the child, where such views and preferences can reasonably be ascertained;
>>
>> (c) the length of time the child has lived in a stable home environment;
>>
>> (d) the ability and willingness of each person applying for custody of the child to provide the child with guidance and education, the necessaries of life and any special needs of the child;

(e) any plans proposed for the care and upbringing of the child;

(f) the permanence and stability of the family unit with which it is proposed that the child will live; and

(g) the relationship by blood or through an adoption order between the child and each person who is a party to the application.

(a) The Meaning of the "Best Interests" Test

Some commentators have argued that the broad and far-reaching nature of the best interests test (as expressed in either statute above) is in practice no test at all. Instead, these observers argue, the best interest test amounts to a "catch all" for personal opinions that influence decision-making. Certainly, one should always be on guard against allowing personal opinions to be determinative of 'best interests' decision-making. While it may seem an anathema to sound jurisprudence that a decision-maker will be influenced by his or her own personal background and beliefs, judges are people too and will be influenced, to an extent, by their own experiences, traditions and beliefs. However, one must also have some confidence in the system itself and the efforts of the legislature to move the "law" towards a more objective and child-focused test. Our family law system invests heavily in the selection, training and education of the judiciary. As a result, in our legal system, the "best interests" test is applied as objectively as possible.

At the same time, one must not lose sight of the benefits that the discretion and latitude inherent in the application of the best interests test brings to the children in the court system. As noted in the quotation at the beginning of the chapter, the best interests test allows a court to properly consider the needs of the specific child before the court, and to recognize and respond to the inherent differences in situation, character, disposition and reaction of each individual.

PAST CONDUCT

It is clear that relatively wide latitude is given to a judge in determining the child's best interests in custody and access matters. However, there is also a restriction on what a court may consider contained in the applicable statutes. Both the *Children's Law Reform Act* and the *Divorce Act* contain a specific restriction on using the past conduct of a party in making custody and access orders unless the "past conduct" impacts on the child's best interests.

In this regard, the *Divorce Act* states:

> 16(9) In making an order under this section, the court shall not take into consideration the past conduct of any person unless the conduct is relevant to the ability of that person to act as a parent of a child.[21]

In the *Children's Law Reform Act*, the provision is similar and states:

> Note: On a day to be named by proclamation of the Lieutenant Governor, subsection (3) is repealed by subsection 78(2) and the following substituted:
>
> (3) Domestic violence to be considered — In assessing a person's ability to act as a parent, the court shall consider the fact that the person has at any time committed violence against his or her spouse or child, against his or her child's parent or against another member of the person's household.[22]

In 2005, Ontario proclaimed in force a new provision concerning the impact of past conduct and its impact on a person's ability to be a parent. Now, a court has a specific jurisdiction to consider a person's previous history of domestic violence (against his or her spouse, child or child's parent or other member of the person's household) in deciding issues relevant

---

[21] Section 16(9), *Divorce Act*, R.S.C. 1985, c. 3 (2nd Supp.).
[22] R.S.O. 1990, c. C.12, s. 78(2); 1999, c. 6, s. 7(1); 2005, c. 5, s. 8(1).

to suitability to be a parent. Aside from the issue of previous domestic violence, a court is not to consider incidents in a person's past conduct in adjusting issues relating to role appropriateness. It is often very difficult to determine whether a person's past conduct is relevant to the ability of that person to act as a proper parent. It is often only through a full examination of the facts that the court can determine whether or not something is a factor that will affect the child.

For example, a person who drinks alcohol to excess may be a wonderful parent. Alternatively, such a person may be a dangerous alcoholic who should not care for a child. Either is a possibility; without a full examination of the facts of the case and the particular circumstances of that particular child[23] it is difficult for a court to know which possibility is correct.

Custody and access disputes are often difficult to determine because it is unclear whether or not past behaviour is a true concern (for the child) or whether the other parent is only now alleging that a past behaviour was a concern (for the child) as it may assist them in "winning" their case. For example, a parent may have used alcohol to excess throughout the marriage. If the other parent did not comment on the behaviour during the time the parents were together, was it really an important issue for the health and safety of the child? Is the past conduct now relevant to act as a parent of a child?

Before the court ever gets asked the question the parents themselves determine whether or not they feel it is relevant.

On separation, if the non-drinking parent does believe the other's use of alcohol is an issue that affects their child then there is no disagreement between them and the matter may

---

[23] See, for example, *Pelletier v. Pelletier*, [2003] O.J. No. 417 (Ont. S.C.J.), where two previous impaired driving convictions were found not to be relevant to parenting given their historical nature.

never become a consideration for the court. However, if one of the parents alleges that the drinking is an issue that will affect the child then they can make an application to the court to determine custody and access.

Upon application, the court will review the evidence and make an order for the child that is in the child's best interests. Once a custody and access order is made, the order (rather than the individuals involved) determines the rights and obligations that the adults have regarding the children.

In the example given, one of the terms of seeing or having the child is that there be no consumption of alcohol. The court will decide whether or not the past conduct is relevant to the parenting of the child and will put in safeguards to control any inappropriate behaviour.

The court will usually do this in a larger context of granting one party the authority to make day-to-day decisions regarding the child. Because so many decisions need to be made in parenting a child, terminology has developed to more easily label the respective rights of the parties. Essentially, these terms are "custody (by one or more party) and "access" (by one or more party). That leads us, of course, to the next question: what are custody and access?

DEFINING CUSTODY AND ACCESS

Perhaps no area of law creates more confusion, controversy and unnecessary litigation than the area of custody and access.

Professor James McLeod, who writes extensively on family law, has noted:

Many parents do not understand the meaning of "custody" or "access", or "joint custody" so that their insistence on, or opposition to, a particular form of order often is more emotional than rational.[24]

One can never hope to remove emotion from a consideration of what is best for a child. However, there is no doubt that a more rational approach to custody and access would likely assist greatly in making custody and access orders work for the benefit of all involved.

What then do we mean by custody and access?

As noted above, custody and access are nothing more than simple terms that help us label the sharing of rights and obligations that adults have to a child or children.

In the ideal world, this sharing of rights and obligations would take place in a neutral manner, with all of the participants recognizing and respecting others' legal rights and complying with their own obligations. This type of arrangement is the case in many areas of law. For example, two parties can share one building as "landlord" and "tenant" and make it work quite well. The landlord has certain rights (have rent paid, obtain the property back at the end of the rental agreement in good condition) and certain obligations (allow for quite enjoyment etc.). The tenant too has certain rights (right of quiet enjoyment etc.) and certain obligations (pay rent, do not damage the premises). Both have rights and obligations over the one common building that they both share.

Custody and access are meant to work in the same fashion. A child is shared amongst adults and each has various rights and obligations to that child. The custodial parent is the parent who has the obligation and the right to make the major decisions regarding the child. Parents and other adults who have

---

[24] James G. McLeod, Alfred A. Mamo, *Annual Review of Family Law 2004* (Toronto: Thomson Carswell, 2004) at 2.

an interest in the child, but who may be limited in their decision-making authority, are the access parent (or person(s) with access).

Like "landlord" and "tenant", "custody" and "access" are labels meant to be neutral in their use and impact. A tenant and landlord are both important and they are both accorded certain deference. Similarly, an access parent is as important to a child as is a custodial parent. However, in custody and access matters, a court determines that it is in the best interests of the child that one of the adults should make decisions regarding the child and so that adult is given "custody".

WHAT IS CUSTODY?

Custody has been defined as, ". . . a bundle of rights and responsibilities dealing with day-to-day care and control of children . . . to promote their long-term best interests."[25]

In determining custody, a court will look at the best interests criteria noted above to determine the child's best interests. Based on the weight and measure of the evidence given in the particular case and the criteria established in the legislation, the court determines that decisions regarding the child should be primarily made by one of the adults in the litigation or the other.

It should be noted that if the court determines that it is best that two (or even more) adults should have the day-to-day decision-making responsibility then more than one adult could be granted custody. These individuals would jointly share this responsibility and have "joint-custody".

Joint custody is rarer than an order of "sole custody". Joint custody is very rarely ordered if there is an indication from

---

[25] *Ibid.* at 4.

one of the parties that they cannot get along with the other party so as to allow a "joint" custody arrangement work for the benefit of the child.

JOINT CUSTODY VERSUS SOLE CUSTODY

The court may grant custody of a child to one or more persons under section 28 of the *Children's Law Reform Act* and subsection 16(4) of the *Divorce Act*. When more that one person is granted custody (i.e., each is fully entitled to make decisions about the child), we refer to the situation as "joint custody". Joint custody is referred to in subsections 20(1) and (3) and section 28 of the *Children's Law Reform Act*, and in subsections 16(4) and (10) of the *Divorce Act*. Also, an application for shared custody can be brought under the same provisions of the *Children's Law Reform Act* and the *Divorce Act*.

Given the fact that it is common to have emotional discord between separating parents, which, in turn often exacerbates any existing differences of opinion regarding raising children, in most custody and access cases, joint custody is not granted.

As joint custody requires parents to make decisions together, such an arrangement is only workable when parents show an ability to co-operate. However, Ontario courts have recently begun to make more orders for joint custody arrangements. Sometimes, these orders are structured within a parallel parenting model, which is discussed further below. Historically, Ontario courts have been reluctant to order joint custody.

The Ontario Court of Appeal set the precedent for joint custody in the 1979 cases of *Baker v. Baker*[26] and *Kruger v. Kruger*.[27] Although these decisions affirmed sole custody as the norm and joint custody as the exception, Wilson J.A.'s dissenting

---

[26] (1979), 8 R.F.L. (2d) 236 (Ont. C.A.).
[27] (1979), 11 R.F.L. (2d) 52 (Ont. C.A.).

judgment in *Kruger v. Kruger* laid the foundation for the recent trend toward joint custody.

In *Baker v. Baker*, the trial judge held that while the parents could no longer live together as spouses, they were capable of working together in the future for the well-being of their child. The trial judge awarded joint custody. The Court of Appeal overturned the trial judge, finding that joint custody is only appropriate in limited circumstances where parents are mature and amicable toward one another.

In *Kruger v. Kruger*, the trial judge awarded the mother sole custody. The father sought joint custody on appeal. The majority of the Court of Appeal dismissed his appeal, but Wilson, J.A. dissented. She held that the parents were capable of working with each other in the children's interests.

The majority in *Kruger v. Kruger* was not convinced that the parents could co-operate, and did not agree that joint custody was the best arrangement for the child. Its judgment emphasized that only the father was seeking joint custody and therefore the parents could not agree on the important issue of custodial arrangements.

Accordingly, in most custody disputes, it is likely that the court would decide it is in the child's best interests that one individual has "sole custody" or "custody" of the child. However, from time to time, based on the case authorities noted above, the court would, from time to time, "force" joint custody if that was deemed to be in the best interests of the child.[28]

The nature of joint custody arrangements vary widely. Generally, joint custody means parents share decision-making about the children. Joint custody typically involves an arrange-

---

[28] See, for example, Justice Wallace's decision in *Nurmi v. Nurmi*, [1988] O.J. No. 1288 (Ont. U.F.C.).

ment where one parent has the day-to-day care and control of the child while the other parent has generous contact with the child and the right to provide input into decisions affecting that child.

The law has developed over time such that an initial tendency by the courts to award sole custody to one parent (over another), has now given way to courts being increasingly receptive to joint custody arrangements. One recent form of joint custody arrangement has been called "parallel parenting".

PARALLEL PARENTING

Particularly in the last decade, courts have become more receptive to claims for joint custody. Joint custody has increasingly been awarded in the form of parallel parenting orders. Parallel parenting can provide a solution (even in high-conflict situations) where neither parent is a better candidate than the other to have sole custody. Within a parallel parenting arrangement, parents are given equal status and are entitled to exercise custodial rights and responsibilities over independent spheres of a child's life, independent of one another.

Parallel parenting plans will often include detailed residential arrangements, rules about contact with the child, and methods for dispute resolution. The dispute resolution mechanism sometimes entails the ongoing involvement of a child care professional who acts as a parenting coordinator to mediate or arbitrate disputes between the parties. It is common in parallel parenting arrangements for parents to use email to convey necessary information to one another, rather than engaging in direct contact by telephone or in person. A "communication book" is also a technique often employed. A communication book is simply a notebook that travels with the child. Each parent can make comments in the book relating to the child during the time they are with the respective parent. The parent receiving the child can then review the communication book and get updated on the health, behaviour and other matters concerning the child without needing to contact the other parent directly and discuss issues in person. Conflict between the parents can be reduced if such a parenting arrangement is structured appropriately. Although studies have found that heightened parental involvement can in fact lead to heightened conflict—a poor outcome for children in separated families—courts sometimes award joint custody where they are convinced that children benefit from the heightened involvement of both parents.

Despite some innovation by the Courts with respect to joint and parallel parenting arrangements, joint custody remains the exception, rather than the rule. In the Court of Appeal case of *Hildinger v. Carroll*,[29] the mother's award of sole custody at trial was upheld on appeal. The parents were fractious, but on appeal, the father sought a parallel parenting plan (as opposed to cooperative joint custody). The case supports the *Baker* line of cases that joint custody remains an exceptional remedy. Laskin J. did observe that, "...assuming without deciding that parallel parenting is now a viable option where the parties are uncooperative, I see no justification for it in this case."[30]

Nonetheless, courts are sometimes willing to order joint custody in the face of conflict and communication problems between the parties. For example, in *South v. Tichelaar*,[31] the Court expressed optimism that a parenting order could foster cooperation between the parents struggling to work together. The Court held that creating a shared custody regime could help improve communication lines between the parents.

However, more recently, the Ontario Court of Justice reviewed a parallel parenting order that had been in place for approxi-

---

[29] [2004] O.J. No. 291 (Ont. C.A.).
[30] *Ibid.* at para. 24.
[31] (2001), 20 R.F.L. (5th) 175 (Ont. S.C.J.).

mately two years involving two parents with a long history of conflict with each other. In *Powers v. Powers*,[32] Zuker J. found that while the Court that had made the parallel parenting order hoped that such an order would be appropriate, the existing parenting regime was not in the best interests of this child.[33]

While it remains to be seen whether the use of "parallel parenting" regimes will increase or decline in the future, it is probably safe to say that in the majority of cases, one "custodial parent" will usually be vested with the entire breadth of rights and responsibilities of day-to-day care and control of the child.

INCIDENTS OF CUSTODY

In deciding between contesting parents, while a court can deal with the totality of rights pertaining to a child, it can also deal with certain aspects of the child's life or "incidents of custody" Again, as Professor McLeod has noted:

> A court may deal with the totality of rights (custody) or one or more individual incidents of custody. In most cases, courts deal with the totality of rights by deciding which parent should be granted custody and then deciding whether on the facts of the case, it is appropriate to sever off an individual incident of custody for special treatment.[34]

Examples of incidents of custody can run the entire breadth of human experience—from religious training to medical decisions to mobility issues. At the end of the day, a court decides an "incident of custody" using the same test that applies to the totality of issues, based upon what is in the "best interests of

---

[32] 2004 ONCJ 281 (Ont. C.J.).
[33] A similar decision by the Ontario Court of Appeal that arrived in January 2005 also seems to indicate that parallel parenting and "joint custody" regimes will remain the exception rather than the rule. See *Kaplanis v. Kaplanis* (2005), 10 R.F.L. (6th) 373 (Ont. C.A.).
[34] McLeod and Mamo, *Annual Review of Family Law 2004*, supra note 24 at 4.

the child". Again, determining what is in "the best interests of the child" is more art than science. However, as a general matter, certain factors carry more weight in the court's determination of a child's best interests than others.

DETERMINING CUSTODY: APPROACHES TO "THE BEST INTERESTS OF THE CHILD"

While the best interests of the child is the overriding test in determining custody and access, there is no doubt that determining who should be the custodial parent between two loving, competent, competing adults can be challenging for the court and for those observing the system from outside.

The following is a review of some of the approaches used by courts in determining what is in the "best interests of the child".

(a) The Traditional Approach

As noted above, the legal system, like much of society, originally believed that the gender should be an important factor in determining custody.

(b) The "Primary Parent" Model or "Status Quo"

Gradually, however, research, study and common sense began to lessen the impact that the parents' gender played in custody decision-making. Instead, parenting and the relationship between the child and the parent began to take on greater importance in determining the best interests of the child.

Barbara Bennett Woodhouse challenged the existing theoretical foundation for the determination of children's interests by demonstrating the extent to which the existing law grounds them in adult rights. She advocated the adoption of a new conceptual foundation she calls "generism". Generism involved attaching greater weight to the child's relationships with adults who respond to a child's needs (functional parenting relationships), and less weight to the genetic relationship that gives a parent a possessory interest in the child irrespective of that parent's functional involvement. In short, her child-centric model of the parent-child relationship would take the concept of "best interest" further in the direction of the child.[35]

The movement within the court toward a child-centric model of the parent-child relationship essentially means that the court, in part, initially tries to determine who the primary parent of the child was prior to the break-up of the family unit. If there was a primary parent then, all things being equal, it is likely in the best interests of the child that this arrangement continues. As such:

> In *K. (M.M.) v. K. (U.)* (1990), 28 R.F.L. (3d) 189, 76 Alta. L.R. (2d) 216 (sub nom. *Kastner v. Kastner*), 109 A.R. 241 (Alta. C.A.), leave to appeal refused (1991), 3 R.F.L. (3rd) 366 (S.C.C.) the Alberta Court of Appeal endorsed the "primary parent" approach to custody. This approach was originally articulated in *Garska v. McCoy* (1981), W. Va. 276 S.E. 357 (S. Ct. of Appeals), and, other things being equal, favours awarding custody to the parent who was primarily responsible for child rearing before the marriage broke down—the parent who *"has wiped* [the children's] *noses, bathed them, maintained their health, driven them to school, tutored* [them], *taken them to church and arranged for their daycare;"* *K.(M.M.) v. K. (U.)* at 204 (R.F.L.).[36]

Lawyers and judges have shortened the phraseology of the "primary parent model" to the term that they use of "status

---

[35] Barbara Bennett Woodhouse, "Hatching the Egg: A Child-Centred Perspective on Parents' Rights" (1993) 14 Cardozo L. Rev. 1747, quoted by Zuker J. in *Bater v. Alessandro* at p. 107, confirmed on appeal: *Bater v. Alessandro* (2002), 2002 CarswellOnt 3573 (Ont. S.C.J.), *per* Low J.

[36] See also Richard Neely, "The Primary Caretaker Parent Rule: Child Custody and the Dynamics of Greed" (1984) 3 Yale L. & Pol'y Rev. 168, from *Bater v. Alessandro* as above.

quo". This means that unless there are significant reasons to change it, the court will attempt to continue the "status quo" of parenting that arose prior to the break up of the family unit.

More simply put, under the "status quo" approach to deciding custody, the court attempts to determine what the parenting arrangement was for the child before the family breakdown and once that is decided, determine whether it remains in the best interests of the child for that to continue.

The "status quo" paradigm is in accordance with the general understanding that stability for the child is in his or her best interests. Further, the logic of the status quo approach is that the parents themselves had developed and agreed upon a pattern of custody prior to the breakdown and so the individuals involved must have felt that this approach was best for their children.

(c) The "Status Quo" in Legislation

When both parents have worked outside of the home, it may be very difficult to determine (as noted above) which of them "...has wiped [the children's] noses, bathed them, maintained their health, driven them to school, tutored [them], taken them to church and arranged for their daycare." Often, both parents contributed to the care of the child, but the court needs to wade through people's memories, recollections and any actual proof that there may be as to who did what and when for the child and determine which one did the most.

For practical purposes, the *Children's Law Reform Act* contains provisions that, in part, make the court's task of re-constructing the past easier by implicitly assuming that the status quo of the recent past is reflective of the status quo when the parents were together as a unit.

Under the *Children's Law Reform Act*, each parent is initially equally entitled to custody. Section 20 of the Act confirms:

> 20(1) Father and mother entitled to custody — Except as otherwise provided in this Part, the father and the mother of a child are equally entitled to custody of the child.

However, despite the initial equality of the parents with respect to custody, under subsection 20(4) of the CLRA, the "status quo" of custody that occurs in the aftermath of a break-up becomes the immediate favourite in any subsequent custody litigation:

> 20(4) Where parents separate — Where the parents of a child live separate and apart and the child lives with one of them with the consent, implied consent or acquiescence of the other of them, the right of the other to exercise the entitlement of custody and the incidents of custody, but not the entitlement to access, is suspended until a separation agreement or order otherwise provides.

Although a parent may have done many, many negative things throughout his or her life, marriage or relationship, if, upon separation, the children are left in his or her care and he or she is parenting reasonably well, then that "status quo" will be given some deference by the court. It is this role as a parent that is crucial to the determination of custody and not their role as a spouse or a "person".

While the court will sift through other evidence, if asked, and determine whether any of it will affect the best interests of the child, the reality is that if there has been successful parenting since separation, any past grievances (unless extremely significant) will not, usually, change the status quo. This is a very difficult concept for many separating parents to comprehend, let alone accept. This can lead to on-going problems between the adults and how they interact with each other.

As discussed above, the hope is that custody is a "value neutral" term, amounting to the one parent continuing the stable pattern of caregiving that existed prior to the family unit breakdown.

However, for a variety of reasons, "custody" has become a very "value laden" term. Certain commentators have argued that the term "custody" naturally connotes both a power struggle between parents (rather than cooperation) and the inherent alienation of the access parent.

The approach of placing sole responsibility with the custodial parent has the advantage of producing consistent decision-making and lifestyle choices for the child. On the other hand, it seems harsh to relegate the access parent to the role of a stranger, simply because the access parent cannot agree with the custodial parent or because the access parent has become inconvenient as a result of the custodial parent's involvement in a new relationship.[37]

A criticism is that the distinction between custody and access sets up a power struggle between the parents that moves the focus of attention away from the child. Although the best interests of the child is the test applied in determining which parent will have custody, this approach has the ring of a contest of rights that exacerbates the relationship between the parents rather than fostering cooperation between them.[38]

Various groups and individuals have sought to develop more neutral language to describe the process of addressing a child's needs rather than focus on the power equation amongst the adults.

---

[37] See James G. McLeod, annotation, *Young v. Young* (1993), 49 R.F.L. (3d) 129 at 132, citing *Carter v. Brooks* (1990), 30 R.F.L. (3d) 53 (Ont. C.A.), from *Bater v. Alessandro, supra* note 35.

[38] Janet Walker, "From Rights to responsibilities for Parent: Old Dilemmas, New Solutions" (1991) 29 Family & Conciliation Courts Review 361 at 361-64, from *Bater v. Alessandro, supra* note 35.

(d) Determining the "Status Quo" for the Purposes of Child Custody Awards

Perhaps using the term "custody" is less important than the flaws in the process involved in awarding custody: it is difficult to objectively assess actual involvement with the child's care prior to separation, i.e., to determine the status quo. The nature of family life is such that it usually occurs at home rather than in the public sphere.

Rather than simply rely on the memories of the participants, the court will also look to corollary evidence that *may* provide a more objective means of determining the status quo during the relationship. In this regard, in a traditional relationship (where one parent works outside of the home and one does not), the parent who works outside of the home is undoubtedly doing that for the benefit of the child. However, the parent working outside the home is unlikely to be the primary caregiver of the child, as this parent is simply not with the child most of the time. Obviously, there may be exceptions to this generalization. Often, the "traditional breadwinner" is surprised to learn that she or he are not seen as a primary caregiver for the child when an independent and objective comparison of time dedicated to the care of the children is made by a court.

In making a custody award, the court will consider all factors in making its decision. However, an important starting point for a court to determine the "best interests of the child" is for the court to uncover the parenting regime that the child has already experienced.

To put it more eloquently:

> In making a determination as to the best interests of the child, courts must attempt to balance such considerations as the age, physical and emotional constitution and psychology of both the child and his or her parents and the particular milieu in which the child will live. . . . Probably one of the most significant factors in many cases will be the rela-

tionship that the child entertains with his or her parents. This must necessarily encompass such considerations as the strength of the emotional ties and the role of the person who has provided primary care in the life of the child.[39]

As a result, teachers, daycare workers, medical professionals and various others who are interacting with children on a daily basis are often asked to provide their observations and evidence to help a court determine who parented the child (or children) prior to family breakdown. Simple tasks such as taking the child to the dentist or to get their hair cut may be the independent information the court requires to determine custody.

OTHERS MAY APPLY FOR CUSTODY

As noted above, sometimes the primary caregiver for the family was not a parent but another family member or even a friend of the family. While parents (and specifically mothers and fathers) are entitled to custody, it should be noted that anyone can (in Ontario) apply for custody of a child. Section 21 of the *Children's Law Reform Act* reads:

> 21. Application for custody or access — A parent of a child *or any other person* may apply to a court for an order respecting custody of or access to the child or determining any aspect of the incidents of custody of the child. [Emphasis added.]

This provision allows grandparents, other members of a child's extended family and even strangers to seek custody of a child. These people also have the ability to apply to the court for custody. In such situations, a court will consider whether it is in the best interests of the child to award custody to this "non-parent party".

---

[39] *Young v. Young, supra* note 12 at para. 162.

Again, the right of "non-parents" to apply for custody is an area that is not well understood by the general public. If a stepfather or stepmother or a grandmother or aunt (or some other person) has been caring for a child successfully then it is likely that an application by this person(s) will be favourably looked upon by the court, regardless of other considerations. As stated above, the current trend in the law is to continue the caregiving regime for the child that existed prior to marital break-up.

The person granted "custody" of a child is cloaked with the legal authority of "parenthood" whether or not they are related to the child by blood. To this end, the *Children's Law Reform Act* (as an example) specifically grants the person(s) awarded custody (regardless of who that person may be) the rights, responsibilities and authority of a parent with respect to the child, which must be exercised in the best interests of that child. Subsections 20(2), (3) of the CLRA read:

> (2) Rights and responsibilities — A person entitled to custody of a child has the rights and responsibilities of a parent in respect of the person of the child and must exercise those rights and responsibilities in the best interests of the child.
>
> (3) Authority to act — Where more than one person is entitled to custody of a child, any one of them may exercise the rights and accept the responsibilities of a parent on behalf of them in respect of the child.

A parent or other person who seeks to change the initial status quo (on an initial application or through any subsequent order) must show that some significant reason (or reasons) exist such that the best interests of the children would be best met by effecting a change in the status quo. In the alternative, such an applicant must show that the "status quo parent" will not act in the future for the best interests of the child.

As noted, practially, displacing the status quo is often a very high legal and evidentiary burden to meet. Frequently, once a court hears evidence establishing the existing care arrangement for a child, it is the determining factor for the purposes of issues of custody in all subsequent litigation.

DE FACTO CUSTODY, INTERIM CUSTODY, FINAL CUSTODY

As a practical matter, family breakdown may entail many stages and processes over the course of a sometimes lengthy period of time. Obviously, child custody is a part of each stage and process. In turn, each stage and process may establish a "status quo" custody arrangement for the purposes of all subsequent steps. The evolution and evocation of the "status quo" over the course of the legal process are usually referred to a *"de facto* custody", "interim custody" and "final custody".

(a) *De Facto* Custody

Upon a family breakdown, one parent or person takes charge of the children to meet their day-to-day needs. At this point, there is usually neither a court application or a separation agreement in place to determine the legal rights of the parents (or others) with respect to the children. However, as seen above, parents are equally entitled to the incidents of custody (at first) and any *consent, implied consent or acquiescence of the other* to a custody arrangement may create a certain status quo that can carry weight with the court. The result is that, whether or not the law formally recognizes the arrangement, one parent has custody of the child. Lawyers call this *"de facto* custody".

For many, *"de facto* custody" is sufficient to confirm the child's best interests and if the consent, implied consent or acquiescence of the other parent continues, then this informal situation can continue as long as everyone is satisfied with that situation.

(b) Formal Custody Arrangements: Separation Agreements and Orders

Unfortunately, there are many cases where people are not satisfied with the *de facto* situation and the informal arrangements for custody need formalization through a separation agreement or a court order.

(i) SEPARATION AGREEMENTS

A separation agreement is a contract between the separating parties setting out the rights, responsibilities and accords between them in respect to the end of their relationship, including matters of custody and access to children of the relationship. A signed separation agreement can be filed with the court and enforced like a court order. If the parties negotiate, have separate legal representation, and sign a separation agreement, then the matter may well be settled and a custody application need not proceed.

(ii) INTERIM ORDERS CONCERNING CUSTODY

In many cases, formal applications for custody will commence. Because court applications can take a lengthy period of time to wind their way through the judicial process, the parties will often ask the court to make a temporary or "interim" order that may remain until the there is a full hearing on the merits. Interim orders are made on limited evidence that has not been fully examined through the trial process.

As a result, while on an interim application for custody a court will still consider all the factors of the child's best interests, an interim order of custody is even more likely to continue a status quo of childcare that has developed, unless there is significant evidence available that this should change.

Because an interim order can last for several months pending trial of a custody matter, the interim hearings into the issue of custody, known as "motions", are very important. While in other areas of the law interim applications or motions are concerned with procedural matters, in the area of custody and access, the subject matter on motions is substantive and often key to the ultimate decision on custody and access that will be made at trial.

However, there are important distinctions between the interim stage and the final stage. On a motion for custody, evidence is presented to the court in written form, called an affidavit. A witness does not usually come to court, but instead takes an oath that the contents of the affidavit are true and this sworn form of evidence is presented to the court. By contrast, a final order of custody (unless the matter is settled out of court) can only be made after a trial rather than by motion. Evidence at a trial is almost always done by the witness attending court and giving oral or *viva voce* testimony. These are obviously quite different experiences in both form and substance and knowing "what to expect" will be invaluable.

Anyone who is working with children and is presented with a copy of a court order purporting to give one person or another "custody" should try to determine whether the order they are reviewing is an interim order or a final order. While an interim order does grant custodial rights along with other rights, it is only temporary and the custody arrangements between the parties may be subject to change when the court makes the final order.

(iii) FINAL ORDERS CONCERNING CUSTODY

Final orders are final. In this regard, once a court makes a final order on an application for custody, that application is no longer before the court. After a final order for custody is made, it will continue until the child is 18 or marries.

MATERIAL CHANGE IN CIRCUMSTANCES

"Final" is a somewhat relative term in custody and access matters. In this regard, because the overriding test for all aspects of custody and access is the best interests of the child and because the needs, interests and circumstances of children do change, the court can always revisit the issues of custody and access upon a subsequent application. A subsequent application to revisit a custody order may be brought at any time. However, to ensure that there is no misadventure caused by those who are just not happy with the original outcome, the applicant seeking to change a final order must show that there has been a "material change in circumstances" (concerning the best interests of the child) that justifies changing the original order.

As a child's needs change, it may be in the child's best interests to change the final order regarding custody. However, in order for the court to revisit custody issues after a final order has been made, something significant or "material" to the best interests of the child must have changed since the court made its last order.

The Supreme Court has described the meaning of the term a "material change in circumstances":

> The requirement of a material change in the situation of the child means that an application to vary custody cannot serve as an indirect route of appeal from the original custody order. The court cannot retry the case, substituting its discretion for that of the original judge; it must assume the correctness of the decision and consider only the *change* in circumstances since the order was issued: *Baynes v. Baynes* (1987), 8 R.F.L. (3d) 139 (B.C. C.A.); *Docherty v. Beckett* (1989), 21 R.F.L. (3d) 92 (Ont. C.A.); *Wesson v. Wesson* (1973), 10 R.F.L. 193 (N.S. T.D.), at p. 194.[40]

---

[40] *Gordon v. Goertz*, [1996] 2 S.C.R. 27 at 189, referred to in *Bater v. Alessandro*, *supra* note 35 at p. 104, *per* Zuker J.

Section 29 of the *Children's Law Reform Act* confirms that a "material change in circumstances" is the threshold for variation of an existing order for custody and access:

> 29(1) Order varying an order — A court shall not make an order under this Part that varies an order in respect of custody or access made by a court in Ontario unless there has been a material change in circumstances that affects or is likely to affect the best interests of the child.

In practice, determining what constitutes "a material change in circumstances" can be a very subjective decision. A change in the child's wishes,[41] a proposed move by the custodial parent, or the custodial parent getting a new romantic partner may all be a material change such that an application is brought to the court to vary an existing custodial order. Unfortunately, because of the subjective nature of the "material change" standard, many families return to court a number of times to "hash out" on-going developments.

One of the most frequent reasons for the return to court is a dispute over access. "Access" is often as misunderstood as custody.

WHAT DOES ACCESS MEAN?

As discussed above, the issue of custody is determined based upon an assessment of the best interests of the child. A parent who does not have custody of a child is usually referred to as an "access parent".

Access parents generally do not have decision-making power regarding the child. It has been stated that the role of the access

---

[41] As children get older, their views and preferences and what they perceive to be in their best interests takes on greater and greater weight with the court. Often a lawyer is appointed for a child so that the evidence of the child's views and preferences can be placed before the court.

parent is "that of a very interested observer, giving love and support to [the child] in the background".[42]

However, an access parent is not without certain rights regarding the child. In this regard, the applicable legislation provides that access parents with two broad categories of rights:

- the right to be informed about the child; and
- the right to make enquires regarding the child.[43]

For example, the *Divorce Act* enumerates a series of rights that the access parent has regarding the information about the child.

> (5) Unless the court orders otherwise, a spouse who is granted access to a child of the marriage has the right to make inquiries, and to be given information, as to the health, education and welfare of the child.[44]

Further, specific provisions of the *Divorce Act* confirm that contact with an access parent is in the child's best interests and that a change in the residence of the child may trigger notice rights regarding the move for the access parent:

> (7) Without limiting the generality of subsection (6), the court may include in an order under this section a term requiring any person who has custody of a child of the marriage and who intends to change the place of residence of that child to notify, at least thirty days before the change or within such other period before the change as the court may specify, any person who is granted access to that child of the change, the time at which the change will be made and the new place of residence of the child.[45]

---

[42] *Pierce v. Pierce*, [1977] 5 W.W.R. 572 (B.C. S.C. [in Chambers]) at 575. See also *Gubody v. Gubody*, [1955] O.W.N. 548 (Ont H.C.) and *Sudeyko v. Sudeyko* (1974), 18 R.F.L. 273 (B.C. S.C.).
[43] See, for example, s. 20(5) of the CLRA.
[44] Section 16(5) of the *Divorce Act, supra* note 21.
[45] *Divorce Act*, s. 16(7).

(10) In making an order under this section, the court shall give effect to the principle that a child of the marriage should have as much contact with each spouse as is consistent with the best interests of the child and, for that purpose, shall take into consideration the willingness of the person for whom custody is sought to facilitate such contact.[46]

The CLRA has similar presumptions about contact with the other spouse. For example, while one can acquiesce to the other parent the "right" of custody, one cannot acquiesce to the right of access.[47] Access specifically includes the right to visit with and be visited by the child.[48]

Given the presumptions that contact with both parents (and significant other persons) is in the best interests of a child, the rights of the custodial parent may not be as pre-eminent as a custodial parent may originally have thought. For example, a custodial parent may wish to relocate to another jurisdiction. Given his or her authority as custodial parent, one may assume that the custodial parent can simply move with the child. However, as noted in the sections above, contact with an access parent is something that is deemed to be in the best interests of the child pending information or evidence to the contrary. As a result, relocation by the custodial parent (which might sever the child's relationship or contact with the access parent) may be considered a "material change in circumstances". As stated above, a "material change in circumstances" justifies the access parent re-opening the issue of child custody.

Many custodial parents are dismayed to learn that if there is a material change in circumstances (of the child); a final order can be revisited time and time again.

One of the largest investments in time by lawyers in custody and access matters is educating clients to the realities of the

---

[46] *Divorce Act*, s. 16(10).
[47] Section 20(4) of the CLRA.
[48] *Supra* note 43.

custody and access regime and managing their reactions to this information. It is important to understand that neither the rights of the custodial parent nor the rights accorded the access parent are absolute or invulnerable to change or amendment. Custodial parents do have rights regarding the child in their care, including certain authority over decision-making. However, with those rights comes the responsibility of acting in the best interests of the child. Other parties can, upon a material change in circumstances, have the court examine whether or not the responsibilities are being fulfilled by the custodial parent.

Similarly, access parents are often dismayed to learn that while they do have certain rights to information and contact with their child, the custodial parent is the primary decision-maker for the child and can make decisions that the access parent might not have made.

Some parents and interested caregivers are able to balance these roles without difficulty, others are not. Unfortunately, sometimes parents' own perpetual reassessment and scrutiny of the other "side" sets up the potential for unwarranted and unnecessary litigation that is not in anyone's best interests.

It should also be noted that while custody is a label that speaks to decision-making power, it may or may not equate with how much time is spent with the child. In this regard, sharing time with the child is different than the "decision making" that goes on in custody and access determinations.

"Custody" is fundamentally about rights to make decisions concerning the child. Having custody of a child does not necessarily provide the custodial parent with a greater allotment of time with the child than that enjoyed by the access parent. However, because they are often linked together, most people equate custody with time-sharing.

TIME-SHARING

As noted above, a core feature of custody and access litigation is that, all things being equal, there should be as much contact with each parent as possible.

Again, subsection 16(10) of the *Divorce Act* puts it succinctly when it states:

> (10) In making an order under this section, the court shall give effect to the principle that a child of the marriage should have as much contact with each spouse as is consistent with the best interests of the child and, for that purpose, shall take into consideration the willingness of the person for whom custody is sought to facilitate such contact.

A child can spend a great deal of time with a custodial parent or very little time with a custodial parent. Custody is a matter of decision-making rather than the quantity of time.

This too is a subtle and often confusing distinction for those involved in the custody and access system. Being the "access" parent does not necessarily mean that you will see the child less. Often, to be fair, this is the case as the custodial parent, as we have seen, is quite often the primary caregiver both by decision-making and in day-to-day physical care of the child.

However, there is an incorrect belief, among some litigants, that they need to apply for "custody" as a means to get time with the children. The reality is that the adults in the family unit will both want to spend time with the child after separation. Often because of school and work commitments in the family, a regime of "every other weekend and a mid-week access visit" develops along with other additional times during major holidays and school holidays. However, the "time-sharing formula" that the parents or the court arrives at is in keeping with the time that is available to share with the child. The labels of custody and access speak to the decision-making authority over the child.

DECISION-MAKING DURING ACCESS

Another area of confusion is the often mistaken belief that a custodial parent gets to make *all* the decisions concerning a child, including everyday decisions that concern or arise while the child is sharing time with the access parent. Just as a tenant can arrange their furniture in an apartment without interference from a landlord, so too an access parent, generally, can make decisions for the child when the child is with them. However, just as a tenant probably cannot knock down a wall without some input from the landlord, neither can the access parent intrude into the area of decision-making that is the right of the custodial parent.

Like so many custody and access issues, this is a subtle and confusing area. What decisions are "custody decisions" differs from family to family and child to child. Depending on the relationship of the adults, matters such as what the child is fed during time-sharing or where a parent got the child's hair cut may lead to disputes and possible court action to determine whether or not an access parent was or was not entitled to make a decision regarding the child.

If required, the court will review the best interests of the child again in the circumstances and in its order detail what the access parent can and cannot do during the periods of access. However, it is well established that unless the custodial parent can show that the access parent's decisions are not in the best interests of the child, the access parent will be given some freedom in ensuring the child knows the other parent, their family and beliefs.[49]

---

[49] See, for example, *Hockey v. Hockey* (1989), 69 O.R. (2d) 338 (Ont. Div. Ct.), where an access parent was allowed to share his religion with the child as there was no evidence that exposure to the two religions would be harmful to the child and, as well, that the mother was wrong to threaten to terminate time with the child unless he stopped.

While the law generally presumes that the child's sharing of both time and information with the access parent is in the child's best interests, this is not always the case. In some cases, an access parent's time-sharing with the child will be terminated completely as this is in the best interests of the child. In certain cases, while time-sharing with an access parent is permitted to continue, contact is regulated by means of certain safeguards, such as court-ordered "supervised access".

"SUPERVISED ACCESS" AND "SUPERVISED ACCESS CENTRE"

As described above "supervised access" is simply when the parties agree (or the court orders) that the time spent with the non-custodial parent should be supervised.

Depending on the circumstances, supervising such access may be done by a family member, a trusted person or it may be contracted with a formal "Supervised Access Centre".

Although "supervised access" may last a long time, generally it is not seen as a long-term situation, but an initial introduction or re-introduction of the adult back into the child's life. The time-sharing is monitored for safety reasons, but invariably, the expectation is that the matter will return to court. Under the circumstances, a court then determines whether the contact should be unsupervised, whether it should remain supervised, or, whether it should terminated entirely. Each case will be determined on the individual facts of that child and the adults involved. Again, the test applied in these circumstances is what is in the best interests of the child.

One of the reasons that access may be supervised is that there is a fear for the child's safety. Secondly, even if the child is kept safe, there is a fear that the "access parent" will not return the child to the "custodial parent" after access.

Should a parent kidnap a child, there are international agreements under the auspices of the *Hague Convention* to sort out the rights of the child to be with their proper, lawful, custodial parent and to affect the safe return of the missing child. That being said, there is little doubt that a parent would rather the child be returned without needing to rely on the *Hague Convention* or other enactment.

HAGUE CONVENTION ON THE CIVIL ASPECTS OF INTERNATIONAL CHILD ABDUCTION

Child abductions are difficult enough when they occur within Canada. When they involve other countries, they are even more trying.

As noted above, there are often differing views between countries regarding: what is best for children; how to raise them; and who should raise them. As a result, if a child is removed to a foreign country it might be very difficult to "enforce" a custodial order made in Canada.

The *Hague Convention on the Civil Aspects of International Child Abduction* (which has become more commonly known as simply the *Hague Convention*), is the main international treaty that can assist parents whose children have been abducted to another country. As of September 2004, 75 countries have adopted the *Hague Convention*, including Canada. It is a mechanism that assists greatly in the case of children abducted to signatory countries.

In 1979, a special committee on the Civil Aspects of International Child Abduction prepared a preliminary draft of the *Hague Convention on the Civil Aspects of International Child Abduction*. From that committee, the *Hague Convention* was adopted by the Hague Conference on October 25, 1980, and came into force on December 1, 1983.

The *Hague Convention* is tacitly renewed every five years. If a signatory denounces it during that period, only the signatory is affected and not the entire agreement.[50]

The *Hague Convention* has two main objectives:

- to secure the prompt return of children wrongfully removed or retained in any contracting State; and,
- to ensure that custody and access rights under the law of one contracting State are respected in other contracting States.

In Ontario, the *Hague Convention* was brought into force by the *Children's Law Reform Amendment Act, 1982*. The *Hague Convention* is adopted in section 46 of the *Children's Law Reform Act*. Between 1983 and 1988, the *Hague Convention* was brought into force in every province and territory in Canada. The *Hague Convention* is international in scope and does not operate interprovincially within Canada.

The various Canadian governments (at both the provincial/ territorial and federal levels) cooperate closely in assisting parents affected by such abductions. These cases can involve both Canadian children who have been wrongfully removed from Canada and those that have been prevented from returning home by one of their parents.

PREVENTION

In many cases, abduction or custody issues arise when the parent prevents the child from returning to Canada. These cases would likely not be considered as abductions as permission was granted when the child was initially taken. To the

---

[50] See http://hcch.e-vision.nl/index_en.php?act=conventions.status& cid=24 for a list of the contracting States (member and non-member), as of June 16, 2005.

surprise of the affected parent they are therefore custody rather than criminal matters.

The country where the child is may not recognize a Canadian custody order or may be unwilling or unable to enforce such an order.

If one is separated or divorced and a child is traveling to a foreign country, one should discuss the planned visit with a Canadian lawyer experienced on such matters. In some instances, it might also be necessary to discuss this with a lawyer in the country that one is visiting. The lawyer(s) can assist in ensuring safeguards are in place to ensure as much as possible that the child is safely returned home. In the alternative, they may be able to assist in ensuring the visit does not occur in the first place.

The *Hague Convention* is only useful in the case of children who are in foreign signature countries. Within Canada, taking a child could be a criminal matter.

PARENTAL ABDUCTION

Parental abduction is a criminal offence under sections 281, 282 and 283 of the Canadian *Criminal Code*. In many situations, the criminal justice system can assist a custodial parent in locating and recovering their child.

Because the administration of criminal justice in Canada is a provincial/territorial responsibility, the *Criminal Code* may be administered in a slightly different way from one province or territory to another.

In some provinces and territories the police can act on child abductions themselves. In other areas the Crown Attorney will need to review the matter first to see whether or not the parent who has the child has abducted the child or whether they had rights to have the child with them (in which case it may be a *Hague Convention* matter rather than a criminal matter).

Using the *Criminal Code* makes it easier for the police to search for and locate a child. An arrest warrant is generally issued, often improving cooperation among police forces both nationally and internationally.

If necessary, an extradition request may be made if there is an extradition treaty with the country in which the alleged abductor is located.

EXTRADITION

Extradition may be helpful in some cases of international abduction. This is the mechanism where a person held by foreign authorities is transferred back to Canada as the alleged crime occurred here.

However, extradition can be a lengthy and uncertain process. As well, there is no guarantee that foreign authorities will return the child, even if they should permit the extradition of the alleged abductor.

Not all countries regard child abduction by one of the parents as a criminal act and often extradition treaties between Canada and other countries require the alleged act to be an offence in both countries.

Despite the difficulties, the *Hague Convention* is probably the best mechanism available at this time to assist in "retrieving" an abducted child or a child whose parent is preventing him or her from returning home from another country.

The hope is, of course, that one will not be forced to use such mechanisms as custody and access will be worked out between both parents in such away that the child will continue to receive the warm, nurturing love and affection that he or she deserves, regardless of the relationship of the parents.

CONCLUSIONS

Custody and access is a large, complex area of law that is really larger than one chapter. There are many subtleties to the determinations that go into making decisions in the area. These subtleties are often confused by participants given the highly emotional nature of the interests at stake and the various factors that may or may not be important depending on the facts of each case.

However, it is hoped that reviewing some of the main areas involved in custody and access will assist your general understanding of this difficult and often contentious area.

6

YOUTH CRIMINAL JUSTICE ACT

HISTORY

Separate consideration for youths in the criminal justice system in Canada began on a systemic basis in 1908 by introducing the *Juvenile Delinquents Act* ("JDA"). This initial statute provided a definition of a "childhood age" (age 7-16) and an interpretive focus upon acting in the best interests of the child.[1] Under the JDA, children in the justice system were not viewed as criminals, but as ". . .misdirected [children]. . .in need of aid, encouragement, help and assistance". A variety of sentencing options were available, from granting an absolute discharge to making the offending youth a ". . .ward of the state".[2] Concern over judicial discretion under the JDA and its "needs-based" approach prompted extensive discussion of reform in the 1960s. The *Young Offenders Act* ("YOA") was introduced in Parliament in 1981 and proclaimed in force in 1984.

The *Young Offenders Act* itself quickly faced a firestorm of criticism, particularly in connection with some widely publicized cases in which youths convicted of murder received what the

---

[1] Alan W. Leschied, *Young Offenders Act in Review: A More Modest Proposal for Change* (Correctional Services Canada, 1999).
[2] *Ibid.* at 1.

public perceived to be light sentences. While attempts were made by amendments to shore-up the inadequacies of the statute, by 1998 the federal Justice Minister had announced that the YOA was to be supplanted by successor legislation. The *Youth Criminal Justice Act* ("YCJA") replaced the *Young Offenders Act* as the law governing young offenders and Canada's youth justice system on April 1, 2003.

APPLICATION OF THE YCJA

The YCJA applies to youths between the ages of 12 and 18. Under the YCJA regime, a "child" (under the age of 12) is not criminally responsible for his or her actions. Refractory behaviour by children is typically addressed as a matter of child protection legislation and/or intervention by the school system.

APPLICATION OF THE *CRIMINAL CODE*

Section 140 of the YCJA states:

> 140. Except to the extent that it is inconsistent with or excluded by this Act, the provisions of the *Criminal Code* apply, with any modifications that the circumstances require, in respect of offences alleged to have been committed by young persons.

DIFFERENCES BETWEEN THE YCJA AND YOA

The YCJA marks a significant departure from the YOA as the governing law on youth justice. The primary differences between the new YCJA and YOA may be stated as follows:

- in Part I of the YCJA, a specific set of governing principles guide the application and interpretation of the YCJA, including the issue of whether a young person will have formal involvement in the justice system at all (extrajudicial measures);

- unlike the YOA, the YCJA contains a presumption in favour of resolving non-violent, first offences without formal involvement of the youth justice system, by means of what the YCJA calls "extrajudicial measures";
- unlike the YOA, the YCJA encourages the use of "extrajudicial measures" in every context where they will be sufficient to ". . .hold a young person accountable for his or her offending behaviour"[3] and if their use is appropriate in considering the other guiding principles of the YCJA stated in Part I of the YCJA;
- the YCJA encourages the involvement of the young person's family (and extended family where appropriate), victims and community members in designing and implementing "extrajudicial measures";
- unlike the YOA, the YCJA gives a youth court the power to impose adult sentences on a young person (under the YOA, to impose an adult sentence, the young person had to be transferred to adult court);
- the YCJA lowers the age limit for the presumption of adult sentences to 14 years old (from the previous 16 under the YOA), but it accords the power to individual provinces to determine how this presumption will apply in each locality;
- the YCJA extends the range of offences to which a presumption of an adult sentence will apply (including a pattern of serious, violent offences) from the YOA, which presumed adult sentences to be appropriate only for: murder, attempted murder, manslaughter and aggravated sexual offences;
- under the YCJA, the Crown Attorney in each case can renounce the application to the case of the presumption of an adult sentence, leaving the youth court to impose an appropriate sentence;
- under the YCJA, publishing the details from a youth court proceeding may be permitted (after a finding of guilt) in

---

[3] *Youth Criminal Justice Act*, s. 4(c).

circumstances where a youth receives an adult sentence or if a youth sentence is imposed for an offence that carries the presumption of an adult sentence, unless the youth court decides that publication is inappropriate. Under the YOA, publishing the particulars was allowed only in circumstances in which a matter was transferred to adult court;
- under the YCJA, there is more recognition of the victim, including reference in the guiding principles of the statute in Part I. Victims are given rights of information, including right to access youth court records and access to information on extrajudicial measures taken with respect to a young person. Under the YOA, victims' rights were more tentative and discretionary and victims' interests did not form part of the guiding principles in respect to its application and interpretation;
- unlike the YOA, under the YCJA, young persons' voluntary statements to police may be admitted into evidence by a youth court, notwithstanding minor irregularities in statutory compliance by police. Under the YOA, such variations were fatal to the consideration of such material by the court;
- under the YCJA, decisions on such matters as extrajudicial measures, conditions of release from pre-trial detention, sentencing, and re-integration (by police and youth courts) may be informed by advisory groups termed "conferences", which can comprise the parents of the young person, the victim, community agencies and professionals. The YOA did not provide for such consultations;
- under the YCJA, all "custodial sentences" include a portion served in custody and a portion to be served "under supervision" in the community. A prepared plan for "re-integration" in the community (for a period of up to 30 days) is required for each youth who receives a custodial sentence. Under the YOA, there was neither a provision for

"supervised re-integration" nor a requirement for a prepared plan in respect to releasing a young offender.

GUIDING PRINCIPLES

The YCJA is organized and interpreted in accordance with the following broad statements of policy and principle.

The intention of the criminal justice system is:

- to prevent crime by addressing the circumstances underlying a young person's offending behaviour;

- to rehabilitate young persons who commit offences and reintegrate them into society; and

- to ensure a young person is subject to meaningful consequences for offences committed.

The youth criminal justice system emphasizes:

- rehabilitation and reintegration;
- fair and proportionate accountability consistent with greater dependency of young persons and their reduced level of maturity;
- timely intervention that reinforces the link between the offending behaviour and its consequences; and
- promptness and speed of actions taken under the YCJA, given young persons' perception of time.

The measures taken against young persons who commit offences should:

- reinforce respect for societal values;
- encourage the repair of harm done to victims and the community; and
- be meaningful to the individual young person, given his

or her individual needs and development and where appropriate, should involve the parents, the extended family, the community, and social/other agencies in rehabilitating and reintegrating the young person.

Special considerations should apply in respect to proceedings against young persons, including:

- the young person's rights and freedoms in their own right, including the right to be heard and to participate in the process (other than the decision to prosecute);
- the special guarantees of the young person's rights and freedoms;
- treating the victims with courtesy, compassion and respect for their dignity and ensuring the victims suffer the minimum degree of inconvenience as a result of their involvement with the criminal justice system;
- providing the victims with information about the proceedings and giving them an opportunity to participate and to be heard;
- informing parents of measures or proceedings involving their children; and
- encouraging parents to support their children in addressing their offending behaviour.

The YCJA is to be "liberally construed" so as to ensure that young persons are dealt with in accordance with these statements of guiding principle.

ORGANIZATION OF THE YCJA

The YCJA has seven core parts, as well as two parts dealing with statutory operation and one Schedule (which gives a listing of offences that apply to section 120 of the statute).

The parts of the YCJA are as follows:

- Part 1—Extrajudicial Measures
- Part 2—Organization of Youth Criminal Justice System
- Part 3—Judicial Measures
- Part 4—Sentencing
- Part 5—Custody and Supervision
- Part 6—Publication, Records and Information
- Part 7—General Provisions
- Part 8—Transitional Provisions
- Part 9—Consequential Amendments, Repeal and Coming into Force of the Act

EXTRAJUDICIAL MEASURES

One of the cornerstones of the YCJA is addressing divergent behaviour by youth outside of the justice system. Part 1 of the YCJA sets out a framework for using a range of measures (other than youth court proceedings) for responding to youth crime, based upon the supplementary statement of principles found in section 4 of the statute, which begins with recognizing that "extrajudicial measures are often the most appropriate and effective way to address youth crime".[4] Extrajudicial measures may be particularly appropriate for responding to less serious youth crime in a timely and effective manner.

(a) Extrajudicial Measures Defined

The YCJA contemplates the following range of extrajudicial measures:

- measures based on police discretion, such as warnings, cautions and referrals to community programs;
- cautions by Crown attorneys; and

---

[4] YCJA, s. 4(a).

- more formal extrajudicial measures called extrajudicial sanctions, formerly known as "alternative measures" under the YOA.

Basically, there are two tiers of extrajudicial measures:

- warnings, cautions and referrals;
- "extrajudicial sanctions".

(b) When to Use Extrajudicial Measures

One of the objectives of the YCJA is to increase the use of effective and timely non-court responses to less serious offences by youth. The YCJA provides that extrajudicial measures should be used for any offence, including more serious offences, if the measures would:

- be adequate to hold the young person accountable for his or her offending behaviour; and
- be consistent with the principles of the Act.

Extrajudicial measures are presumed to be adequate to hold a young person accountable if the young person has committed a less serious offence and has not previously been found guilty of any offence. Beyond this presumption, under the YCJA, extrajudicial measures may still be used to address behaviour by individuals who have previously been dealt with by way of extrajudicial measures or who have been previously found guilty of an offence.[5]

(c) The Aim of Extrajudicial Measures

Extrajudicial measures are intended to allow early intervention with young people and provide the opportunity for the broader community to play an important role in developing

---

[5] YCJA, s. 4(d).

community-based responses to youth crime. Increasing the use of non-court responses not only improves the response to less serious youth crime, but also enables the courts to focus on more serious cases.

(d) Who Considers Extrajudicial Measures?

The focus under the YCJA is to encourage considering extrajudicial resolution at the earliest stage in the intervention process. Accordingly, the focus is on extrajudicial measures being considered by police officers. The YCJA states:

> A police officer shall, before starting judicial proceedings or taking any other measure under this Act against a young person alleged to have committed an offence, consider whether it would be sufficient, having regard to the principles set out in section 4, to take no further action, warn the young person, administer a caution, if a program has been established under section 7, or, with the consent of the young person, refer the young person to a program or agency in the community that may assist they young person not to commit offences.[6]

The potential practical and systemic advantages of this approach are numerous. When police use extrajudicial measures, it:

- provides an alternative to formal charges to respond to youth offences;
- minimizes case preparation time by officer(s);
- provides swift consequences to youths who offend;
- reduces the amount of minor offences processed by youth courts, allowing police and the court to focus on serious offences;
- allows quick provision of accountable intervention.

---

[6] YCJA, s. 6(1).

(e) Extrajudicial Sanctions Defined

Extrajudicial sanctions are essentially the second (and more serious) level of extrajudicial measures after cautions, warnings and referrals, which are used when this first group of strategies is inadequate because of:

- the seriousness of the offence;
- the nature and number of the previous offences committed by the young person; and
- any other aggravating circumstances in the particular case.

Known as "alternative measures" under the YOA, extrajudicial sanctions entail a young person participating in a government-authorized program that is appropriate to the young person and the "interests of society".

(f) Using Extrajudicial Sanctions

An extrajudicial sanction can be used only if:

- it is government authorized;
- it is appropriate to the young person's needs and society's interest;
- the young person has been informed about the extrajudicial sanction and fully and freely consents to be subject to it and the young person has been previously advised of his or her right to counsel and has been given a reasonable opportunity to consult with counsel;
- the young person accepts responsibility for the act or omission that forms the basis of the offence that he or she is alleged to have committed;
- in the view of the Crown, there is sufficient evidence to proceed with prosecution of the offence; and

- the prosecution of the offence is not barred in any way by law.[7]

The YCJA prohibits using extrajudicial matters where a young person:

- denies he or she participated, or was involved, in committing the offence; or
- expresses the wish to have the charge dealt with by a youth justice court.

(g) Admissions for Purposes of Extrajudicial Sanctions as Evidence

As noted above, a condition for imposing an extrajudicial sanction is accepting responsibility for the acts or omissions of the alleged offence. Accordingly, subsection 10(4) makes such "admission, confession or statement" inadmissible in evidence for the purpose of any civil or criminal proceeding.

(h) Extrajudicial Sanctions and Criminal Charges

If an extrajudicial sanction is imposed, criminal charges can still be laid. However, under subsection 10(5) of the YCJA, if a charge is laid, the youth court must dismiss the charge if it is satisfied that the young person has fully complied with the terms and conditions of the program. Where there is partial compliance with the terms and conditions, the court has discretion to dismiss the charge(s) if ". . .prosecution of the charge would be unfair having regard to the circumstances and the young person's performance with respect to the extrajudicial sanction".

---

[7] YCJA, s. 10(2).

(i) Success with Extrajudicial Programs

Extrajudicial programs have been successful in the past. Nearly all of the young persons who participated in alternative measures programs under the YOA successfully completed the required measure.

(j) The Role of Extrajudicial Measures in Youth Criminal Justice

Extrajudicial measures play a big role in the youth criminal justice system. Most cases in youth court are non-violent. Nearly half of the violent offences are minor assault. More than 40 per cent of the cases in youth court fall into four categories of less serious offences:

- theft under $5,000 (e.g., shoplifting);
- possession of stolen property;
- failure to appear in court; and
- failure to comply with a disposition (e.g., breach of a condition of probation).

COMMITTEES AND CONFERENCES

Other than the courts, the YCJA permits the creation of other bodies that facilitate intervention with young persons who are involved with the police or the criminal justice process.

(a) Youth Justice Committees

A youth justice committee is a group of people who are appointed (typically by a province) to assist in aspects of implementing or administering the YCJA.[8] A committee may have involvement in a situation with or without specific charges

---

[8] YCJA, s. 18(1).

being brought against a youth. Under the YCJA, the functions of a youth justice committee include (where a young person is alleged to have committed an offence):

- giving advice on the appropriate extrajudicial measure to be used in respect to a young person;
- supporting any victim of an alleged offence by soliciting their concerns and facilitating the reconciliation of the victim and the young person;
- ensuring the availability of community support to a young person by arranging services from the community including "...short-term mentoring and supervision"; and
- helping to coordinate the interaction between the agency/group and youth criminal justice system when the youth is also being dealt with by a child protection body or community group.

As more general matters, committees may also:

- advise the federal and provincial governments on the rights and protections of young persons, or policies and procedures under the YCJA;
- provide information to the public in respect to the YCJA and the youth justice system;
- fulfill any other functions assigned to them (typically by the Province).[9]

A referral to a committee may be made by police prior to a charge being laid or by a Crown Attorney after a charge has been laid. Generally, committees deal with matters concerning less serious offences, rather than many crimes involving violence or serious property damage.

---

[9] YCJA, s. 18.

(b) Conferences

A conference is a group of people put together to make a decision required under the YCJA, which may be called by a youth justice court judge, a province's YCJA director, a justice of the peace or a prosecutor (such as a Crown Attorney).[10]

A wide range of matters may be addressed by a conference, including giving advice and direction on:

- appropriate extrajudicial measures;
- conditions for judicial interim release;
- sentences (including the review of sentences); and
- reintegration plans.[11]

Under the YCJA, the provinces are given the power to establish rules for convening or conducting conferences other than those ordered by a youth court or a justice of the peace.[12] In provinces where such rules are adopted, these diktats are binding.[13]

YOUTH COURT

Part 2 of the YCJA addresses the Organization of the Youth Criminal Justice system, which a young person may face if a situation is not addressed by means of extrajudicial measures.

(a) Youth Court and Adult Court Differences

A youth does not go before the same court as an adult. The YCJA dispenses with the possibility that existed under the YOA that a youth charged with a serious crime would be transferred to a court for adults. Instead, the YCJA contem-

---

[10] YCJA, s. 19(1).
[11] YCJA, s. 19(2).
[12] YCJA, s. 19(3).
[13] YCJA, s. 19(4).

plates all youth matters, including the most serious of situations, being handled in a special youth court system for young persons. However, a youth appearing in youth court is charged with the offences under the *Criminal Code* (or other applicable federal statute); the YCJA does not contain a separate listing of offences that can be committed by youths as opposed to adults.

A youth court does not necessarily deal with a young person like a court for adults. The idea of a specialized court system for youths is to recognize and address the unique situation and vulnerabilities of young persons. However, the YCJA does allow a youth court to impose adult sentences on young persons in certain situations.

(b) Youth Court Jurisdiction and Powers

Youth court has jurisdiction over offences alleged to have been committed by a person 18 years old or older who is alleged to have committed an offence while a young person.[14] If a person turns 18 during the course of a youth court proceeding, the youth court maintains jurisdiction over that proceeding, rather than passing the matter to an adult court.[15]

For the most part, a youth court has the same powers as adult court. For the purposes of carrying out the provisions of the YCJA, a provincial court judge sitting in youth justice court has the same powers as in summary conviction court under the *Criminal Code*.[16] When deemed to be a youth court judge for the purposes of a proceeding, a superior court judge possesses the same powers of a superior court of criminal jurisdiction.[17] Furthermore, a youth court has the same powers as

---

[14] YCJA, s. 14(5).
[15] YCJA, s. 14(4).
[16] YCJA, s, 14(6).
[17] YCJA, s, 14(7).

an adult court to address and punish someone for contempt of court, with the added option that contempt of court by a youth may yield a youth sentence for an infraction by a young person.[18]

(c) Youth's Age Unknown at Time of Offence

The YCJA allows the youth court to retain jurisdiction if it is unclear as to whether an alleged offence occurred (or did not occur as the case may be) during a period when the accused was a youth (and therefore subject to the provisions of the YCJA) or over 18 (and an adult whose offences are addressed under the *Criminal Code*).[19] After making the necessary findings of fact in respect to an offence, the YCJA allows a youth court to sentence a person under the YCJA (if the factual resolution is that the matter was committed while a youth), or to impose an appropriate penalty under the *Criminal Code* (or other applicable Act of federal Parliament), if the facts disclose that the illegal act was committed while the person was over the age of 18.[20]

(d) Enactments to Youth Court Proceedings

Obviously, the YCJA is the primary source of guidance for how a young person is dealt with by the justice system. As previously stated, when criminal charges are brought against youths, the offences are drawn from the *Criminal Code* (or other applicable federal statutes, such as the *Narcotics Control Act*) rather than YCJA itself. The YCJA also allows each province to establish its own procedural rules for youth court, so long as these provisions are not inconsistent with the YCJA or its regulations. Many provinces and territories have separate pro-

---

[18] YCJA, s, 15.
[19] YCJA, s, 16
[20] YCJA, s. 16(b)

cedural legislation (many of them simply updated versions of statutes from the days of the YOA), which regulates youth court proceedings in the province[21] while others merely deal with the designation and organization of youth courts in the province as a part of larger statutes that govern court matters.[22]

(e) Involving a Justice of the Peace in Youth Court

A justice of the peace is a magistrate (often not a lawyer) who is often responsible for many critical aspects of administering criminal justice (particularly at the entry point into the system), such as bail hearings and issuing search warrants. While the role of a justice of the peace in the criminal justice system will vary from province to province, they perform many important functions that facilitate important aspects of legal administration.

The YCJA specifically provides that any proceeding that may be carried on before a justice of the peace under the *Criminal Code* (e.g., a bail hearing)—other than a plea, a trial or adjudication—may be carried out in respect to an offence committed by a young person.[23] The YCJA specifically allows that a justice of the peace has jurisdiction to make an order under section 810 of the *Criminal Code* with respect to a young person (i.e., to compel the young person to enter into a recognizance or bond, with or without sureties, to keep the peace and be of good behaviour for a specific period of time) in circumstances where there is fear of injury or damage to persons or property.[24]

---

[21] See, for example, Alberta's *Youth Justice Act*, R.S.A. 2000, c. Y-1 and *Rules of Youth Court Regulation*, Alta. Reg. 297/88; Northwest Territories' *Youth Justice Act*, S.N.W.T. 2003, c. 31.
[22] See, for example, Ontario's, *Courts of Justice Act*, R.S.O. 1990, c. C.43 (as amended); and Quebec's *Courts of Justice Act*, R.S.Q. c. T-16.
[23] YCJA, s. 20(1).
[24] YCJA, s. 20(2).

(f) The Role of the Court Clerk in Youth Court

A court clerk is someone who assists in the process of justice. The YCJA provides that, in addition to the abilities given a court clerk under the *Criminal Code*, a court clerk also may:

- administer oaths and affirmations in all matters relating to the business of criminal justice; and
- in the absence of a youth court judge, exercise all the powers of a youth court judge with respect to adjournments.[25]

JUDICIAL MEASURES

Part 3 of the *Youth Criminal Justice Act* deals with the conduct of judicial proceedings against young persons. The decision to charge a youth with an offence exposes him or her to the regimen of the formal judicial process and its consequences, including the potential for deprivation of liberty. Accordingly, in addition to the initiatives listed above (such as extrajudicial measures and conferences), to avert a young person's formal involvement in the criminal process, the YCJA also allows each province to set up a "pre-charge screening" mechanism that sets out circumstances in which the consent of the Attorney General (of the Province) is required prior to proceeding.[26] Such a program has been established in Nova Scotia, with the Crown Caution/Pre-Charge screening program in place in Halifax. The pre-charge screening component primarily relates to non-violent property offences of a minor nature.[27]

Private prosecutions of young persons are prohibited under section 24 of the YCJA.

---

[25] YCJA, s. 21.
[26] YCJA, s. 23.
[27] Department of Justice, Canada website: http://canada.justice.gc.ca/en/ps/yj/partnership/fundtd.html, "Pilot Projects Funded to Date."

(a) A Young Person's Right to Counsel

Like adults, on arrest or "detention" youths have:

- the right to retain and instruct counsel without delay;
- the right to exercise the right to retain and to instruct counsel personally at any stage of proceedings against them, including before and during the consideration of using extrajudicial measures;[28]
- on arrest or "detention", the right to be advised without delay of the right to retain and instruct counsel without delay.[29]

(b) Specific Procedural Protections for Young People

Procedural protections arise under the YCJA that are specific to youth and apply to them in addition to those already provided for adults. Obligations on the part of various officials are set out, as is the role of parents, in proceedings and obligations unique to young persons throughout the judicial process, beginning with the decision to charge a young person to when finding of guilt is made or a charge is dismissed, withdrawn or stayed. These specific protections include:

- safeguards to address a situation where a young person attends a hearing or in court without counsel including allowing for the appointment of counsel for a young person and appointing an adult to assist the young person;[30]
- having reminders of the right to counsel included on notices and summons from a youth court;[31]
- providing notice of steps in the criminal justice process to

---

[28] YCJA, s. 25(1).
[29] YCJA, s. 25(2).
[30] YCJA, ss. 25(3) to (8)
[31] YCJA, s. 25(9).

a young person's parents (or a substitute) with particulars as specified in the YCJA;[32] and
- allowing that a court may require the attendance of a parent before a youth justice court in respect to proceedings against a young person and providing for penalties in the event of the parent's non-attendance.[33]

(c) Privacy Protections for Young People

There is a general prohibition on publishing the identify of a young person (or details that may serve to identify a young person) who has been dealt with under the YCJA.[34] There are exceptions to this non-disclosure rule,[35] where:

- a young person has been found guilty of an offence and given an adult sentence;
- a young person has been convicted of a "presumptive offence", but has received a youth sentence where no publication ban has been made by a youth court;
- disclosure in the course of ". . .the administration of justice" is made where the purpose of the disclosure is not to make the information known in the community;
- disclosure is necessary to allow authorities to seek the public's assistance (by means of an application to court) in apprehending a young person who is unlawfully at large if he or she is dangerous;
- with leave of a court, where a young person wants to disclose the fact that he or she has been dealt with under the YCJA and disclosure is neither contrary to the young person's best interests or the public interest; and
- a person who has turned 18 years of age (and who is not

---

[32] YCJA, s. 26.
[33] YCJA, s. 27.
[34] YCJA, s. 110.
[35] YCJA, s. 110(2).

in custody) discloses the information him- or herself. After such disclosure, there is no further ban on publication.[36]

PRE-TRIAL DETENTION

One of the objectives of the *Youth Criminal Justice Act* is to reduce youth incarceration at the pre-trial stage of the youth justice process.

A youth may be detained before trial under the YCJA, as the provisions of Part VI of the *Criminal Code* are incorporated by reference in the YCJA (except to the extent that they are inconsistent).[37]

Despite the inclusion of these *Criminal Code* provisions by reference, the YCJA is based on a general presumption of release. The YCJA provisions in this respect emphasize that detaining young persons should occur only as an exception. Accordingly, the YCJA restricts pre-trial detention by means of provisions that:

- prohibit detention from being used as a ". . .substitute for appropriate child protection, mental health or other social measures";[38]
- presume against imposing custody in respect to offences for which a young person could not be sentenced to custody if found guilty of the offence;[39] and
- require a judge to look into the availability of a responsible person into whose care a young person can be released as an alternative to custody.[40]

---

[36] YCJA, s. 112.
[37] YCJA, s. 28.
[38] YCJA, s. 29(1).
[39] YCJA, s. 29(2).
[40] YCJA, s. 31(2).

COURT APPEARANCES

Where a criminal matter gives rise to a charge, the charge must be adjudicated by a youth court.

(a) First Appearance

At a first appearance in youth court, the presiding judge must make sure that certain steps are taken as required under section 32 of the YCJA. These include the following:

- reading the information (for summary conviction offences) or indictment (in cases of indictable offences) to the young person (the document that sets out the details of the allegations against the young person including the sections of the law he or she is alleged to have violated);
- advising the young person of the right to retain and instruct counsel where the young person is not represented by counsel;
- informing the young person that an adult sentence may be imposed on him or her if the court is aware that the Crown intends to seek an adult sentence for the offence charged, or the status of the accused at the time of the offence is uncertain (i.e. as a youth or as an adult);
- reading the following caution if the young person is charged with having committed a "presumptive offence": "An adult sentence will be imposed if you are found guilty unless the court orders that you are not liable to an adult sentence and that a youth sentence must be imposed."

A young person can waive the requirement to receive the cautions noted above where he or she is represented by counsel and the lawyer advises that the young person has been advised of the information under section 32.

(b) "Presumptive Offence"

The term "presumptive offence" is defined in subsection 2(1) of the YCJA. It is an offence committed (or alleged to have been committed) by a young person who has attained the age of 14 years (or an older age than 14 set by individual provinces), including:

- first or second degree murder (under section 231 or section 235 of the *Criminal Code*);
- attempted murder (under section 239 of the *Criminal Code*);
- manslaughter (under any of sections 232, 234 and 236 of the *Criminal Code*);
- aggravated sexual assault (under section 273 of the *Criminal Code*); and
- a "serious violent offence" (defined also in subsection 2(1) to mean an offence in the commission of which a young person causes or attempts to cause serious bodily harm) for which an adult may be sentenced to imprisonment for two years or more, if at the time of the commission (or alleged commission) of the offence, the young person has had at least two prior findings made against him or her (in different proceedings) of having committed a "serious violent offence."

(c) Pleading Guilty

An unrepresented youth can simply plead guilty. However, prior to accepting the guilty plea of an unrepresented young person, the court must:

- be satisfied that the young person understands the charge;
- explain to the young person the consequences of being liable to an adult sentence, if the young person faces an adult sentence, and the procedure by which a young person may apply for an order that a youth sentence be imposed; and

- explain that the young person may plead guilty or not guilty to the charge or if subsection 67(1) (election for court for trial – adult sentence) or 67(3) (election of court for trial Nunavut – adult sentence) applies, explain that the young person may elect to be tried by a youth court justice judge without a jury and without a preliminary inquiry or to have a preliminary inquiry and be tried with a judge without a jury or to have a preliminary inquiry and to be tried by a court composed of a judge and a jury and, in either or the latter two cases, a preliminary inquiry will only be conducted if requested by the young person or the prosecutor.

If the court is not satisfied that the young person understands the charge, the court must (unless the young person faces an adult sentence in which case he or she is put to an election as to the mode of trial in accordance with section 67 of the YCJA) enter a plea of not guilty on behalf of the young person and proceed with a trial of the matter.[41]

If the youth court is not satisfied that the young person understands the procedural explanations given to him or her (as set out above), the court must order that the young person be represented by counsel.

If the court is satisfied that the young person understands the charge and the consequences and the youth court determines that the facts support the charge, the court must find the young person guilty of the offence.[42]

(d) Release from Custody

If a young person is denied bail by order of a justice of the peace, at any time after such an order is made, an application may be made to youth court (if at least two clear days' notice

---

[41] YCJA, s. 32(4).
[42] YCJA, s. 36(1).

in writing is given to the prosecutor or the prosecutor waives the requirement of notice) to have the young person released from detention.[43]

(e) Medical or Psychological Evaluation

At any stage of proceedings, a youth court may order a young person to be assessed by a "qualified person" where:

- the young person and the prosecutor consent; and
- on the court's own motion, or on application by either the Crown or the young person, if the court believes that a medical, psychological or psychiatric report is necessary to (a) consider an application for release/detention in custody; (b) make a decision on an application in respect to adult sentencing for the young person; (c) make or review an adult sentence; (d) consider an application for continuing custody; (e) set conditions of supervision and/or make an order of supervision; (f) authorize disclosure of information about a young person.

To grant a motion or application for a medical or psychological examination (which is not on consent), the court must be satisfied that:

- there are reasonable grounds to believe that the young person may be suffering from: a physical or mental illness or disorder; a psychological disorder; an emotional disturbance; a learning disability; or a mental instability;
- the young person's history shows "repeated findings of guilt" under the YCJA or YOA; or
- the young person is alleged to have committed a "serious violent offence" (defined in subsection 2(1) as an offence in the commission of which a young person causes or attempts to cause serious bodily harm.).

---

[43] YCJA, s. 33.

(f) Assessing a Young Person

The YCJA refers to an assessment being done by a "qualified person", which is defined as:

- a person duly qualified by provincial law to practice medicine or psychiatry;
- a person duly qualified by provincial law to carry out psychological examinations or assessments; and
- in the absence of a regulating provincial law, a person who is, in the opinion of the court, qualified to carry out psychological examinations or assessments. (A province has the power under the YCJA to compile a list designated classes of persons who are qualified.)[44]

(g) Custody for the Purposes of Assessment

A young person can be remanded in custody for the purposes of an assessment for up to 30 days if the youth court is satisfied that:

- on the evidence presented (which may be in the form of a report), custody is necessary to conduct the assessment; or
- on the evidence of a qualified person (which may be in the form of a report), detention is desirable to conduct the assessment and the young person consents to custody.

A young person may also be detained in custody in respect of any other matter or by virtue of any provision of the *Criminal Code*.[45] The youth court retains discretion to vary the terms or conditions of an order for an assessment in any manner the court considers appropriate.

---

[44] YCJA, s. 34(14).
[45] YCJA, ss. 34(1) to (5).

(h) The Assessment Report

In the ordinary course of events, a copy of an assessment report on a young person is given to:

- the young person;
- any parent of the young person who is in attendance at the proceedings;
- counsel for the young person; and the prosecutor.[46]

In certain circumstances, the report may be withheld from the young person and his/her parents if the court is satisfied that disclosing the report would seriously impair the treatment or recovery of the young person or would likely endanger the life or safety of another person or result in serious psychological harm to another person.[47] Notwithstanding these circumstances, a youth court may still release all or portions of the report where it is satisfied that is in the interests of justice to make the disclosure.[48] A young person (or his or her counsel or adult representative as the case may be) has a right to ask the court for permission to cross-examine the expert who made the report.[49] A report of this nature generally forms part of the court record of the case.[50]

The YCJA contains a provision that allows an assessor to disclose immediately to "any person who has care or custody of the young person" that a young person held in detention or committed to custody is likely to endanger his or her own life or safety or to endanger the life of, or cause bodily harm to another person, whether or not this aspect is contained in the assessor's report. This permission to make immediate disclo-

---

[46] YCJA, s. 34(7).
[47] YCJA, s. 34(10).
[48] YCJA, s. 34(11).
[49] YCJA, s. 34(8).
[50] YCJA, s. 34(12).

sure to a parent, caregiver or other supervisor of the youth applies "...despite any other provision..." of the YCJA.[51]

(i) Involving Children's Aid or Child Welfare Agencies in the Youth Court Process

A youth court has the specific power (in addition to any other order it may make) to refer a young person to a child welfare agency for assessment to determine whether the young person can be helped by such an institution.[52]

(j) Proceeding to Trial

A matter will proceed to trial in youth court if an accused pleads not guilty to a charge(s) or if a youth pleads guilty but the youth court is not satisfied that the facts alleged support the charge. After the matter is heard at trial, it is open for the youth court to find a youth guilty or not guilty as the case may be.[53] If the youth is acquitted, the matter ends (subject to an appeal by the Crown). If the youth is found guilty/convicted, the matter proceeds to sentencing.

(k) Mode of Trial

In situations where a young person is charged with an offence for which an adult would face a term of imprisonment of five years or more, he or she is given the right to elect the mode of trial.[54] The right to elect the mode of trial applies only where an "adult sentence" may be imposed (as discussed below) and not where the young person faces only a "youth sentence" (again discussed below) as such allotments carry only the pos-

---

[51] YCJA, s. 34(13).
[52] YCJA, s. 35.
[53] YCJA, s. 36(2).
[54] YCJA, ss. 66 and 67.

sibility of three years in custody or less, except in cases of first or second degree murder.[55] Unlike under the YOA, all trials of young persons take place in youth court—there is no transfer to "adult court". Under these circumstances, a young person can choose to be tried:

- by a youth court judge without a jury;
- by a youth court judge following a "preliminary inquiry";
- by judge and jury without "preliminary inquiry".

A "preliminary inquiry" is a pre-trial hearing to determine whether there is sufficient evidence to warrant that an accused stand trial. It allows the young person (usually through counsel) the opportunity to find out information about the case he or she is facing by asking questions of the witnesses called by the prosecution at the preliminary inquiry (under oath). The process of a preliminary inquiry is governed by Part XVIII of Canada's *Criminal Code*.

Where this election by a young person arises, the youth court points these options out to the young person by reading the election to the young person prior to the entry of a plea.

(l) Rules for Trial Conduct

The YCJA incorporates by reference parts of the *Criminal Code* with respect to the conduct of trials (e.g., Part XIX–Trial without a Jury; Part XX–Trial with a Jury). However, special protections with respect to privacy and entitlement to counsel, in addition to the *Criminal Code* provisions, are built into youth court processes under the YCJA.

---

[55] Department of Justice, *YCJA Explained*, "Adult Sentences—Trial Process"; website: http://canada.justice.gc.ca/en/ps/yj/repository/3modules/05adult/3050301e.html.

Further, the YCJA contains specific evidentiary safeguards, apart from the rules of evidence applicable to adults, directed at protecting the procedural rights of young persons.[56]

SENTENCING UNDER THE YCJA

A young person found guilty of a criminal offence will be sentenced under one of two sentencing regimes: under the "youth sentencing" scheme of the YCJA or sentencing as an adult as provided in sections 61-81 of the statute. Under the YCJA, a youth court may only consider sentencing a young person as an adult where:

- the person was at least 14 years of age when the offence was committed;
- the offence is one for which an adult could receive a sentence of at least two years;

Certain offences are "presumptive offences" (murder, attempted murder, manslaughter, aggravated sexual assault or a serious violent offence in which a person causes or attempts to cause serious bodily harm) for which an adult sentence is presumed to be appropriate upon a finding of guilt for a certain offence. Each province is given the ability to determine at what age (14, 15 or 16) the presumption of an adult sentence will apply. The presumption of the appropriateness of an adult sentence does not mean that an adult sentence will be automatically imposed; the presumed appropriateness of an adult sentence is subject to being displaced where it can be shown that a youth sentence is of sufficient duration to hold a young person accountable for their conduct.

---

[56] For a thorough review of this regime, see the Department of Justice publication, *YCJA Explained*, "Evidence, Statements and Reports" at http://canada.justice.gc.ca/en/ps/yj/repository/3modules/11eviden/3110001a.html.

(a) Youth Sentencing

The YCJA contains many provisions speaking to the purpose, principles and factors to be considered in imposing "youth sentences" on young persons under the statute. The purpose of this express guidance is to address concerns expressed about lack of clear guidance on sentencing under the YOA.[57] Particularly disquieting about the process of sentencing under the YOA was the very high number of custodial sentences given to young people, particularly in connection with minor and non-violent offences.[58] The express guidelines under the YCJA are intended to address some of these aspects by means of particular directives and guiding principles.

(b) Purpose

The stated purpose of sentencing under the YCJA is to hold a young person accountable for an offence:

- by means of imposing just sanctions with meaningful consequences; and
- in a way that promotes his or her rehabilitation and reintegration into society.

The societal goal to be achieved through sentencing under the YCJA is contribution to the "...long-term protection of the public".[59]

---

[57] Department of Justice, *YCJA Explained*, "Approach to Sentencing" at http://canada.justice.gc.ca/en/ps/yj/repository/3modules/04youth/3040001a.html.
[58] *Ibid.*
[59] YCJA, s. 38(1).

(c) General Principles

Sentencing under the YCJA is to be guided by the general principles of the statute stated in section 3, as well as the following ideas from section 38 of the YCJA:

- a young person should not be sentenced to a punishment greater than that given to an adult convicted of the same offence;
- a sentence given must be similar to sentences imposed in the region on similar young persons found guilty of the same offence in similar circumstances;
- the sentence given must be proportionate to the seriousness of the offence and the degree of responsibility of the young person for the offence;
- all available sanctions *other than custody* that are reasonable under the circumstances should be considered for all young persons, with particular attention to the circumstances of aboriginal young persons;
- subject to the requirement of proportionality stated above, the sentence must be the least restrictive to achieve the purpose of sentencing (stated above); be the most likely to rehabilitate and reintegrate the young person into society; and to promote a sense of responsibility in the young person and an acknowledgement of the harm done to victims and the community.

(d) Factors to Consider

In sentencing a young person under the YCJA, a youth court is required to consider:

- the young person's degree of participation in the commission of the offence (i.e., was he or she a central actor or a peripheral part);
- the harm done to victims and whether such injury was intentional or reasonably foreseeable;

- any reparation by the young person to the victim or to the community;
- the time spent in detention by the young person as a result of the offence;
- the previous findings of guilt against the young person; and
- any other aggravating and mitigating circumstances related to the young person or the offence that are relevant to the purpose and principles above.[60]

(e) Outside Help on Sentencing

In addition to relying on what has actually been presented to the court in evidence, in determining the appropriate sentence to be imposed on a young person who has been found guilty of a crime, a court can rely on a "pre-sentence report" as discussed below. Also, section 34 of the YCJA allows a court to order a medical or psychological assessment of a young person, which also may form part of the considerations for sentencing.

Further, a youth court may convene (or cause to be convened) a "conference"; essentially a consultation group that is called upon for input into the appropriate sentence for the young person, in consideration of all the circumstances of the case. The composition of a "conference" will vary according to the situation, and may include the young person's parents, the victim, people who are familiar with the young person, members of community agencies, professionals, etc.[61] While the wealth of information and perspectives available through the conferring model may greatly assist the youth justice process, a practical problem arises in accessing such human resources for conferencing. Participation in conferencing adds yet more

---

[60] YCJA, s. 38.
[61] Department of Justice, *YCJA Explained* at http://canada.justice.gc.ca/en/ps/yj/repository/3Modules/04youth/3040301g.html

time commitments to the calendars of people who are already fully committed to their roles in the lives of young people.[62]

By virtue of section 50 of the YCJA, the victim impact provisions of the *Criminal Code* are incorporated into youth court proceedings. Accordingly, victim impact statements may also play a role in youth court sentencing procedures.[63]

(f) Pre-Sentence Report

A Pre-sentence report ("PSR") is usually a written report[64] on the personal and family history and "present environment" of a young person[65] that is prepared by a youth justice worker. The YCJA provides direction as to the contents of such reports, only insofar as such information is relevant to the sentencing principles set out in section 38 above (see heading (c) "General Principles", above).[66] The elements contained in a PSR under the YCJA include:

- the results of an interview with the young person and, if reasonably possible, the parents of the young person and "...if appropriate and reasonably possible", interviews with members of the young person's extended family;
- the results of an interview with the victim in the case "...if applicable and reasonably possible";
- the recommendations from any "conference" convened with respect to sentencing;[67]
- any information applicable to the case, including:

---

[62] For a discussion of practical and legal issues surrounding the conferencing process, please see *R. v. M. (B.)*, [2003] 2003 SKCA 135 (Sask. C.A.), beginning at para. 46 of the judgment.

[63] *Supra* note 55, "Sentencing" module at p. 12.

[64] Although in exceptional circumstances as provided in s. 40(3) of the YCJA, a PSR can be submitted orally.

[65] See definition, s. 2(1) of the YCJA.

[66] YCJA, s. 40.

[67] YCJA, s. 41.

1. the age, maturity, character, behaviour and attitude of the young person and his or her "...willingness to make amends"
2. any plans put forward by the young person to change his or her conduct or to participate in activities or undertake measures to improve himself or herself
3. the young person's youth justice record and her or his social services involvement in this respect
4. the history of "alternative measures" or extrajudicial sanctions used with respect to the young person under the YOA and YCJA and the response of the young person to those measures
5. the availability and appropriateness of community services and facilities for young persons and the willingness of the young person to use those services
6. the young person's relationship with his or her parents (including the degree of control and influence of the parents over the young person) and if appropriate and reasonably possible, a description of his or her relationship with his or her extended family (including information concerning their degree of control and influence over the young person) and
7. the school attendance and performance record of the young person as well as his or her employment record;
- any information to assist the court in determining whether there is an alternative to a custodial sentence;[68] and
- any information from the provincial director (i.e., the delegate for the purposes of the YCJA for a particular Province).

(g) Other Sentencing Recommendations

In addition to considering the contents of a pre-sentence report and/or medical or psychological reports concerning a young

---

[68] As discussed below and as is required by s. 38(2) of the YCJA.

person, a youth court must also consider the following inputs on the question of sentencing:

- any recommendations of a conference (convened under section 41 of the YCJA);
- any recommendations made by the parties to the proceedings (i.e., the prosecution and the young person or his or her counsel/agent; and
- the parents of the young person.[69]

In addition to the foregoing, the youth court has an obligation to consider "...any other relevant information before the Court".[70]

(h) Custodial Sentences

As stated above, great concern was expressed with the number of custodial sentences that resulted from sentencing practices under the YOA. Accordingly, the YCJA states specific guidelines that control when a disposition directs a young person into custody. The YCJA provides that a young person cannot be given a custodial sentence unless:

- the young person has committed a violent offence;
- the young person has failed to comply with non-custodial sentences;
- the young person has committed an indictable offence for which an adult offender could be sentenced to prison for two years or more and the young person has a "pattern of findings of guilt" under either the YCJA or YOA; or
- in exceptional cases, where the young person has committed an indictable offence, and imposing a "non-custodial" sentence would be contrary to the sentencing principles expressed in section 38 of the YCJA (i.e., see the principles

---

[69] YCJA, s. 42(1).
[70] Ibid.

stated under the heading (c) above, "General Principles").[71]

The YCJA specifies that a custodial sentence is not to be used "as a substitute" for "...appropriate child protection, mental health or other social measures." This would appear to suggest that where child protection measures or psychological intervention, on the particular circumstances of the case, are appropriate; those initiatives should be pursued rather than subjecting the young person to the institutional correction of a custodial sentence.

To impose a sentence that commits a young person to custody (in "non-exceptional" cases), at least one of the three regular pre-conditions mentioned above must be present in the case (i.e., committing a violent offence; failing to comply with non-custodial sentences; and committing an offence for which an adult would be subject to two years or more plus a record of findings of guilt under the YCJA or YOA). Further, the court must have considered "all alternatives to custody" that were raised at the sentencing hearing that are "reasonable under the circumstances".[72] In other words, in keeping with the emphasis under the YCJA, on sentencing, the court has an obligation to opt for a non-custodial sentence if such an alternative to custody is "reasonable under the circumstances". However, with respect to first or second degree murder, a custodial sentence (within the options for custody and "community supervision" specified) is mandated by the statute.[73]

---

[71] For a discussion of these factors, see, for example, *R. v. C. (D.L.)* 2003 CanLII 32877 (N.L.P.C.) at paras. 49-75.
[72] YCJA, s. 39(5).
[73] YCJA, ss. 42 (2)(preamble) and 42(2)(q), (r).

(i) Determining a "Reasonable Alternative to Custody"

Subsection 39(3) of the YCJA directs that in answering the question of whether there is a "reasonable alternative" to custody, a youth court must consider:

- the alternatives to custody that are available;
- the likelihood that a young person will comply with a non-custodial sentence, taking into account his or her history in previous non-custodial dispositions; and
- the alternatives to custody that have been used in respect of young persons for "similar offences committed in similar circumstances".

The subsection obliges the court to "consider" the submissions, not necessarily to accept them, although the thrust of the Act and the suggestion of reliance on previous dispositions for "similar offences committed in similar circumstances" would appear to auger against custodial dispositions that depart from previous sentences for the same occurrence. The fact that a young person has been subject, on a previous occasion, to a non-custodial sentence, does not mean that a youth court is precluded from imposing the same or another type of non-custodial sentence on a young person.[74]

(j) Records and Documents for Sentencing

Before sentencing a young person to custody, there are records and documents that require consideration. In the ordinary course, where the prosecutor (i.e., the Crown) suggests that a young person be sentenced to custody, the court must consider a "pre-sentence report" (as described above), unless the consideration of a pre-sentence report is waived by the young person or his/her counsel.[75]

---

[74] YCJA, s. 39(4).
[75] YCJA, s. 39(7).

(k) Length of Custody

While the length of custodial sentences for first and second degree murder is guided by specific directives in the YCJA,[76] in the ordinary course, the length of a custodial sentence is determined by a youth court by reference to the sentencing principles given in section 38 (see heading (c) "General Principles" above) as well as rules on sentence calculation developed with reference to the YCJA, the *Criminal Code* and related statutes.[77] In determining the length of a sentence for violent offences requiring treatment, courts may determine the length in a manner that provides sufficient time to assess the young person and to develop a rehabilitative plan specific to his or her needs.[78] For most offences, the maximum "custody and supervision" order is two years, except offences for which an adult would be liable to life imprisonment (other than murder) for which a young person may receive a maximum three-year sentence. A period of community supervision is imposed that is at least half the length of the custody period.

In terms of the length of sentences by number of offences, the general approach under the YCJA is that a sentence for a single offence is limited to two years while the combined duration of two offences will draw time up to three years.

The offence of murder requires a custody and supervision order under the YCJA. The maximum length of such an order is ten years for first degree murder and seven years for second degree murder, with the period of supervision after custody set by the court according to the circumstances of the particular case.

---

[76] YCJA, 42(2)(q) and (r).
[77] *Supra* note 55 at p. 19.
[78] See *R. v. C. (D.L.)*, *supra* note 71 at para. 77.

(l) Alternatives to Youth Sentencing

Section 42 of the YCJA lists the range of sanctions that may be imposed upon a young person after he or she is found guilty of an offence by a youth court that may be used alone or in combination where "...they are not inconsistent with each other". As stated above, the section does restrict the range of sentencing options for the serious offences of first and second degree murder to the sanctions listed in paragraphs 42(2)(q) and (r) that include custodial components. The following dispositions may also be given by a youth court:

- a reprimand (i.e., a formal denunciation by the court of the young person's behaviour);
- an absolute discharge (i.e., a condition-free disposition in which no further consequences are imposed by a court) in circumstances where such a resolution is in the "...best interests of the young person and not contrary to the public interest";
- a conditional discharge (i.e., a young person is released on his or her own recognizance, subject to complying with certain specified conditions);
- a fine of up to $1,000, with the court having the ability to determine when and how such a fine may be paid. Some portion of the fine may be allocated by individual provinces to compensate victims of crime;[79]
- payment of an amount of compensation to a victim for loss, damage or injury (bearing in mind the young person's ability to pay);
- restitution of property to the person who owned it prior to the offence;
- reimbursement to an innocent purchaser (i.e., the young person may have to compensate or repay money that was received from an innocent third party who purchased stolen property);

---

[79] *Supra* note 57 at p. 14.

YOUTH CRIMINAL JUSTICE ACT ♦ 201

- personal service by a young person to a person suffering loss, damage or injury where the injured person consents to such an arrangement and such work does not interfere with the young person's education or work, and does not exceed 240 hours over 12 months;[80]
- community service (that does not exceed 240 hours of service, which can be completed over 12 months) in an activity that has either been approved by the province's director for the YCJA or consented to by the person or organization for whom the work is to be performed;
- a prohibition, seizure or forfeiture order authorized by federal legislation. (Certain prohibition orders with respect to weapons are mandatory if the young person is convicted of specified violent offences punishable by imprisonment of ten years or more);
- probation for a period of up to two years (in accordance with the provisions concerning probation orders set out in sections 55 and 56 of the YCJA);
- order a young person be placed in an "intensive support and supervision program" (if such facilities and programs exist in the province in which the young person is situated).[81] The idea here is a more vigilant, hands-on version of probation with an emphasis on support and prospective behaviour modification. Again, resource limitations have been an issue with respect to "intensive support and supervision programs;"[82]
- attendance order (a young person attends a non-residential program of a maximum of 240 hours over six months to address his or her individual issues and behaviour, again if such facilities and programs exist or are available where the young person is situated). Again, while novel sentenc-

---
[80] Ibid.
[81] YCJA, s. 42(3).
[82] See, for example, the discussion in R. v. D. (W.A.L.) (1), [2004] 2004 SKPC 40 (Sask. Prov. Ct.) and R. v. C. (K.L.), [2004] 2004 SKPC 98 (Sask. Prov. Ct.) at paras. 32-42.

ing options exist, courts are troubled by the lack of facilities available to implement this remediation even though these sentencing options are on the books;[83]
- a "deferred custody and supervision order" (where an offence is not a "serious violent offence")[84] (and where such is consistent with the sentencing principles and the provisions governing the imposition of custodial sentences) for a specified period of up to six months in which a young person essentially serves her or his sentence in the community following certain specified conditions, the breach of which render the conditions vulnerable to being changed or alternatively, the disposition being converted into a custodial sentence;
- a custody and supervision order. Under the YCJA, all committals to custody include a period of supervision in the community to provide for a period of support and supervision during a young person's reintegration into the community.[85] The community portion, however, can be converted to custody where there are reasonable grounds to believe that the young person will commit an offence causing death or serious bodily harm during the community allotment. During the community portion of a custody and supervision order, mandatory conditions are stipulated in the YCJA[86], namely, the young person must:
  1. keep the peace and be of good behaviour
  2. report to the "provincial director" under the YCJA and be under its supervision
  3. inform the "provincial director" immediately upon being arrested or questioned by the police

---

[83] See *R. v. C. (K.L.)*, *ibid.* at paras. 32-42.
[84] See YCJA, s. 2(1). A "serious, violent offence" is an offence in the commission of which a young person "causes or attempts to cause serious bodily harm."
[85] The particulars of how this regime is to be handled are contained in Part 5 of the YCJA.
[86] YCJA, s. 97(1).

4. advise the provincial director under the YCJA of his or her address of residence and any changes in address, normal occupation, family or financial situation, or anything that may affect the young person's ability to comply with the conditions of her or his sentence and
5. not own, possess or have the control of any weapon, ammunition, "prohibited device" or explosive substance (except with written authorization by the provincial director for the purpose of a specific program);
- intensive rehabilitative custody and supervision order, which is generally directed to the needs of the most violent youth offenders, who meet the following criteria:
  1. the young person has been found guilty of murder, attempted murder, manslaughter, aggravated sexual assault or a third "serious violent offence"
  2. the young person suffers from a mental or psychological disorder
  3. an individualized treatment plan for the young person has been developed or
  4. the provincial director for the YCJA determines that such a program is available and is appropriate for the young person.

ADULT SENTENCING

Under the YCJA, all proceedings take place in youth court. The YCJA has dispensed with the practice, as was the case under the YOA, of transferring more serious matters to adult court. However, under the YCJA, a young person may still be vulnerable to receiving an "adult sentence" (as opposed to a "youth sentence" as discussed below) under certain circumstances.

(a) Imposing an "Adult Sentence"

The threshold for receiving an "adult sentence" under the YCJA has two components as follows:

- the youth must have been found guilty of an offence for which an adult could receive a sentence of 2 years or more;
- the person must have been at least 14 years old at the time of the commission of the offence.

For certain offences, called "presumptive offences", an adult sentence is presumed to be appropriate. These are as follows:

- murder, attempted murder, manslaughter, aggravated sexual assault; and
- where a youth has been found guilty on at least two previous occasions of an offence involving violence and the court has made a determination that the acts involved constituted a "serious violent offence" under the YCJA (an offence that involves causing or attempting to cause serious bodily harm).

All other offences that could yield a sentence of over two years for an adult (and therefore may attract an adult sentence), but are not listed in the YCJA as "presumptive offences" are known as "non-presumptive offences".

The YCJA contains different procedures leading up to a court's consideration of the issue of an adult sentence for each of: the first group of presumptive offences; the second group of presumptive offences; and "non-presumptive" offences.

(b) Adult Sentencing Process

(i) MURDER, ATTEMPTED MURDER, MANSLAUGHTER AND AGGRAVATED SEXUAL ASSAULT

When a young person is charged with any of the above-noted offences, the law presumes that an adult sentence will apply if a youth is found guilty. This does not mean that imposing an adult sentence is automatic: only that a young person, upon being aware of these potential consequences, must take steps to displace this presumption. Accordingly, the court is obligated to advise the young person, at his or her first appearance, that an adult sentence will apply to the offence if he or she is found guilty at trial.[87] After being apprised of this unenviable fact, the young person has the ability, under section 61 of the YCJA, to apply to the youth court (at any time prior to sentencing) for an order that a youth sentence be imposed, instead of an adult sentence.[88] The court then considers this application at the time of sentencing, unless the Crown has decided to forgo an adult sentence. The Crown prosecutor may also elect not to pursue an adult sentence having in mind the particular circumstances of the case.

(ii) "SERIOUS VIOLENT OFFENCE"

As stated above, a second type of situation that leads to the presumption that an adult sentence is appropriate is where a young person has been found guilty on at least two previous occasions of an offence involving violence and the court has made a determination that the acts involved constituted a "serious violent offence" under the YCJA (an offence involving causing, or attempting to cause, serious bodily harm). Unlike the presumptive offences such as murder, etc., in dealing with a "serious violent offence", the prosecution must seek a finding

---

[87] YCJA, s. 32(1)(d).
[88] YCJA, s. 63.

from the court, on notice to the young person[89] that it will be seeking an adult sentence. Upon receiving word of the Crown's intention to seek an adult sentence, the court has an obligation to explain to the young person that an adult sentence will apply on conviction.[90] The young person, in turn, has the ability to make an application to the court to show why a youth sentence should apply under the circumstances. The application or applications concerning the appropriate sentence then proceeds after a finding of guilt.

(c) Adult Sentences for "Non-presumptive Offences"

With respect to all other offences, the prosecution may still seek an adult sentence, and it must give notice of this intention to seek such a disposition (to both the court and the young person[91]) before the young person has entered a plea to the charge (or afterward with leave of the court). The court then must advise the young person of this possibility. If the youth does not oppose the request to seek an adult sentence, then sentencing proceeds on this basis. If the youth opposes the imposition of an adult sentence, a hearing is held after a finding of guilt (or a plea by the young person) to determine the appropriate sentence.

(d) Determining Which Sentence to Impose

On an application to determine whether an adult sentence or a youth sentence is appropriate for a young person, a youth court is guided by many provisions of the YCJA, namely:

- the governing principles of the YCJA stated in section 3;
- the purposes for youth sentences expressed in section 38;

---

[89] YCJA, ss. 64(2) and (4).
[90] YCJA, s. 32(1)(c).
[91] YCJA, s. 64(2).

- the criteria for committing an individual to custody pursuant to a youth sentence under section 39;
- the test for imposing an adult sentence expressed in section 72.

The essential question a youth court must consider in deciding to impose an adult sentence or a youth sentence is whether imposing a youth sentence would be sufficient (particularly in terms of length) to hold a young person accountable for his or her behaviour. The aim of all sentencing regimes under the YCJA is to impose meaningful consequences on a young person for criminal acts, so as to facilitate a young person's rehabilitation and reintegration into society.

(e) Factors to Review in Determining an Adult or Youth Sentence

As stated above, the basic question facing a youth court on an application to decide between an adult sentence and a youth sentence is whether a youth sentence will be sufficient (and sufficiently long) to hold a young person accountable for his or her behaviour. The factors considered by a youth court in making this crucial determination (in addition to the statutory touchstones above) are:

- the age of the young person;
- his or her character and background;
- his or her previous record; and
- any other factors of the case that the court considers relevant.

The onus of proof on an application to seek an adult sentence lies with the prosecution. During this process, the court is to consider any pre-sentence report available concerning the young person and the submissions of the parties and, when available, the submissions of the young person's parents.

(f) Sentencing Length

Generally, with the YCJA taking a philosophical approach that de-emphasizes custody, when an adult sentence is deemed appropriate, the sentence given to a young person is generally shorter than a sentence that might be imposed on an adult for the same offence.

(g) Youth Identification in Adult Sentencing

As stated below, the general ban on publication under the YCJA does not apply where a young person receives an adult sentence. If a young person receives a youth sentence with respect to a presumptive offence, the youth court must inquire as to whether either the Crown or the young person wants a publication ban. In these circumstances, a determination is made as to whether a publication ban is appropriate, having regard to the circumstances of the case and the balancing of the public interest and the goal of rehabilitating the young person?

CUSTODY

The fact that a young person receives an adult sentence does not necessarily mean that in serving this sentence, he or she will be placed among adult offenders. Young persons sentenced as adults may be placed:

- in a youth facility;
- the adult provincial correctional system (for sentences less than two years); or
- the adult federal penitentiary system (for sentences more than two years).

There is a presumption under the YCJA that a youth custody placement is the appropriate assignment for a person who is under the age of 18 at the time of sentencing. This presumption can be rebutted where an adult sentence is given and it is in the best interests of the young person or the interests of others' safety. Similarly, it is presumed that a person who is 18 or over at the time of sentencing should be addressed by adult provincial or federal correctional facilities. The philosophical thrust of this separation is that in most cases, young offenders should be housed separately from adult offenders, whose influence on them may not be congruent with their rehabilitation.[92]

The court also has the ability to split the sentence between different contexts (i.e., part in a youth facility and later transfer to an adult institution), with the presumption that no person is to remain in a youth facility beyond the age of 20.[93]

INFORMATION AND PRIVACY

As outlined above, the general theme of the YCJA is to protect the privacy of young persons who are involved in criminal justice. The goal of the YCJA is to rehabilitate and reintegrate young people who have had involvement with the system of procedures under the YCJA without stigma, such that these individuals may continue with a blemish-free adult life without reference to youthful mistakes. Accordingly, Part 6 of the YCJA establishes a complicated regime entitled "Publication, Records and Information", which:

- classifies YCJA records and reports into categories;
- governs who may retain and have access to such records;
- constructs an access and disclosure guidelines for YCJA records;
- regulates the periods of time in which such records can be accessed;
- provides for the destruction of YCJA records;

---

[92] *Supra* note 55.
[93] *Ibid.*

- sets out consequences for breaches of the privacy provisions; and
- deals with the admissibility of YCJA records into evidence.

A review of the complexity of this regime is beyond the scope of this book. However, it is important to mention that while the general thrust of the YCJA's privacy guidelines favour non-disclosure, this framework under the YCJA recognizes that the youth criminal justice system does not operate in isolation from other systems in which a young person (or individuals whom a young person's conduct has touched) may be involved, such as the school system. As such, there are specific exceptions to the rules in favour of protecting a young person's privacy, For example, subsection 125(6) of the YCJA allows limited disclosure, where necessary, of necessary portions of court records, police records or government records[94] connected to the YCJA to "...any professional or other person engaged in the supervision or care of a young person—including a representative of any school board or school or any other educational or training institution..." where the disclosure is necessary:

- to ensure the young person's compliance with conditions of a court order or conditions of "reintegration leave";
- to ensure the safety of staff, students or other persons; and
- to facilitate the young person's reintegration.

These exceptions to permit disclosure are essentially the same ones as listed in section 38.1(13) of the YCJA. It is crucial to understand that the permission under the subsection to make disclosure to school or other authorities on the basis of the broad categories stated in subsection 125(6) of the YCJA and for the specific purposes enumerated in that statute does not amount to either:

---

[94] YCJA, ss. 114-116.

1. a general authorization to authorities to disclose information to school boards/school representatives (or other listed category of person) based upon a potential future need (i.e., they *may* require information or documents in the future); or
2. a general authorization to the recipients to disseminate or apply the information received for any purpose, outside the purposes listed in the statute.

As stated by the Supreme Court of Canada in the case of *N. (F.), Re*,[95] as was the case with the sharing of information under the YOA, "...communication will have to be more tightly tailored to comply with the non-disclosure provisions of the Act".[96] In that case, the routine disclosure by an advisory body to all local school boards of the weekly youth court dockets was contrary to the YOA. In making its decision, the Supreme Court of Canada slammed both the practice of general distribution of youth court information to school boards on the basis that they might need it, and the use of the information for purposes other than those specifically authorized under the YOA. As the top Court stated at paragraph 35 of the judgment:

> School boards do have a legitimate interest in knowing of members of its student body that could present a danger to themselves or others. The schools may well desire the information for their own purposes. (The letter of the Chief Judge, *supra*, identified one of the objectives as the control of truancy, but this is not a purpose recognized as valid under the statutory scheme.) In my opinion, the school boards have not made a convincing case that their specific interest in the confidential information is related to the administration of justice as opposed to the administration of the schools.
>
> Order and discipline in the schools are a very important consideration but Parliament's restrictions in s. 44.1(1)(k) have to be respected.[97]

---

[95] [2000] 1 S.C.R. 880 (S.C.C.).
[96] *Ibid.* at para. 54.
[97] *Ibid.* at paras. 35 and 36.

In the decision, the Supreme Court did not interfere with a school board's ability to take necessary steps to address genuine safety concerns:

> Once the information is lawfully in the hands of the school, of course, the school may take steps to address its safety concerns (as, of course, it is entitled to do on the basis of any information that raises safety issues). This remedial action may include, where appropriate, an expulsion hearing: *G. (F.) v. Scarborough (City) Board of Education* (1994), 68 O.A.C. 308 (Ont. Div. Ct.); or other restriction seven prior to trial where necessary: *H. (G.) v. Shamrock School Division No. 38*, [1987] 3 W.W.R. 270 (Sask. Q.B.). As stated by Smith Prov. Ct. J. in *G. (R.), Re* (February 10, 1999), Doc. Quesnel 9280 (B.C. Prov. Ct.), at para. 33, albeit he was dealing with an application under s. 38(1.5): "As important as privacy is for youth records under the YOA, there is an overriding importance, in certain circumstances, of allowing disclosure in order to protect other children".[98]

However, in the decision, the Court sharply criticized both the dissemination and application of information beyond the statutory categories:

> ... young persons charged with offences such as shoplifting, which ordinarily would not raise safety concerns at all, should be (but are not now) excluded from the general distribution to school boards linking specific accused with specific offences. The docket as presently distributed identifies all young persons in trouble under the Act, whether or not they are on bail, probation or conditional supervision, whether or not they are a threat to safety of the staff, students or other persons, and whether or not they attend school.[99]

The regime of privacy protection and permitted disclosure of YCJA records under the statute are exceedingly complex, textured by numerous exceptions and complicated by specific permitted disclosure agents authorized to give limited categories or items of information to specific people. As such, it is strongly recommended that proper legal advice be obtained

---

[98] *Ibid.* at para. 55.
[99] *Ibid.* at para. 51.

prior to seeking or using information in relation to a YCJA proceeding.

The foregoing is a very broad outline of the YCJA, an extensive and complicated statute, which contains special regimes and rules applicable to young people and imports the rules of criminal law and procedure from such laws as the *Criminal Code*. The foregoing is offered to give the reader a flavour and overview of the YCJA.

7
Dealing with Children and the Boundaries of Using Force

Children need to be protected from abusive treatment. They are vulnerable members of Canadian society and Parliament and the Executive act admirably when they shield children from psychological and physical harm. In so acting, the government responds to the critical need of all children for a safe environment. Yet this is not the only need of children. Children also depend on parents and teachers for guidance and discipline, to protect them from harm and to promote their healthy development within society. A stable and secure family and school setting is essential to this growth process.

Chief Justice Beverley McLachlin,
Canadian Foundation for Children v. Canada[1]

"Always be nice to your children because they are the ones who will choose your rest home."

Phyllis Diller

As a general matter, children lack the experience, judgment and self-control that are characteristic of most adults. Further, as anyone dealing with children professionally or personally on a regular basis can attest, boundaries of acceptable behaviour set for children by adult caregivers are often tested, breached or even ignored altogether. As a matter of the psychosocial development of children, both individually and in

---

[1] [2004] 1 S.C.R. 76 (S.C.C.) at para. 58.

groups, and sometimes as a matter of their immediate safety and security, adult caregivers are frequently called upon to assert or re-assert the boundaries demarking acceptable and unacceptable behaviour.

While the decision to intervene with respect to a child's behaviour by an adult is often obvious, particularly in the context of immediate physical danger to the child or others, what is less sure is what intervention is appropriate, and to what extent. Is physical force called for? If physical means are used, is it legally acceptable or appropriate under the circumstances, or will the end result of an apparently necessary disciplinary intervention be criminal sanctions to the adult actor? The answer to this question is a difficult one, which content has varied tremendously over different contexts, particularly the effusion of time. Judicial determinations of "reasonable force" in correcting a child have stretched from the early threshold of acts being prohibited where done with ". . .a dangerous weapon, improper for correction. . .and likely to kill or maim"[2] in the early part of the 20th century, all the way to recently questioning the very legitimacy of using any physical force.

SECTION 43 OF CANADA'S *CRIMINAL CODE*

As noted in Chapter 2, child abuse is proscribed behaviour under the child protection statutes of our Provinces in Canada, including Ontario's *Child and Family Services Act*. However, in addition to recognizing the need to protect children from the infliction of abuse, the law also recognizes the necessity of protecting their adult caregivers from criminal jeopardy if physical contact ensues from dealing with a child, so long as the force is applied for correction and is "reasonable under the circumstances". The primary legal recognition of this principle

---

[2] *R. v. Hilton*, as quoted in *R. v. Metcalfe* (1927), 49 C.C.C. 260 (Sask. Dist. Ct.) at para. 26.

stems from section 43 of the *Criminal Code* ("the Code"), which reads as follows:

> 43. Every schoolteacher, parent or person standing in the place of a parent is justified in using force by way of correction toward a pupil or child, as the case may be, who is under his care, if the force does not exceed what is reasonable under the circumstances.

It is important to read this law in the context in which it occurs. The Code, one of the chief legal mechanisms of social control in our society, is not a wholesale permission for adults to use physical force against children but rather a justification that is raised as a defence by an adult who might otherwise be imperiled by criminal jeopardy. Applying physical force in many circumstances amounts to the criminal offence of assault. Section 43 provides a defence to assault where force is used in a particular way and in a particular context. Further, it is a defence only to certain specific people; it in no way constitutes permission to a stranger to a child to randomly strike or abuse a child apart from the context of a *relationship* between the correcting adult and the child receiving the correction. More specifically, section 43 very loosely can be described as conforming to the following basic structures and parameters:

- by whom: any of a teacher, parent, or person standing in the place of a parent;
- to whom: a child under the care of a teacher/parent/person standing in the place of a parent
- what: using force;
- why: by way of correction;
- when: when a child is under his (or her) care; and
- how: force is not beyond what is reasonable under the circumstances

By far the largest point of legal debate since the inception of section 43 has focused on the last of these categories: *How*. How much force will be tolerated by the law and what meaning or content can be given to the nebulous words "reasonable under the circumstances"? What circumstances? As we will see through a review of the section's history, content has been poured through this section like sand through the hourglass; shifting standards in societal norms have imbued the section with substance that at first fixed it as justifying a "spare the rod and spoil the child" level of tolerance (short of ruinous physical injury); moved to a level of scrutiny such that virtually every physical contact could potentially be criminalized; and finally found partial resolution in a 2004 decision of the Supreme Court of Canada that drew some more lasting guidelines for interpreting this long puzzled-over provision of law.

HISTORY OF SECTION 43

A version of the defence currently found in the Code was included in Canada's first *Criminal Code*, which was enacted in 1892. Section 55, as it was numbered at the time, was little different from the current version of the provision. It read:

> 55. It is lawful for every parent, or person in the place of a parent, schoolmaster or master, to use force by way of correction towards any child, pupil or apprentice under his care, provided that such force is reasonable under the circumstances.

Essentially the same components of the current section are present (reasonable force by way of correction applied by parents and teachers), despite the fact they are expressed in the language of the time (e.g., schoolmaster or master). However, the permissiveness of the interpretation following from this early version was somewhat more elastic than generally given to the law in succeeding years.

In *R. v. Robinson*,[3] a principal was charged with assault in connection with his interaction with a 14-year old student of the school. Reacting to the teen's refractory conduct in cracking

---

[3] (1899), 7 C.C.C. 52 (N.S. Co. Ct.).

DEALING WITH CHILDREN & BOUNDARIES OF USING FORCE ♦ 219

the schoolhouse steps, and failing to offer an accompanying admission when confronted, the schoolmaster proceeded to vigorously whip the pupil on his hands with a leather strap. After reviewing the landscape of appropriate English and American authorities on the question of what "reasonable force under the circumstances" denoted, the Court enunciated the following broad guidelines for application of the section:

- the section applied to force applied as "corporal punishment";
- corporal punishment inflicted by a school teacher upon a pupil is presumed to be reasonable and for sufficient cause until the contrary is shown;
- where there is sufficient cause for punishing a pupil and the result is only temporary with no serious injury, it will be presumed to be reasonable; and
- punishment "beyond the child's power of endurance" or that seriously endangers life, limb or health, disfigures the child or causes permanent injury is unreasonable and unlawful.

This general trend of criminalizing only serious and permanent injury to a child was continued in the early 20th century case, *R. v. Gaul*[4] in which a 9-year-old truant was meted out the rather extensive punishment of being strapped on his hands; then progressively receiving a series of lashes on his buttocks, thighs, backs and legs; and then being slapped on the face with a force that caused him to fall to the ground, and, upon righting himself, being slapped to the ground again. The resulting injuries to the put-upon pupil included bleeding and bruising; a mark on the side of his face; sickness and vomiting; headaches; and a limp that lasted several days. Nonetheless, the accused principal was acquitted of any criminal wrongdoing, with the Court dismissing the charges on the basis that the Crown had failed to establish to the requisite standard that

---

[4] (1904), 8 C.C.C. 178 (N.S. C.A.).

the force was "...actuated by malice" or that the acts resulted in "...permanent injury to the child".

Judicial acceptance of an "interventionist" approach with respect to correcting a child by force persisted beyond the early part of the 20th century. In the aforementioned decision of the Saskatchewan District Court in *R. v. Metcalfe*, the following rather extraordinarily permissive remarks are made in respect to the applicable provision of the *Criminal Code*:

> I have consulted many authorities and so far as my reading extends the only case in which the schoolmaster or mistress has been found guilty of an assault is where the act was done with a dangerous weapon, improper for correction, and likely, (the age and strength of the pupil being duly considered) to kill or maim, such as an iron bar, etc., or where the pupil is kicked to the ground or otherwise illtreated, or where the chastisement is flagrantly excessive, or the master has been actuated with malice or illwill towards the pupil...[5]

On a more substantive basis, it was only in the early 1970s, after the current version of the section had been put in place, that the law began to develop an approach to how section 43 should be applied on more than just a situation-specific basis. In the 1970 case of *R. v. Haberstock*,[6] upon reviewing the earlier case law, the Court gave a statement of principles to be applied in section 43 cases, namely:

- what would otherwise be an assault is justified under section 43, provided that the force used is "reasonable and appropriate";
- whether the force used is reasonable or excessive is a question of fact to be determined on the circumstances of each case;
- in determining whether the force used is reasonable under the circumstances, the test is whether, at the time the punishment was administered, it was reasonable.

---

[5] *Supra* note 2.
[6] (1970), 1 C.C.C. (2d) 433 (Sask. C.A.).

DEALING WITH CHILDREN & BOUNDARIES OF USING FORCE ◆ 221

As the 1970s gave way to the 1980s, and following from the attempt at substantive content given to the section in the *Haberstock* decision, some of the discussion about section 43 turned to a review of what or whose standards would be used to judge the reasonableness of any circumstance in which the defence to assault was raised. In the case of *R. v. Baptiste*,[7] the accused raised the defence that the punishment of a 15-year-old with a belt and an extension cord accorded with the standards of tolerance accepted during the accused's childhood in Trinidad. The Court rejected this argument, noting that the community context for judging reasonableness was that of the contemporary Canadian society.

The section eventually reached the Supreme Court of Canada in 1984 in the decision of *R. v. Ogg-Moss*.[8] In that case, the Court clarified that section 43 amounts to a justification of the application of force, where it is applied for the rightful purpose of correcting a child's errant behaviour:

> ...Section 43 is, in other words, a *justification*. It exculpates a parent, schoolteacher or person standing in the place of a parent who uses force in the correction of a child, because it considers such an action not a wrongful, but a *rightful*, one. It follows that, unless the force is "by way of correction", that is, for the benefit of the education of the child, the use of force will not be justified.[9]

Further analytical aid in giving meaning to the section was provided in the roughly contemporaneous ruling by the Saskatchewan Court of Appeal in the case of *R. v. Dupperon*.[10] More than any previous ruling to that date, this case provided an analytical framework for looking at section 43 issues. The Court offered:

---

[7] (1980), 61 C.C.C. (2d) 438 (Ont. Prov. Ct.).
[8] (1984), 14 C.C.C. (3d) 116 (S.C.C.).
[9] *Ibid.* at para. 51.
[10] (1984) 16 C.C.C. (3d) 453 (Sask. C.A.).

...In determining that question [of whether the force used by way of correction was reasonable under the circumstances] the court will consider, from both an objective and a subjective standpoint, such matters as the nature of the offence calling for correction, the age and character of the child and the likely effect of the punishment on this particular child, the degree of gravity of the punishment, the circumstances under which it was inflicted, and the injuries, if any, suffered. If the child suffers injuries which may endanger life, limbs or health or is disfigured, that alone would be sufficient to find that the punishment administered was unreasonable under the circumstances.[11]

The Court added that "...any punishment motivated by arbitrariness, caprice, anger or bad humour may constitute an offence and punishment for correction must never be administered with the intention of physically injuring the child."[12]

Out of these series of cases, and primarily from the guidance in *Dupperon*, a modern test under section 43 emerged. To use section 43:

- the force in question must be applied by a person who fits within the definition of a "...schoolteacher, parent of person standing in the place of a parent";
- the force must be applied to a "pupil" or a "child" under the person's care;
- the force must be applied for the purpose of correction;
- the application of force must *not* be motivated by "...arbitrariness, caprice, anger or bad humour"; and
- the force applied must be "reasonable under the circumstances".

From these decisions, it became clear that "reasonableness" would be assessed in the circumstances of any case by looking at, from both an objective and subjective standpoint:

- the nature of the offence calling for correction;

---

[11] *Ibid.* at 460.
[12] *Ibid.* at 460-61.

- the age and character of the child involved;
- the likely effect of the punishment on the child;
- the degree of gravity of the punishment;
- the circumstances under which the force is applied; and
- the injuries, if any, suffered by the child.

As we will see below, the Supreme Court of Canada in a landmark decision in 2004 specifically directed that the ". . .nature of the offence calling for correction" is not a relevant consideration under section 43, but paid particular attention to age as a factor in applying the section 43 defence.

THE CURRENT APPROACH: THE *CANADIAN FOUNDATION CHARTER* CHALLENGE

The Canadian approach to section 43 has recently been criticized by a ruling made by the Supreme Court of Canada in 2004 in the case of *Canadian Foundation for Children, Youth & the Law v. Canada (Attorney General)*.[13] In 1999, the Applicant ("the Foundation"), a non-profit advocacy group on behalf of children and youth, sought a declaration that section 43 of the Code:
- violated section 7 of the *Canadian Charter of Rights and Freedoms* ("the *Charter*") (right to safety and security of the person) because it fails to give procedural protection to children; does not further the "best interests of the child;" and is both overbroad and vague;
- violated section 12 of the *Charter* (right to be free from cruel and unusual punishment) because it constitutes cruel and unusual punishment; and
- violated section 15 of the *Charter* (equality before the law), because it denies children the legal protection against assaults that is accorded to adults.

---

[13] [2004] 1 S.C.R. 76 (S.C.C.) [hereinafter "Section 43 Challenge"].

The Foundation's challenge to section 43 was rejected both at first instance in the Ontario Superior Court and later on appeal to the Ontario Court of Appeal. The matter finally made its way to the Supreme Court of Canada in June 2003, which resulted in a decision by the Court that was released in late January 2004.

The Court rejected the Foundation's argument that the rights of children under section 7 of the *Charter* were violated by section 43. On the issue of whether section 43 denies procedural rights to children as a matter of fundamental justice (or basic civil rights), the Court concluded that section 43 provided adequate protection to a child's procedural rights:

> . . .s. 43 provides adequate procedural safeguards to protect [the procedural rights of children]. The child's interests are represented at trial by the Crown. The Crown's decision to prosecute and its conduct of the prosecution will necessarily reflect society's concern for the physical and mental security of the child. There is no reason to suppose that, as in other offences involving children as victims or witnesses, the Crown will not discharge that duty properly. Nor is there any reason to conclude on the arguments before us that providing separate representation for the child is either necessary or useful. I conclude that no failure of procedural safeguards has been established.[14]

Next, the majority of the Court rejected the argument that in failing to serve the legal principle of "the best interests of the child" it was in violation of the guarantee under section 7 of the *Charter* to safeguard the principles of fundamental justice. The Court made clear that while the "best interests of the child" is an important tenet of the law, ". . .this legal principle is not a principle of fundamental justice".[15] The Court pointed out that the legal standard of "best interests of the child" is not vital or fundamental to the societal norm of justice and hence is not a principle of fundamental justice.[16] In so doing, the top

---

[14] *Ibid.* at para. 6.
[15] *Ibid.* at para 7.
[16] *Ibid.* at para 10.

Court ruled that while this aspect of the law was important in many contexts, its weight would not govern every situation, including in some criminal law situations:

> It follows that the legal principle of the "best interests of the child" may be subordinated to other concerns in appropriate contexts. For example, a person convicted of a crime may be sentenced to prison even where it may not be in his or her child's best interests. Society does not always deem it essential that the "best interests of the child" trump all other concerns in the administration of justice....[17]

The Supreme Court also turned back the argument by the Foundation that section 43, with its nebulous idea of reasonable force under the circumstances, was unconstitutionally vague. In this section, the Supreme Court surveyed the indicators of what the term "reasonable force" means in the context of Canadian law, noting that section 43:

- is limited to the "mildest forms of assault" where there is neither harm nor the prospect of bodily harm;
- does not apply to force that either harms or degrades a child and is therefore unreasonable;
- should not focus on the gravity of the child's wrongdoing (as urged in *R. v. Dupperon*[18]), but rather whether the force was applied by way of correction);
- should not be interpreted on the basis of what individual judges or caregivers think is subjectively reasonable, but rather on "...an objective appraisal based upon learning and consensus";
- should not provide a defence to teachers who employ "corporal punishment" instead of "corrective force to remove children from classrooms or secure compliance with instructions"; and
- should admit an approach that concedes an "evolutive" approach to the standards of reasonableness that takes ac-

---

[17] *Ibid.* at para. 10.
[18] (1984), 16 C.C.C. (3d) 453 (Sask. C.A.).

count of the information reflected in previous decisions as well as the research and expert evidence that might be disclosed in some cases.

In dealing with the vagueness argument, the Supreme Court pointed out that standards of reasonableness evolve over time. In surveying current standards to determine whether there was sufficient content in the section to withstand the legal attack of being unconstitutionally vague, the Court pronounced what behaviour is currently found to be acceptable, and what behaviour is unacceptable, under section 43. The Court ruled:

- section 43 does *not* apply to children under 2 years of age or to teenagers;
- "degrading, inhuman or harmful conduct" is not protected by section 43;
- "discipline by the use of objects or blows or slaps to the head is unreasonable";
- teachers may apply force to remove a child from a classroom or to secure compliance with instructions, but not merely as corporal punishment;
- conduct must be corrective; section 43 "...rules out conduct stemming from caregiver's frustration, loss of temper or abusive personality";
- the gravity of the event that precipitates the use of force is not a relevant consideration under section 43; and
- the test under section 43 is objective, *not* subjective and is to be considered "...in context and in light of all the circumstances of the case".[19]

After giving specific guidance on the standards of reasonable behaviour toward children under section 43, the majority of the Court then rejected the Applicant's argument that section 43 was overbroad in that it potentially includes children who

---

[19] *Supra* note 13 at para. 40.

cannot benefit from correction; i.e., children under the age of 2 as well as teenagers. The Court ruled that in enacting section 43 with a stipulation that only "reasonable" force is acceptable, government had adequately addressed the potential over breadth: unreasonable behaviour such as striking a child under 2 or using corporal punishment on teenagers is widely recognized as unreasonable and outside the breadth of the enactment. Therefore, section 43 is not overbroad.

The Applicant advanced that section 43 exposed children to "cruel and unusual treatment or punishment" in violation of section 12 of the *Charter*. The Court quickly declined that argument, pointing out first that parents are not state actors so as to be covered by the provisions of the *Charter*. While the Court allowed that "teachers" may be emanations of the state for the purposes of the *Charter*, it quickly dispensed with this question, averring that none of the conduct permitted pursuant to section 43 was "cruel and unusual" or ". . .excessive so as to outrage the standards of decency".

The Court then faced the pressing question of whether section 43 transgressed section 15 of the *Charter*, which guarantees equality before the law. The Applicant was advancing that the behaviour permitted under section 43, if applied towards adults, would be assuredly criminal. Therefore, the argument advanced that the existence of section 43 permits unequal treatment at law on the grounds of age and contains an implicit message that children are ". . .less capable, or less worthy of recognition or value as a human being or as a member of Canadian society". The fault in this argument, the Court identified, is that it draws an equivalency between *equal* treatment before the law and *identical* treatment. The Court's reasoning was that the decision not to criminalize minor interventions with children was in fact "age-appropriate" as a legal response bearing in mind the child's context in the family and at school:

...In fact, declining to bring the blunt hand of the criminal law down on minor disciplinary contacts of the nature described in the previous section reflects the resultant impact this would have on the interests of the child and on family and school relationships. Parliament's choice not to criminalize this conduct does not devalue or discriminate against children, but responds to the reality of their lives by addressing their need for safety and security in an age-appropriate manner.[20]

In scrutinizing section 43 in the context of section 15 of the *Charter*, the Court reviewed previous decisions that found that a law that "....properly accommodates the claimant's needs, capacities, and circumstances" does not generally offend section 15 of the *Charter*. The Court acknowledged that one of the needs of children is to be protected from abuse, but also recognized the simultaneous requirements of guidance and discipline provided in a safe environment. At paragraph 59 of the judgment, the Court explained the balance between these concurrent requirements as addressed in section 43 of the Code:

> Section 43 is Parliament's attempt to accommodate both of these needs. It provides parents and teachers with the ability to carry out the reasonable education of the child without the threat of sanction by the criminal law. The criminal law will decisively condemn and punish force that harms children, is part of a pattern of abuse, or is simply the angry or frustrated imposition of violence against children; in this way, by decriminalizing only minimal force of transient or trivial impact, s. 43 is sensitive to children's need for a safe environment. But s. 43 also ensures the criminal law will not be used where the force is part of a genuine effort to educate the child, poses no reasonable risk of harm that is more than transitory and trifling, and is reasonable under the circumstances. Introducing the criminal law into children's families and educational environments in such circumstances would harm children more than help them. So Parliament has decided not to do so, preferring the approach of educating parents against physical discipline.

In light of the potentially ruinous consequences that may be imposed by the "blunt instrument"[21] of the criminal law in

---

[20] *Ibid.* at para. 51.
[21] *Ibid.* at para. 60.

contexts of non-abusive contact, the Court concluded that section 43 was not an endorsement of using force against children, but an exemption from criminal consequences for reasonable intervention by way of correction.

Citing the practical approach of section 43 in proscribing abusive conduct but excepting reasonable force by way of correction as "...firmly grounded in the actual needs and circumstances of children...", the Court concluded that section 43 does not offend section 15 of the *Charter*. The Court concluded on the question by stating plainly that section 43 prevents the broad definition of "assault" under the *Criminal Code* from reaching interventions with children that fall far short of "corporal punishment". As stated as paragraph 62:

> The reality is that without s. 43, Canada's broad assault law would criminalize force falling far short of what we think of as corporal punishment, like placing an unwilling child in a chair for a five-minute "time-out". The decision not to criminalize such conduct is not grounded in devaluation of the child, but in a concern that to do so risks ruining lives and breaking up families—a burden that in large part would be borne by children and outweigh any benefit derived from applying the criminal process.

In so finding, the Court recognized that the criminal law—with its potentially dire consequences for the family unit, the education setting and therefore the child—may have a far greater and deleterious impact on the child (in removing the offending adult) than the perhaps transitory conduct permitted by section 43.

The Court then responded to the argument that even if the "big picture" effect of section 43 is "salutary", permitting harm to individual children in service of a systemic societal goal is intolerable as a matter of law. The Court reinforced that harmful or abusive conduct toward children is not justified under section 43. Further, the Court stated, the *Charter* does not demand perfect conformance to all individuals to remain valid.

In the final analysis, the majority of the Supreme Court in the case upheld the defence under section 43 of the *Criminal Code* and found that it did not violate sections 7, 12 or 15 of the *Charter*.

PERMISSIBLE "CORRECTION" AFTER THE SECTION 43 CHALLENGE

The Supreme Court of Canada in the Section 43 Challenge provided some basic ground rules applicable to the defence under that provision of the *Criminal Code*. The basic grounds rules under section 43 are:

- the force used must be applied for purposes of correction;
- the child must be capable of benefiting by the correction (children under 2 and disabled children would not be capable);
- the force used must be *reasonable* under the circumstances;
- "reasonableness" is to be assessed *objectively* having regard to the all the circumstances of the case; and
- the *gravity* of the precipitating event is *not* relevant to assessing whether the force is reasonable under the circumstances.

It is also now clear that section 43 does *not* permit:

- corporal punishment of children under 2 (because of the lack of corrective value);
- corporal punishment of teenagers (because it may induce aggressive or anti-social behaviour);
- corporal punishment using objects (e.g., belts or rulers) because it is physically and emotionally harmful;
- corporal punishment by mean of slaps or blows to the head because it is harmful;
- punishment that is abusive or part of a pattern of abuse; or
- behaviour that is ". . .simply the angry or frustrated imposition of violence against children".

The decision in the Section 43 Challenge also draws a distinction between permissible behaviour by parents (or those in place of a parent) and teachers. It makes clear that teachers can use corrective force to remove children from classrooms or secure compliance with instructions. However, teachers may *not* use corporal punishment to correct students. By contrast, parents may still use corporal punishment for the purposes permitted by the section; in the other words, force that is reasonable under the circumstances.

The Section 43 Challenge ruling does not clarify a difficult aspect of many of these cases: how to distinguish between the "angry or frustrated imposition of violence against children" and corrective force that is reasonable under the circumstances, which is accompanied by anger and frustration by the intervening actor. Indeed, it is a feature of many decisions predating the Section 43 Challenge that virtually any significant evidence of anger and/or frustration accompanying the corrective action was held to be enough to deny the accused the benefit of a section 43 defence. However, since the decision in the Section 43 Challenge, at least some courts appear to recognizing that reasonable corrective force may be applied that is protected under section 43 in circumstances where the precipitating event angers or outrages the parent.[22]

In a strange way, the decision in the Section 43 Challenge may have made the law in the area more unstable. In specifically disagreeing with the Court in *R. v. Dupperon* (long the leading case under section 43) that the "nature of the offence calling for correction" was a relevant consideration, the Court has weakened the precedent value of one of the few cases in this subject area providing some specific guidance on the analytical

---

[22] See, for example, *R. v. Boyd*, [2004] 2004 ABPC 125 (Alta. Prov. Ct.), in which a parent was permitted a defence under s. 43 after spanking his 8-year-old child who had told him to "shut up" as well as threatening him with a lawsuit.

framework to be used in these situations. While the Section 43 Challenge decision is very specific on what behaviour is and is not permitted in disciplining children under the provision, the guidance it provides for the analytical framework in such cases is somewhat wanting. Specifically eschewing an approach in which the Court assesses the reasonableness of the intervention from the subjective perspective of the trier of fact (because this approach sends a "muddled message as to what is and is not permitted"[23]), the new approach to be taken to the question of reasonable force is "...an objective appraisal based on current learning and consensus". [24]

> Determining what is "reasonable under the circumstances" in the case of child discipline is also assisted by social consensus and expert evidence on what constitutes reasonable corrective discipline. The criminal law often uses the concept of reasonableness to accommodate evolving mores and avoid successive "fine-tuning" amendments. It is implicit in this technique that current social consensus on what is reasonable may be considered. It is wrong for caregivers or judges to apply their own subjective notions of what is reasonable; s. 43 demands an objective appraisal based on current learning and consensus. Substantial consensus, particularly when supported by expert evidence, can provide guidance and reduce the danger of arbitrary, subjective decision making.[25]

Essentially, the decision in the Section 43 Challenge posits the resolution of issues as a battle of experts (or expert material) in which each side ostensibly provides support by reference to universal standards of tolerated behaviour, such as that provided by statute(s), human rights conventions (e.g., Human Rights Committee of the United Nations), and scholarly work.

The logic of the Section 43 Challenge turns upon the existence of actual consensus as to acceptable behaviour toward children. While the top Court admitted that these will evolve, the

---

[23] *Supra* note 13 at para. 39.
[24] *Ibid.* at para. 36.
[25] *Ibid.*

decision seems to have abrogated the analytical framework from *Dupperon* in favour of a list of specific proscribed behaviours and the hope that the facts of future cases will be amenable to resolution with reference to clear notions of permitted behaviour. As of this writing, the evolution of the law in this area remains to be seen.

8

CHILDREN AT SCHOOL

"The object of education is to prepare the young to educate themselves throughout their lives."
Robert Maynard Hutchins

If you are planning for a year, sow rice; if you are planning for a decade, plant trees; if you are planning for a lifetime, educate people.
Chinese proverb

One of the most prominent (and time-intensive) aspects of a child's life outside his or her home is attending a school or an educational institution. It is obvious that a central part of a child's life at school involves receiving instruction in accordance with considered curriculum content that is delivered in an organized and systematic fashion. However, the law recognizes that the time a child spends at school is not simply an exercise in pedagogy, but also a cornerstone of both personal enlightenment and societal development. As stated by the Supreme Court of Canada:

> A school is a communication centre for a whole range of values and aspirations of a society. In large part, it defines the values that transcend society through the educational medium. The school is an arena for the exchange of ideas and must, therefore, be premised upon principles of tolerance and impartiality so that all persons within the school environment feel equally free to participate....[1]

---

[1] *Ross v. New Brunswick School District No. 15*, [1996] 1 S.C.R. 825 (S.C.C.) at para. 42.

In the same decision, the Supreme Court of Canada adopted the classic statement of the school's role in society made by the United States Supreme Court in the groundbreaking civil rights' case of *Brown v. Board of Education of Topeka*:

> Today, education is perhaps the most important function of state and local governments. . . . It is the very foundation of good citizenship. Today it is a principal instrument in awakening the child to cultural values, in preparing him [or her] for later professional training, and in helping him [or her] to adjust normally to his environment.[2]

Essentially, the law views the schools as the forum by which a society will shape its future through the impact on its children. Given the fact that a large percentage of a child's time is spent in school and the pivotal place education plays in social engineering, this chapter will examine some aspects of a child's life at school. Please note, however, that this chapter is an overview only. Given the complexity of the topic, and the governing laws that vary from province to province, it is difficult to definitively set out the law governing education. Nonetheless, the following material should function as a guide to some of the general matters of concern that are common to many jurisdictions on the topic.

LAWS GOVERNING SCHOOLS

Under the Canadian Constitution, education falls within the legislative domain of the individual provinces of Canada to regulate.[3] At the same time, the Constitution of Canada also protects the fundamental rights of the Roman Catholics in Ontario (the only Province to have denominational rights conferred by law at the time of Canadian Confederation) and to a

---

[2] 347 U.S. 483, U.S. 1954 at para. 2.
[3] *Constitution Act, 1867*, s. 93.

lesser degree those in Manitoba, Saskatchewan and Alberta.[4] Section 23 of the *Constitution Act, 1982* also specifically provides protection to minority language education rights.

In most provinces and territories, the legal framework for public education lies in one or more statutes governing school matters, commonly by means of creating or continuing school boards or school districts that operate schools and provide educational services. Regulations are also frequently important implementers of the general skeleton of the legal system for education.[5]

While education statutes and regulations provide much of the specifics and substance of the law governing education in each province and territory, the law made through the decisions of judges (or other official decision-makers)—referred to as the common law—also have a role to play in the law governing schools. A simple example of applying the common law to a statutory context in education is where a student is injured. In such cases, many education statutes provide for specific statutory duties on boards and educators to take steps to secure the safety of students. However, determining whether liability will be imposed for a student injury in a particular case often rests on consideration of the decisions of previous cases and the standards of expected conduct developed through those rulings.

---

[4] *Constitution Act, 1867*, s. 93(1). For a discussion of the complicated way in which s. 93(1) applies to the various provinces, see the Supreme Court of Canada's discussion of the issue in *Ontario English Catholic Teachers' Assn. v. Ontario (Attorney General)*, [2001] 1 S.C.R. 470 (S.C.C.) beginning at para. 4.

[5] For example, O. Reg. 298, *Operation of Schools–General*, contains many diverse and important provisions mandating how a school is to be operated, including the parameters of the school day, the duties of teachers and principals, etc.

CHARTER APPLICATION TO SCHOOLS

The *Charter* applies only to government or bodies and organizations that are part, or are found to be part, of government. The Supreme Court of Canada has held that ". . .schools constitute part of government".[6] Therefore, the *Charter* applies to schools and school boards/districts or authorities.

Over the years, the *Charter* has been invoked with respect to many diverse aspects of the educational experience, including:

- the rights of school boards to financial management and control over funding;[7]
- the question of funding private religious schools;[8]
- separate school funding in Ontario;[9]
- languages of instruction;[10]
- the nature of the relationship between teacher and student for the purposes of certain criminal offences;[11]
- selection of books for use in classrooms;[12]
- school announcements;[13]
- special education/pupil placement;[14]

---

[6] *R. v. M. (M.R.)*, [1998] 3 S.C.R. 393 (S.C.C.) at para. 25.
[7] See, for example, *Ontario English Catholic Teachers' Assn. v. Ontario (Attorney General)*, *supra* note 4.
[8] See, for example, *Adler v. Ontario*, [1996] 3 S.C.R. 609 (S.C.C.).
[9] See, for example, *Reference re Bill 30, an Act to amend the Education Act* , [1987] 1 S.C.R. 1148 (S.C.C.).
[10] See, for example, *Quebec Assn. of Protestant School Boards v. Quebec (Attorney General) (No. 2)*, [1984] 2 S.C.R. 66 (S.C.C.); *Gosselin c. Québec (Procureur général)*, 2005 SCC 15 (S.C.C.); and *Solski c. Québec (Procureure générale)*, 2005 SCC 14 (S.C.C.).
[11] See, for example, *R. c. Audet*, [1996] 2 S.C.R 171 (S.C.C.).
[12] See, for example, *Chamberlain v. Surrey School District No. 36*, [2002] 4 S.C.R. 710 (S.C.C.).
[13] See, for example, *Zylberberg v. Sudbury (Board of Education)* (1988), 65 O.R. (2d) 641 (Ont. C.A.).
[14] See, for example, *Eaton v. Board of Education of Brant County*, [1997] 1 S.C.R. 241 (S.C.C.).

CHILDREN AT SCHOOL ♦ 239

- the funding of educational services for autistic students;[15]
- search and seizure involving students in schools;[16]
- promotion of hatred during instruction;[17]
- the right of students to be educated in an environment that is not "poisoned" by the out-of-school discriminatory statements of a teacher[18]; and
- the right of school officials to procedural fairness in the process of termination/dismissal.[19]

Despite the application of the *Charter* to schools and the numerous examples of situations in which the *Charter* has been applied in school-related litigation, it is also important to recognize the fact that some degree of discretion is accorded by the law to educators to make reasonable decisions in their particular school contexts or while supervising students outside of school. The Supreme Court made the following statement in the context of a search and seizure case involving students:

> School authorities must be accorded a reasonable degree of discretion and flexibility to enable them to ensure the safety of their students and to enforce school regulations. Ordinarily, school authorities will be in the best position to evaluate the information they receive. As a result of their training, background and experience, they will be in the best possible position to assess both the propensity and credibility of their students and to relate the information they receive to the situation existing in their particular school. For these reasons, courts should recognize the preferred position of school authorities to determine whether reasonable grounds existed for the search.[20]

---

[15] See, for example, *Auton v. British Columbia (Minister of Health)*, [2004] 3 S.C.R. 657 (S.C.C.).
[16] See, for example, *R. v. M. (M.R.)*, *supra* note 6.
[17] See, for example, *R. v. Keegstra* [1990] 3 S.C.R. 697 (S.C.C.).
[18] See, for example, *Ross v. New Brunswick School District No. 15*, *supra* note 1.
[19] See, for example, *Knight v. Indian Head School Division No. 19*, [1990] 1 S.C.R. 653 (S.C.C.).
[20] See *R. v. M. (M .R.)*, *supra* note 6 at para. 49.

Obviously, this lenience will not necessarily be accorded to every decision made by a teacher or school authority in every context, particularly where the action taken subverts the interest of pupils to the individual's self-interest.[21] However, there appears to be some basic recognition in the law (including the decisions under the *Charter*) that individuals who make decisions for *bona fide* reasons, absent some compelling legal reasons otherwise, should not be second-guessed by the courts or other decision-makers.

HUMAN RIGHTS LEGISLATION APPLICATION TO SCHOOLS

While the application of the *Charter* is limited to government and emanations of government, the reach of human rights legislation extends both to public institutions and to private actors. School boards are therefore bound by the requirements of human rights legislation, which proscribes discrimination and harassment on the prohibited grounds listed in such statutes.[22] While human rights legislation does not have "constitutional" recognition (as does the *Charter*, which is part of the *Constitution Act, 1982*), it does have a special position as a matter of law, and is to be interpreted in a flexible manner in recognition of its distinct, quasi-constitutional status.[23] At its most basic, the law expects institutions to which human rights legislation applies (such as school boards or school divisions) to: (a) have a general awareness of the provisions of the gov-

---

[21] An obvious example is the sexual exploitation of pupils: see, for example, the discussion in *R. c. Audet, supra* note 11.

[22] For a general discussion of human rights in the school context and particularly in the Province of Manitoba, see, for example, *Human Rights in the School* by the Manitoba Human Rights Commission found at http://www.gov.mb.ca/hrc/english/publications/school/chap1.html.

[23] In this regard, see *Ontario Human Rights Commission v. Simpsons-Sears Ltd.*, [1985] 2 S.C.R. 536 at para. 12.

CHILDREN AT SCHOOL ♦ 241

erning human rights legislation; and (b) to have some mechanism in place by which complaints can be made.

It is also important to recognize in Ontario that special recognition is given to the rights of separate schools in the Province in section 19 of the Ontario *Human Rights Code*, which reads that the statute is not to be interpreted so as to ". . .adversely affect any right or privilege respecting separate schools. . ." under the Constitution or the Ontario *Education Act*. Separate school boards in Ontario may therefore consider denominational matters in their employment practices, including with respect to hiring[24] and dismissal.[25]

As at this writing, two very prominent topics in the intersection of human rights and education law are accommodating students with disabilities, including students with autism spectrum disorder (which has been the subject of numerous recent human rights complaints against school boards in Ontario)[26] and the obligation of school authorities to take steps to address bullying.[27]

---

[24] See, for example, *Morra v. Metropolitan (Separate School Board)* (1981), 3 C.H.R.R. D/1034 (Ont. Bd. of Inquiry).

[25] See, for example, *Essex (County) Roman Catholic Separate School Board v. Porter* (1978), 21 O.R. (2d) 255 (Ont. C.A.) and *Essex (County) Roman Catholic Separate School Board v. Tremblay-Webster* (1983), 142 D.L.R. (3d) 479 (Ont. Div. Ct.), affirmed (1984), 5 D.L.R. (4th) 665 (Ont. C.A.).

[26] On this topic generally, see the *Guidelines on Accessible Education* released by the Ontario Human Rights Commission in September 2004, which may be accessed on its website at www.ohrc.ca. See also the decision of the Supreme Court of Canada in *Auton v. British Columbia (Minister of Health)*, *supra* note 15. However, in this regard, see also the recent decision of Justice Frances Kiteley in *Wynberg v. Ontario* (2005), 2005 CarswellOnt 1242 (Ont. S.C.J.).

[27] See, for example, *North Vancouver School District No. 44 v. Jubran*, [2003] 3 W.W.R. 288 (B.C. S.C.), reversed (2005) 39 B.C.L.R. (4th) 153 (B.C. C.A.). See discussion of the *Jubran* case at pages 279 to 281.

MANDATORY SCHOOL ATTENDANCE

Simply stated, children do have to attend school. The reason is that the provinces and territories (which have constitutional jurisdiction over education) have enacted compulsory school laws that mandate school attendance for children between certain ages.[28] While some statutes contain limited exceptions to the rules of mandatory public school attendance[29] (some of which apply on an ongoing basis, e.g., a private school, or on a temporary or event basis, e.g., a religious holiday), the general rule is that children of the prescribed age who are not excused pursuant to an exception in the governing statute have an obligation to attend school.

A CHILD'S RIGHT TO ATTEND SCHOOL

Most education statutes in Canada confer a basic right to children of a certain age to attend a publicly funded school in one's area of residence.[30] However, beyond this basic statement of right, the rules concerning the practical application of the right

---

[28] See, for example, the Ontario *Education Act*, R.S.O. 1990, c. E.2, s. 21(1), which requires that children attend school between the ages of 6 and 16.

[29] See, for example, the Ontario *Education Act*, s. 21(2), which allows a child to be excused including where "(a) the child is receiving satisfactory instruction at home or elsewhere" or "(b) the child is unable to attend school by reason of sickness or other unavoidable cause. . .."

[30] See, for example, Alberta's *School Act*, R.S.A. 2000, c. S-3, s. 8; British Columbia's *School Act*, R.S.B.C. 1996, c. 411, s. 3; Manitoba's *Public Schools Act*, R.S.M. 1987, c. P250, s. 259(1); New Brunswick's *Education Act*, S.N.B. 1997, c. E-12, s. 8; Newfoundland & Labrador's *Schools Act*, S.N.L. 1997, c. S-12.2, s. 3; Northwest Territories' *Education Act*, S.N.W.T. 1995, ss. 5 and 28; Nova Scotia's *Education Act*, R.S.N.S. 1995-96, c. 1, s. 5(2); Prince Edward Island's *School Act*, R.S.P.E.I. 1988, c. S-21, s. 68; Quebec's *Education Act*, R.S.Q. I-13.3, s. 1; Saskatchewan's *Education Act*, S.S. 1995, c. E-0.2 s. 142; and Yukon's *Education Act*, R.S.Y. 2002, s. 10.

to attend schools can become very complicated indeed.[31] As a very general statement (subject, of course, to the particular rules applicable in one's province), most attendance rights turn fundamentally on:

- whether the student has attained school age;
- whether the student is resident within a jurisdiction;
- whether the student is enrolled in a school operated by a local school board; and
- the "school support" (i.e., the payment of school levies) of that person's parent or guardian.

A fine general summary of the school attendance scheme in Ontario was provided by Perkins J. in a recent case decision:[32]

> To try to boil down a fairly complex statutory scheme to its essential elements, I think the scheme can be summarized as follows:
>
> 1. Resident pupils do not have to pay fees to go to school (section 32 (1)).
> 2. A pupil is a resident pupil if both the pupil and the pupil's parent or "guardian" reside in the geographical area of the school section (section 33 (1)).
> 3. A "guardian" for this purpose is a person (other than a parent) who has lawful custody of the pupil (section 1 (1)).
> 4. Pupils must attend school, whether they qualify as resident pupils or not section 21 (1)).
> 5. A parent or "guardian" of a pupil must see to it that the pupil attends school, on penalty of an offence punishable by a $200 fine (section 30 (1)).
> 6. A "guardian" for the purpose of liability for this offence is a person (other than a parent) who has
>   (a) lawful custody of the pupil (section 1 (1));
>   (b) received into his or her home a pupil who resides with the person or is in his or her care (section 18).

---

[31] For a thorough, step-by-step discussion of the seemingly Byzantine rules with respect to school attendance rights in Ontario, see Anthony F. Brown, *Legal Handbook for Educators*, 5th ed. (Toronto: Carswell, 2004) at chapter 2.

[32] *Chou v. Chou*, [2005] O.J. No. 1374 (Ont. S.C.J.) at paras. 48 and 49.

Under this attendance scheme Canadian citizenship, by birth or naturalization, and landed immigrant status are irrelevant. The only thing that matters is residence of the pupil and the parent or guardian in the school section on the relevant date. Note that the pupil and the parent or guardian do not have to reside together in order for the pupil to qualify as resident—they both have to live in the same school section, but could be in separate residences.

The right to attend a publicly funded school is frequently confused with a pupil's right to attend the school of his or her choice within a particular area. Generally, the law offers the former but does not extend any right to the latter. The statutory right to attend a school does not translate to the right to choose a particular school.[33]

ENFORCING ATTENDANCE

Most provinces have some mechanisms to enforce school attendance, often by means of statutory empowerment to an "attendance officer"[34] or "attendance counselor"[35] to intervene where an unexcused child does not attend school. In some jurisdictions, the parents/guardians of a non-attending pupil may also be subject to prosecution for offences contained in the applicable education statutes.[36] Proceedings may also be initiated against parents who cause their children to attend a

---

[33] In this respect, see for example *Robertson v. Niagara South Board of Education* (1973), 1 O.R. (2d) 548 (Ont. Div. Ct.); *Hatch v. London (City) Board of Education* (1979), 25 O.R. (2d) 481 (Ont. H.C.); *D. v. North York (City) Board of Education* (1980), 13 M.P.L.R. 1 (Ont. H.C.).
[34] See, for example, Alberta's *School Act*, R.S.A. 2000, c. S-3, ss. 14-16.
[35] See, for example, Ontario's *Education Act*, R.S.O. 1990, c. E-2, s. 24.
[36] See, for example, Ontario's *Education Act*, R.S.O. 1990, c. E-2, s. 30. See also the case law under this provision, including *Lambton (County) Board of Education v. Beauchamp* (1979), 10 R.F.L. (2d) 354 (Ont. Prov. Ct.) and *R. v. Prentice* (1983), 14 W.C.B. 39 (Ont. Fam. Ct.).

school that is not deemed to be suitable for education by the intervening authorities.[37]

ENTITIES PROVIDING PUBLIC EDUCATION SERVICES

In addition to creating a substantive right of a student to attend school, education statutes also provide explicitly for a means by which the education program is to be delivered: the vehicle of the school board or school district.[38] Often, school boards are accorded the status of statutory corporations.[39] It is common for education statutes to create a list of fundamental duties for educational institutions, including basic matters of corporate infrastructure such as the duty to:

- appoint officers to run the board (including a secretary and a treasurer);
- authorize the appointed treasurer to pay bills on the board's behalf;
- fix times for board meetings and hold them accordingly;
- establish and operate out of a head office;
- provide instruction and "adequate accommodation" for

---

[37] See, for example, *R. v. Kotelmach* (1989), 76 Sask. R. 116 (Sask. Q.B.) and *R. v. Jones*, [1986] 2 S.C.R. 284 (S.C.C.), in which a pastor of a fundamentalist church schooled his children in a program run in his church's basement. No exemption from the ordinary attendance rules was sought under Alberta's *School Act* (although a request could have been made for a provincial inspector to approve the program under the applicable legislation). Charges under the statute were defended by means of a challenge to the charging provision on the grounds of freedom of religion under s. 2(a) of the *Charter*. On appeal, the Supreme Court of Canada found that the "interference" in a person's religious freedom did not offend ss. 2(a) and 7 of the *Charter*, particularly as the section built-in the opportunity to parents to have their church-based instruction certified as "sufficient" by a provincial inspector.

[38] See, for example, s. 58.1(2) of the Ontario *Education Act*.

[39] See, for example, s. 58.1(5) of the Ontario *Education Act*.

students who have a right to attend schools in the jurisdiction of the board;
- operate kindergartens;
- provide special education services (in accordance with statute or regulations);
- repair property;
- make provision for adequate insurance for the property, buildings and equipment of the board;
- operate schools in accordance with the governing education statutes and regulations;
- keep schools open during the whole period of the school year in accordance with regulations; and
- appoint an adequate number of principals and teachers to operate the schools.[40]

While an oversimplification, the basic statutory duties of a school board in Ontario amount to:

- an obligation to develop a corporate infrastructure (i.e., human and real property resources, including a head office) through which to operate;
- hiring an adequate number of people (including supervisory officers,[41] principals and teachers) to the number of schools to provide "adequate accommodation";
- operating schools in accordance with the *Education Act* and its regulations (and other applicable laws);
- providing adequate instruction and accommodation for students who have a legal right to attend schools operated by the board, including ". . .special education programs and special education services for its exceptional pupils".

---

[40] See, for example, s. 170(1) – duties of boards under Ontario's *Education Act*, R.S.O. 1990, c. E-2.
[41] See Part X of the Ontario *Education Act*, including s. 279 (obligation to hire supervisory officers) and s. 280 (obligation to hire a director of education).

Education legislation such as the Ontario *Education Act* lists a broad array of legal obligations with which a board is required to comply. As a practical matter, however, these legal duties are expressed in rather general, somewhat theoretical language that provides little plain indication of their substantive content. For example, any person who has attended school has an intuitive appreciation of what constitutes "instruction" for the purposes of the duty of a school board to provide ". . .instruction and adequate accommodation". The matter of what constitutes ". . .adequate accommodation" in turn, does not bring to mind many tangible, non-legal images. The lofty nature of some of the language under Ontario's *Education Act* has provoked, with respect to some duties, extensive litigation to "flesh out" the more obliquely stated subsections listed therein. In Ontario, there has been extensive litigation around the concept of the concept of the duty to provide "instruction and adequate accommodation" particularly in contexts where parents/guardians have challenged the legality of school closures[42] and more recently with respect to the statutory obligation to provide special education services.

WHAT IS A SCHOOL BOARD IN LAW?

In Ontario, as stated above,[43] school boards are not-for-profit corporations. However, unlike private corporations, the members of the board of directors of school boards are elected by the public (and are colloquially known as "trustees"). To serve as a school board member, an individual must be "qualified" to be elected as a board member pursuant to Part VIII of the

---

[42] See, for example, *Alexander v. Etobicoke Board of Education* (1981), 34 O.R. (2d) 76 (Ont. H.C.); *MacDonald v. Lambton County Board of Education* (1982), 37 O.R. (2d) 221 (Ont. H.C.); and *Eddington v. Kent (County) Board of Education* (1986), 56 O.R. (2d) 403 (Ont. Dist. Ct.).
[43] See s. 58.5 of the Ontario *Education Act*.

Education Act[44] and under the *Municipal Elections Act, 1996*[45] and must be a successful candidate in an election or by-election held in accordance with the *Municipal Elections Act, 1996*.

The practical significance of a school board's status as a corporation is the way in which it must transact official business. As a corporation, a school board may only officially act in one of two ways: by passing resolutions at a meeting of its board of directors (i.e., meeting of the board members/trustees) or by by-law. The former is disproportionately the more common means by which a school board gets things done. While it is true that a board's administrators may make administrative decisions concerning a board's day-to-day operations on behalf of a board, fundamental matters such as making and terminating contracts (including employment contracts) and expelling students must be considered and approved by board members.[46]

THE SCHOOL BOARD'S DUTIES WITH RESPECT TO INSTRUCTION

Flowing from a board's statutory obligation to provide instruction, as a general matter, a board of education should deliver curriculum content (for courses of study often prescribed for them by the province and developed in accordance with provincial guidelines[47]) as delivered and facilitated by qualified

---

[44] See in particular s. 219.
[45] See ss. 29-30 *Municipal Elections Act, 1996*.
[46] Under s. 309(13) of the *Education Act*, the statutory duties of a school board may be delegated by the board to a committee of the board. This act of delegation, however, must be officially transacted by the board itself so as to properly clothe this committee with statutory jurisdiction.
[47] See, for example, s. 8(1), paras. 3 and 4 of the Ontario *Education Act* and s. 168(2)(c) of the British Columbia *School Act*, R.S.B.C. 1996, c. 412.

principals and teachers.[48] While there have been several high-profile cases concerning the materials used in the course of instruction,[49] there have very few cases—outside the context of special education[50]—which have raised the issue of the level or quality of instruction provided to students as selected or provided by school boards.[51]

THE SCHOOL BOARD'S DUTIES WITH RESPECT TO SPECIAL EDUCATION

Special education is aimed at serving the needs of "exceptional pupils" i.e., a student whose ". . .behavioural, communicational, intellectual, physical or multiple exceptionalities are such that he or she is considered to need placement in a special education program. . ."[52] on a full- or part-time basis. As stated above, the obligation of a board to provide special education services in many provinces arise from statute and associated regulations that map out the particulars of process. In Ontario,

---

[48] See, for example, s. 170(1), para. 12 of the Ontario *Education Act* and s. 19 of the British Columbia *School Act*. Under both regimes, exceptions to the requirement of qualification exist in emergency situations: see O. Reg. 298, R.R.O. 1990, s. 21 and the British Columbia *School Act*, s. 19(2).

[49] See, for example, the decision in *Chamberlain v. Surrey School District No. 36, supra* note 12, which concerned a school board's rejection for use as supplementary learning materials three books that portrayed same-sex couples.

[50] See, for example, *Eaton v. Brant County Board of Education, supra* note 14, which involved a challenge by parents of a severely handicapped child to the removal of that student from a placement with non-special education learners into a special education learning environment.

[51] See, for example, *Hicks v. Etobicoke (City) Board of Education*, [1988] O.J. No. 1900 (Ont. Dist. Ct.), in which an allegation of ". . .failing to provide proper education" was dismissed as disclosing ". . .no reasonable cause of action." In so doing, the Court relied on the Supreme Court of Canada decision in *R. v. Jones, supra* note 37, para. 80, in which it was stated ". . .The courtroom is simply not the best arena for the debate of issues of educational policy and the measurement of educational quality."

[52] Ontario *Education Act*, s. 1(1).

for example, there is a specific statutory duty placed upon school boards "....to provide exceptional pupils with special education programs and special education services that are appropriate for their needs."[53] The range of characteristics that may be categorized as exceptional include: "....children who have behavioural or communication disorders, or intellectual, physical or multiple disabilities...".[54]

In Ontario, the implementation of the broadly worded duty to provide special education is largely undertaken pursuant to the process set out in Ontario Regulation 181/98 – *Identification and Placement of Exceptional Pupils*.

The process leading to the provision of special education services to a pupil in Ontario may be described roughly as follows:

- identifying that a student may have special learning needs (by request of the parent/guardian or by referral from the principal on notice to the child's parent/guardian);
- referring the student to the Board's Identification, Placement Review Committee (IPRC) ("IPRC Committee");
- having the IPRC Committee decide whether the student is an exceptional pupil and if so, the proper placement for the pupil, including: placement in a regular class for all or part of the school day; placement in a special education class for all or part of the school day; placement in a special education class with partial integration in a regular class; or referral to a Provincial Committee (where appropriate) with respect to eligibility for admission to a Provincial school for the Blind or Deaf or a Provincial Demonstration school serving pupils with severe learning disabilities;

---

[53] A straightforward outline of the system of special education in Ontario is given at the Ministry of Education website at http://www.edu.gov.on.ca/eng/general/elemsec/speced/ontario.html, "An Introduction to Special Education in Ontario".
[54] *Ibid.*

- hearing of any appeal or appeals by parents/guardians in respect to the IPRC Committee's decision on the child's placement (a first appeal is usually made to an internal committee of the board, while a follow-up appeal can be made to an outside Tribunal called the Ontario Special Education Tribunal);
- developing an "Individual Education Plan ("IEP") for a child with input from a child's parent or guardian (or from the child where he or she is over the age of 16). The IEP essentially expresses the goals for the particular student's education; expresses what services or placements are going to be made to addresses those goals; the personnel to be involved; and the timeline targets for reaching these learning milestones. The IEP also provides the methodology by which a learner's progress is going to be reviewed;
- placing the student in accordance with the IPRC decision (or subsequent appeal decision as the case may be); and
- ongoing monitoring and review of the chosen placement for a pupil. A parent may request a review of a child's placement after the child has been in the placement for at least three months.[55]

As noted above, as at this writing, extensive litigation is ongoing in the special education field with respect to funding for treatment and intervention for autism spectrum disorder. While some of these cases address autism as a health services or social services issue (because the therapy sought begins before a child reaches school age), an Ontario case has attacked the appropriateness of current special education programs for autistic children, arguing that,

> ...compulsorily subjecting the child with autism to special education that is useless or harmful is a breach of the child's security of the person, and depriving the parent of choice with respect to the child's special education and the ability to secure for the child the intervention that is

---

[55] Ontario Reg. 181/98, s. 21(2).

clinically indicated is a breach of the parent's right to security of the person.[56]

In that case, among other things, the Ontario government (as represented by the Ministry of Community and Social Services) was found to have breached the rights of autistic children guaranteed under section 15 of the *Charter* by failing to fund early Intensive Behavioural Intervention (IBI) and other therapies.[57] Undoubtedly, in light of the Supreme Court of Canada's decision in *Auton v. British Columbia (Minister of Health)*[58] (in which a similar decision in British Columbia was overturned on appeal to the Supreme Court of Canada), the case will be appealed.

SCHOOL BOARD ADMINISTRATION

Obviously, teachers and principals are part of a board's staff in providing educational services. However, as a corporation, a board needs other staff to administrate its many services. While elected board trustees do have final decision-making power on behalf of a board, work must be done in order to present matters (and the information concerning those matters) to the elected officials, as well as to keep the corporation functioning on a day-to-day basis. As such, many education statutes, such as Ontario's *Education Act*, call for a board to hire a chief executive officer (and chief education officer) called a "director of education"[59] who must also be qualified as a teacher.[60] To assist in the administration of a board of education, a board must also hire a sufficient number of administrative executives called "supervisory officers"[61] (also referred to

---

[56] *Wynberg v. Ontario, supra* note 26 at para. 5.
[57] *Ibid.*, paras. 871-873.
[58] *Supra* note 15.
[59] Ontario *Education Act*, ss. 279-280.
[60] *Ibid.*, s. 283(1).
[61] *Ibid.*, s. 279.

as superintendents) who are to be assigned specific titles and areas of responsibility.[62] Supervisory officers have specific statutory duties for which they are responsible under education legislation.[63]

Given the fact that a school board has to attend to both pedagogical matters of program delivery and corporate matters of business and operation, supervisory officers typically fall into two categories: academic supervisory officers (who are assigned to administrate the ". . .development, implementation, operation and supervision of educational programs in schools"[64]) and business supervisory officers who have qualifications and experience in matters of business administration.[65]

In addition to obligations to have a basic administrative team in place as required by the legislation, school boards are also empowered to engage other employees as are necessary to operate their enterprises[66] as well as having specific powers to retain psychologists or psychiatrists.[67]

SPECIFIC STATUTORY DUTIES OF SCHOOL BOARD EMPLOYEES

As institutions, school boards have certain prescribed statutory duties in education legislation[68] and in other legislation

---

[62] *Ibid.*, s. 285(1).
[63] *Ibid.*, s. 286.
[64] Ontario Reg. 309, R.R.O. 1990 – *Supervisory Officers*, s. 3(1).
[65] *Ibid.* at s. 2.1.
[66] Ontario *Education Act*, s. 171(1), para. 3.
[67] *Ibid.* at para. 6.
[68] See, for example, the Ontario *Education Act*, s. 170; the *Ontario College of Teachers Act, 1996*, S.O. 1996, c. 12; and the *Regulation made under the Teaching Profession Act* (updated by the Ontario Teachers' Federation) at ss. 14-18.

that impinges upon education.[69] In addition to the duties specifically residing with school boards, each of supervisory officers,[70] principals,[71] and teachers[72] are given specific statutory obligations. Directors of education and supervisory officers, as part of the administrative team of a board of education, are charged with the responsibility of making decisions that implement a board's fulfillment of its statutory duties.

In addition to duties set out in education legislation, educators (and principals especially as the operational heads of schools) face statutory duties from general public welfare statutes, including health promotion legislation.[73]

SCHOOL BOARDS' STATUTORY DUTIES WITH RESPECT TO CHILD PROTECTION

Fundamentally, many of the specific statutory duties to secure the health and welfare of students on a day-to-day basis are expressed as duties of principals, who are the operational heads of schools. For example, Ontario's *Education Act*[74] ex-

---

[69] See, for example, the Ontario *Municipal Freedom of Information and Protection of Privacy Act*, R.S.O. 1990, c. M.56, which defines "institution" to include a "school board."
[70] See Ontario *Education Act*, s. 286.
[71] See Ontario *Education Act*, ss. 265-266 and O. Reg. 298 – *Operation of Schools – General*, s. 11.
[72] See Ontario *Education Act*, s. 264 and O. Reg. 298, *Operation of Schools – General*, s. 20. See also the *Regulation made under the Teaching Profession Act* updated by the Ontario Teachers' Federation.
[73] See, for example, the *Health Protection and Promotion Act*, R.S.O. 1990, c. H.7, s. 28, which obligates a school principal "...who is of the opinion that a pupil in the school has or may have a communicable disease shall, as soon as possible after forming the opinion, report thereon to the medical officer of health of the health unit in which the school is located." In this respect, see also O. Reg. 569, R.R.O. 1990, s. 2, which specifies the required contents for such a report.
[74] R.S.O. 1990, c. E.2 (as amended).

presses specific obligations on school principals with respect to health and welfare of pupils in subsections 265(j)-(m):

> It is the duty of a principal of a school, in addition to the principal's duties as a teacher,
>
> . . .
>
> (j) to give assiduous attention to the health and comfort of pupils, to the cleanliness, temperature and ventilation of the school, to the care of all teaching materials and other school property, and the condition and appearance of the school buildings and grounds;
>
> (k) to report promptly to the board and to the medical officer of health when the principal has reason to suspect the existence of any communicable disease in the school, and of the unsanitary condition of any part of the school building or the school grounds;
>
> (l) to refuse admission to the school of any person who the principal believes is infected with or exposed to communicable diseases requiring an order under section 22 of the *Health Protection and Promotion Act* until furnished with a certificate of a medical officer of health or of a legally qualified medical practitioner approved by the medical officer of health that all danger from exposure to contact with such person has passed;
>
> (m) subject to an appeal to the board, to refuse to admit to the school or classroom a person whose presence in the school or classroom would in the principal's judgment be detrimental to the physical or mental wellbeing of the pupils.[75]
>
> . . .

Also, principals (as well as teachers) are specifically named in subsection 72(5) as among the categories of professionals who have a duty to report child abuse under section 72 of the *Child and Family Services Act*.[76]

---

[75] With respect to admitting individuals to school premises, see also the somewhat overlapping provision of the Ontario *Education Act*, s. 306 and O. Reg. 474/00, which deals specifically with access to school premises.

[76] R.S.O. 1990, c. C.11.

School boards also have miscellaneous duties expressed in the Ontario *Education Act* with respect to the safety and welfare of children.[77] Further, a board, in service of the safety and security of all the school community, is obligated under Part VIII of the *Education Act* to enact and enforce a local "Code of Conduct" applicable to schools operated by the board.[78]

Following from the Robins Report,[79] an investigation by former Ontario Court of Appeal Justice Syndey L. Robins into the events arising from a particularly long-standing abuse by a teacher in Northern Ontario, the Ontario Government introduced new reporting obligations by way of the *Student Protection Act, 2002* (a bill amending the *Education Act* and other Acts). The *Student Protection Act, 2002* imposed new reporting obligations on boards of education. In Ontario, a board is obligated to report to the Ontario College of Teachers (within 30 days of the respective occurrence) where:

- it terminates a member of the College (or imposes restrictions on a member of the College) for reasons of "professional misconduct";[80]
- a member resigns before a termination (or restriction) is placed upon him or her for reasons of "professional misconduct";[81] or
- a member resigns while facing an investigation into alle-

---

[77] See, for example, s. 170(1), para. 8 (keep buildings and premises in proper repair and in proper sanitary condition); para. 12.1 (treatment of teacher charged with or convicted of sexual offence or other offence which may place students at risk); para. 15 (report children not enrolled); see generally also Part VII – Behaviour, Discipline and Safety (which puts in place the Province-wide "Code of Conduct" and the means by which it is enforced).

[78] See Ontario *Education Act*, s. 302.

[79] *Protecting Our Students: A Review to Identify and Prevent Sexual Misconduct in Ontario* (Toronto: Queen's Printer, 2000).

[80] See *Ontario College of Teachers Act, 1996*, s. 43.2(1). For the definition of "professional misconduct" see also O. Reg. 437/97.

[81] See *Ontario College of Teachers Act, 1996*, s. 43.2(2).

gations of an act or omission by the member that would, if proven, have caused the employer to terminate the member's employment or to impose restrictions on the member's duties for reasons of professional misconduct.[82]

Under these amendments (incorporated largely into the *Education Act* and the *Ontario College of Teachers Act, 1996*), a board of education also has specific obligations to make a report "promptly" to the Ontario College of Teachers where it becomes aware of charges or convictions in respect to certain criminal offences, where the member:

- has been charged with or convicted of an offence under Canada's *Criminal Code* involving sexual conduct and minors;
- has been charged with or convicted of an offence under the *Criminal Code*, which, in the opinion of the employer, indicates that students may be at risk of harm or injury; or
- has engaged in conduct or taken action that, in the opinion of the board, should be reviewed by a Committee of the Ontario College of Teachers (either the Fitness to Practise Committee or the Discipline Committee).

The board must also make a follow-up report to the College where a member who is subject to a report made pursuant to the duties above:

- has the charge(s) against him or her withdrawn;
- is discharged (from further prosecution) after a preliminary inquiry;
- has the charge(s) against him or her stayed;
- is acquitted at trial.[83]

---

[82] *Ibid.* at s. 43.2(3).
[83] *Ibid* at s. 43.3.

The College of Teachers also has specific duties to report certain matters to employers, including outcomes from its Fitness to Practise and Discipline Committees.

It is an offence for a board to fail to report on the matters listed above. On conviction, an offending employer faces a fine of up to $25,000.[84]

The Minister of Education also has a largely overlooked power under section 263 of the Ontario *Education Act* to cause the termination of a teacher (on 30 days' written notice) despite the provisions of any collective agreement where ". . .a matter arises that in the opinion of the Minister adversely affects the welfare of the school in which the teacher is employed."[85]

The *Student Protection Act, 2002* also made changes to the longstanding *Teaching Profession Act*, amending the collegial duty to share an "adverse report" with a fellow member where the subject matter of the report is the "sexual abuse" of a student by the member.[86]

STATUTORY DUTIES CONCERNING STUDENT RECORDS

In Ontario, each elementary and secondary school student is assigned an Ontario Education number, which is used as an identifier on student's records.[87] A principal must keep a rec-

---

[84] *Ibid.* at s. 48.1.
[85] This section allows an emergency situation to be addressed rather than speaking to misconduct or fault of a particular teacher: see *Etobicoke (Borough) Board of Education v. O.S.S.T.F., District 12* (1981), 2 L.A.C. (3d) 265 (Ont. Arb. Bd.).
[86] "Sexual abuse" includes sexual intercourse or other physical sexual relations; sexual touching; or behaviour or remarks by the member toward a student of a sexual nature: see *Teaching Profession Act*, s. 12(3).
[87] Ontario *Education Act*, s. 266.2.

ord concerning each student.[88] The ground rules for compiling, maintaining, using and retaining a student record (or "Ontario Student Record" or "OSR") in Ontario are set out in the Ontario Student Record Guideline from the Ontario Ministry of Education.[89] The purpose of a student record is so that educators may reference it for the purposes of "...the improvement of instruction of the pupil."

A parent (or a pupil who is over the age of 18) has a right to access a student's "record",[90] and there is an express procedure in the statute to resolve disagreements with respect to the content of the OSR.[91] However, the information to which a parent (or guardian) has access as part of a student's school "record" is not as wide as might it originally appear. Courts have found that the notes kept by a school guidance counselor do not form part of a student "record" for the purposes of section 266(2) of the Ontario *Education Act*.[92] Further, requests by biological parents for access to school counselor's notes (outside the context of a criminal trial that might raise issues) have been denied on the basis that "...communications between the guidance counsellor and the student, as well as notes relating to those communications, are properly the subject of a privileged level of confidentiality."[93] In that case, the Court observed, at paragraph 36:

> In my opinion, a student is entitled to enjoy a high level of expectation of privacy concerning communications made to a guidance counsellor at school, and concerning any notes made by the counsellor in connection with those communications, in the context of a child protection hearing.

---

[88] See s. 265(1)(d) of the *Education Act*.
[89] The text of the Guideline is found at http://www.edu.gov.on.ca/eng/document/curricul/osr/osr.html
[90] Ontario *Education Act*, s. 266(3).
[91] Ontario *Education Act*, s. 266(4) and (5).
[92] *Children's Aid Society of Waterloo (Regional Municipality) v. L. (T.)*, [1990] O.J. No. 1174 (Ont. Fam. Ct.).
[93] *Children's Aid Society of Ottawa v. S. (N.)*, [2005] O.J. 1070 (Ont. S.C.J.).

Confidentiality provisions in the *Education Act* protect the privacy of the student record[94] and the collection, use and disclosure of its contents are also regulated by the parallel and paramount regime under the *Municipal Freedom of Information and Protection of Privacy Act*.[95] Certain information from a student record must be disclosed to the local medical officer of health as specified in the applicable section of the *Education Act*.[96]

As stated in the *Municipal Freedom of Information and Protection of Privacy Act*, ("MFIPPA")[97] notwithstanding the existence of confidentiality provisions with respect to student records under both the *Education Act* and MFIPPA, a court still retains jurisdiction to order the disclosure of material from a student's record where the interests of justice so require. A common circumstance in which this sort of situation may arise is in a criminal proceeding where a student is the complainant. In this context, a defence attorney may bring an application to the court asking the court to order the disclosure of records in the custody of a third party, i.e., the school. This type of application is colloquially referred to as an "O'Connor application" named for the decision of the Supreme Court of Canada decision that outlined the process to be followed in the circumstances of such requests.[98] The process to be followed in such a court application is described in our chapter concerning going to court.

---

[94] See *Education Act*, s. 266(2), (9) and (10).
[95] R.S.O. 1990, c. M.56. The *Municipal Freedom of Information and Protection of Privacy Act* contains a paramountcy provision in s. 53(1) that states that it prevails over the confidentiality provisions in any other Act unless the other statute provides otherwise. The *Education Act* contains no such provision.
[96] Ontario *Education Act*, s. 266(2.1).
[97] *Supra* note 95 at s. 51(2). See also *R. v. K. (A.J.)* (1995), 23 O.R. (3d) 582 (Ont. Gen. Div.).
[98] *R. v. O'Connor*, [1995] 4 S.C.R. 411 (S.C.C.).

SCHOOL BOARD DUTIES TO CHILDREN BEYOND THOSE STATED IN THE STATUTE

Obviously, the various statutes governing education in Canada set out specific duties that a school board must fulfill, including the duty to enroll and provide instruction to children as well as the duty to report where a child is in need of protection under child protection legislation.[99] However, related to these statutory obligations is a basic common law obligation (i.e., a duty arising from judge-made law rather than from statutes or regulations) imposed on boards to be mindful of the health and well-being of students while the pupils are in their care. The basic nature of this legal burden was aptly expressed by Teresa Hepburn and Melanie Warner:

> The common law in Canada clearly establishes that school authorities have a special duty of care toward students in their charge. This duty is imposed upon them due to the unique nature of their work. Because parents are obligated to either send their child (or children) to school or provide home schooling, they are entitled to expect that schools will take reasonable measures to prevent risk of harms with the school environment or on school-sponsored excursions."[100]

As a matter of law, educators are seen to be *in loco parentis*, which roughly translated from Latin means they act 'in place of a parent'.

---

[99] See, for example, Ontario's *Child and Family Services Act*, R.S.O. 1990, c. C.11.

[100] Teresa Hepburn and Melanie Warner, "Excursions – An Important Educational Tool" in Roderick C. Flynn, ed., *In Support of Lifelong Learning* (Proceedings of the 13th Annual Conference of the Canadian Association of the Practical Study of Law in Education, held in St. Andrews-by-the-Sea, New Brunswick, May 4-7, 2002), at para. 6.04.

A SCHOOL BOARD'S DUTY OF CARE TOWARD A STUDENT

If a school board (and by implication, those acting on a school board's behalf such as principals and teachers) has a special common law obligation to take care to protect a student from harm, the question naturally arises, as a practical matter, what is the content of this duty? Courts have stated that the content of the duty of care owed to a student is not the same in every case and will vary according to the circumstances. Rather than precisely defining the nature of the duty of care owed to students, courts have generally stated that "...the standard of care to be exercised by school authorities in providing for the supervision and protection of students for whom they are responsible is that of the careful or prudent parent."[101] Determining whether this standard of care has been met in each case is reached by referring to a number of variables, which include:

- the number of students being supervised at any given time;
- the age of the students being supervised;
- the nature of the exercise or activity that is being supervised;
- the degree of skill or training the students may have in respect to the activity in question;
- the nature or condition of the equipment being used;
- the competency and capacity of the students involved; and
- any additional relevant factors.[102]

As a very general matter, courts have been somewhat reluctant to hold educators liable for accidental injuries to students absent fairly pronounced thoughtlessness or lack of planning that either greatly increases the likelihood of injury or results

---

[101] *Myers v. Peel (County) Board of Education*, [1981] 2 S.C.R. 21 (S.C.C.).
[102] *Ibid.*

in children being beyond rescue when foreseeable trouble occurs.[103]

However, in certain circumstances, a school board may be found vicariously liable for the negligent acts of its employees and agents, where:

- the relationship between the employee and the school board is sufficiently close so as to make the imposition of liability appropriate;
- the wrongful or negligent act is sufficiently connected to the employee or agent's assigned tasks that the tort can be regarded as a materialization of the risks created by the enterprise.[104]

Care should be taken in trying to apply these somewhat abstract legal standards quickly and easily to everyday situations. The law of "vicarious liability" has been puzzled over extensively over the years, including numerous pronouncements by the Supreme Court of Canada. Suffice it to say that this complex area of the law does not lend itself to either clear statements of law or easy application to a given set of facts. As such, if a situation arises where responsibility for an accident or occurrence is in question, it is best to seek legal advice immediately.

---

[103] The classic case in this regard is *Moddejonge v. Huron (County) Board of Education*, [1972] 2 O.R. 437 (Ont. H.C.), in which a number of students drowned after being given permission to swim in a reservoir at a conservation area (which had a steep drop-off) by a supervising education coordinator who could not swim.

[104] See *K.L.B. v. British Columbia* [2003] 2 S.C.R. 403 (S.C.C.) at paras. 18-19, citing *G.T.-J. v. Griffiths*, [1999] 2 S.C.R. 570.

THE COMMON LAW DUTY OF CARE BEYOND THE CLASSROOM (AND SCHOOL-RELATED ACTIVITIES)

As noted above, those involved in education (including students and teachers) owe a special duty of care to students in their care. In discharging this duty, teachers and principals have a legal obligation to take steps to prevent students from harm. Obviously, this standard applies to activities carried on in school and on school-sponsored trips or excursions. But does this duty transcend the classroom into conduct outside the classroom? Where a teacher encounters a student outside of school in his or her private life, does the student-teacher dynamic (and the duties which accompany it) continue?

In 1996, the Supreme Court of Canada answered 'generally yes' to this question in its decision in the case of *R. c. Audet*.[105] The case involved a 22-year old teacher who encountered a 14-year old female student (accompanied by her cousins who were in their 20s) whom he had taught as a Grade 8 pupil during the previous school year. Over the course of the evening, the teacher engaged in some sexual activity. The teacher was later charged with the offence of sexual exploitation.[106] The teacher argued that as he was no longer the student's teacher, he was no longer in a position of "trust or authority" toward her. While both the trial court and the first level of appeal accepted this argument, the Supreme Court of Canada overturned these decisions, finding that in most cases, even outside of school, a teacher is in a position of trust and confidence toward his or her students:

---

[105] *Supra* note 11.
[106] Pursuant to s. 153 of the *Criminal Code* of Canada. The offence of sexual exploitation is an exception to the age of consent of 14 years of age. Where a person is in a relationship of "trust and authority" toward a young person between the age of 14 and 18, the defence of consent is negated and the offence of "sexual exploitation" applies.

...it would be excessively formalistic to refuse to recognize that certain persons, by reason of the role entrusted to them by society, will *in fact* and in the vast majority of cases come within the ambit of s. 153(1) by reason of their status *vis-à-vis* the young person and, in particular, the relationship they are engaged in with that young person as a consequence of such status....[107]

The Supreme Court concluded at paragraph 43:

In short, I am of the view that in the vast majority of cases teachers will indeed be in a position of trust and authority towards their students. It must also be recognized that there may be situations where, owing to exceptional factual circumstances, this is not the case because, even though the accused has the status of a teacher, his or her relationship with a particular student is such that the element of trust or authority is totally absent. I will refrain from speculating and suggesting hypothetical examples to illustrate this. However, in the absence of evidence raising a reasonable doubt in the mind of the trier of fact, it cannot be concluded that a teacher is not in a position of trust and authority towards his or her students without going against common sense.

The decision in the *Audet* case is consistent with earlier rulings of the top Court on the topic of the standards of behaviour expected of educators, including the behaviour in their private lives. In the case of *Ross v. New Brunswick School Division No. 15*,[108] the Supreme Court provided the template for the evaluation of a teacher's conduct:

... teachers as "medium" must be perceived to uphold the values, beliefs and knowledge sought to be transmitted by the school system. The conduct of a teacher is evaluated on the basis of his or her position, rather than whether the conduct occurs within the classroom or beyond. Teachers are seen by the community to be the medium for the educational message and because of the community position they occupy, they are not able to "choose which hat they will wear on what occasion"...[109]

---

[107] *R. c. Audet, supra* note 11 at para. 40.
[108] *Supra* note 1.
[109] *Ibid.* at para. 44.

The Supreme Court made additional comments on this point at paragraph 45:

> It is on the basis of the position of trust and influence that we hold the teacher to high standards both on and off duty, and it is an erosion of these standards that may lead to a loss in the community of confidence in the public school system. I do not wish to be understood as advocating an approach that subjects the entire lives of teachers to inordinate scrutiny on the basis of more onerous moral standards of behaviour. This could lead to a substantial invasion of the privacy rights and fundamental freedoms of teachers. However, where a "poisoned" environment within the school system is traceable to the off-duty conduct of a teacher that is likely to produce a corresponding loss of confidence in the teacher and the system as a whole, then the off-duty conduct of the teacher is relevant.

In the third case from a trilogy of cases on the topic of the off-duty conduct of educators,[110] the Supreme Court extended the reasoning given above to the issue of whether a teacher who engages in off-duty misconduct should be retained as an employee:

> . . .it is essential that [labour] arbitrators recognize the sensitivity of the educational setting and ensure that a person who is clearly incapable of adequately fulfilling the duties of a teacher both inside and outside the classroom is not returned to the classroom. Both the vulnerability of students and the need for public confidence in the education system demand such caution.....[111]

It is clear from the above statements that an educator's obligation to maintain a higher standard of conduct continues outside the classroom. While his or her obligation to provide instruction or supervision may not extend beyond school-authorized activities, conduct towards students in the world at large must be above board in all respects, in the context of both

---

[110] *Toronto (City) Board of Education v. O.S.S.T.F., District 15*, [1997] 1 S.C.R. 487 (S.C.C.). This was the last of three Supreme Court of Canada decisions including *Ross* and *Audet*.
[111] *Ibid.* at para. 57.

contact with students beyond school and as part of an educator's everyday life.

THE SCHOOL BOARD'S LEGAL RESPONSIBILITY FOR STUDENT ABUSE BY A TEACHER OR OTHER EMPLOYEE

As stated above, a school board may be found in certain circumstances to be vicariously liable (i.e., an employer or principal party is found responsible in the place of a non-innocent employee, actor or agent) for the wrongful acts of its employees, although generally courts are reluctant to find an employer liable for intentional acts that are not authorized by the school board or where the perpetrator's employment did not "...significantly contribute to the occurrence of the harm."[112]

However, a more common basis for liability is negligence: that the facts disclose that a school board knew or ought to have known (based upon certain usually plain clues) that wrongful acts were taking place and the institution failed to take steps or sufficient steps to stop or curtail the wrongful acts.

In a 2003 case, the Supreme Court of Canada clarified that a school board's statutory and common law duties to take steps to protect a child from harm do not amount to ultimate responsibility to ensure that no harm comes to the student while he or she is at school or engaged in school related activities.[113] The case involved a young female student who was subjected to sexual assaults by a school janitor over the course of two

---

[112] See *G.T.-J. v. Griffiths*, [1999] 2 S.C.R. 570 (S.C.C.). For specific applications, see, for example, *H. (S.G.) v. Gorsline*, [2004] 2004 ABCA 186 (Alta. C.A.), leave to appeal refused (2005), 2005 CarswellAlta 62 (S.C.C.), but see also *John Doe v. Avalon East School Board* (2004), 244 Nfld. & P.E.I.R. 153 (N.L. T.D.), in which vicariously liability was imposed on a school board arising from sexual assaults by one of the board's teachers.

[113] See *G. (E.D.) v. Hammer*, [2003] 2 S.C.R. 459 (S.C.C.).

years. The employing school board had no knowledge of the assaults and it was found to have no reason to suspect that the janitor was acting inappropriately (which may have rendered it vulnerable to allegations of negligence). At paragraph 20 of the decision, the Supreme Court of Canada distinguished between the existence of statutory and common law duties on school boards to protect students and an automatic conclusion that school boards are responsible if any injury occurs to a student under its care where it has neither knowledge of the wrongful acts nor reason to suspect any malfeasance was taking place:

> These specific duties [with respect to student health and safety] do not permit the inference that boards are generally and ultimately responsible for the health and safety of school children on school premises, in a way as would render them liable for abuse at the hands of a school employee. The same is true of the provisions laying out the general duties of school boards. None of the general duties gives school boards full responsibility for students' welfare while on school premises... [T]he [British Columbia School] Act does not appear to impose a general non-delegable duty upon school boards to ensure that children are kept safe while on school premises, such as would render the Board liable for abuse of a child by an employee on school premises.

In the *Hammer* case, the Supreme Court of Canada clarified that while a school board has statutory and common law duties to take care of children (while children are in the care of the board through its employees), these obligations do not mean that any time a children is injured or assaulted at school, a board is necessarily legally responsible. In turn, this ruling does not mean that negligence by a board is excused. Instead, the top Court, wrestling with some fine points of law (e.g., whether a school board has a "non-delegable duty of care"), found that in situations where a board is not negligent (particularly in its supervision of employees who have engaged in criminal activities) an injured student does not necessarily have a right to recover damages from a school board.

As is evident from the above-noted passage, the legal responsibility of a school board for injuries or criminal acts committed against its students is a complex subject. Again, if such an issue arises, it is important to seek legal advice that specifically addresses the situation at hand.

SCHOOL BOARD RESPONSIBILITY AND HEALTH AND SAFETY

While trips outside of school are often supported by permission slips that are required to be signed by a parent or guardian (often pursuant to a board's excursion policy), a day-to-day issue that is assuming greater and greater prominence in schools in the area of duty to care for students is the issue of an educator's obligation to respond or intervene with respect to student health care emergencies, particularly situations involving allergies and anaphylaxis[114] or to protect students (including special needs students) from injuring themselves or others. Ordinarily, the law does not impose upon an individual the duty to rescue another, and will only require that a person refrain from making a bad situation worse. However, an educator has specific statutory and common law duties to protect students and therefore, the question naturally arises, when a student has a health crisis, what steps, if any, do educators have to take to intervene? In some circumstances, an educator's own health and safety may be imperiled by intervention, triggering obligations and responsibility issues for employers, particularly under applicable occupational health and safety legislation. The answer to this question will depend upon the particular circumstances. Obviously, an educator who does not intervene to help a child in a benign situation that can be addressed with minimal effort will be assessed with a different eye by a court or other tribunal than a teacher who does not

---

[114] In this respect, see Health Canada's *Anaphylaxis: A Handbook for School Boards*, which may be found at http://www.hc-sc.gc.ca/fn-an/nutrition/child-enfant/anaphylaxis-anaphylaxie_e.html.

jump into a situation that poses great physical danger. General guidance on how to respond in such situations may often be gathered from board policies covering such topics, as well as information or positions from an educator's union or professional organization.

SCHOOL BOARD POWERS

As noted above, school boards have a long list of statutory and common law responsibilities, the most important of which relate to taking steps to educate and protect the children under their care.

To allow school boards to function, both as educational institutions and as corporate entities, it is common for education statutes to provide school boards with powers to enable them both to take care of the necessities of everyday functioning (e.g., to hire staff, to acquire land, and to build schools, etc.) and to offer programs and services on a discretionary basis.[115] Also, in provinces such as Ontario where school boards are deemed to be non-profit corporations, school boards also enjoy the general list of abilities given to such entities under applicable corporate legislation.[116]

---

[115] See, for example, the Ontario *Education Act*, s. 171(1) – a general listing of the powers of school boards, which includes such diverse abilities as the ability to appoint officers and employees (para. 3) all the way to allowing boards to host free public lectures (para. 30) and have school fairs (para. 35).

[116] See Ontario *Education Act*, ss. 58.5(1) and (3) as to the applicability of s. 180(7) of the Ontario *Business Corporations Act*. See also Part III of the *Corporations Act*, R.S.O. 1990, c. C.38, which in s. 117(c) applies ". . . to every corporation incorporated by or under a general or special Act of the Legislature" and arguably applies to school boards as creatures of the *Education Act*. In addition to extending specific powers to corporations without share capital created by the legislature, s. 133 of Part III of the *Corporations Act* also incorporates by reference other general corporate powers relating to management given in Parts II and III of the statute.

SUSPENSION AND EXPULSION

While the discipline of students in schools by way of corporal punishment has generally fallen into disuse over the past 25 years (and now has been officially outlawed by the Supreme Court of Canada),[117] most education statutes give school boards (or committees of school boards) the power to discipline students by way of suspension or expulsion.[118] In a number of provinces, including Ontario, teachers are given the power to suspend students for certain offences, although they are also given the option to refer the matter to school administration.[119]

In most provinces, student discipline is imposed for violations of some template that states or affirms standards of appropriate conduct and which proscribes unacceptable behaviour for students. This template is either a set document that is incorporated by reference or a standard(s) stated explicitly in the legislation itself or a related regulation. The template for student discipline in Ontario is the Provincial "Code of Conduct"[120] (a document that sets out the behavioural standards expected of ". . .all members of the school community").[121] The

---

[117] See *Canadian Foundation for Children v. Canada*, [2004] 1 S.C.R. 76 at para. 38.

[118] In this context, it is important to pay attention to the definition (or a lack of a particular definition) of the terms "expulsion" and "suspension" in specific statutory contexts. For example, the Alberta *School Act* considers an "expulsion" to be essentially any banishment from school for more than ten school days, while Prince Edward Island defines the term "expulsion" to connote banishment to the end of the current school year.

[119] See Ontario *Education Act*, s. 306(3).

[120] *Ibid.*, s. 301.

[121] In addition to the Code of Conduct (applicable to all members of the school community), O. Reg. 298, *Operation of Schools—General* in s. 23 contains a list of "Requirements for Pupils." Despite this list, few, if any, references are made to this student-only behavioural guideline since introducing the new discipline regime under the *Safe Schools Act*.

"Code of Conduct" is a policy of the Ontario Minister of Education and it is enforced through references contained in the text of the *Education Act*. In other provinces, the behavioural template may arise at the school or board level.[122] Certain infractions (which are derived from the Code of Conduct) draw mandatory consequences of suspension[123] and expulsion[124] in the *Education Act*, subject to regulations that relax these compulsory penalties where the pupil is unable to control his or her behaviour; the student does not understand the foreseeable consequences of his or her behaviour; or the continuing presence of the student does not create an unacceptable safety risk.

As stated above, the Ontario *Education Act* makes a suspension (i.e., a temporary banishment up to a maximum of 20 days) mandatory for certain offences, including:

- uttering a threat to inflict serious bodily harm on another person;
- possessing alcohol or illegal drugs;
- being under the influence of alcohol;
- swearing at a teacher or at another person in a position of authority;
- committing an act of vandalism that causes extensive damage to school property at the pupil's school or to property located on the premises of the pupil's school; or
- engaging in another activity that, under a policy of the board, is one for which a suspension is mandatory.[125]

A pupil's parent or guardian (or the pupil him- or herself if 18 years of age or over) or such other person authorized to do so

---

[122] See, for example, the British Columbia *School Act*, s. 6 which requires a student to comply with a school- or board-imposed Code of Conduct.
[123] See Ontario *Education Act*, s. 306(1).
[124] Ontario Reg. 37/01 – *Expulsion of a Pupil* and O. Reg. 106/01 – *Suspension of a Pupil*.
[125] Ontario *Education Act*, s. 306(1).

under a policy of the board may request that a decision to suspend a pupil be reviewed and such a review is to be conducted in accordance with the applicable board policy.[126] An appeal from the review decision lies to the board of education or a committee of the board and it is to be conducted in accordance with a policy on suspension appeals passed by the board.[127]

In the case of expulsions, in Ontario, a principal faced with the possible commission of an infraction for which expulsion is mandatory must suspend the accused pupil[128] (upon providing written notice to his or her parent or guardian or to the pupil him- or herself where they are 18 or over) and may either refer the matter to a hearing by the board or elect to conduct an investigation of the matter. Such infractions include:

- possessing a weapon, including possessing a firearm;
- using a weapon to cause harm or to threaten bodily harm to a person;
- committing a physical assault on another person that causes bodily harm requiring treatment by a medical practitioner;
- committing sexual assault;
- trafficking in weapons or illegal drugs;
- committing robbery;
- giving alcohol to a minor;
- engaging in an activity for which expulsion is mandatory under a policy of the board.

After an investigation, the principal may either refer the matter to the board for a hearing or impose a "limited expulsion" for

---

[126] Ontario *Education Act*, s. 308.
[127] *Ibid.*
[128] *Ibid.*, s. 309(2). The duty to suspend a pupil is subject to the noted stipulations in the regulations mentioned in O. Reg. 106/01 --*Suspension of a Pupil*.

a period of up to a year.[129] However, under the Ontario *Education Act*, a principal lacks the ability to expel a pupil if more than 20 days have elapsed since the original suspension unless the parties agree to a later deadline.[130] A principal's decision to expel a pupil may be appealed to the school board (or a committee to which such work is delegated), which must conduct such an appeal in accordance with board policy on the subject.[131]

An expulsion hearing by a school board (or a committee of a board as authorized by section 309(13)) is to be conducted in accordance with the board's policy on expulsions.[132] If the board determines after a hearing that the student committed an infraction for which expulsion is mandatory, the board must impose either a "limited expulsion" or a "full expulsion".[133] A limited expulsion means that the student is prohibited from attending the school (and school-related activities) he or she attended at the time of the expulsion until either the date set out in the expulsion (which cannot be more than one year after the date of the principal's suspension) or until the student meets the requirements set by the board for his or her return to school.[134] A "full expulsion" bans a student from attending any school in Ontario or any school-related activity until he or she has met the requirements "set by regulation" for returning to school.[135] In Ontario, the applicable regulation stipulates that a student must complete a "strict discipline program" in order to return to school.[136] School boards are required by the Ministry of Education to provide programs, courses, and services for students who have received a full

---

[129] Ontario *Education Act*, ss. 309(6) and (7).
[130] *Ibid.*, s. 309(8).
[131] *Ibid.*, s. 311(3).
[132] *Ibid.*, s. 309(10).
[133] *Ibid.*, s. 309(11).
[134] *Ibid.*, s. 309(14).
[135] *Ibid.*, s. 309(16).
[136] Ontario Reg. 37/01 – *Expulsion of a Pupil*, s. 3.

expulsion.[137] The Ministry of Education approved seven strict discipline program providers across Ontario in May 2001. Many school boards proceeded to make agreements with these service providers in order to service their students who were in need of access to "strict discipline programs". However, where others did not, these institutions were required to follow the provisions of a policy memorandum on strict discipline programs in implementing these services.[138]

Decisions to expel a pupil may be appealed by a parent or guardian; the pupil who is over 18; or another person authorized to do so by an applicable board policy. As stated above, decisions by a principal to impose a limited expulsion (of up to a year in duration) must be made to the board. In Ontario, a decision made by a school board to expel a pupil is made to the Ontario Child and Family Services Review Board ("CFSRB"), an entity continued under the *Child and Family Services Act* ("CFSA").[139] The ground rules for the operation of the CFSRB are stated in a regulation under the CFSA[140] and the *Expulsion of a Pupil* Regulation under the *Education Act*.[141] A party wishing to appeal a school board's expulsion decision has 60 days of the decision being appealed to give the CFSRB written notice of appeal.[142] The CFSRB does have discretion to extend the time for making an appeal where there exist reasonable grounds for doing so.[143] The notice of appeal must:

- set out the date of the decision that is being appealed;

---

[137] See Ontario *Education Act*, s. 312, and Policy/Program Memorandum No. 130 of the Ministry of Education, which is found at http://www.edu.gov.on.ca/extra/eng/ppm/130.html.
[138] *Ibid.*
[139] See *Child and Family Services Act*, R.S.O. 1990, c. C.11, s. 271.
[140] See O. Reg. 70, R.R.O. 1990, ss. 67 to 69.1.
[141] Ontario Reg. 37/01 – *Expulsion of a Pupil.*
[142] Ontario Reg. 70, R.R.O. 1990, s. 69.1(2).
[143] *Ibid.*, s. 69.1(3).

- set out the name of the district school board or school authority that made the decision;
- state whether the decision imposes a limited expulsion as described in subsection 309(14) of the *Education Act* or a full expulsion as described in subsection 309(16) of that Act; and
- be in the form, if any, approved by the Minister and available from the CFSRB.[144]

Despite the formal requirements for the Notice of Appeal, the CFRSB is not to decline to deal with an appeal on the basis of deficiencies in the notice or deviations from the form required.[145] The parties to an appeal are: the person who provided the notice of appeal; the school board; and any other person specified by the CFSRB.[146] The CFSRB is to convene a hearing within 30 days of receipt of the notice of appeal, although the CFSRB has discretion to extend the time for commencing the hearing upon request from one of the parties.[147] The CFSRB has established its own rules of procedure applicable to expulsion appeals, which provide:[148]

- appeals are governed by the *Statutory Powers Procedure Act*;
- CFSRB hearings are a new hearing: the expulsion matter is heard afresh rather than the decision of the original decision maker (i.e.. the school board) being scrutinized;
- pre-hearing conferences may be required;
- CFSRB hearings can be written, electronic or heard orally;
- the parties to the hearing may bring motions; and

---

[144] *Ibid.*, s. 69.1(4).
[145] *Ibid.*, s. 69.1(5).
[146] *Ibid.*, s. 69.1(6).
[147] *Ibid.*, s. 69.1(7), (8).
[148] John Bell & Jennifer Trepanier, "The Safe Schools Act: One Year Later" in Roderick C. Flynn, ed., *In Support of Lifelong Learning* (Proceedings of the 13th Annual Conference of the Canadian Association for the Practical Study of Law in Education, held in St. Andrew's-by-the-Sea New Brunswick, May 4-7, 2002; Toronto: CAPSLE, 2005).

- the CFSRB may make rulings concerning pre-hearing disclosure of documentation.

The CFSRB is to provide the parties (or their counsel/agent on their behalf) with a copy of the Board's decision on the appeal within ten days after the hearing is completed.[149] The range of outcomes from a CFSRB hearing include:

- confirming the board's decision;
- modifying the type or duration of the expulsion;
- imposing, changing or removing conditions that must be satisfied if the pupil is to return to school in Ontario following the expulsion;
- overruling the decision of the board of education and reinstating the pupil.

THE ISSUE OF BULLYING IN SCHOOLS

The issue of bullying in schools (including by means of the Internet also known as "cyber-bullying") has generated a considerable amount of both discussion and press attention in recent years. As a result, many educational institutions have adopted policies and procedures to address these issues, leading to the invocation of both suspension and expulsion penalties where applicable. At the same time, in an increasingly technological world, school authorities have been challenged to respond to bullying situations that have taken increasingly technologically complex forms, including web pages devoted to belittling and demeaning intended targets. The results of bullying can be devastating, even driving some victims to suicide. To address these situations, anti-bullying advocates have taken to cyberspace themselves, starting anti-bullying

---

[149] Ontario Reg. 70, R.R.O. 1990, s. 69.1(9).

websites or web pages[150] to provide information and support to educators, parents and victims of bullying alike.

There are many different definitions of bullying. A simple definition of "bullying" is offered by Public Safety and Emergency Preparedness Canada ("PSEPC") as follows: "bullying is assertion of power through aggression".[151] The PSEPC also cites a national survey of school children from 1997 that reports that at least 6 per cent of children admitted having bullied other children "once or twice" over a six-week period and 15 per cent of children reported that they had been bullied over the same time period.[152]

The legal constraints against bullying are obvious: codes of conduct (at various levels—local and provincial), carrying with them the discipline penalties of suspension and expulsion; and in certain cases, criminal law. The difficulty with policing bullying by way of imposing disciplinary consequences after improper conduct has occurred (whether internally within the school board or outside using the criminal law) is that many victims of bullying (and many witnesses to such treatment) do not report it.

The PSPEC advocates that to "...be effective, bullying interventions must focus beyond the aggressive child and the victim to include peers, school staff, parents and the broader

---

[150] See, for example, www.bullying.org; www.stopbullyingme.ab.ca; www.rcmp.ca/youth/bebrightbully_e.htm; www.bewebaware.ca; and www.prevention.gc.ca/en/library/publications/fact_sheets/bullying.

[151] See www.prevention.gc.ca/en/library/publications/fact_sheets/bullying/#1.

[152] W. Craig and D. Pepler, "Naturalistic observations of bullying and victimization on the playground" (LaMarsh Centre for Research on Violence and Conflict Resolution, York University, 1997) [unpublished report].

community"[153] citing research that ". . ...comprehensive anti-bullying initiatives can help reduce occurrences of bullying".[154]

Some victims of bullying have attempted to address bullying issues by seeking redress by means of civil lawsuits or human rights complaints against school boards and educators alleging failure to prevent the cruel treatment.[155] One of the most prominent cases in recent years is the case of a former British Columbia high school student who alleged in a complaint to the British Columbia Human Rights Tribunal that the North Vancouver School District had violated his human rights on the grounds of sexual orientation in that he was exposed to five years of homophobic bullying during his years at high school.[156] In 2002, the British Columbia Human Rights Tribunal found that Mr. Jubran's human rights had been violated and that the School Board was legally responsible for the discrimination as it had failed to provide an educational environment free from discriminatory harassment. On appeal, however, the Human Rights Tribunal's decision was overturned on the basis that Mr. Jubran ". . .is not a homosexual and the students who attacked him did not believe he was a homosexual. . ." and therefore he was not discriminated against on the grounds of sexual orientation.[157] However, in April 2005, the

---

[153] See http://www.prevention.gc.ca/en/library/publications/fact__ sheets/bullying/#9.
[154] D. Olweus, "Bully/victim problems among school children: Some basic facts and effects of a school-based intervention program" in D. Pepler and K. Rubin, eds., *The Development and Treatment of Childhood Aggression* (Hillsdale, N.J.: Erlbaum, 1991) at 411-448.
[155] See, for example, the cases of *Toronto (City) Board of Education v. Higgs* (1959), 22 D.L.R. (2d) 49 (S.C.C.); *Mainville v. Ottawa (Board of Education)* (1990), 75 O.R. (2d) 315 (Ont. Prov. Ct.); and *Hentze (Guardian ad litem of) v. Campbell River School District No. 72* (1994), 1994 CarswellBC 1047 (B.C. C.A.).
[156] *Jubran v. North Vancouver School District No. 44*, [2002] 2002 BCHRT 10 (B.C. Human Rights Trib.).
[157] (2003), 9 B.C.L.R. (4th) 338 (B.C. S.C.).

British Columbia Court of Appeal reversed the lower Court's decision in a ruling released April 6, 2005.[158] The Court first held that Mr. Jubran could rely on section 8 of the British Columbia Human Rights Code despite the fact that he did not identify himself as gay and turned to the issue of the school board's responsibility. In so doing, the Court recounted the School Board's approach to the bullying against Mr. Jubran, which the earlier Tribunal had found to be inconsistent and ineffective. The British Columbia Court of Appeal made the following comments at paragraph 96:

> In concluding that the School Board had not responded in an effective way to the students' discriminatory conduct, the Tribunal found that the school staff was pursuing a disciplinary approach that was not effective, and lacked resources to adopt a broader, educative approach to deal with the difficult issues of harassment, homophobia and discrimination. The School Board failed to provide those resources to the school staff during Mr. Jubran's years at Handsworth, though some were available. Some steps were taken by school staff to educate themselves about these issues after Mr. Jubran complained to the Human Rights Commission. Only after he graduated, however, did the School Board establish a strategy to address harassment and discrimination.

The Court of Appeal linked this analysis to the special role of schools in society and the lives of students in earlier comments at paragraph 92 of the judgment:

> In my opinion, the legal reasoning of the Tribunal on this question is sound. Contrary to the position taken by the School Board, she did not impose a standard of "strict liability". The Tribunal relied on *Attis* for the Supreme Court of Canada's articulation of the importance of a discrimination-free school environment and the duty of the School Board to provide it. That environment is mandated by the special position educational institutions occupy in fostering the values of our society and by the *Code*, which requires those who provide services to the public to do so in a nondiscriminatory way, so as to foster the full participation of individuals in the life of British Columbia, in a climate of understand-

---

[158] 2005 BCCA 201 (B.C. C.A.).

ing, mutual respect and equality of dignity and rights (see s. 3 of the *Code*).

The Court of Appeal added at paragraph 94, "The goal of a discrimination-free school environment is the ideal against which the School Board's response to the harassment of Mr. Jubran may be measured."

The British Columbia Court of Appeal restored the earlier decision of the British Columbia Human Rights Tribunal.

While it is difficult to derive broad principles of general application from the *Jubran* decision—involving as it does a violation of a fundamental human right—at very least, *Jubran* will no doubt prompt greater vigilance of bullying that may entail violations of human rights legislation (e.g., anti-gay name calling and harassment), it may also spur school boards to step up proactive measures to address bullying for fear of legal responsibility for the behaviour of the perpetrators.[159]

SCHOOL AUTHORITIES' POWER TO PREVENT TRESPASSING

Despite its key role as a public institution, a school is private property to which the public does not have access as a matter of right. Section 305(2) of the Ontario *Education Act* reads: "No person shall enter or remain on school premises unless he or

---

[159] For a detailed description of both the legal and practical issues around bullying, see Teresa Hepburn and Eric M. Roher, "What Should We Do about Bullying?" in Roderick C. Flynn, ed., *Law in Education: Help or Hindrance?* (Proceedings of the Fourteenth Annual Conference of the Canadian Association for the Practical Study of Law in Education, held in Jasper, Alberta, April 27-30, 2003; Toronto: CAPSLE, 2005) beginning at p. 447 and Dr. Shaheen Shariff "Keeping Schools Out of Court: Reasonable Tort Standards to Address Psychological Harm" in the same volume, beginning at p. 655.

she is authorized by regulation to be there on that day or at that time."

Under the applicable regulation,[160] the following individuals have a right to be on school premises on any day and at any time:

- a person enrolled as a pupil of the school;
- a parent or guardian of a pupil;
- a person employed or retained by the board; and
- a person who is otherwise on the premises of a school for a "lawful purpose".[161]

Special categories of invitees are also permitted to be on school premises for limited time periods, including:

- a person who is invited to attend an event, a class or a meeting, but only for the purposes of attending the event, class or meeting;
- a person who is invited onto the school premises for a particular purpose by the principal, vice-principal or by another person specifically authorized by board policy.[162]

A person who is not one of the categories of persons listed above commits an offence[163] and may be directed to leave the school by the principal. Subsection 305(4) of the Ontario *Education Act* reads: "The principal of a school may direct a person to leave the school premises if the principal believes that the person is prohibited by regulation or under a board policy from being there".

Further, notwithstanding a person's legal right to be present on school premises, the school's principal or vice-principal

---

[160] Ontario Reg. 474/00.
[161] *Ibid.*, s. 2(1).
[162] *Ibid.*, ss. 2(2) and 2(3).
[163] Ontario *Education Act*, s. 305(5).

CHILDREN AT SCHOOL ♦ 283

may exclude a person from the school if that person's presence on school premises is detrimental to the "safety or well-being of a person on the premises".[164] A separate enactment from the *Education Act* allows a principal to exclude a person from a school or class, subject to an appeal to the board, where a person's continuing presence in the school would ". . .in the principal's judgment be detrimental to the physical or mental well-being of the pupils".[165]

Individuals who are listed in the applicable regulation as having a right of access to the school do not necessarily have a right of access to all areas of the school premises.[166] This provision means that while certain people have a general right of access to school property, this licence does not extend to a general right to have access to areas to which entry is implicitly or expressly denied.

As a practical matter, while a general statutory right to exclude individuals from a school may be somewhat comforting (including the offence provision given in section 305(5) of the *Education Act*), faced with an individual who refuses to leave, contact with police (or other appropriate emergency authority) may be necessary to quell an obstreperous or out-of-control trespasser or stubborn guest. In addition to obvious resort to the *Criminal Code*, a peace officer has specific authorization under the *Trespass to Property Act*[167] to ". . .arrest without warrant any person he or she believes on reasonable and probable grounds to be on the premises"[168] who has no right or authority to be on school property. The *Trespass to Property Act* specifically includes a school board as an "occupier" (confer-

---

[164] Ontario Reg. 474/00 – *Access to School Premises*, s. 3(1).
[165] Ontario *Education Act*, s. 265(1)(m).
[166] Ontario Reg. 474/00 – *Access to School Premises*.
[167] R.S.O. 1990, c. T.21.
[168] *Ibid.*, ss. 9-11.

ring a right to exclude people from private property) for the purposes of the statute.[169]

RIGHTS OF PARENTS

While obviously parents have specific choices to make prior to a child's attendance at school (including to which school system one's school tax support will be directed), in recent years (particularly with respect to special needs education), concern has been expressed by parents with respect to their role in education once a student starts to attend school, noting that a parent has many responsibilities but comparatively few legal rights. A parent, as a matter of law, has legal responsibility for a child, including potential responsibility for damage done by a child.[170] A parent also has the obligation to ensure that a child of mandatory school age attends school, failing which he or she faces potential prosecution.[171]

While Division 2 of British Columbia's *School Act*[172] contains a specific list of entitlements of parents of school children,[173] few other provinces, including Ontario, have in place a direct and localized statement of parent rights with respect to school participation, opting instead for indirect reference by inclusion on school councils,[174] in volunteer activities, and through separate parent advocacy groups.[175]

---

[169] *Ibid.*, s. 1(2).
[170] This is a common law principle and also one expressed in statute: see, for example, the Ontario *Parental Responsibility Act, 2000*, S.O. 2000, c. 4.
[171] See Ontario *Education Act*, ss. 21(5) and 30.
[172] R.S.B.C. 1996, c. 412, s. 7.
[173] These include the right to be informed, in accordance with the orders of the Minister of the student's attendance, progress and behaviour at the school.
[174] See Ontario *Education Act*, s. 170(1), para. 17.1, and O. Reg. 612/00 – *School Councils*.
[175] See Ontario *Education Act*, s. 17.1, which continues the "Ontario Parent Council."

In Ontario, however, the issue of parental involvement and input in schools is being examined with a "Parent Voice in Education" Task Force, which was formed in November 2004. The Task Force delivered a report in April 2005 that suggested improvements in the area, including:

- a Provincial policy on parental involvement;
- a stronger role and support for parents at a local and provincial levels;
- a new office of Parental Involvement in the Ministry of Education; and
- the establishment of an advisory board of parents.[176]

While the implementation of some, or any of the Report's recommendations, as at this writing remains to be seen, it does provide a template for potential future discussion of the role of the parent in the education system.[177]

WHAT ELSE?

Like so many other issues in connection with children, education law is exceedingly complex because it touches so many areas of both statute and common law, including labour law, health law, privacy law and civil litigation to name just a few. In this chapter, we have focused deliberately on the child's interaction in school, rather than the extensive duties, obligations and rights of the other professionals and employees who function in a school environment. Due to the breadth of the topic, the nature of the treatment of these topics is necessarily short. If any issue develops that is specific to you or your child with respect to school, please consult a qualified legal professional.

---

[176] See www.edu.gov.on.ca/eng/document/reports/parentVoice.pdf.
[177] Information for parents on education and their involvement in their child's education may be found at the Ontario Ministry of Education's website at www.edu.gov.on.ca/eng/parents.

9
AN INTRODUCTION TO CHILD SUPPORT

Arguably, a parent is obligated to provide proper support for his or her child without being asked.
Zuker J., from Balo v. Motlagh[1]

As you have seen in Chapter 5, there are times when parents need to separate from each other. When they separate, they may or may not continue to have financial responsibilities and obligations to their former partner. However, when they separate they will definitely continue to have financial obligations and responsibility for their children.

Regrettably, one of the more controversial and least understood issues regarding parenthood is the absolute obligation to be financially responsible for the child. The obligation continues whether or not they wanted the child, ever intended to have a child or, for that matter, even continue to see the child.[2] "Child support" is the financial responsibility and obligation

---

[1] [2004] O.J. No. 3611 (Ont. C.J.) at para. 41.
[2] Some even make the argument that a child that has been made a Crown ward and in care of a Children's Aid Society should continue to be a child of the marriage for support purposes. See, for example, the case of *S. (J.M.) v. M. (F.J.)* (2004) 6 R.F.L. (6th) 191 (Ont. S.C.J.). It was subsequently reversed on appeal at *Seabrook v. Major* (2005), CarswellOnt 3168 (Ont. Div. Ct.), but note the dissenting opinion of Molloy J. Also see s. 60 of the CFSA.

of continuing to care for a child whether it is done voluntarily or by court order.

As Zuker J. noted in the quotation above, one would assume that each parent would assume the obligation that they have to their children and take financial responsibility for their children without being asked. This does happen and in those cases, one never hears about the matter: the parents "work it out" between them.[3] However, there are also many parents who do not wish or who do not feel they should pay child support and do not do so voluntarily.

As a result, the law has stepped in and has made it a legislated requirement to pay child support for dependent children. Both the *Divorce Act*[4] and the provincial Acts dealing with children include authority to the court to order support for dependent children.

The court's powers in this regard are quite extensive. As can be seen in the Ontario's *Family Law Act* example below, the obligation to provide support may even extend to costs that arose before the children were even born.[5]

> 34(1) Powers of court — In an application under section 33, the court may make an interim or final order,
>
> (a) requiring that an amount be paid periodically, whether annually or otherwise and whether for an indefinite or limited period, or until the happening of a specified event;
>
> (b) requiring that a lump sum be paid or held in trust;
>
> (c) requiring that property be transferred to or in trust for or vested in the dependant, whether absolutely, for life or for a term of years;

---

[3] Although it should be noted the court may set aside any agreement between parents that does not make proper arrangements for the children's financial support.
[4] *Divorce Act*, R.S.C., 1985, c. 3 (2nd Supp.), as amended.
[5] *Family Law Act*, R.S.O. 1990, c. F.3, as amended. See ss. 33 and 34.

(d) respecting any matter authorized to be ordered under clause 24 (1) (a), (b), (c), (d) or (e) (matrimonial home);

(e) requiring that some or all of the money payable under the order be paid into court or to another appropriate person or agency for the dependant's benefit;

(f) requiring that support be paid in respect of any period before the date of the order;

(g) requiring payment to an agency referred to in subsection 33 (3) of an amount in reimbursement for a benefit or assistance referred to in that subsection, including a benefit or assistance provided before the date of the order;

(h) requiring payment of expenses in respect of a child's prenatal care and birth;

(i) requiring that a spouse who has a policy of life insurance as defined in the *Insurance Act* designate the other spouse or a child as the beneficiary irrevocably;

. . .

Generally, however, when one thinks of child support, one thinks of an amount of money that is (usually) paid monthly from one parent to another to assist in the costs associated with raising children.

Although parents are primarily affected by "child support" as will be noted further below, a child's caregiver and others involved in the day-to-day care of children can also become involved in the process of determining the proper amount of "support". Specifically, you may be required to confirm the amounts of remuneration received as it relates to extraordinary expenses that can be added on to basic child support amounts under the current regime. As such it is hoped that this brief introduction can provide some guidance to you and your organization should you become involved in a child support dispute.

However, this is a very brief and simple introduction. Despite the attempts of various governments to simplify it, child support law remains extremely complex. As always, anyone dealing with a child support issue should seek independent legal advice in the area where the matter is being heard.

BACKGROUND

Historically the issue of child support has progressed along with our society's view of children and the obligations of parents to those children. Certainly, by the 1970s, child support was an established "right" of children and an "obligation" for parents.[6] Both the *Divorce Act* and many of the various Provinces, including Ontario, had special provisions in their laws, outlining the obligation to provide support for children.[7]

Unfortunately, for a variety of reasons, the "system" before 1997 became a "hodgepodge" of different rulings that varied from jurisdiction to jurisdiction and seemed to depend more on the sympathies of the particular judge than any rational connection to the children's needs.[8] The lack of predictability in the system was seen as inappropriate. It was also believed that it fostered litigation because the unpredictability of the outcome encouraged litigants to "give it a try" before the courts.

As well, the tax consequences of paying and receiving support did not seem to make much sense and were not very equitable for anyone involved in the system. Child support was tax deductible for the parent paying support and taxable as in-

---

[6] Perhaps it should also be noted that a child also has an obligation in law to support dependent parents if that is necessary. For example, see s. 33 of the *Family Law Act*.
[7] See, for example, s. 15.1 of the *Divorce Act* and s. 31 of the *Family Law Act*.
[8] For a review of the events leading up to the introduction of the Guidelines and a review of their impact, please see "Children Come First: A Report to Parliament on the Provisions and Operation of the 'Federal Child Support Guidelines'" (Department of Justice Canada, available on the Department of Justice website) at Volumes 1 and 2.

come for the parent receiving support. The paying parent was invariably in a higher tax bracket than the receiving parent. There were cases when the tax saving benefits the payor received (by way of tax deduction) exceeded the benefit the children received from the support after taxes. Often adjustments were made up front by lawyers and judges to account for the "tax consequences". However, even then the "tracking" of the tax made the system bulky and difficult. This was especially unhelpful for the support recipient who already had the challenge of primarily raising the children and had little time or resources to calculate all of the applicable tax factors.

Finally, the enforceability of child support was sporadic at best. If a support recipient wanted to enforce payment of support, he or she had to take steps to initiate and prosecute a garnishment process. This was a difficult process that was often too expensive to pursue when the monies that the recipient had were already being expended to "make up" for the missing or late support payments.

Given these difficulties, a complete revamping of the system was explored throughout the 1980s and earlier 1990s. By 1997, there was an implementation of a new, dramatically different approach to child support. Specifically, child support guidelines were introduced at both the federal and provincial levels.

The "guidelines" are based on a "grid" that sets support levels in increments based on the income of the support "payor" and the number of children. It is believed and hoped that this provides a consistent, objective amount of support across the "grid" or "table" regardless of any subjective considerations.

The Province of Ontario guidelines[9] for example, set out the following objectives for the *Child Support Guidelines*:

---

[9] For ease of explanation, references to the *Child Support Guidelines* in this Chapter will be referring to the Ontario version, O. Reg. 391/97 [here-

The objectives of these guidelines are,

(a) to establish a fair standard of support for children that ensures that they benefit from the financial means of their parents and, in the case of divorce, from the financial means of both spouses after separation;
(b) to reduce conflict and tension between parents or spouses by making the calculation of child support more objective;
(c) to improve the efficiency of the legal process by giving courts, and parents and spouses, guidance in setting the levels of child support and encouraging settlement; and
(d) to ensure consistent treatment of parents or spouses and their children who are in similar circumstances.

The guidelines have made a significant change to the area of child support and are generally regarded has having been successful in obtaining their objectives. However, there remains significant litigation over the issue of child support.

WHO IS ENTITLED TO CHILD SUPPORT?

One of most disputed areas of litigation in the area of child support is whether or not a child should receive support at all. Just as there have been various definitions of a "child" noted in other chapters in this book, as well there is a definition regarding which children are entitled to support. These vary from location to location and from Act to Act. Under section 15.1 of the *Divorce Act*, a "child of the marriage" is entitled to support. A "child of the marriage" is defined in subsection 2(1) as one who has not "withdrawn from their charge":

> "child of the marriage" means a child of two spouses or former spouses who, at the material time,
>
> (a) is under the age of majority and who has not withdrawn from their charge, or

---

inafter "the Guidelines"] (in force on December 1, 1997), made under the *Family Law Act*, as amended. (See O. Reg. 26/00, in force on March 1, 2000 and O. Reg. 446/01, in force on January 1, 2002.)

(b) is the age of majority or over and under their charge but unable, by reason of illness, disability or other cause, to withdraw from their charge or to obtain the necessaries of life;

Unfortunately, one needs to look at case law in order to determine when a child has "withdrawn from their charge". This determination often turns on the facts of the particular circumstances of the child before the court at the time and, essentially relates to whether of not the court finds that the child is still a "dependent".

Similarly, section 31 of Ontario's *Family Law Act* is unclear. Rather than using the words "withdrawn from their charge", it substitutes "control".

> 31(1) Obligation of parent to support child — Every parent has an obligation to provide support for his or her unmarried child who is a minor or is enrolled in a full time program of education, to the extent that the parent is capable of doing so.
>
> (2) Idem — The obligation under subsection (1) does not extend to a child who is sixteen years of age or older and has withdrawn from parental control.

As one can see in the second part of the definitions, the support obligation does not end based on an objective criteria of age or, the termination of all schooling (although it can). Instead, the obligation of support flows from the far more nebulous concept of withdrawing from parental control or charge.

Accordingly, there may be some adult children in their 20s who are entitled to support as they are continuing with their education and they may be dependent on the parents. On the other hand, there may be a minor child of 17 who is not entitled to support as they have withdrawn from parental control and they are not in school. As can be imagined, there can be immense disagreement between separated partners (and the children themselves) as to when or if the child has left parental control.

Invariably, the court must make a complex examination of: the child's living arrangements; whether the child has his or her own source of income; the parent's historical expectations as to how long they would have been supporting their child's scholastic endeavours; and some subjective guesswork as to whether or not the child is still a "child". Unfortunately, the guidelines do not assist in this initial contest and litigation continues to occur as a result.

What has changed from the previous regime is that if a child is entitled to support, then the courts have a tool to assist them in determining the amount that should be paid. However, how the final amount of support is arrived at is not without dispute.

DETERMINING THE AMOUNT OF SUPPORT

Under the *Family Law Act* in Ontario (and in other similar legislation), it is has long been a common philosophy that both parents have an obligation to provide support for their child.

What is new is that the apportionment of the support that is to be paid is an amount that is determined in accordance with the *Child Support Guidelines*, rather than the parent's ability to pay or what their discretionary income might be.

As noted, there is, in essence, a basic grid or table that outlines an amount of support based on the payor's gross income and the number of children receiving support. Section 3 of the Guidelines sets out a presumptive rule that for the majority of families, this is the amount of support paid. The bulk of the other portions of the Guidelines outlines "exceptions" that may be considered to move away from the "table amount" should there be just reasons for doing so.

> **3(1) Presumptive rule** — Unless otherwise provided under these guidelines, the amount of an order for the support of a child for children under the age of majority is,

(a) the amount set out in the applicable table, according to the number of children under the age of majority to whom the order relates and the income of the parent or spouse against whom the order is sought; and

(b) the amount, if any, determined under section 7.[10]

As noted above, one of the most controversial and confusing areas regarding support entitlement is the case of an adult child. The "guidelines" also factor in whether or not the table amount should apply to adult children.

ADULT CHILDREN

Subsection 3(2) of the Guidelines makes it a presumption that the table amount of support will be paid to the adult child just as if they were a minor. However, with adult children, the court has discretion to go "outside" of the grid, should that be in the child's best interests. In that case, the court will factor in the circumstances of the child as well as the financial ability of the parents to contribute.

(2) Child the age of majority or over — Unless otherwise provided under these guidelines, where a child to whom an order for the support of a child relates is the age of majority or over, the amount of an order for the support of a child is,

(a) the amount determined by applying these guidelines as if the child were under the age of majority; or

(b) if the court considers that approach to be inappropriate, the amount that it considers appropriate, having regard to the condition, means, needs and other circumstances of the child and the financial ability of each parent or spouse to contribute to the support of the child.

There is also discretion given to the court when the paying parent makes an income in excess of $150,000 per annum.

---

[10] Ontario Reg. 391/97, s. 3(1).

DISCRETION REGARDING HIGH INCOME

Section 4 of the Guidelines have included some discretion for the court when the payor has a high income level.

> 4. Incomes over $150,000 — Where the income of the parent or spouse against whom an order for the support of a child is sought is over $150,000, the amount of an order for the support of a child is,
>
> (a) the amount determined under section 3; or
> (b) if the court considers that amount to be inappropriate,
>
> (i) in respect of the first $150,000 of the parent's or spouse's income, the amount set out in the table for the number of children under the age of majority to whom the order relates,
> (ii) in respect of the balance of the parent's or spouse's income, the amount that the court considers appropriate, having regard to the condition, means, needs and other circumstances of the children who are entitled to support and the financial ability of each parent or spouse to contribute to the support of the children, and
> (iii) the amount, if any, determined under section 7.

It has been argued that when using the "table amount" for a high income, it is unfair to the support payor as the support funds are (likely) in excess of the amounts that are actually needed to care for the children. One view suggests that this is unfair as the "excess" under such a child support amount is in reality a form of spousal support as it is of benefit to the other parent(s) rather than to the child. The court has been clear that while discretion is available to a court, the presumption continues to be in favour of the table amount even in the case of extremely high incomes.[11]

This is perhaps most understandable when one considers the philosophy behind the support in the first place. If the parents continued to reside together the children of the relationship would benefit, both directly and indirectly, from the total economic resources of the parents. The philosophy behind child

---

[11] See *Francis v. Baker*, [1999] 3. S.C.R. 250 (S.C.C.).

support is that children will continue to receive the benefit of the economic support of all of their parents whether they have separated or not. Accordingly, it would seem to be in keeping with the philosophy of the support regime that both those with very high incomes and with very low incomes would pay a table amount.

However, it would likely be more understandable for a payor with a low income to argue that the table amount should not apply. To this end, the Guidelines allow a payor to claim "Hardship" as a reason for the court to go "outside" the table amounts.

HARDSHIP

A support payor who has an extremely high income may be able to pay an amount that is different then the Guidelines would indicate.

Similarly, those parents who are of less income may wish to have the court order an amount different then the table amount. Given the presumptive rule that we have seen, the first choice for the court is that the table amount applies. However, if the payor can establish that they are under a "hardship" from the table amount, then the court does have some discretion to go "outside the tables", as stated in subsection 10(2) of the Guidelines:

> 10(1) Undue hardship — On the application of either spouse or an applicant under section 33 of the Act, a court may award an amount of child support that is different from the amount determined under any of sections 3 to 5, 8 or 9 if the court finds that the parent or spouse making the request, or a child in respect of whom the request is made, would otherwise suffer undue hardship.

The test for hardship sets quite a high threshold. It is a two-part test. First the payor must come under one of the enumerated heads of the "Undue Hardship" test outlined in section 10(2) of the Guideline regulation:

> 10(2) Circumstances that may cause undue hardship — Circumstances that may cause a parent, spouse or child to suffer undue hardship include,
>
> > (a) the parent or spouse has responsibility for an unusually high level of debts reasonably incurred to support the parents or spouses and their children during cohabitation or to earn a living;
> > (b) the parent or spouse has unusually high expenses in relation to exercising access to a child;
> > (c) the parent or spouse has a legal duty under a judgment, order or written separation agreement to support any person;
> > (d) the spouse has a legal duty to support a child, other than a child of the marriage, who is,
> > > (i) under the age of majority, or
> > > (ii) the age of majority or over but is unable, by reason of illness, disability or other cause, to obtain the necessaries of life;
> > (e) the parent has a legal duty to support a child, other than the child who is the subject of this application, who is under the age of majority or who is enrolled in a full time course of education;
> > (f) the parent or spouse has a legal duty to support any person who is unable to obtain the necessaries of life due to an illness or disability.

The list of circumstances that bring one into the hardship test is exhaustive. As a result, it is often difficult for a parent to fit under one of the enumerated headings.

Even if one can show that they meet the first part of the test, then they must also meet the second part of the test in subsections 10(3), (4), namely, that they have a lower household standard of living then the support recipient's household.

> (3) Standards of living must be considered — Despite a determination of undue hardship under subsection (1), an application under that subsection must be denied by the court if it is of the opinion that the household of the parent or spouse who claims undue hardship would, after

determining the amount of child support under any of sections 3 to 5, 8 or 9, have a higher standard of living than the household of the other parent or spouse.

(4) Standards of living test — In comparing standards of living for the purpose of subsection (3), the court may use the comparison of household standards of living test set out in Schedule II.

Although there may be situations where the hardship test is met, it is very rare. The reality is that most support payors have a higher standard of living than the recipient of the support. The fact is that the recipient will have the on-going expenses of the children. This obligation usually results in a lower standard of living. If this were not the case, then support likely would not be payable in the first place.

Just as the payor may wish to convince the court to use its discretion to not apply the table amount, the recipient may also ask for monies above and beyond the table amount. There may be additional costs related to the children's care that can be quantified and these can be looked at by the court.

ADD-ONS/EXTRAORDINARY BENEFITS

While the payor(s) may feel the "table amount" is too high, the support recipient may feel the amount is too low. The recipient also has a mechanism to seek an amount different than the table amount. In this regard, the recipient is entitled to seek a contribution of "extraordinary expenses" that are specific to this child or children.

The issue of extraordinary benefits has created a great deal of litigation since the introduction of the guidelines. Some have argued that the extraordinary benefits section was intended to assist with costs that were truly "extraordinary". Others have taken a much more pragmatic view of the "extraordinary benefits", arguing that they are simply additional costs or "add-ons" to which each parent should contribute.

It would seem from a plain reading of the Guideline's subsection 7(1) that most are not so extraordinary and contain such things as assisting with daycare, school costs, health care costs, etc.

> 7(1) Special or extraordinary expenses — In an order for the support of a child, the court may, on the request of either parent or spouse or of an applicant under section 33 of the Act, provide for an amount to cover all or any portion of the following expenses, which expenses may be estimated, taking into account the necessity of the expense in relation to the child's best interests and the reasonableness of the expense in relation to the means of the parents or spouses and those of the child and to the spending pattern of the parents or spouses in respect of the child during cohabitation:
>
>> (a) child care expenses incurred as a result of the custodial parent's employment, illness, disability or education or training for employment;
>> (b) that portion of the medical and dental insurance premiums attributable to the child;
>> (c) health-related expenses that exceed insurance reimbursement by at least $100 annually, including orthodontic treatment, professional counselling provided by a psychologist, social worker, psychiatrist or any other person, physiotherapy, occupational therapy, speech therapy, prescription drugs, hearing aids, glasses and contact lenses;
>> (d) extraordinary expenses for primary or secondary school education or for any other educational programs that meet the child's particular needs;
>> (e) expenses for post-secondary education; and
>> (f) extraordinary expenses for extracurricular activities.

Once it is determined that the extra cost is one that is covered by the Guideline section, then the presumption is that the parents will share the expense in proportion to their respective ability to pay and factoring in any tax or other benefit that might be invoked.

> 7(2) Sharing of expense — The guiding principle in determining the amount of an expense referred to in subsection (1) is that the expense is shared by the parents or spouses in proportion to their respective in-

comes after deducting from the expense, the contribution, if any, from the child.

(3) Subsidies, tax deductions, etc. — In determining the amount of an expense referred to in subsection (1), the court must take into account any subsidies, benefits or income tax deductions or credits relating to the expense, and any eligibility to claim a subsidy, benefit or income tax deduction or credit relating to the expense.

On the surface, then the Guidelines seem fairly simple. They commence presuming the table amount is correct and just. The payor can try and reduce the table amount. The primary mechanism for this to be tried is by claiming hardship. The recipient will try and increase the table amount by asking that "add-ons" be also ordered for the various items that are specific to the costs of the child.

However, despite the simplicity of the system on the surface, there are in practice a number of perils that create litigation and frustration for the parties.

DISCLOSURE

One of the most difficult issues in dealing with support is obtaining disclosure of the financial circumstances of the parties (and in some cases the children). Given that the table amounts are based on the income level of the support payor, full financial disclosure is critical.

There are a number of requirements in the various Acts and the Family Court Rules obligating all parties to make on-going financial disclosure of their income, tax returns as well as sworn financial statements.

On occasion, disclosure of a person's financial circumstances is not forthcoming and the court has been granted authority to "impute" the income of a potential payor. In this way, the court will arrive at an income for child support purposes based on any information that the potential recipient can provide even if the amount that is arrived at is erroneous.

It should also be noted that the obligation to disclose financial circumstances is required of the person requesting child support as well. This is particularly so in the case of "extraordinary" expenses. In order to make the claim for "add-on" money, the court must find that the expenses are occurring for the benefit of the child. For those working with children, you should be aware that the receipts you provide for daycare, after-school activities, clubs, sports, etc., may come under the court's scrutiny as they try to determine the appropriate amount to be paid by each parent.

SPLIT CUSTODY

Another issue of contention, despite the Guidelines, is the issue of "split custody". This is the situation where one spouse has one child (or more) from the relationship and the other parent has one (or more) of the children from the relationship.

In that situation, the support is "set off" against each other in that the order for support is made against each as to what they should be paying if custody was not split, as determined in section 8 of the Guidelines:

> 8. Where each parent or spouse has custody of one or more children, the amount of an order for the support of a child is the difference between the amount that each parent or spouse would otherwise pay if such an order were sought against each of the parents or spouses.

Usually, this termination is worked out fairly easily. However the "splitting" of the extraordinary benefits can "bog down" the set off of the two parties.

More confusing is the issue of "shared custody".

SHARED CUSTODY

Of greater confusion than "split custody" is the concept of "shared parenting". If the child is with the paying parent at least 40 per cent of the time, then the Guidelines suggest that the care of the child is "shared" (for child support purposes) and the court has some discretion to go outside of the table amount. Section 9 states:

> 9. Where a parent or spouse exercises a right of access to, or has physical custody of, a child for not less than 40 per cent of the time over the course of a year, the amount of the order for the support of a child must be determined by taking into account,
>
> (a) the amounts set out in the applicable tables for each of the parents or spouses;
> (b) the increased costs of shared custody arrangements; and
> (c) the condition, means, needs and other circumstances of each parent or spouse and of any child for whom support is sought.

Courts have attempted to deal with support under the "40/60 split" of shared custody in a variety of ways. This has resulted in different approaches and outcomes.[12] Needless to say, this uncertainty is what the implementation of the Guidelines was meant to avoid. Therefore, it is perhaps not surprising that a case was recently argued before the Supreme Court of Canada on this issue. It is hoped that the Supreme Court's decision will lead to clearer direction in this area.[13]

---

[12] For a review of the case law in this area, see Kim Hart Wensley's article "Shared Custody – Section 9 of the Federal Child Support Guidelines: Formulaic? Pure Discretion? Structured Discretion" 23 C.F.L.Q. 63.

[13] *Contino v. Leonelli-Contino* (2002), 30 R.F.L. (5th) 266 (Ont. Div. Ct.), varied (2003), 42 R.F.L. (5th) 295 (Ont. C.A.), leave to appeal allowed (2004), [2003] S.C.A.A. No. 557 (S.C.C.) heard by the S.C.C. on January 14, 2005 and on reserve.

PREDICTABILITY?

As you can see from the brief introduction noted above, while the Guidelines have provided some measure of predictability in the application and determination of support, there are still many areas of contention. What has been resolved, however, is the confusion that previously arose over tax consequences and enforceability.

TAX CONSEQUENCE CHANGES

The 1996 federal budget brought changes to the way child support was calculated for tax purposes. The changes came into effect on May 1, 1997 to coincide with the introduction of the Guidelines.

Under the Guidelines, child support paid or received under orders or agreements made after the introduction of the Guidelines are (generally) not taxable to the recipient and are not deductible by the payor.

It should be noted that there was some limited ability of parents (if they agreed) to maintain the "old" taxation system, but this was very rare and for almost all child support orders the payments are "tax neutral" to both sides.

ENFORCEMENT

This chapter cannot cover the myriad of mechanisms that are in place to enforce support payment. However, it is acknowledged that the new mechanisms that have been initiated after the introduction of the Guidelines have been substantially "beefed up". For both positive and negative reasons, the changes in enforcement—and the task of carrying out the enforcement—are more obvious to the public than the Guidelines themselves.

Along with the introduction of the Guidelines and the changes to the tax system, the Provinces enacted new legislation to enforce the guidelines. In Ontario, the *Family Responsibility and Support Arrears Enforcement Act, 1996*[14] was passed, setting up a new government enforcement agency called the Director of the Family Responsibility Office.[15]

Unlike the previous enforcement agencies that were only implemented once the support recipient pursued enforcement remedies, the new regime ensured FRO has a mandate to enforce every child support order unless specifically withdrawn from their office. In this regard, the court is obligated to include as part of the order an operative part that ensures the order will be enforced by the Director of FRO.[16] This enforcement part is considered a separate "Support Deduction Order". Both the support order and the Support Deduction Order must be filed with FRO.[17] The Support Deduction Order can only be withdrawn on the written request of the recipient and only if the support order itself is being withdrawn.[18] In fact, the court can include a provision that the order cannot be withdrawn if it feels this is necessary.[19]

Numerous other implementations were also made to ensure enforcement was a priority. Provisions for enforcing orders made in other jurisdictions were included.[20] Also of importance was that the income source (i.e., the employer) of the payor could become responsible for the child support if it/they failed to deduct the support at source or forward to FRO.[21]

---

[14] S.O. 1996, c. 31, as amended.
[15] *Ibid.* at s. 2.
[16] *Ibid.* at s. 9(1).
[17] *Ibid.* at ss. 12(1) and (2).
[18] *Ibid.* at s. 16(5).
[19] *Ibid.* at s. 9(2).
[20] *Ibid.* at s. 13.
[21] *Ibid.* at s. 26(7).

In addition to these changes, numerous new and surprising "penalties" were included to assist payors to meet their obligations. Perhaps most well known is the penalty to suspend a driver's licenses for failing to pay child support.[22] Less well known is that many other licenses including federally issued licenses such as pilot and boat licenses can also be suspended under similar Acts. In addition, liens can be put on homes and personal property and ultimately jail time can be ordered for a non-payor.[23]

In essence, child support and the non-payment of it has become a very serious and important issue. Some would say this was long overdue. Be that as it may, anyone who owes child support would be well advised to seek independent legal advice as soon as possible. There are limits on what remedies and options are available once the FRO starts certain enforcement steps and any delay might be detrimental to the payor and others who rely on him or her in their day-to-day activities.

CONCLUSION

Although the *Child Support Guidelines* have gone a long way to simplifying the area, there remains much complexity in how child support is applied and how it is enforced. It is hoped that this brief introduction will provide an overview to assist in understanding some of the key terms and aspects of it. As always though, one should consider legal advice if involved, as a lawyer can assist in guiding one through the complexities that may be unique to the situation and jurisdiction.

---

[22] *Ibid.* at ss. 33 through 39
[23] *Ibid.* at ss. 40 through 50.

10
INFORMATION AND DISCLOSURE/ ASSESSMENTS/ CHILDREN'S LAWYER

If you work with children, eventually someone will want to know what a child has said to you. You may also be asked to describe what you have observed a child do. This chapter is intended to be a guide to how to handle such requests, including the situations in which you may be asked to provide information to a court.

As reviewed in Chapter 2, a professional has a legal obligation to immediately report suspected child abuse. In Ontario, this is a personal obligation that cannot be delegated by a professional who receives the information during the course of his or her duties. Distinct from a situation that involves suspected child abuse, on-going interaction with a child will involve observations and perhaps recordings of what occurred. Therefore, the information retained by a professional during the course of this relationship may be important "evidence" to a court in determining an issue before it. Such evidence may your verbal "testimony". If you are called upon to give evidence, your testimony may also involve disclosing any documents (notes, records etc.) that you might have kept regarding the job you do.

A request to disclose information concerning a child may be troubling for the professional who receives it. There are many, many restrictions on disclosure of personal information in various jurisdictions and these laws change frequently, including by means of the introduction of new laws. In Ontario for example, the new *Personal Health Information Protection Act, 2004*[1] has only recently come into effect.

In addition to the privacy laws, there may also be confidentiality agreements and protocols that your employer has in place (and that you have signed) limiting the information you can release. There may also be a procedure governing how that information should be disclosed. These aspects must also be considered.

You should certainly consult with your own procedure and your organization's own legal resources and lawyers before proceeding to release any information. This will ensure that every disclosure is lawful and does not create serious difficulties for yourself or your organization.

The following is intended as a general review of the processes and terminology involved in providing evidence about a child. It is intended to familiarize you with this often anxiety-inducing process and to assist you to obtain your own legal advice.

SUBPOENA OR SUMMONS TO ATTEND AT TRIAL

The easiest (and most common) means of getting a witness before the court (or other official body such as a tribunal) is to serve him or her with a legal document requiring the person's attendance in court. If a matter is in criminal courts, the document requiring the witness' attendance is called a "subpoena". In non-criminal matters, the document is called a "summons".

---

[1] *Personal Health Information Protection Act, 2004*, S.O. 2004, c. 3.

In practice, however, the terms "subpoena" and "summons" are often used interchangeably by lawyers, judges and laypersons alike. In this chapter, for the sake of simplicity, we will refer to the document which served on a witness as a "summons".

A summons is a document typed on a standard court form. It is often issued and signed by a court staff member (although not always). It will advise a person that they are required to attend at some event that involves a court case, stating the date that the witness is required, as well as the time.

In most situations, the witness is asked to attend to give evidence at a trial or at a tribunal hearing. However, a witness may also receive a summons to give evidence at an "examination for discovery" (popularly known as a "discovery" or "discoveries"), which is a deposition given during the course of a civil lawsuit. An "examination for discovery" is a meeting (which is not held at a court or tribunal but instead at an office) where a witness can be asked questions under oath before an "Official Examiner" (not a judge). The Official Examiner will make a transcript of all of the questions asked and answers given. The transcript from an examination for discovery may be used at the trial of the civil action for comparison purposes: to see if the answers given by the witness at examination for discovery are different from the answers later by the same witness in testifying in court at trial.

Almost all boards, tribunals and courts have rules permitting the serving of a summons on a prospective witness. For example, in a Family Court matter in Ontario, other than the Unified Family Court, a party who wants a witness to give evidence in court (or to bring documents or other things to the court) may serve a witness with a summons along with a small fee prescribed by Rule 23 applicable to that court.[2]

---

[2] Rule 23(3) of the *Family Law Rules*, O. Reg. 114/99, as amended.

There are many rules governing whether a summons is properly served. As soon as you are served with a summons (i.e., it comes to your attention), you should seek legal advice to determine whether or not it has been lawfully served.

At a minimum, contact should be made with the lawyer or party that had the summons delivered to you. It may be that a date other than the one listed on the summons can be negotiated if the date listed on the summons is inconvenient. In certain situations, after you speak with the lawyer or party who served you with the summons, that party may conclude that your testimony would not be of assistance to the court in determining the issues in dispute.

However, please be aware that your personal convenience or lack of desire to attend court does not change the fact that you have received an official court document when you receive a summons. You should never ignore such a document. If the summons has been served on you correctly, then you need to attend court on the date and time listed on the summons. Failure to comply with a summons may subject you to consequences that are quite severe. If you fail to comply with a summons, the court may issue a warrant for your arrest.

As an example, Rule 23(7) of the *Family Law Rules* gives the court specific authority to issue an arrest warrant where a person does not obey a summons. It reads:

> 23(7) Failure to obey summons — the court may issue a warrant for arrest (form 32b) to bring a witness before the court if,
>
> (a) the witness has been served as subrule (3) requires, but has not obeyed the summons; and
>
> (b) it is necessary to have the witness present in court or at a questioning.

As you can see, it is important to deal immediately with a summons once one has been received. Usually a summons to a witness indicates that a witness is expected to testify under oath. However on other occasions, only your documents and records are being sought. Again, it is important that you communicate with whoever sent the summons in order to find out (as much as possible) what is expected of you on the date specified.

A common situation in which documents may be requested of a third party (e.g., a school; an institution; a counsellor) occurs in the context of a trial in the criminal courts. In these situations, a very set procedure governs how records are obtained from a third party (e.g., you or your institution). This process has become known as an "O'Connor Application".

O'CONNOR APPLICATION (CRIMINAL)

An O'Connor Application gets its name from a Supreme Court of Canada case[3] that set out the steps the parties and court will take to obtain records that may (or may not) ultimately be used in the criminal proceedings. For certainty, the steps arising from this Court decision have been incorporated into the *Criminal Code*. However, many peoples still refer to applications to obtain records from third parties as an "O'Connor Application" in reference to the case of the same name.

What is being sought by means of an O'Connor Application are the records held by someone other than the accused or the Crown. The party who makes such an application believes that somehow that records in the hands of these "third parties" will have an impact on the outcome (or process) of the criminal proceedings.

The prescribed steps in an O'Connor Application represent an attempt to balance the rights of an accused to fully defend him- or herself against the privacy interests of anyone who may have custody of, or be mentioned in, "third party records".

---

[3] *R. v. O'Connor*, [1995] 4 S.C.R. 411 (S.C.C.).

A "record" for the purposes of an "O'Connor Application" is very broadly defined in section 278.1 of the *Criminal Code*:[4]

> 278.1. For the purposes of sections 278.2 to 278.9, "record" means any form of record that contains personal information for which there is a reasonable expectation of privacy and includes, without limiting the generality of the foregoing, medical, psychiatric, therapeutic, counselling, education, employment, child welfare, adoption and social services records, personal journals and diaries, and records containing personal information the production or disclosure of which is protected by any other Act of Parliament or a provincial legislature, but does not include records made by persons responsible for the investigation or prosecution of the offence.

The *Criminal Code* sets out a two-part mechanism by which a party to a criminal trial may seek to obtain records in the custody of a third party on the basis that these records are "relevant" to the proceedings.

First, an application must be made to the trial judge and only the trial judge to obtain the third party record(s):

> 278.3(2) An accused who seeks production of a record referred to in subsection 278.2(1) must make an application to the judge before whom the accused is to be, or is being, tried.

The *Criminal Code* also contains specific requirements of the application for third-party records. In addition to the requirement that the application be in writing, the applicant must also provide some indication of what the records are and who has "custody or control" of the records. In addition, the party seeking the records must indicate why it is thought that the requested records will be "likely relevant" to the matters before the court.

> 278.3(3) An application must be made in writing and set out
>
> > (a) particulars identifying the record that the accused seeks to have produced and the name of the person who has possession or control of the record; and

---

[4] *Criminal Code*, R.S.C. 1985, c. C-46.

(b) the grounds on which the accused relies to establish that the record is likely relevant to an issue at trial or to the competence of a witness to testify.

It is critical that the party seeking the third-party records demonstrates the relevancy of the documents. The *Criminal Code* emphasizes that the existence of certain facts with respect to third-party records does not automatically mean that the requested documents are relevant. As stated in the *Criminal Code*:

> 278.3(4) Any one or more of the following assertions by the accused are not sufficient on their own to establish that the record is likely relevant to an issue at trial or to the competence of a witness to testify:
>
> (a) that the record exists;
>
> (b) that the record relates to medical or psychiatric treatment, therapy or counselling that the complainant or witness has received or is receiving;
>
> (c) that the record relates to the incident that is the subject-matter of the proceedings;
>
> (d) that the record may disclose a prior inconsistent statement of the complainant or witness;
>
> (e) that the record may relate to the credibility of the complainant or witness;
>
> (f) that the record may relate to the reliability of the testimony of the complainant or witness merely because the complainant or witness has received or is receiving psychiatric treatment, therapy or counselling;
>
> (g) that the record may reveal allegations of sexual abuse of the complainant by a person other than the accused;
>
> (h) that the record relates to the sexual activity of the complainant with any person, including the accused;
>
> (i) that the record relates to the presence or absence of a recent complaint;
>
> (j) that the record relates to the complainant's sexual reputation; or
>
> (k) that the record was made close in time to a complaint or to the activity that forms the subject-matter of the charge against the accused.

In addition to issuing and serving the application on the other parties to the criminal proceeding (usually this involves the accused serving the application on the Crown), in an O'Connor application, the keeper of the records (whether an institution or individual) must also be served with a copy of the application and a summons to appear with the records when the O'Connor application is heard in court. It should be noted that a copy of the application and the summons must also be delivered or served on any person affected by the records (i.e., the person to whom the records pertain or who are mentioned in the records). Frequently, in criminal matters, records are sought pertaining to the complainant in the proceeding. However, such records may also make reference to other individuals, in addition to the complainant. This requirement to serve the application and summons on any person affected by the records is often particularly troublesome for the party seeking access. It is often the case that because the contents of the records are not fully known, the identity of individuals referred to in the records, similarly, is not known. The *Criminal Code*, nonetheless, states as follows:

> 278.3(5) The accused shall serve the application on the prosecutor, on the person who has possession or control of the record, on the complainant or witness, as the case may be, and on any other person to whom, to the knowledge of the accused, the record relates, at least seven days before the hearing referred to in subsection 278.4(1) or any shorter interval that the judge may allow in the interests of justice. The accused shall also serve a subpoena issued under Part XXII in Form 16.1 on the person who has possession or control of the record at the same time as the application is served.

Because of this practical issue, a judge hearing an O'Connor application has the power to order that notice of the application be given to a party affected by the records at any time.[5]

When an O'Connor application is heard in court, it proceeds roughly as follows. The judge will hold a private small hearing

---

[5] *Criminal Code*, s. 278.3(6).

to determine whether or not the court should review the third-party records. In the course of this small hearing, the holder of the records and others are invited to make representations as to whether they think the records should be reviewed by the court or not. As per the *Criminal Code*:

> 278.4(1) The judge shall hold a hearing *in camera* to determine whether to order the person who has possession or control of the record to produce it to the court for review by the judge.
>
> (2) The person who has possession or control of the record, the complainant or witness, as the case may be, and any other person to whom the record relates may appear and make submissions at the hearing, but they are not compellable as witnesses at the hearing.

After hearing the positions of those who have made submissions, the judge must consider the question of whether or not the records should be released. In doing so, the judge is guided by specific criteria stated in the *Criminal Code*. As follows:

> 278.5(2) In determining whether to order the production of the record or part of the record for review pursuant to subsection (1), the judge shall consider the salutary and deleterious effects of the determination on the accused's right to make a full answer and defence and on the right to privacy and equality of the complainant or witness, as the case may be, and any other person to whom the record relates. In particular, the judge shall take the following factors into account:
>
> (a) the extent to which the record is necessary for the accused to make a full answer and defence;
>
> (b) the probative value of the record;
>
> (c) the nature and extent of the reasonable expectation of privacy with respect to the record;
>
> (d) whether production of the record is based on a discriminatory belief or bias;
>
> (e) the potential prejudice to the personal dignity and right to privacy of any person to whom the record relates;
>
> (f) society's interest in encouraging the reporting of sexual offences;
>
> (g) society's interest in encouraging the obtaining of treatment by complainants of sexual offences; and

(h) the effect of the determination on the integrity of the trial process.

Based on these criteria, the court has the power to order the production of the documents to the court. The relevant section of the *Criminal Code* is as follows:

> 278.5(1) The judge may order the person who has possession or control of the record to produce the record or part of the record to the court for review by the judge if, after the hearing referred to in subsection 278.4(1), the judge is satisfied that
>
> (a) the application was made in accordance with subsections 278.3(2) to (6);
>
> (b) the accused has established that the record is likely relevant to an issue at trial or to the competence of a witness to testify; and
>
> (c) the production of the record is necessary in the interests of justice.

Obviously, the person or institution holding records, as well as the individuals mentioned in the records, may have concerns about releasing the records to the court for the purposes of determining which ones will be released to the moving party (usually the accused). Therefore, these individuals may take the position that the records should not be released to the court for review. Ultimately, however, the decision lies with the court to determine whether or not the documents should be reviewed As stated in the sections above, in deciding the application, the judge must weigh the interests of the holders of the records and those mentioned in the records balanced against the accused's right to make full answer and defence and to receive a fair trial.

If the judge decides to review the records for the purposing of determining which ones should be released to the accused (usually the moving party), he or she will review them in private.[6]

---

[6] *Criminal Code*, s. 278.6(1).

After the court reviews the records, the judge has the power under the *Criminal Code* to release to the accused the records that the judge feels are relevant to an "issue at trial" or the "competence of a witness to testify". In making this determination, the judge balances the accused's rights to make "full answer and defence" against the privacy interests of the individuals to whom the records relate:

> 278.7(1) Where the judge is satisfied that the record or part of the record is likely relevant to an issue at trial or to the competence of a witness to testify and its production is necessary in the interests of justice, the judge may order that the record or part of the record that is likely relevant be produced to the accused, subject to any conditions that may be imposed pursuant to subsection (3).
>
> (2) In determining whether to order the production of the record or part of the record to the accused, the judge shall consider the salutary and deleterious effects of the determination on the accused's right to make a full answer and defence and on the right to privacy and equality of the complainant or witness, as the case may be, and any other person to whom the record relates and, in particular, shall take the factors specified in paragraphs 278.5(2)(a) to (h) into account.

Obviously an O'Connor Application can be quite a complex proceeding and anyone served with such a request should contact their legal counsel to get advice on how to manage the request.

While the receipt of a subpoena or summons usually indicates that a trial has commenced and that one will be testifying at a trial or hearing, there are also many other methods of obtaining documents and information prior to a trial or hearing.

PRE-TRIAL MOTION FOR DOCUMENTS

Like an O'Connor application in criminal proceedings, in civil and family law proceedings, a motion can be brought to request the records of a third party at any time.

The Rules of most courts allow for some form of pre-trial disclosure of materials from third-party record holders.

For example, the *Family Law Rules* provide for such a motion under Rule 19(11):

> 19(11) Document in non-party's control — if a document is in a non-party's control, or is available only to the non-party, and is not protected by a legal privilege, and it would be unfair to a party to go on with the case without the document, the court may, on motion with notice served on every party and served on the non-party by special service,
>
> (a) order the non-party to let the party examine the document and to supply the party with a copy at the legal aid rate; and
>
> (b) order that a copy be prepared and used for all purposes of the case instead of the original.

In most cases, these motions are brought well in advance of a trial in order for everyone to know "what is out there". In some cases, the fact that the documents exist may even make a trial unnecessary: reviewing the documents may convince one of the parties that they do not want to proceed to a contested hearing.

In addition to the Rules of the various courts and tribunals, some legislation allows documents to be obtained from third parties. For example, under section 74 of the *Child and Family Services Act* ("CFSA"), a Children's Aid Society has a broad right to obtain records from third parties.

The operation of section 74 is very similar to that of an O'Connor Application in the criminal court. However, on a section 74 application, the court can order that the information be disclosed by the record holder prior to the trial, and even after a trial if it is necessary to enforce compliance with an order that has been made under section 57 of the CFSA (an order for child protection). Section 74 of the CFSA reads:

Court-Ordered Access to Records

74(1) Record — In this section and sections 74.1 and 74.2,

"record" means recorded information, regardless of physical form or characteristics;

"record of personal health information" has the same meaning as in the Mental Health Act.

(2) Motion or application, production of record — A Director or a society may at any time make a motion or an application for an order under subsection (3) or (3.1) for the production of a record or part of a record.

(3) Order — Where the court is satisfied that a record or part of a record that is the subject of a motion referred to in subsection (2) contains information that may be relevant to a proceeding under this Part and that the person in possession or control of the record has refused to permit a Director or the society to inspect it, the court may order that the person in possession or control of the record produce it or a specified part of it for inspection and copying by the Director, by the society or by the court.

(3.1) Same — Where the court is satisfied that a record or part of a record that is the subject of an application referred to in subsection (2) may be relevant to assessing compliance with one of the following and that the person in possession or control of the record has refused to permit a Director or the society to inspect it, the court may order that the person in possession or control of the record produce it or a specified part of it for inspection and copying by the Director, by the society or by the court:

1. An order under clause 51(2)(b) or (c) that is subject to supervision.
2. An order under clause 51(2)(c) or (d) with respect to access.
3. A supervision order under section 57.
4. An access order under section 58.
5. An order under section 65 with respect to access or supervision.
6. A restraining order under section 80. 1999, c. 2, s. 24(1).

(4) Court may examine record — In considering whether to make an order under subsection (3) or (3.1), the court may examine the record.

The information that the Society can obtain under section 74 must be kept confidential, except where a court order authorizes its disclosure, or as it is disclosed in testimony in a proceeding under the CFSA under which the documents were sought.[7]

The right to obtain documents through section 74 of the CFSA is quite broad and prevails over many confidentiality provisions in statutes, including the *new Personal Health Information Protection Act, 2004.*[8]

However, there are limits to the nature of the information that can be obtained on an application under section 74 of the CFSA. Information that is solicitor-client privileged is exempt from disclosure.[9] Further, in order to obtain records on an application under section 74, the Children's Aid Society must always demonstrate to the court that the third-party records being sought are relevant to the issues being decided before the court.[10] If the Society cannot show that the information is relevant to the protection of children, then the court will not order the third party to disclose its records. The ability to apply to obtain disclosure of third-party records under section 74 is not a justification for a Children's Aid Society to go on a "fishing expedition" so as to intrude unnecessarily into a parent's life, without demonstrating the relevance of the records sought.

ASSESSMENT REPORTS

In addition to potential involvement in a pre-trial motion or application for disclosure of records, another way in which individuals working with children may become involved in legal proceedings involving children is in the course of preparing an "assessment report".

---

[7] CFSA, R.S.O. 1990, c. C.11, s. 74(5).
[8] S.O. 2004, c. 3, Sch. A.
[9] *Supra* note 7 at s. 74(6).
[10] See Madame Justice Patricia H. Wallace's comments in *Children's Aid Society of Hamilton-Wentworth v. T. (S.)*, [1996] O.J. No. 3578 (Ont. Gen. Div.), confirmed on appeal to the Divisional Court [unreported].

Sometimes a court is unsure about what the relevant issues in a proceeding involving children really are, without obtaining further information. As we saw in previous chapters, allegations that are made in family courts are often made in wholly subjective terms, without detailed background facts about the context giving rise to the allegations or background or details concerning the lives of the children involved. In these circumstances, the parties and the court may ask that an assessor review the situation and prepare a report to the court. As part of preparing an assessment report, the assessor often wants to speak to people who interact with a child (or children) on a day-to-day basis.

As noted, an assessor is someone with some form of expertise, someone qualified to perform the particular assessment ordered (usually regarding children or some aspect of children). The assessor will take a variety of steps to form an opinion regarding the child and will make certain recommendations (usually in a written report) to the court about what he or she thinks would be best for the child. A court is not obligated to accept and implement an assessment report. A court can always order what it believes is in the best interests of the children in accordance with the governing law. However, an assessment report does often carry a great deal of weight with the court and will influence the eventual income of a proceeding. Often, the influence an assessment report will have on the outcome of a case will be affected by the level of expertise possessed by the assessor. For example, an assessment done by a social worker may carry less weight than an assessment report prepared by a psychologist. In turn, an assessment report prepared by a psychologist may carry less weight then one completed by a psychiatrist. In addition to an assessor's credentials, consideration may be also given to the background, experience, and independence of the author of a report.

Another factor affecting the impact of an assessment report is the way in which the assessment is conducted. If the Assessor is overly selective about whom he/she meets and excludes certain relevant individuals or is unduly influenced by one side's version of the facts then the assessment report may have less influence with the court.

Each assessor has different means of conducting an assessment. Assessors usually want to witness the children's interaction with the parents (or parties to the court case). However, assessors may also want to know whether their observation of the children's behaviour and conduct is the "norm". Accordingly, assessors will often seek out information from daycare providers, teachers and others who see the children interacting with the parents (or parties) on a more frequent and candid basis.

Once again, if you are contacted by an assessor, you should always consult with your own legal advisors to determine what information you can and cannot give to the assessor. When you are approached by someone who wants to do on an assessment on a child, you will want to enquire and ascertain what authority the assessor has (which may affect what or how much information you may disclose) as there are many types of assessments.

Some assessments are informal and have nothing to do with a court. For example, a parent who suspects that his or her child has Attention Deficit Disorder may commission a psychologist to complete a "psycho-educational assessment". Also, a family that is undergoing counselling may also have a social worker "assess" the child to assist in working out some issue that is of concern to the family. Because these are private personal assessments, the amount that you will want to disclose (or are willing to disclose) may be very different than an assessment that is ordered by the court.

A court can order an assessment of a child in both the child protection case and in custody and access matters. In many respects the assessments in both types of cases are similar. One of the key differences between them is that the custody and access assessment, like a custody and access matter generally, can be requested at any time. On the other hand, a child protection assessment has an initial "threshold" that a Children's Aid Society must meet before it can start "assessing" the private life of the family. In this regard, a child protection assessment can only be ordered by the court once the child has been found to be "in need of protection" as defined in the CFSA.

The authority for an assessment in the child protection area is found in section 54 of the CFSA. An assessment (especially in the child protection context but sometimes in the custody and access context as well) is often mistakenly referred to as a "parenting capacity assessment". In fact, there is no ability to fully assess whether or not someone is, or will obtain the capacity to be, a "good parent". Indeed, it might be impossible to define what a "good parent" is. However, section 54 does allow for a variety of different types assessments to be ordered ranging from psychological to educational. In an assessment ordered under section 54 of the CFSA, the assessor will likely look at a number of factors to prepare a report to assist a court in determining whether or not someone has the strengths to safely parent a child in his or her care. Section 54 of the CFSA reads:

> 54(1) Order for assessment — Where a child has been found to be in need of protection, the court may order that within a specified time,
>
> (a) the child; or
>
> (b) a parent or a person, except a foster parent, in whose charge the child has been or may be,
>
> attend before and undergo an assessment by a specified person who is qualified, in the court's opinion, to perform medical, emotional, developmental, psychological, educational or social assessments and has consented to perform the assessment.

Technically, an assessment report in a child protection matter is to be completed within 30 days[11] unless the court orders otherwise. In practice, it is extremely rare for one to be completed that quickly. Once completed, an assessment report is forwarded to the court, to the parties, and to a number of other entities listed in the CFSA. A court can also order that a report be forwarded to parties that it feels should receive a copy.[12] In addition, children themselves may see an assessment report depending on their age. Children in child protection proceedings have certain rights under the *Child and Family Services Act*, once they are 12 years of age. The relevant provision of the CFSA reads:

> 54(4) Child under twelve — Where the person assessed is a child less than twelve years of age, the child shall not receive a copy of the report unless the court considers it desirable that the child receive a copy of the report.
>
> (5) Child twelve or older — Where the person assessed is a child twelve years of age or more, the child shall receive a copy of the report, except that where the court is satisfied that disclosure of all or part of the report to the child would cause the child emotional harm, the court may withhold all or part of the report from the child.

The report will be reviewed and will be included as evidence in the child protection proceedings before the court.[13]

As noted, an assessment conducted in a custody and access proceeding is similar to the child protection assessment. The only difference is that in a custody and access proceeding, an assessment can be requested at any time.[14] The authority for ordering an assessment in a custody and access case comes from section 30 of the *Children's Law Reform Act*. To a certain degree, the authority for the assessment in custody and access

---

[11] CFSA, s. 54(2).
[12] CFSA, s. 54(3).
[13] CFSA, s. 54(6).
[14] *Children's Law Reform Act*, R.S.O. 1990, c. C.12, as amended, s. 30(2) ("CLRA").

matters is even broader than in child protection proceedings: there are few limits on what type of assessment may be requested in order to assist the court, as long as an assessor has a technical or professional skill and consent to act. Section 30(1)-(4) of the *Children's Law Reform Act* reads:

> 30(1) Assessment of needs of child — The court before which an application is brought in respect of custody of or access to a child, by order, may appoint a person who has technical or professional skill to assess and report to the court on the needs of the child and the ability and willingness of the parties or any of them to satisfy the needs of the child.
>
> (2) When order may be made — An order may be made under subsection (1) on or before the hearing of the application in respect of custody of or access to the child and with or without a request by a party to the application.
>
> (3) Agreement by parties — The court shall, if possible, appoint a person agreed upon by the parties, but if the parties do not agree the court shall choose and appoint the person.
>
> (4) Consent to act — The court shall not appoint a person under subsection (1) unless the person has consented to make the assessment and to report to the court within the period of time specified by the court.

While a child protection assessment is limited to a person who has "charge of a child", it is interesting to note that, by contrast, a custody and access assessment can conceivably be undertaken concerning any person who is given notice, although the chances of that being ordered is unlikely.

> 30(5) Attendance for assessment — In an order under subsection (1), the court may require the parties, the child and any other person who has been given notice of the proposed order, or any of them, to attend for assessment by the person appointed by the order.

Once an Assessment Report in a custody and access matter is completed, it is filed with the court and copies are distributed to the parties.[15] Unlike a child protection assessment, there is no specific provision that addresses whether or not the child

---

[15] CLRA, s. 30(7), (8).

should obtain a copy of the assessment. However, if the child is represented by a lawyer then the lawyer for the child will be given a copy.[16]

Like a child protection assessment, the assessment under section 30 of the CLRA is automatically admissible as evidence in the proceeding. Accordingly, the assessor may be called as a witness by either side.[17]

While a court-ordered assessment report has a great deal of influence on the outcome of a custody and access proceeding, this does not mean that a report or its author will necessarily go unchallenged. At the end of the day, the reality is that the court may not agree with the methodology used in an assessment report or its conclusions or both. The right of the parties to a custody and access matter to present other expert opinions to the court is specifically protected under the *Children's Law Reform Act*. The relevant provision is as follows:

> 30(15) Other expert evidence — The appointment of a person under subsection (1) does not prevent the parties or counsel representing the child from submitting other expert evidence as to the needs of the child and the ability and willingness of the parties or any of them to satisfy the needs of the child.

In summary, court-ordered assessments of children are either "section 54" child protection assessments or "section 30" custody and access assessments.

In addition, there can sometimes be an "investigation" done through the office that appoints lawyers for children. These "investigations" are sometimes, mistakenly, also referred to as assessments and you may also be contacted when one of these is being completed.

---

[16] CLRA, s. 30(8).
[17] CLRA, s. 30(9), (10).

LEGAL REPRESENTATION OF CHILDREN

In Ontario, when a matter comes before the court that involves the interests of a child, the court has authority to ensure the child's interests are protected by providing the child with his or her own legal representation.

A division of the Ministry of the Attorney General has been set up to provide children with this assistance. Now known as the Office of the Children's Lawyer ("OCL"), the OCL provides a number of services to children before the courts. The most common role of the OCL is to appoint a lawyer for a child.

A lawyer can be important for the child and the court in determining a child's best interests as the child's own views and preferences are factors to be considered in determining those best interests. There is no set rule of when a child's views and preferences begin to become important to the court, but generally the views and preferences of very young children are not believed to be of much importance in determining best interests. As a child gets older though, and certainly by the time the child is in his or her teens, the court will usually give great deference to the views and preferences of the child.

Optimistically, the view is that an older child will have greater insight and objectivity into what is in his or her own best interests. Cynically, one recognizes the reality of the situation. The child who is the subject of the order can arbitrarily change the terms of the Order anytime he or she wants by getting onto a bus or driving over to the other parent's home. Given this fact, a court should strongly consider making orders that conform to a child's wishes.

Regardless of the reasons why, a Children's Lawyer is appointed for children over the age of 12, but also for children certainly younger.

The lawyer who is appointed to act for a child is the child's lawyer. The Children's Lawyer is obligated to take his or her client's instructions and make the child's position known to the court regardless of whether (in the lawyer's opinion) that position is in the best interests of the child. Technically, the lawyer is also obligated to follow usual rules of evidence to get evidence regarding the child's wishes before the court rather than becoming a witness themselves regarding what the child told them.[18]

Given this, an appointment for a Children's Lawyer is usually only made (and perhaps should only be made) when the child is old enough and competent to give instructions to a lawyer. When a child is too young to give instructions, an assessment of the child or a social worker investigation (described in greater detail below) is likely more appropriate to assist the court.

Despite the fact that a Children's Lawyer is typically appointed only for older children (who have the ability to provide instructions to such counsel), there is no rule that says that a Children's Lawyer cannot be appointed for young children. In fact, on some occasions, a court will appoint a lawyer for a child who may be too young to provide meaningful instructions to a lawyer. Even in these situations where a child is too young to instruct counsel, a Children's Lawyer must attempt to put before a court the child's views and preferences, rather than the appointed lawyer's personal opinion about what is best for the child. The appointed Children's Lawyer remains an advocate for the child, rather than an *amicus curiae* or "friend of the Court".

There remains some debate as to the practical difference between the role of *amicus curiae* and the role of an advocate for children, particularly where the child involved is very young. The courts remain clear in their view (in both custody and

---

[18] *Strobridge v. Strobridge* (1994), 4 R.F.L. (4th) 169 (Ont. C.A.).

access matters and in child protection cases) that a Children's Lawyer is that child's advocate, rather than a friend of the court. As Justice Czutrin J. noted in a child protection case involving children too young to give instructions:

> ... It is for the children's counsel, ultimately, to present whatever evidence they have or to review the evidence and make submissions to protect the children's best interests. These should not be personal views, but based on a position the Children's Lawyer takes, based on the evidence and the law, to advance a position to protect the children. It is not for counsel to stand up and give personal views or to give evidence from the counsel table.
>
> Ultimately, it is for the court to decide the issues in this case. Counsel is not the legal guardian in this case or *amicus curiae*, but the legal representative. The relation between the child's counsel and the child is one of solicitor and client. . . .[19]

The lawyers themselves are usually local lawyers who represent children on behalf of the OCL.

Under the *Child and Family Services Act*, at any stage of proceedings, legal representation may be requested for a child. A court is obligated to consider whether or not the child should have their own lawyer as early in the process as possible. The relevant provision reads:

> 38(1) Legal representation of child — A child may have legal representation at any stage in a proceeding under this Part.
>
> (2) Court to consider issue — Where a child does not have legal representation in a proceeding under this Part, the court,
>
>> (a) shall, as soon as practicable after the commencement of the proceeding; and
>>
>> (b) may, at any later stage in the proceeding,
>
> determine whether legal representation is desirable to protect the child's interests.

---

[19] *R. (C.) v. Children's Aid Society of Hamilton* (2004), 4 R.F.L. (6th) 98 (Ont. S.C.J.) at paras. 30, 31.

In this regard, the views and preferences of the child as to what he or she believes to be in his or her best interests becomes more of a factor as the child gets older. Accordingly, if a court determines that legal representation in a particular case is desirable to protect a child's interests, the court shall direct that legal representation be provided for the child.[20]

In making a decision as to whether to appoint a lawyer for a child, the court has criteria to guide it including whether or not the child's best interests are protected by other means. Section 38(4) of the CFSA reads as follows:

> 38(4) Criteria — Where,
>
> (a) the court is of the opinion that there is a difference of views between the child and a parent or a society, and the society proposes that the child be removed from a person's care or be made a society or Crown ward under paragraph 2 or 3 of subsection 57(1);
>
> (b) the child is in the society's care and,
>
> > (i) no parent appears before the court, or
> >
> > (ii) it is alleged that the child is in need of protection within the meaning of clause 37(2)(a), (c), (f), (f.1) or (h); or
>
> (c) the child is not permitted to be present at the hearing,
>
> legal representation shall be deemed to be desirable to protect the child's interests, unless the court is satisfied, taking into account the child's views and wishes if they can be reasonably ascertained, that the child's interests are otherwise adequately protected.

On some occasions, the "parent" in child protection matters is a person who is legally defined to be "a child". In such instances, the appointment of a Children's Lawyer is mandatory.

> 38(5) Where parent a minor — Where a child's parent is less than eighteen years of age, the Children's Lawyer shall represent the parent in a proceeding under this Part unless the court orders otherwise.[21]

---

[20] CFSA, s. 38(3).
[21] CFSA, s. 38(5).

The Children's Lawyer can also be appointed under the *Children's Law Reform Act*.

In addition to the lawyer, the OCL can provide the lawyer with a "social work assist". This is a social worker assigned to the lawyer who will meet with the client (the child) and through those interviews, seek to put the evidence of the child (and their views and preferences) before the court.

Instead of having a lawyer represent the child (either with or without a social work assist) in a custody and access matter, the parties, the OCL or the court can request, and the court can order,[22] that the OCL conduct an investigation of matters concerning the custody, access, child support or education of the child. The *Courts of Justice Act* states:

> 112(1) Investigation and report of Children's Lawyer — In a proceeding under the *Divorce Act* (Canada) or the *Children's Law Reform Act* in which a question concerning custody of or access to a child is before the court, the Children's Lawyer may cause an investigation to be made and may report and make recommendations to the court on all matters concerning custody of or access to the child and the child's support and education.

In these circumstances, someone from the OCL (usually a social worker) is appointed by the OCL to conduct an investigation. This investigation often includes meeting with the parents and children and others involved with the children's day-to-day care, such as teachers and daycare providers. As a result of this investigation, a report is provided to the court as evidence and the maker of the report can be compelled to attend at the trial to explain or be examined on the contents of the Report:

> (3) Report as evidence — An affidavit of the person making the investigation, verifying the report as to facts that are within the person's knowledge and setting out the source of the person's information and belief as to other facts, with the report attached as an exhibit thereto,

---

[22] *Courts of Justice Act*, R.S.O. 1990, c. C.43, as amended, s. 112.

shall be served on the parties and filed and on being filed shall form part of the evidence at the hearing of the proceeding.

(4) Attendance on report — Where a party to the proceeding disputes the facts set out in the report, the Children's Lawyer shall if directed by the court, and may when not so directed, attend the hearing on behalf of the child and cause the person who made the investigation to attend as a witness.[23]

As can be seen, in many ways, there is little difference between a Children's Lawyer Investigation Report and an Assessment Report. However, for your purposes, you may wish to know the basis of the request made to you, should anyone contact you for information in making a report concerning a child.

CONCLUSIONS

As noted above, there are many methods of seeking out information from professionals involved with children's care. Some of the more common methods to ascertain information concerning children that are used in Ontario's legal system are discussed above.

It is hoped that by having some exposure to some of these terms, you will have a better understanding what is being asked when you are met with a request for information. In that way, you can better serve yourself, your organization and, most importantly, the children to which you provide care.

---

[23] *Courts of Justice Act*, s. 112(3), (4).

APPENDIX

ONTARIO

Child and Family Services Act – sections 1-3; 15; 27; 37; 38; 72; and 79 335

Children's Law Reform Act – sections 1-10; 20-24; 30; 35; and 36 365

Education Act – sections 170-171; 264; 265; and 300-316 385

    Ontario Regulation 298 – Operation of Schools, General 443

Family Law Act – sections 1; 29; 30-34; and 46 473

    Child Support Guidelines – sections 1-21 487

FEDERAL

Canadian Charter of Rights and Freedoms – sections 1-34; and 52 503

Divorce Act – sections 1; 2; 8; 15; and 16 517

Youth Criminal Justice Act – sections 1-13; and 125 525

Child and Family Services Act

R.S.O. 1990, c. C.11 [ss. 130, 131, 132(4), (5), 178, 179(1), (2)(a)–(c), (e)–(g), 180–182, 184–191 not in force at date of publication.] as am. S.O. 1992, c. 32, s. 3; 1993, c. 27, Sched.; 1994, c. 27, s. 43(2); 1996, c. 2, s. 62; 1999, c. 2 [ss. 2(3), 11, 23(2), 27, 28, 30(2), (3), (5), 31, 33(2) not in force at date of publication.]; 1999, c. 6, s. 6; 1999, c. 12, Sched. E, s. 1 (Fr.); 1999, c. 12, Sched. G, s. 16; 2001, c. 13, s. 5; 2002, c. 17, Sched. F, s. 1; 2002, c. 18, Sched. D, s. 1; 2004, c. 3, Sched. A, s. 78; 2005, c. 5, s. 7

Paramount purpose

1. (1) The paramount purpose of this Act is to promote the best interests, protection and well being of children.

Other purposes

(2) The additional purposes of this Act, so long as they are consistent with the best interests, protection and well being of children, are:

1. To recognize that while parents may need help in caring for their children, that help should give support to the autonomy and integrity of the family unit and, wherever possible, be provided on the basis of mutual consent.
2. To recognize that the least disruptive course of action that is available and is appropriate in a particular case to help a child should be considered.
3. To recognize that children's services should be provided in a manner that,
    i. respects children's needs for continuity of care and for stable family relationships, and
    ii. takes into account physical and mental developmental differences among children.
4. To recognize that, wherever possible, services to children and their families should be provided in a manner that respects cultural, religious and regional differences.

5. To recognize that Indian and native people should be entitled to provide, wherever possible, their own child and family services, and that all services to Indian and native children and families should be provided in a manner that recognizes their culture, heritage and traditions and the concept of the extended family.

1999, c. 2, s. 1

Transitional Provision

Pursuant to 1999, c. 2, s. 37(5), section 1 of the Child and Family Services Act, *as it read on the day before the March 31, 2000 proclamation of 1999, c. 2, s. 1, continues to apply to any proceeding under Part III, including a status review proceeding, commenced before that date.*

On the day before the proclamation, s. 1 read as follows:

1. **Declaration of principles** — *The purposes of this Act are,*

   (a) as a paramount objective, to promote the best interests, protection and well-being of children;

   (b) to recognize that while parents often need help in caring for their children, that help should give support to the autonomy and integrity of the family unit and, wherever possible, be provided on the basis of mutual consent;

   (c) to recognize that the least restrictive or disruptive course of action that is available and is appropriate in a particular case to help a child or family should be followed;

   (d) to recognize that children's services should be provided in a manner that,

       (i) respects children's needs for continuity of care and for stable family relationships, and

       (ii) takes into account physical and mental developmental differences among children;

   (e) to recognize that, wherever possible, services to children and their families should be provided in a manner that respects cultural, religious and regional differences; and

(f) *to recognize that Indian and native people should be entitled to provide, wherever possible, their own child and family services, and that all services to Indian and native children and families should be provided in a manner that recognizes their culture, heritage and traditions and the concept of the extended family.*

French language services

2. (1) Service providers shall, where appropriate, make services to children and their families available in the French language.

Duties of service providers

(2) Service providers shall ensure,

(a) that children and their parents have an opportunity where appropriate to be heard and represented when decisions affecting their interests are made and to be heard when they have concerns about the services they are receiving; and

(b) that decisions affecting the interests and rights of children and their parents are made according to clear, consistent criteria and are subject to procedural safeguards.

Interpretation

Definitions

3. (1) In this Act,

"agency" means a corporation; "agence"

"approved agency" means an agency that is approved under subsection 8(1) of Part I (Flexible Services); "agence agréé"

"approved service" means a service provided,

(a) under subsection 7(1) of Part I or with the support of a grant or contribution made under subsection 7(2) of that Part,

(b) by an approved agency, or

(c) under the authority of a licence; "service agréé"

"band" has the same meaning as in the *Indian Act* (Canada); "bande"

"Board" means the Child and Family Services Review Board continued under Part IX (Licensing); "Commission"

"child" means a person under the age of eighteen years; "enfant"

"child development service" means a service for a child with a developmental disability or physical disability, for the family of a child with a developmental disability or physical disability, or for the child and the family; "service de développement de l'enfant"

"child treatment service" means a service for a child with a mental or psychiatric disorder, for the family of a child with a mental or psychiatric disorder, or for the child and the family; "service de traitement de l'enfant"

"child welfare service" means,

(a) a residential or non-residential service, including a prevention service,

(b) a service provided under Part III (Child Protection),

(c) a service provided under Part VII (Adoption), or

(d) individual or family counselling; "service de bien-être de l'enfance"

"community support service" means a support service or prevention service provided in the community for children and their families; "service communautaire d'appoint"

"court" means the Ontario Court of Justice or the Family Court of the Superior Court of Justice; "tribunal"

"developmental disability" means a condition of mental impairment present or occurring in a person's formative years that is associated with limitations in adaptive behaviour; "déficience intellectuelle"

"developmental handicap" [Repealed 2001, c. 13, s. 5(2).]

"Director" means a Director appointed under subsection 5(1) of Part I (Flexible Services); "directeur"

"foster care" means the provision of residential care to a child, by and in the home of a person who,

>   (a) receives compensation for caring for the child, except under the *Ontario Works Act, 1997*, the *Ontario Disability Support Program Act, 1997* or the *Family Benefits Act*, and
>   (b) is not the child's parent or a person with whom the child has been placed for adoption under Part VII,

and "foster home" and "foster parent" have corresponding meanings; "soins fournis par une famille d'accueil", "famille d'accueil", "père de famille d'accueil", "mère de famille d'accueil"

Proposed Amendment — 3(1) "foster care"

"foster care" means the provision of residential care to a child, by and in the home of a person who,

>   (a) receives compensation for caring for the child, except under the *Ontario Works Act, 1997* or the *Ontario Disability Support Program Act, 1997*, and
>   (b) is not the child's parent or a person with whom the child has been placed for adoption under Part VII,

and "foster home" and "foster parent" have corresponding meanings; "soins fournis par une famille d'accueil", "famille d'accueil", "père de famille d'accueil", "mère de famille d'accueil"

>   1999, c. 2, s. 2(3) [Not in force at date of publication.]

"**Indian**" has the same meaning as in the *Indian Act* (Canada); "Indien"

"**licence**" means a licence issued under Part IX (Licensing), and "licensed" and "licensee" have corresponding meanings; "permis", "autorisé en vertu d'un permis", "titulaire de permis"

"**local director**" means a local director appointed under section 16 of Part I (Flexible Services); "directeur local"

"**Minister**" means the Minister of Community and Social Services; "ministre"

"**municipality**" does not include a lower-tier municipality that is situated within a regional municipality; "municipalité"

"**native community**" means a community designated by the Minister under section 209 of Part X (Indian and Native Child and Family Services; "communauté autochtone"

"**native person**" means a person who is a member of a native community but is not a member of a band, and "native child" has a corresponding meaning; "autochtone", "enfant autochtone"

"**order**" includes a refusal to make an order; "arrêté, order et ordonnance"

"**prescribed**" means prescribed by the regulations; "prescrit"

"**program supervisor**" means a program supervisor appointed under subsection 5(2) of Part I (Flexible Services); "superviseur de programme"

"**regulations**" means the regulations made under this Act; "règlements"

"**residential service**" means boarding, lodging and associated supervisory, sheltered or group care provided for a child away from the home of the child's parent, and "residential care" and "residential placement" have corresponding meanings; "service en établissement", "soins en établissement", "placement en établissement"

"service" means

(a) a child development service,
(b) a child treatment service,
(c) a child welfare service,
(d) a community support service, or
(e) a young offenders service; "service"

"service provider" means,

(a) the Minister,
(b) an approved agency,
(c) a society,
(d) a licensee, or
(e) a person who provides an approved service or provides a service purchased by the Minister or an approved agency,

but does not include a foster parent; "fournisseur de services"

"society" means an approved agency designated as a children's aid society under subsection 15(2) of Part I (Flexible Services); "société"

"Tribunal" means the Licence Appeal Tribunal; "Tribunal"

"young offenders service" means a service provided under Part IV (Young Offenders) or under a program established under that Part. "service aux jeunes contrevenants".

Idem: "parent"

(2) In this Act, a reference to a child's parent shall be deemed to be a reference to,

(a) both parents, where both have custody of the child;
(b) one parent, where that parent has lawful custody of the child or the other parent is unavailable or unable to act as the context requires; or

(c) another individual, where that individual has lawful custody of the child, except where this Act provides otherwise.

1999, c. 2, s. 2(1), (2); 1999, c. 12, Sched. G, s. 16(1); 2001, c. 13, s. 5(1)–(3); 2002, c. 17, Sched. F, s. 1

. . .

**Part I
Flexible Services**

. . .

Children's Aid Societies

Definition

15. (1) In this section, **"prescribed"** means prescribed in a regulation made by the Minister under subsection 214(4) of Part XI (Regulations). "prescrit"

Designation of children's aid society

(2) The Minister may designate an approved agency as a children's aid society for a specified territorial jurisdiction and for any or all of the functions set out in subsection (3), may impose terms and conditions on a designation and may vary, remove or amend the terms and conditions or impose new terms and conditions or impose new terms and conditions at any time, and may at any time amend a designation to provide that the society is no longer designated for a particular function set out in subsection (3) or to alter the society's territorial jurisdiction.

Functions of society

(3) The functions of a children's aid society are to,

(a) investigate allegations or evidence that children who are under the age of sixteen years or are in the society's care or under its supervision may be in need of protection;

(b) protect, where necessary, children who are under the age of sixteen years or are in the society's care or under its supervision;

(c) provide guidance, counselling and other services to families for protecting children or for the prevention of circumstances requiring the protection of children;

(d) provide care for children assigned or committed to its care under this Act;

(e) supervise children assigned to its supervision under this Act;

(f) place children for adoption under Part VII; and

(g) perform any other duties given to it by this or any other Act.

Prescribed standards, etc.

(4) A society shall,

(a) provide the prescribed standard of services in its performance of its functions; and

(b) follow the prescribed procedures and practices.

(5) [Repealed 2002, c. 18, Sched. D, s. 1.]

Protection from personal liability

(6) No action shall be instituted against an officer or employee of a society for an act done in good faith in the execution or intended execution of the person's duty or for an alleged neglect or default in the execution in good faith of the person's duty.

2002, c. 18, Sched. D, s. 1

. . .

Part II
Voluntary Access to Services

. . .

Consents

Consent to service: person over sixteen

27. (1) A service provider may provide a service to a person who is sixteen years of age or older only with the person's consent, except where the court orders under this Act that the service be provided to the person.

Consent to residential service: child under sixteen

(2) A service provider may provide a residential service to a child who is less than sixteen years of age only with the consent of the child's parent or, where the child is in a society's lawful custody, the society's consent, except where this Act provides otherwise.

Exception

(3) Subsections (1) and (2) do not apply where a service is provided to a child under Part IV (Young Offenders).

Discharge from residential placement

(4) A child who is placed in a residential placement with the consent referred to in subsection (2) may only be discharged from the placement,

(a) with the consent that would be required for a new residential placement; or
(b) where the placement is made under the authority of an agreement made under subsection 29(1) (temporary care agreements) or subsection 30(1) or (2) (special needs agreements), in accordance with section 33 (termination by notice).

Transfer to another placement

(5) A child who is placed in a residential placement with the consent referred to in subsection (2) shall not be transferred from one placement to another unless the consent that would be required for a new residential placement is given.

Child's wishes

(6) Before a child is placed in or discharged from a residential placement or transferred from one residential placement to another with the consent referred to in subsection (2), the service provider shall take the child's wishes into account, if they can be reasonably ascertained.

. . .

Part III
Child Protection

Definitions

37. (1) In this Part,

"child" does not include a child as defined in subsection 3(1) who is actually or apparently sixteen years of age or older, unless the child is the subject of an order under this Part; "enfant"

"child protection worker" means a Director, a local director or a person authorized by a Director or local director for the purposes of section 40 (commencing child protection proceedings); "préposé à la protection de l'enfance"

"extended family", when used in reference to a child, means the persons to whom the child is related by blood, marriage or adoption; "famille élargie"

"parent", when used in reference to a child, means each of,

(a) the child's mother,
(b) an individual described in one of paragraphs 1 to 6 of

subsection 8(1) of the *Children's Law Reform Act*, unless it is proved on a balance of probabilities that he is not the child's natural father,

(c) the individual having lawful custody of the child,

(d) an individual who, during the twelve months before intervention under this Part, has demonstrated a settled intention to treat the child as a child of his or her family, or has acknowledged parentage of the child and provided for the child's support,

(e) an individual who, under a written agreement or a court order, is required to provide for the child, has custody of the child or has a right of access to the child, and

(f) an individual who has acknowledged parentage of the child in writing under section 12 of the *Children's Law Reform Act*,

but does not include a foster parent; "père ou mère"

"place of safety" means a foster home, a hospital, and a place or one of a class of places designated as such by a Director under subsection 17(2) of Part I (Flexible Services), but does not include,

(a) a place of secure custody as defined in Part IV (Young Offenders), or

(b) a place of secure temporary detention as defined in Part IV. "lieu sûr"

Child in need of protection

(2) A child is in need of protection where,

(a) the child has suffered physical harm, inflicted by the person having charge of the child or caused by or resulting from that person's,

    (i) failure to adequately care for, provide for, supervise or protect the child, or

(ii) pattern of neglect in caring for, providing for, supervising or protecting the child.

(b) there is a risk that the child is likely to suffer physical harm inflicted by the person having charge of the child or caused by or resulting from that person's,

(i) failure to adequately care for, provide for, supervise or protect the child, or
(ii) pattern of neglect in caring for, providing for, supervising or protecting the child.

(c) the child has been sexually molested or sexually exploited, by the person having charge of the child or by another person where the person having charge of the child knows or should know of the possibility of sexual molestation or sexual exploitation and fails to protect the child;

(d) there is a risk that the child is likely to be sexually molested or sexually exploited as described in clause (c).

(e) the child requires medical treatment to cure, prevent or alleviate physical harm or suffering and the child's parent or the person having charge of the child does not provide, or refuses or is unavailable or unable to consent to, the treatment;

(f) the child has suffered emotional harm, demonstrated by serious,

(i) anxiety,
(ii) depression,
(iii) withdrawal,
(iv) self-destructive or aggressive behaviour, or
(v) delayed development,

and there are reasonable grounds to believe that the emotional harm suffered by the child results from the actions, failure to act or pattern of neglect on the part of the child's parent or the person having charge of the child;

(f.1) the child has suffered emotional harm of the kind described in subclause (f)(i), (ii), (iii), (iv) or (v) and the child's parent or the person having charge of the child does not provide, or refuses or is unavailable or unable to consent to, services or treatment to remedy or alleviate the harm;

(g) there is a risk that the child is likely to suffer emotional harm of the kind described in subclause (f)(i), (ii), (iii), (iv) or (v) resulting from the actions, failure to act or pattern of neglect on the part of the child's parent or the person having charge of the child;

(g.1) there is a risk that the child is likely to suffer emotional harm of the kind described in subclause (f)(i), (ii), (iii), (iv) or (v) and that the child's parent or the person having charge of the child does not provide, or refuses or is unavailable or unable to consent to, services or treatment to prevent the harm.

(h) the child suffers from a mental, emotional or developmental condition that, if not remedied, could seriously impair the child's development and the child's parent or the person having charge of the child does not provide, or refuses or is unavailable or unable to consent to, treatment to remedy or alleviate the condition;

(i) the child has been abandoned, the child's parent has died or is unavailable to exercise his or her custodial rights over the child and has not made adequate provision for the child's care and custody, or the child is in a residential placement and the parent refuses or is unable or unwilling to resume the child's care and custody;

(j) the child is less than twelve years old and has killed or seriously injured another person or caused serious damage to another person's property, services or treatment are necessary to prevent a recurrence and the child's parent or the person having charge of the child

does not provide, or refuses or is unavailable or unable to consent to, those services or treatment;
(k) the child is less than twelve years old and has on more than one occasion injured another person or caused loss or damage to another person's property, with the encouragement of the person having charge of the child or because of that person's failure or inability to supervise the child adequately; or
(l) the child's parent is unable to care for the child and the child is brought before the court with the parent's consent and, where the child is twelve years of age or older, with the child's consent, to be dealt with under this Part.

Best interests of child

(3) Where a person is directed in this Part to make an order or determination in the best interests of a child, the person shall take into consideration those of the following circumstances of the case that he or she considers relevant:

1. The child's physical, mental and emotional needs, and the appropriate care or treatment to meet those needs.
2. The child's physical, mental and emotional level of development.
3. The child's cultural background.
4. The religious faith, if any, in which the child is being raised.
5. The importance for the child's development of a positive relationship with a parent and a secure place as a member of a family.
6. The child's relationships by blood or through an adoption order.
7. The importance of continuity in the child's care and the possible effect on the child of disruption of that continuity.
8. The merits of a plan for the child's care proposed by a society, including a proposal that the child be placed

for adoption or adopted, compared with the merits of the child remaining with or returning to a parent.
9. The child's views and wishes, if they can be reasonably ascertained.
10. The effects on the child of delay in the disposition of the case.
11. The risk that the child may suffer harm through being removed from, kept away from, returned to or allowed to remain in the care of a parent.
12. The degree of risk, if any, that justified the finding that the child is in need of protection.
13. Any other relevant circumstance.

Where child an Indian or native person

(4) Where a person is directed in this Part to make an order or determination in the best interests of a child and the child is an Indian or native person, the person shall take into consideration the importance, in recognition of the uniqueness of Indian and native culture, heritage and traditions, of preserving the child's cultural identity.

1999, c. 2, s. 9

Transitional Provision

Pursuant to 1999, c. 2, s. 37(5), section 37 of the Child and Family Services Act, *as it read on the day before the March 31, 2000 proclamation of 1999, c. 2, s. 9, continues to apply to any proceeding under Part III, including a status review proceeding, commenced before that date.*

On the day before the proclamation, section 37 read as follows:

Definitions

37. (1) *Is this Part,*

"child" does not include a child as defined in subsection 3(1) who is actually or apparently sixteen years of age or older,

unless the child is the subject of an order under this Part; *"enfant"*

"child protection worker" means a Director, a local director or a person authorized by a Director or local director for the purposes of section 40 (commencing child protection proceedings); *"préposé à la protection de l'enfance"*

"extended family", when used in reference to a child, means the persons to whom the child is related by blood, marriage or adoption; *"famille élargie"*

"parent", when used in reference to a child, means each of,

(a) the child's mother,
(b) an individual described in one of paragraphs 1 to 6 of subsection 8(1) of the Children's Law Reform Act, unless it is proved on a balance of probabilities that he is not the child's natural father,
(c) the individual having lawful custody of the child,
(d) an individual who, during the twelve months before intervention under this Part, has demonstrated a settled intention to treat the child as a child of his or her family, or has acknowledged parentage of the child and provided for the child's support,
(e) an individual who, under a written agreement or a court order, is required to provide for the child, has custody of the child or has a right of access to the child, and
(f) an individual who has acknowledged parentage of the child in writing under section 12 of the Children's Law Reform Act,

but does not include a foster parent; *"pére ou mére"*

"place of safety" means a foster home, a hospital and a place or one of a class of places designated as such by a Director under subsection 17(2) of Part I (Flexible Services), but does not include,

(a) a place of secure custody as defined in Part IV (Young Offenders), or

(b) *a place of secure temporary detention as defined in Part IV.*

"lieu sûr"

Child in need of protection

(2) A child is in need of protection where,

(a) the child has suffered physical harm inflicted by the person having charge of the child or caused by that person's failure to care and provide for or supervise and protect the child adequately;

(b) there is a substantial risk that the child will suffer physical harm inflicted or caused as described in clause (a);

(c) the child has been sexually molested or sexually exploited, by the person having charge of the child or by another person where the person having charge of the child knows or should know of the possibility of sexual molestation or sexual exploitation and fails to protect the child;

(d) there is a substantial risk that the child will be sexually molested or sexually exploited as described in clause (c);

(e) the child requires medical treatment to cure, prevent or alleviate physical harm or suffering and the child's parent or the person having charge of the child does not provide, or refuses or is unavailable or unable to consent to, the treatment;

(f) the child has suffered emotional harm, demonstrated by severe,

(i) anxiety,
(ii) depression,
(iii) withdrawal, or
(iv) self-destructive or aggressive behaviour,

and the child's parent or the person having charge of the child does not provide, or refuses or is unavailable or unable to consent to, services or treatment to remedy or alleviate the harm;

(g) there is a substantial risk that the child will suffer emotional harm of the kind described in clause (f), and the child's parent or the person having charge of the child does not provide, or refuses or is unavailable or unable to consent to, services or treatment to prevent the harm;

(h) the child suffers from a mental, emotional or developmental condition that, if not remedied, could seriously impair the child's development and the child's parent or the person having charge of the child does not provide, or refuses or is unavailable or unable to consent to, treatment to remedy or alleviate the condition;

(i) the child has been abandoned, the child's parent has died or is unavailable to exercise his or her custodial rights over the child and has not made adequate provision for the child's care and custody, or the child is in a residential placement and the parent refuses or is unable or unwilling to resume the child's care and custody;

(j) the child is less than twelve years old and has killed or seriously injured another person or caused serious damage to another person's property, services or treatment are necessary to prevent a recurrence and the child's parent or the person having charge of the child does not provide, or refuses or is unavailable or unable to consent to, those services or treatment;

(k) the child is less than twelve years old and has on more than one occasion injured another person or caused loss or damage to another person's property, with the encouragement of the person having charge of the child or because of that person's failure or inability to supervise the child adequately; or

(l) the child's parent is unable to care for the child and the child is brought before the court with the parent's consent and, where the child is twelve years of age or older, with the child's consent, to be dealt with under this Part.

Best interests of child

(3) Where a person is directed in this Part to make an order or determination in the best interests of a child, the person shall take into consideration those of the following circumstances of the case that he or she considers relevant:

1. *The child's physical, mental and emotional needs, and the appropriate care or treatment to meet those needs.*
2. *The child's physical, mental and emotional level of development.*
3. *The child's cultural background.*
4. *The religious faith, if any, in which the child is being raised.*
5. *The importance for the child's development of a positive relationship with a parent and a secure place as a member of a family.*
6. *The child's relationships by blood or through an adoption order.*
7. *The importance of continuity in the child's care and the possible effect on the child of disruption of that continuity.*
8. *The merits of a plan for the child's care proposed by a society, including a proposal that the child be placed for adoption or adopted, compared with the merits of the child remaining with or returning to a parent.*
9. *The child's views and wishes, if they can be reasonably ascertained.*
10. *The effects on the child of delay in the disposition of the case.*
11. *The risk that the child may suffer harm through being removed from, kept away from, returned to or allowed to remain in the care of a parent.*
12. *The degree of risk, if any, that justified the finding that the child is in need of protection.*
13. *Any other relevant circumstance.*

Where child an Indian or native person

(4) Where a person is directed in this Part to make an order or determination in the best interests of a child and the child is an Indian or native person, the person shall take into consideration the importance, in recognition of the uniqueness of Indian and native culture, heritage and traditions, of preserving the child's cultural identity.

Legal Representation

Legal representation of child

38. (1) A child may have legal representation at any stage in a proceeding under this Part.

Court to consider issue

(2) Where a child does not have legal representation in a proceeding under this Part, the court,

(a) shall, as soon as practicable after the commencement of the proceeding; and
(b) may, at any later stage in the proceeding,

determine whether legal representation is desirable to protect the child's interests.

Direction for legal representation

(3) Where the court determines that legal representation is desirable to protect a child's interests, the court shall direct that legal representation be provided for the child.

Criteria

(4) Where,

(a) the court is of the opinion that there is a difference of views between the child and a parent or a society, and the society proposes that the child be removed from a person's care or be made a society or Crown ward under paragraph 2 or 3 of subsection 57(1);

(b) the child is in the society's care and,

   (i) no parent appears before the court, or
   (ii) it is alleged that the child is in need of protection within the meaning of clause 37(2)(a), (c), (f), (f.1) or (h); or

(c) the child is not permitted to be present at the hearing,

legal representation shall be deemed to be desirable to protect the child's interests, unless the court is satisfied, taking into account the child's views and wishes if they can be reasonably ascertained, that the child's interests are otherwise adequately protected.

Where parent a minor

(5) Where a child's parent is less than eighteen years of age, the Children's Lawyer shall represent the parent in a proceeding under this Part unless the court orders otherwise.

1994, c. 27, s. 43(2); 1999, c. 2, s. 10

Transitional Provision

Pursuant to 1999, c. 2, s. 37(5), section 38 of the Child and Family Services Act, *as it read on the day before the March 31, 2000 proclamation of 1999, c. 2, s. 10, continues to apply to any proceeding under Part III, including a status review proceeding, commenced before that date.*

On the day before the proclamation, section 38 read as follows:

Legal representation of child

38. (1) *A child may have legal representation at any stage in a proceeding under this Part.*

Court to consider issue

(2) Where a child does not have legal representation in a proceeding under this Part, the court,

> (a) shall, as soon as practicable after the commencement of the proceeding, and
>
> (b) may, at any later stage in the proceeding,

determine whether legal representation is desirable to protect the child's interests.

Direction for legal representation

(3) Where the court determines that legal representation is desirable to protect a child's interests, the court shall direct that legal representation be provided for the child.

Criteria

> (4) Where,
>
> > (a) the court is of the opinion that there is a difference of views between the child and a parent or a society, and the society proposes that the child be removed fro a person's care or be made a society or Crown ward under paragraph 2 or 3 of subsection 57(1);
> >
> > (b) the child is in the society's care and,
> >
> > > (i) no parent appears before the court, or
> > >
> > > (ii) it is alleged that the child is in need of protection within the meaning of clause 37(2)(a), (c), (f) or (h); or
> >
> > (c) the child is not permitted to be present at the hearing,

legal representation shall be deemed to be desirable to protect the child's interests, unless the court is satisfied, taking into account the child's views and wishes if they can be reasonably ascertained, that the child's interests are otherwise adequately protected.

Where parent a minor

(5) *Where a child's parent is less than eighteen years of age, the Children's Lawyer shall represent the parent in a proceeding under this Part unless the court orders otherwise.*

. . .

Duty to Report

Duty to report child in need of protection

72. (1) Despite the provisions of any other Act, if a person, including a person who performs professional or official duties with respect to children, has reasonable grounds to suspect one of the following, the person shall forthwith report the suspicion and the information on which it is based to a society:

1. The child has suffered physical harm, inflicted by the person having charge of the child or caused by or resulting from that person's,
    i. failure to adequately care for, provide for, supervise or protect the child, or
    ii. pattern of neglect in caring for, providing for, supervising or protecting the child.
2. There is a risk that the child is likely to suffer physical harm inflicted by the person having charge of the child or caused by or resulting from that person's,
    i. failure to adequately care for, provide for, supervise or protect the child, or
    ii. pattern of neglect in caring for, providing for, supervising or protecting the child.
3. The child has been sexually molested or sexually exploited, by the person having charge of the child or by another person where the person having charge of the child knows or should know of the possibility of sexual

molestation or sexual exploitation and fails to protect the child.
4. There is a risk that the child is likely to be sexually molested or sexually exploited as described in paragraph 3.
5. The child requires medical treatment to cure, prevent or alleviate physical harm or suffering and the child's parent or the person having charge of the child does not provide, or refuses or is unavailable or unable to consent to, the treatment.
6. The child has suffered emotional harm, demonstrated by serious,
   i. anxiety,
   ii. depression,
   iii. withdrawal,
   iv. self-destructive or aggressive behaviour, or
   v. delayed development,

   and there are reasonable grounds to believe that the emotional harm suffered by the child results from the actions, failure to act or pattern of neglect on the part of the child's parent or the person having charge of the child.
7. The child has suffered emotional harm of the kind described in subparagraph i, ii, iii, iv or v of paragraph 6 and the child's parent or the person having charge of the child does not provide, or refuses or is unavailable or unable to consent to, services or treatment to remedy or alleviate the harm.
8. There is a risk that the child is likely to suffer emotional harm of the kind described in subparagraph i, ii, iii, iv or v of paragraph 6 resulting from the actions, failure to act or pattern of neglect on the part of the child's parent or the person having charge of the child.
9. There is a risk that the child is likely to suffer emotional harm of the kind described in subparagraph i, ii, iii, iv

or v of paragraph 6 and that the child's parent or the person having charge of the child does not provide, or refuses or is unavailable or unable to consent to, services or treatment to prevent the harm.
10. The child suffers from a mental, emotional or developmental condition that, if not remedied, could seriously impair the child's development and the child's parent or the person having charge of the child does not provide, or refuses or is unavailable or unable to consent to, treatment to remedy or alleviate the condition.
11. The child has been abandoned, the child's parent has died or is unavailable to exercise his or her custodial rights over the child and has not made adequate provision for the child's care and custody, or the child is in a residential placement and the parent refuses or is unable or unwilling to resume the child's care and custody.
12. The child is less than 12 years old and has killed or seriously injured another person or caused serious damage to another person's property, services or treatment are necessary to prevent a recurrence and the child's parent or the person having charge of the child does not provide, or refuses or is unavailable or unable to consent to, those services or treatment.
13. The child is less than 12 years old and has on more than one occasion injured another person or caused loss or damage to another person's property, with the encouragement of the person having charge of the child or because of that person's failure or inability to supervise the child adequately.

Ongoing duty to report

(2) A person who has additional reasonable grounds to suspect one of the matters set out in subsection (1) shall make a further report under subsection (1) even if he or she has made previous reports with respect to the same child.

Person must report directly

(3) A person who has a duty to report a matter under subsection (1) or (2) shall make the report directly to the society and shall not rely on any other person to report on his or her behalf.

Offence

(4) A person referred to in subsection (5) is guilty of an offence if,
- (a) he or she contravenes subsection (1) or (2) by not reporting a suspicion; and
- (b) the information on which it was based was obtained in the course of his or her professional or official duties.

Same

(5) Subsection (4) applies to every person who performs professional or official duties with respect to children including,
- (a) a health care professional, including a physician, nurse, dentist, pharmacist and psychologist;
- (b) a teacher, school principal, social worker, family counsellor, priest, rabbi, member of the clergy, operator or employee of a day nursery and youth and recreation worker;
- (c) a peace officer and a coroner;
- (d) a solicitor; and
- (e) a service provider and an employee of a service provider.

Same

(6) In clause (5)(b), **"youth and recreation worker"** does not include a volunteer.

Same

(6.1) A director, officer or employee of a corporation who authorizes, permits or concurs in a contravention of an offence under subsection (4) by an employee of the corporation is guilty of an offence.

Same

(6.2) A person convicted of an offence under subsection (4) or (6.1) is liable to a fine of not more than $1,000.

Section overrides privilege

(7) This section applies although the information reported may be confidential or privileged, and no action for making the report shall be instituted against a person who acts in accordance with this section unless the person acts maliciously or without reasonable grounds for the suspicion.

Exception: solicitor client privilege

(8) Nothing in this section abrogates any privilege that may exist between a solicitor and his or her client.

Conflict

(9) This section prevails despite anything in the *Personal Health Information Protection Act, 2004*.
   1993, c. 27, Sched.; 1999, c. 2, s. 22; 2004, c. 3, Sched. A, s. 78(2)

. . .

Offences, Restraining Orders, Recovery on Child's Behalf

Definition

79. (1) In this section, **"abuse"** means a state or condition of being physically harmed, sexually molested or sexually exploited. "mauvais traitements"

Child abuse

(2) No person having charge of a child shall,

(a) inflict abuse on the child; or
(b) by failing to care and provide for or supervise and protect the child adequately,

　　(i) permit the child to suffer abuse, or
　　(ii) permit the child to suffer from a mental, emotional or developmental condition that, if not remedied, could seriously impair the child's development.

Leaving child unattended

(3) No person having charge of a child less than sixteen years of age shall leave the child without making provision for his or her supervision and care that is reasonable in the circumstances.

Reverse onus

(4) Where a person is charged with contravening subsection (3) and the child is less than ten years of age, the onus of establishing that the person made provision for the child's supervision and care that was reasonable in the circumstances rests with the person.

Allowing child to loiter, etc.

(5) No parent of a child less than sixteen years of age shall permit the child to,

(a) loiter in a public place between the hours of midnight and 6 a.m.; or
(b) be in a place of public entertainment between the hours of midnight and 6 a.m., unless the parent accompanies the child or authorizes a specified individual eighteen years of age or older to accompany the child.

Police may take child home or to place of safety

(6) Where a child who is actually or apparently less than sixteen years of age is in a place to which the public has access between the hours of midnight and 6 a.m. and is not accompanied by a person described in clause (5)(b), a peace officer may apprehend the child without a warrant and proceed as if the child has been apprehended under subsection 42(1).

Child protection hearing

(7) The court may, in connection with a case arising under subsection (2), (3) or (5), proceed under this Part as if an application had been made under subsection 40(1) (child protection proceeding) in respect of the child.

. . .

Children's Law Reform Act

R.S.O. 1990, c. C.12 [ss. 77–84 not in force at date of publication.] as am. R.S.O. 1990, c. C.12, ss. 77–84 [Not in force at date of publication.]; S.O. 1992, c. 32, s. 4; 1993, c. 27, Sched.; 1996, c. 2, s. 63; 1996, c. 25, s. 3; 1998, c. 26, s. 101; 1999, c. 6, s. 7; 2000, c. 33, s. 21 [Not in force at date of publication.]; 2001, c. 9, Sched. B, s. 4; 2005, c. 5, s. 8

Part I
Equal Status of Children

Rule of parentage

1. (1) Subject to subsection (2), for all purposes of the law of Ontario a person is the child of his or her natural parents and his or her status as their child is independent of whether the child is born within or outside marriage.

Exception for adopted children

(2) Where an adoption order has been made, section 158 or 159 of the *Child and Family Services Act* applies and the child is the child of the adopting parents as if they were the natural parents.

Kindred relationships

(3) The parent and child relationships as determined under subsections (1) and (2) shall be followed in the determination of other kindred relationships flowing therefrom.

Common law distinction of legitimacy abolished

(4) Any distinction at common law between the status of children born in wedlock and born out of wedlock is abolished and the relationship of parent and child and kindred relationships flowing therefrom shall be determined for the purposes of the common law in accordance with this section.

Rule of construction

2. (1) For the purposes of construing any instrument, Act or regulation, unless the contrary intention appears, a reference to a person or group or class of persons described in terms of relationship by blood or marriage to another person shall be construed to refer to or include a person who comes within the description by reason of the relationship of parent and child as determined under section 1.

Application

(2) Subsection (1) applies to,

(a) any Act of the Legislature or any regulation, order or by-law made under an Act of the Legislature enacted or made before, on or after the 31st day of March, 1978; and

(b) any instrument made on or after the 31st day of March, 1978.

Part II
Establishment of Parentage

Court under ss. 4 to 7

3. The court having jurisdiction for the purposes of sections 4 to 7 is,

(a) the Family Court, in the areas where it has jurisdiction under subsection 21.1(4) of the *Courts of Justice Act*;
(b) the Superior Court of Justice, in the rest of Ontario.
 1996, c. 25, s. 3(1); 2001, c. 9, Sched. B, s. 4(7)

Application for declaration

4. (1) Any person having an interest may apply to a court for a declaration that a male person is recognized in law to be the father of a child or that a female person is the mother of a child.

Declaration of paternity recognized at law

(2) Where the court finds that a presumption of paternity exists under section 8 and unless it is established, on the balance of probabilities, that the presumed father is not the father of the child, the court shall make a declaratory order confirming that the paternity is recognized in law.

Declaration of maternity

(3) Where the court finds on the balance of probabilities that the relationship of mother and child has been established, the court may make a declaratory order to that effect.

Idem

(4) Subject to sections 6 and 7, an order made under this section shall be recognized for all purposes.

Application for declaration of paternity where no presumption

5. (1) Where there is no person recognized in law under section 8 to be the father of a child, any person may apply to the court for a declaration that a male person is his or her father, or any male person may apply to the court for a declaration that a person is his child.

Limitation

(2) An application shall not be made under subsection (1) unless both the persons whose relationship is sought to be established are living.

Declaratory order

(3) Where the court finds on the balance of probabilities that the relationship of father and child has been established, the court may make a declaratory order to that effect and, subject to sections 6 and 7, the order shall be recognized for all purposes.

Reopening on new evidence

6. Where a declaration has been made under section 4 or 5 and evidence becomes available that was not available at the previous hearing, the court may, upon application, discharge or vary the order and make such other orders or directions as are ancillary thereto.

Appeal

7. An appeal lies from an order under section 4 or 5 or a decision under section 6 in accordance with the rules of the court.

Recognition in law of parentage

8. (1) Unless the contrary is proven on a balance of probabilities, there is a presumption that a male person is, and he shall be recognized in law to be, the father of a child in any one of the following circumstances:

1. The person is married to the mother of the child at the time of the birth of the child.
2. The person was married to the mother of the child by a marriage that was terminated by death or judgment of nullity within 300 days before the birth of the child or by divorce where the decree *nisi* was granted within 300 days before the birth of the child.
3. The person marries the mother of the child after the birth of the child and acknowledges that he is the natural father.
4. The person was cohabiting with the mother of the child in a relationship of some permanence at the time of the birth of the child or the child is born within 300 days after they ceased to cohabit.
5. The person has certified the child's birth, as the child's father, under the *Vital Statistics Act* or a similar Act in another jurisdiction in Canada.
6. The person has been found or recognized in his lifetime

by a court of competent jurisdiction in Canada to be the father of the child.

Where marriage void

(2) For the purpose of subsection (1), where a man and woman go through a form of marriage with each other, in good faith, that is void and cohabit, they shall be deemed to be married during the time they cohabit and the marriage shall be deemed to be terminated when they cease to cohabit.

Conflicting presumptions

(3) Where circumstances exist that give rise to a presumption or presumptions of paternity by more than one father under subsection (1), no presumption shall be made as to paternity and no person is recognized in law to be the father.

Admissibility in evidence of acknowledgment against interest

9. A written acknowledgment of parentage that is admitted in evidence in any civil proceeding against the interest of the person making the acknowledgment is proof, in the absence of evidence to the contrary, of the fact.

Approved blood tests

10. (1) Upon the application of a party in a civil proceeding in which the court is called upon to determine the parentage of a child, the court may give the party leave to obtain blood tests of such persons as are named in the order granting leave and to submit the results in evidence.

Conditions attached

(2) Leave under subsection (1) may be given subject to such terms and conditions as the court thinks proper.

Inference from refusal

(3) Where leave is given under subsection (1) and a person named therein refuses to submit to the blood test, the court may draw such inferences as it thinks appropriate.

Consent to procedure

(4) The *Health Care Consent Act, 1996* applies to the blood test as if it were treatment under that Act.

1992, c. 32, s. 4; 1996, c. 2, s. 63

. . .

Part III
Custody, Access and Guardianship Interpretation

. . .

Custody and Access

Father and mother entitled to custody

20. (1) Except as otherwise provided in this Part, the father and the mother are equally entitled to custody of the child.

Rights and responsibilities

(2) A person entitled to custody of a child has the rights and responsibilities of a parent in respect of the person of the child and must exercise those rights and responsibilities in the best interests of the child.

Authority to act

(3) Where more than one person is entitled to custody of a child, any one of them may exercise the rights and accept the responsibilities of a parent on behalf of them in respect of the child.

Where parents separate

(4) Where the parents of a child live separate and apart and the child lives with one of them with the consent, implied consent or acquiescence of the other of them, the right of the other to exercise the entitlement of custody and the incidents of custody, but not the entitlement to access, is suspended until a separation agreement or order otherwise provides.

Proposed Addition — 20(4a)
Duty of separated parents

(4a) Where the parents of a child live separate and apart and the child is in the custody of one of them and the other is entitled to access under the terms of a separation agreement or order, each shall, in the best interests of the child, encourage and support the child's continuing parent-child relationship with the other.
R.S.O. 1990, c. C.12, s. 77 [Not in force at date of publication.]

Access

(5) The entitlement to access to a child includes the right to visit with and be visited by the child and the same right as a parent to make inquiries and to be given information as to the health, education and welfare of the child.

Marriage of child

(6) The entitlement to custody of or access to a child terminates on the marriage of the child.

Entitlement subject to agreement or order

(7) Any entitlement to custody or access or incidents of custody under this section is subject to alteration by an order of the court or by separation agreement.

Application for order

21. A parent of a child or any other person may apply to a court for an order respecting custody of or access to the child or determining any aspect of the incidents of custody of the child.

Jurisdiction

22. (1) A court shall only exercise its jurisdiction to make an order for custody of or access to a child where,

> (a) the child is habitually resident in Ontario at the commencement of the application for the order;
> (b) although the child is not habitually resident in Ontario, the court is satisfied,
>> (i) that the child is physically present in Ontario at the commencement of the application for the order,
>> (ii) that substantial evidence concerning the best interests of the child is available in Ontario,
>> (iii) that no application for custody of or access to the child is pending before an extra-provincial tribunal in another place where the child is habitually resident,
>> (iv) that no extra-provincial order in respect of custody of or access to the child has been recognized by a court in Ontario,
>> (v) that the child has a real and substantial connection with Ontario, and
>> (vi) that, on the balance of convenience, it is appropriate for jurisdiction to be exercised in Ontario.

Habitual residence

(2) A child is habitually resident in the place where he or she resided,

> (a) with both parents;
> (b) where the parents are living separate and apart, with

one parent under a separation agreement or with the consent, implied consent or acquiescence of the other or under a court order; or

(c) with a person other than a parent on a permanent basis for a significant period of time,

whichever last occurred.

Abduction

(3) The removal or withholding of a child without the consent of the person having custody of the child does not alter the habitual residence of the child unless there has been acquiescence or undue delay in commencing due process by the person from whom the child is removed or withheld.

Serious harm to child

23. Despite sections 22 and 41, a court may exercise its jurisdiction to make or to vary an order in respect of the custody of or access to a child where,

(a) the child is physically present in Ontario; and
(b) the court is satisfied that the child would, on the balance of probabilities, suffer serious harm if,
   (i) the child remains in the custody of the person legally entitled to custody of the child,
   (ii) the child is returned to the custody of the person legally entitled to custody of the child, or
   (iii) the child is removed from Ontario.

Merits of application for custody or access

24. (1) The merits of an application under this Part in respect of custody of or access to a child shall be determined on the basis of the best interests of the child.

> **Proposed Amendment — 24(1)**
>
> **Merits of application for custody or access**
>
> (1) The merits of an application or motion under this Part in respect of custody of or access to a child shall be determined on the basis of the best interests of the child.
>
> R.S.O. 1990, c. C.12, s. 78(1) [Not in force at date of publication.]

Best interests of child

(2) In determining the best interests of a child for the purposes of an application under this Part in respect of custody of or access to a child, a court shall consider all the needs and circumstances of the child including,

- (a) the love, affection and emotional ties between the child and,
    - (i) each person entitled to or claiming custody of or access to the child,
    - (ii) other members of the child's family who reside with the child, and
    - (iii) persons involved in the care and upbringing of the child;
- (b) the views and preferences of the child, where such views and preferences can reasonably be ascertained;
- (c) the length of time the child has lived in a stable home environment;
- (d) the ability and willingness of each person applying for custody of the child to provide the child with guidance and education, the necessaries of life and any special needs of the child;
- (e) any plans proposed for the care and upbringing of the child;
- (f) the permanence and stability of the family unit with which it is proposed that the child will live; and
- (g) the relationship by blood or through an adoption order

between the child and each person who is party to the application.

Proposed Amendment — 24(2)

Best interests of child

(2) In determining the best interests of a child for the purpose of an application or motion under this Part in respect of custody of or access to a child, a court shall consider all the child's needs and circumstances, including,

    (a) the love, affection and emotional ties between the child and,

        (i) each person seeking custody or access,
        (ii) other members of the child's family residing with him or her, and
        (iii) persons involved in the child's care and upbringing;

    (b) the child's views and preferences, if they can reasonably be ascertained;

    (c) the length of time the child has lived in a stable home environment;

    (d) the ability of each person seeking custody or access to act as a parent;

    (e) the ability and willingness of each person seeking custody to provide the child with guidance, education and necessities of life and to meet any special needs of the child;

    (f) any plans proposed for the child's care and upbringing;

    (g) the permanence and stability of the family unit with which it is proposed that the child will live; and

    (h) the relationship, by blood or through an adoption order, between the child and each person who is a party to the application or motion.

    R.S.O. 1990, c. C.12, s. 78(2) [Not in force at date of publication.]

Past conduct

(3) The past conduct of a person is not relevant to a determination of an application under this Part in respect of custody of or access to a child unless the conduct is relevant to the ability of the person to act as a parent of a child.

Proposed Amendment — 24(3)

Domestic violence to be considered

(3) In assessing a person's ability to act as a parent, the court shall consider the fact that the person has at any time committed violence against his or her spouse or child, against his or her child's parent or against another member of the person's household.

R.S.O. 1990, c. C.12, s. 78(2) [Not in force at date of publication. Amended 1999, c. 6, s. 7(1); 2005, c. 5, s. 8(1).]

Proposed Addition — 24(3.1)

Definitions

(3.1) In subsection (3),

"same-sex partner" [Repealed 2005, c. 5, s. 8(2).]

"spouse" means,

(a) a spouse as defined in section 1 of the *Family Law Act*, or

(b) either of two persons who live together in a conjugal relationship outside marriage. "conjoint"

R.S.O. 1990, c. C.12, s. 78(2) [Not in force at date of publication. Amended 1999, c. 6, s. 7(2); 2005, c. 5, s. 8(2), (3).]

> **Proposed Addition — 24(4)**
>
> **Restrictions on consideration of other past conduct**
>
> (4) Other than the conduct referred to in subsection (3), a person's past conduct may be considered only if the court is satisfied that it is relevant to the person's ability to act as a parent.
>
> R.S.O. 1990, c. C.12, s. 78(2) [Not in force at date of publication.]

. . .

Custody and Access—Assistance to Court

Assessment of needs of child

30. (1) The court before which an application is brought in respect of custody of or access to a child, by order, may appoint a person who has technical or professional skill to assess and report to the court on the needs of the child and the ability and willingness of the parties or any of them to satisfy the needs of the child.

When order may be made

(2) An order may be made under subsection (1) on or before the hearing of the application in respect of custody of or access to the child and with or without a request by a party to the application.

Agreement by parties

(3) The court shall, if possible, appoint a person agreed upon by the parties, but if the parties do not agree the court shall choose and appoint the person.

Consent to act

(4) The court shall not appoint a person under subsection (1) unless the person has consented to make the assessment

and to report to the court within the period of time specified by the court.

Attendance for assessment

(5) In an order under subsection (1), the court may require the parties, the child and any other person who has been given notice of the proposed order, or any of them, to attend for assessment by the person appointed by the order.

Refusal to attend

(6) Where a person ordered under this section to attend for assessment refuses to attend or to undergo the assessment, the court may draw such inferences in respect of the ability and willingness of any person to satisfy the needs of the child as the court considers appropriate.

Report

(7) The person appointed under subsection (1) shall file his or her report with the clerk and local registrar of the court.

Copies of report

(8) The clerk or local registrar of the court shall give a copy of the report to each of the parties and to counsel, if any, representing the child.

Admissibility of report

(9) The report mentioned in subsection (7), is admissible in evidence in the application.

Assessor may be witness

(10) Any of the parties, and counsel, if any, representing the child, may require the person appointed under subsection (1) to attend as a witness at the hearing of the application.

Directions

(11) Upon motion, the court by order may give such directions in respect of the assessment as the court considers appropriate.

Fees and expenses

(12) The court shall require the parties to pay the fees and expenses of the person appointed under subsection (1).

Idem, proportions or amounts

(13) The court shall specify in the order the proportions or amounts of the fees and expenses that the court requires each party to pay.

Idem, serious financial hardship

(14) The court may relieve a party from responsibility for payment of any of the fees and expenses of the person appointed under subsection (1) where the court is satisfied that payment would cause serious financial hardship to the party.

Proposed Amendment — 30(14)

Idem, serious financial hardship

(14) The court may require one party to pay all the fees and expenses of the person appointed under subsection (1) if the court is satisfied that payment would cause the other party or parties serious financial hardship.
R.S.O. 1990, c. C.12, s. 81 [Not in force at date of publication.]

Other expert evidence

(15) The appointment of a person under subsection (1) does not prevent the parties or counsel representing the child from submitting other expert evidence as to the needs of the child and the ability and willingness of the parties or any of them to satisfy the needs of the child.

. . .

Custody and Access—Enforcement

. . .

Order restraining harassment

35. (1) On application, a court may make an interim or final order restraining a person from molesting, annoying or harassing the applicant or children in the applicant's lawful custody and may require the person to enter into the recognizance or post the bond that the court considers appropriate.

Proposed Amendment — s. 35(1)
Order restraining harassment

(1) On application, a court may make an interim or final order restraining a person from molesting, annoying or harassing the applicant or children in the applicant's lawful custody, or from communicating with the applicant or children, except as the order provides, and may require the person to enter into the recognizance that the court considers appropriate.

R.S.O. 1990, c. C.12, s. 84 [Not in force at date of publication.]

Offence

(2) A person who contravenes a restraining order is guilty of an offence and on conviction is liable to either or both a fine of $5,000 and imprisonment for a term of not more than three months for a first offence and not more than two years for a subsequent offence.

Proposed Repeal — 35(2)

(2) [Repealed 2000, c. 33, s. 21(1). Not in force at date of publication.]

Arrest without warrant

(3) A police officer may arrest without warrant a person the police officer believes on reasonable and probable grounds to have contravened a restraining order.

Existing orders

(4) Subsections (2) and (3) also apply in respect of contraventions committed after those subsections come into force, of restraining orders made under a predecessor of this section.

Proposed Repeal — 35

35. [Repealed 2000, c. 33, s. 21(2). Not in force at date of publication.]

[Editor's note: Subsection 21(3) of S.O. 2000, c. 33 provides that despite the repeal of subsection 35(2) of the Children's Law Reform Act, any prosecution begun under that subsection before its repeal shall continue as if it were still in force. Subsection 21(4) of S.O. 2000, c. 33 provides that despite the repeal of section 35 of the Children's Law Reform Act, any proceeding begun under that section before its repeal shall continue as if that section were still in force and any order made under that section before its repeal or pursuant to clause 21(4)(a) of S.O. 2000, c. 33 after the repeal of section 35 of the Children's Law Reform Act remains in force until it terminates by its own terms or is rescinded or terminated by a court.]

Order where child unlawfully withheld

36. (1) Where a court is satisfied upon application by a person in whose favour an order has been made for custody of or access to a child that there are reasonable and probable

grounds for believing that any person is unlawfully withholding the child from the applicant, the court by order may authorize the applicant or someone on his or her behalf to apprehend the child for the purpose of giving effect to the rights of the applicant to custody or access, as the case may be.

Order to locate and take child

(2) Where a court is satisfied upon application that there are reasonable and probable grounds for believing,

- (a) that any person is unlawfully withholding a child from a person entitled to custody of or access to the child;
- (b) that a person who is prohibited by court order or separation agreement from removing a child from Ontario proposes to remove the child or have the child removed from Ontario; or
- (c) that a person who is entitled to access to a child proposes to remove the child or to have the child removed from Ontario and that the child is not likely to return,

the court by order may direct a police force, having jurisdiction in any area where it appears to the court that the child may be, to locate, apprehend and deliver the child to the person named in the order.

Application without notice

(3) An order may be made under subsection (2) upon an application without notice where the court is satisfied that it is necessary that action be taken without delay.

Duty to act

(4) The police force directed to act by an order under subsection (2) shall do all things reasonably able to be done to locate, apprehend and deliver the child in accordance with the order.

Entry and search

(5) For the purpose of locating and apprehending a child in accordance with an order under subsection (2), a member of a police force may enter and search any place where he or she has reasonable and probable grounds for believing that the child may be with such assistance and such force as are reasonable in the circumstances.

Time

(6) An entry or a search referred to in subsection (5) shall be made only between 6 a.m. and 9 p.m. standard time unless the court, in the order, authorizes entry and search at another time.

Expiration of order

(7) An order made under subsection (2) shall name a date on which it expires, which shall be a date not later than six months after it is made unless the court is satisfied that a longer period of time is necessary in the circumstances.

Wen application may be made

(8) An application under subsection (1) or (2) may be made in an application for custody or access or at any other time.

. . .

Education Act

R.S.O. 1990, c. E.2 as am. R.S.O. 1990, c. E.2, s. 277.6(1), (2); S.O. 1991, c. 10; 1991, c. 15, s. 36; 1992, c. 15, ss. 85–89; 1992, c. 16; 1992, c. 17, ss. 1–3; 1992, c. 27, s. 59; 1992, c. 32, s. 9; 1993, c. 11, ss. 8–43; 1993, c. 23, s. 67; 1993, c. 26, ss. 44, 45; 1993, c. 27, Sched.; 1993, c. 41; 1994, c. 1, s. 22; 1994, c. 17, s. 48; 1994, c. 23, s. 65 [Not in force at date of publication. Repealed 2002, c. 17, Sched. F, s. 1.]; 1994, c. 27, ss. 45, 108; 1995, c. 4, s. 2; 1996, c. 2, s. 65; 1996, c. 11, s. 29; 1996, c. 12, s. 64; 1996, c. 13; 1996, c. 32, s. 70; 1997, c. 3, ss. 2–10; 1997, c. 16, s. 5; 1997, c. 19, s. 33; 1997, c. 22, s. 1; 1997, c. 27, s. 71 [Not in force at date of publication; obsolete.]; 1997, c. 31, ss. 1–142 [s. 101(4) not in force at date of publication.]; 1997, c. 32, s. 10; 1997, c. 43, Sched. G, s. 20; 1998, c. 3, s. 34; 1998, c. 14, s. 1; 1998, c. 33, ss. 39–46; 1999, c. 6, s. 20(1) (Fr.), (2)–(6); 1999, c. 9, ss. 98–100; 2000, c. 5, s. 11; 2000, c. 11, ss. 1–4, 5(1), (2) (Fr.), (3)–(7), 6–25 [ss. 2(1), 3(1), (3)–(5), 17–19, 22(1) not in force at date of publication; ss. 3(3)–(5), 17, 18 obsolete.]; 2000, c. 12, ss. 1–3; 2000, c. 25, s. 45; 2000, c. 26, Sched. C, s. 1; 2001, c. 8, s. 204; 2001, c. 13, s. 16 (Fr.); 2001, c. 14, Sched. A, ss. 1–12; 2001, c. 17, s. 1; 2001, c. 23, s. 65; 2001, c. 24, ss. 1–5 [s. 5 not in force at date of publication.]; 2002, c. 7, s. 1; 2002, c. 8, Sched. A, Sched. I, s. 8; 2002, c. 17, Sched. C, ss. 7–9, Sched. D, ss. 36, 37, Sched. F, s. 1; 2002, c. 18, Sched. G, ss. 1, 2, 3 (Fr.), 4 (Fr.), 5–12; 2002, c. 22, ss. 57–60; 2003, c. 2, s. 20; 2004, c. 8, s. 46 [Not in force at date of publication.]; 2004, c. 31, Sched. 10; 2005, c. 4; 2005, c. 5, s. 21

. . .

Part VI
Boards

Duties and Powers

Duties of boards

170. (1) Every board shall,

1. **appoint secretary-treasurer** — appoint a secretary and a treasurer or a secretary-treasurer who, in the case of a board of not more than five elected members, may be a member of the board;

2. **security of treasurer** — take proper security from the treasurer or secretary-treasurer;

3. **order payment of bills** — give the necessary orders on the treasurer for payment of all money expended for school purposes and of such other expenses for promoting the interests of the schools under the jurisdiction of the board as may be authorized by this Act or the regulations and by the board;

4. **meetings** — fix the times and places for the meetings of the board and the mode of calling and conducting them, and ensure that a full and correct account of the proceedings thereat is kept;

5. **head office** — establish and maintain a head office and notify the Ministry of its location and address and notify the Ministry of any change in the location or address of the head office within ten days of such change;

6. **provide instruction and accommodation** — provide instruction and adequate accommodation during each school year for the pupils who have a right to attend a school under the jurisdiction of the board;

6.1 **kindergarten** — operate kindergartens;

6.2 [Repealed 1996, c. 13, s. 5(1).]

7. **Special education programs and services** — provide or enter into an agreement with another board to provide in accordance with the regulations special education programs and special education services for its exceptional pupils;

Proposed Addition — 170(1), para. 7.1

7.1 **co-instructional activities — elementary** — in accordance with any guidelines issued under paragraph 26.1 of subsection 8(1), develop and implement a plan to provide for co-instructional activities for pupils enrolled in elementary schools operated by the board, in respect of each school year.

> 2000, c. 11, s. 3(1) [Not in force at date of publication.]

7.2 **co-instructional activities—secondary** — in accordance with any guidelines issued under paragraph 26.2 of subsection 8(1), develop and implement a plan to provide for co-instructional activities for pupils enrolled in secondary schools operated by the board, in respect of each school year.

8. **repair property** — keep the school buildings and premises in proper repair and in a proper sanitary condition, provide suitable furniture and equipment and keep it in proper repair, and protect the property of the board;

9. **insurance** — make provision for insuring adequately the buildings and equipment of the board and for insuring the board and its employees and volunteers who are assigned duties by the principal against claims in respect of accidents incurred by pupils while under the jurisdiction or supervision of the board;

10. **conduct schools** — ensure that every school under its charge is conducted in accordance with this Act and the regulations;

11. **school open** — keep open its schools during the whole period of the school year determined under the regulations, except where it is otherwise provided under this Act;

12. **appoint principal and teachers** — appoint for each school that it operates a principal and an adequate number of teachers, all of whom shall be members of the Ontario College of Teachers;

12.1 **duties—charges, convictions** — on becoming aware that a teacher or temporary teacher who is employed by the board has been charged with or convicted of an offence under the *Criminal Code* (Canada) involving sexual conduct and minors, or of any other offence under the *Criminal Code* (Canada) that in the opinion of the board indicates that pupils may be at risk, take prompt steps to ensure that the teacher or temporary teacher performs no duties in the classroom and no duties involving contact with pupils, pending withdrawal of the charge, discharge following a preliminary inquiry, stay of the charge or acquittal, as the case may be;

13. **provide textbooks** — subject to paragraph 31.1 of subsection 171(1) provide, without charge, for the use of the pupils attending the school or schools operated by the board, the textbooks that are required by the regulations to be purchased by the board;

14. **vehicle insurance** — where it furnishes transportation for pupils in a vehicle that is owned by the board, provide and carry with an insurer licensed under the *Insurance Act* for each such vehicle at least the amount of insurance that is required to be provided in respect of such a vehicle by the licensee of a school vehicle under the *Public Vehicles Act*;

15. **report children not enrolled** — ascertain and report to the Ministry at least once in each year in the manner required by the Minister the names and ages of all children of compulsory school age within its jurisdiction who are not enrolled in any school or private school and the reasons therefor;

16. **reports** — transmit to the Minister all reports and returns required by this Act and the regulations;

17. **statement of sick leave credits** — where applicable, issue to an employee, upon the termination of his or her employment with the board, a statement of the sick leave credits standing to the employee's credit with the board at the time of such termination;

17.1 **School councils** — establish a school council for each school operated by the board, in accordance with the regulations;

18. **requirements** — do anything that a board is required to do under any other provision of this Act or under any other Act.

19. [Repealed 1997, c. 31, s. 80.]

20. [Repealed 1997, c. 31, s. 80.]

S. 67 school districts

(2) Paragraph 6.1 of subsection (1) does not apply to the board of a secondary school district established under section 67.

(2.1) [Repealed 2001, c. 14, Sched. A, s. 2(1).]

(2.2) [Repealed 2001, c. 14, Sched. A, s. 2(1).]

(2.3) [Repealed 2001, c. 14, Sched. A, s. 2(1).]

(2.4) [Repealed 2001, c. 14, Sched. A, s. 2(1).]

Plans, reports

(2.5) The Minister may require boards to,

(a) submit a plan required under paragraph 7.1 of subsection (1) in respect of any school year;
(b) submit a plan required under paragraph 7.2 of subsection (1) in respect of any school year; and
(c) report on any matter related to compliance with paragraph 7.1 or 7.2 of subsection (1).

Same

(2.6) A requirement under subsection (2.5) may apply to all boards or to specified boards and every board to which the requirement applies shall comply with it.

Same

(2.7) The Minister may give such directions as he or she considers appropriate respecting the form, content and deadline for submission of a plan or report required under subsection (2.5) and boards shall comply with those directions.

Alterations

(2.8) Where the Minister has concerns that a plan submitted by a board under clause (2.5)(a) or (2.5)(b) may not comply with the requirements of paragraph 7.1 or 7.2 of subsection (1), as the case may be, the Minister may direct the board to alter the plan, in the manner directed by the Minister, and the board shall make the alteration and implement the plan as altered.

Non-application of *Regulations Act*

(2.9) An act of the Minister under this section is not a regulation within the meaning of the *Regulations Act*.

Regulations re school councils

(3) The Lieutenant Governor in Council may make regulations respecting school councils, including regulations relating to their establishment, composition and functions.
1993, c. 11, s. 30; 1996, c. 11, s. 29; 1996, c. 12, s. 64; 1996, c. 13, ss. 5, 12; 1997, c. 31, s. 80; 2000, c. 11, s. 3(2)–(6); 2001, c. 14, Sched. A, s. 2; 2002, c. 7, s. 1

Transitional Provisions

2000, c. 11, s. 3 amended s. 170 by adding paragraphs 7.1 and 7.2 to s. 170(1) and by adding s. 170(2.1) to (2.9).

2000, c. 11, subss. 22(1) [not in force as at date of publication] and (5) provide as follows:

> *22. (1) Paragraphs 7.1 and 7.2 of subsection 170(1) of the Act do not apply in respect of the 1999-2000 school year.*
>
> *(5) In this section,*

"school year" has the same meaning as in the Act.

Class size, primary division

170.1 (1) Every board shall ensure that the average size of its elementary school classes in the primary division, in the aggregate, does not exceed 24 pupils.

Class size, elementary schools

(2) Every board shall ensure that the average size of its elementary school classes, in the aggregate, does not exceed 24.5 pupils.

Class size, secondary schools

(3) Subject to subsection (4.4), every board shall ensure that the average size of its secondary school classes, in the aggregate, does not exceed 21 pupils.

Exception, board resolution

(4) A board may pass a resolution specifying that the average size of its secondary school classes, in the aggregate, may exceed 21 pupils by an amount that is equal to or less than one pupil.

Same

(4.1) A resolution under subsection (4) shall be passed at a meeting that is open to the public.

Same

(4.2) The Minister may make regulations governing resolutions under subsection (4), including but not limited to regulations,

- (a) respecting processes and timing related to the passing of a resolution under subsection (4);
- (b) respecting the period of time in respect of which a resolution under subsection (4) may apply;

(c) specifying any matter related to the increase in the maximum average aggregate size of secondary school classes that a resolution under subsection (4) must set out or provide for;
(d) requiring boards to implement provisions contained in a resolution under subsection (4);
(e) requiring boards to make copies of a resolution under subsection (4) available to the public, in the manner specified in the regulation;
(f) requiring boards to provide copies of a resolution under subsection (4) to persons specified in the regulation.

Same

(4.3) A regulation made under subsection (4.2) may be general or specific.

Same

(4.4) A board that has passed a resolution in accordance with subsections (4) and (4.1) and any regulations made under subsection (4.2) shall ensure that the average size of its secondary school classes, in the aggregate, does not exceed the maximum average aggregate class size specified in the resolution.

Exception, permission of Minister

(4.5) The average size of a board's classes, in the aggregate, may exceed the maximum average class size specified in subsection (1), (2), (3) or (4.4), as the case may be, to the extent that the Minister, at the request of the board, may permit.

Same

(4.6) In giving permission under subsection (4.5), the Minister may impose conditions and the board shall comply with those conditions.

Regulations

(5) The Lieutenant Governor in Council may, by regulation,

(a) establish the methods to be used by a board to determine average aggregate class sizes for the purposes of this section;
(b) exclude any type of class, course or program from the determination of average class size;
(c) require boards to prepare reports containing such information relating to class size as is specified by the regulation;
(d) require boards to make reports required under clause (c) available to the public, in such manner as is specified in the regulation;
(e) require boards to submit reports required under clause (c) to the Minister, in such manner as is specified in the regulation;
(f) specify dates as of which determinations shall be made under this section;
(g) define terms used in this section for the purposes of a regulation made under this section.
1997, c. 31, s. 81; 2000, c. 11, s. 4; 2001, c. 14, Sched. A, s. 3

Transitional Provisions

2000, c. 11, s. 4 repealed and substituted s. 170.1.

2000, c. 11, subss. 22(2) and (5) provide as follows:

22. (2) Despite section ... 4 ... of this Act, section ... 170.1 ... of the Act and any regulations made under ... [that] section ... as ... [that] ... section and those regulations read immediately before this Act receives Royal Assent, continue to apply in respect of the 1999-2000 school year.

(5) In this section,

"school year" has the same meaning as in the Act.

Immediately before 2000, c. 11 received Royal Assent on June 23, 2000, s. 170.1 read as follows:

Class size

170.1 (1) Every board shall ensure that the average size of its elementary school classes, in the aggregate, does not exceed 25 pupils.

Same, secondary schools

(2) Every board shall ensure that the average size of its secondary school classes, in the aggregate, does not exceed 22 pupils.

Exception

(3) The average size of a board's classes, in the aggregate, may exceed the maximum average class size specified in subsection (1) or (2), as the case may be, to the extent that the Minister, at the request of the board, may permit.

Determination date

(4) A board shall determine the average size of its classes, in the aggregate, as of October 31 each year.

Regulations

(5) The Lieutenant Governor in Council may, by regulation,

    (a) establish the method to be used by a board to determine the average size of its classes, in the aggregate;

    (b) exclude special education classes from the determination of average class size;

    (c) require boards to prepare reports (containing the information specified by the regulation) concerning the average size of its classes and to make the reports available to the public;

(d) define terms used in this section for the purposes of a regulation made under this section.

Review of maximum amount

(6) Every three years, the Minister shall review the amount of the maximum average class sizes specified in subsections (1) and (2).

Definition

170.2 (1) In this section,

"**classroom teacher**" means a teacher who is assigned in a regular timetable to provide instruction to pupils and includes a temporary teacher who is assigned in a regular timetable to provide instruction to pupils but does not include a principal or vice-principal.

Minimum teaching time, elementary school

(2) Every board shall ensure that, in the aggregate, its classroom teachers in elementary schools are assigned to provide instruction to pupils for an average of at least 1300 minutes (during the instructional program) for each period of five instructional days during the school year.

(3) [Repealed 2000, c. 11, s. 5(3).]

Allocation to schools

(4) A board shall allocate to each elementary school a share of the board's aggregate minimum time for a school year for all of its classroom teachers (during which they must be assigned to provide instruction to pupils).

Allocation by principal

(5) The principal of an elementary school, in his or her sole discretion, shall allocate among the classroom teachers in the

school the school's share of the board's aggregate minimum time, as described in subsection (4), for the school year.

Same

(6) The principal shall make the allocation in accordance with such policies as the board may establish.

Effect on collective agreements

(7) An allocation under subsection (4) or (5) may be made despite any applicable conditions or restrictions in a collective agreement.

Calculation

(8) The calculation of the amount of time that a board's classroom teachers are assigned as required by subsection (2) shall be based on all of the board's classroom teachers in elementary schools and their assignments, on a regular timetable, on every instructional day during the school year.

Part-time employees

(9) For the purposes of subsection (2), the minimum time required in respect of each classroom teacher who is employed on a part-time basis by the board is correspondingly reduced.

(10) [Repealed 2000, c. 11, s. 5(7).]

(11) [Repealed 2000, c. 11, s. 5(7).]

(12) [Repealed 2000, c. 11, s. 5(7).]

(13) [Repealed 2000, c. 11, s. 5(7).]
    1997, c. 31, s. 81; 1998, c. 14, s. 1; 2000, c. 11, s. 5

Transitional Provisions

2000, c. 11, s. 5 amended s. 170.2 by repealing subss. (4) and (10) to (12) and by repealing and substituting subss. (1), (4), (5), (8) and (9).

2000, c. 11, subss. 22(2), (3) and (5) provide as follows:

22. (2) *Despite section 4 and 5 of this Act, sections 170.1 and 170.2 of the Act and any regulations made under those sections, as those sections and those regulations read immediately before this Act receives Royal Assent, continue to apply in respect of the 1999-2000 school year.*

(3) *Despite subsection (2), where section 23 of this Act applies [see below], the regulations made under section 170.2 of the Act, as they read immediately before this Act receives Royal Assent, do not apply in respect of the 1999-2000 school year.*

(5) *In this section,*

"school year" has the same meaning as in the Act.

2000, c. 11, subss. 23(1), (2), (3) and (5) provide as follows:

23. (1) *Subject to subsection (2), this section applies where the first collective agreement entered into after December 31, 1997 between a board and a designated bargaining agent,*

  (a) *provided, at the time that it was first entered into, for a three year term of operation;*
  (b) *is in operation on the day this Act receives Royal Assent; and*
  (c) *provides that it continues to operate until August 31, 2001.*

(2) *If any amendment is made to the collective agreement on or after May 10, 2000, this section does not apply, or ceases to apply, as the case may be.*

(3) *Despite section 5 of this Act, section 170.2 of the Act, as that section read immediately before this Act receives Royal Assent, continues to apply in respect of secondary schools during the 2000-2001 school year.*

(5) *In this section,*

"board" has the same meaning as in the Act;

"designated bargaining agent" has the same meaning as in Part X.1 of the Act.

"school year" has the same meaning as in the Act.

Immediately before 2000, c. 11 received Royal Assent on June 23, 2000, s. 170.2 read as follows:

Teaching time

170.2 (1) In this section,

"classroom teacher" means a teacher who is assigned in a regular timetable to provide instruction to pupils but does not include a principal or vice-principal.

Minimum teaching time, elementary school

(2) Every board shall ensure that, in the aggregate, its classroom teachers in elementary schools are assigned to provide instruction to pupils for an average of at least 1300 minutes (during the instructional program) for each period of five instructional days during the school year.

Minimum teaching time, secondary school

(3) Every board shall ensure that, in the aggregate, its classroom teachers in secondary schools are assigned to provide instruction to pupils for an average of at least 1250 minutes (during the instructional program) for each period of five instructional days during the school year.

Allocation to schools

(4) A board may allocate to each school a share of the board's aggregate minimum time for a school year for all of its classroom teachers (during which they must be assigned to provide instruction to pupils).

Allocation by principal

(5) The principal of a school, in his or her sole discretion, shall allocate among the classroom teachers in the school the school's share of the board's aggregate minimum time (as described in subsection (4)) for the school year.

Same

(6) The principal shall make the allocation in accordance with such policies as the board may establish.

Effect on collective agreements

(7) An allocation under subsection (4) or (5) may be made despite any applicable conditions or restrictions in a collective agreement.

Calculation

(8) The calculation of the amount of time that a board's classroom teachers are assigned as required by subsection (2) or (3) shall be based upon all of the board's classroom teachers and their assignments (on a regular timetable) on every instructional day during the school year.

Part-time employees

(9) For the purposes of subsection (2) or (3), the minimum time required in respect of each classroom teacher who is employed on a part-time basis by the board is correspondingly reduced.

Definition

(10) In subsection (11),

"credit" includes a credit equivalent awarded in connection with a grade nine program in the 1998-99 school year.

Interpretation: provision of instruction in a secondary school

(11) For the purposes of this section, a classroom teacher in a secondary school is assigned to provide instruction only when he or she is assigned in a regular timetable to invigilate examinations or to provide instruction in,

(a) a course or program that is eligible for credit;
(b) a special education program;
(c) a remedial class the purpose of which is to assist one or more pupils in completing a course or program that is eligible for credit or required for an Ontario secondary school diploma;
(d) an English as a second language or actualisation linguistique en français program;
(e) an apprenticeship program;
(f) a co-operative education program; or
(g) any other class, course or program specified or described in a regulation made under clause (13)(a).

Co-operative education programs: interpretation

(12) For the purposes of clause (11)(f), a teacher is assigned to provide instruction in a co-operative education program when he or she is assigned in a regular timetable to arrange placements for the program or to make site visits to monitor or evaluate the performance of pupils in such placements.

Regulations

(13) The Lieutenant Governor in Council may make regulations,

(a) specifying or describing classes, courses or programs for the purposes of clause (11)(g); and
(b) clarifying the meaning of any word or expression used in subsection (11) or (12).

Definitions

170.2.1 (1) In this section,

"**classroom teacher**" means a teacher who is assigned in a regular timetable to provide instruction in a credit course or credit-equivalent course to pupils and includes a temporary teacher who is assigned in a regular timetable to provide instruction in a credit course or credit-equivalent course to pupils but does not include a principal or vice-principal; "enseignant chargé de cours"

"**credit course**" means a course or program in which a credit or part of a credit may be earned; "cours donnant droit à des crédits"

"**credit-equivalent course**" means a course or program that is prescribed as a credit-equivalent course by the regulations made under this section; "cours donnant droit à des équivalences en crédits"

"**eligible course**" [Repealed 2001, c. 14, Sched. A, s. 4(1).]

"**eligible program**" means a credit course, a credit-equivalent course, an equivalent program or a program of special duties; "programme admissible"

"**equivalent program**" means a course or program that is prescribed as an equivalent program by the regulations made under this section; "programme équivalent"

"**program of special duties**" means a program that is prescribed as a program of special duties by the regulations made under this section. "programme d'affectations spéciales"

Minimum teaching assignments, secondary school

(2) Every board shall ensure that, in the aggregate, its classroom teachers in secondary schools are assigned to provide instruction to or supervision of pupils or to perform duties in

an average of at least 6.67 eligible programs in a day school program during the school year.

Allocation to schools

(3) A board shall allocate to each secondary school a share of the board's aggregate minimum eligible program obligations for a school year for all its classroom teachers.

Allocation by principal

(4) The principal of a secondary school, in his or her sole discretion, shall allocate among the classroom teachers in the school the school's share of the board's aggregate minimum obligations, as described in subsection (3), for the school year.

Same

(5) The principal shall make the allocation in accordance with such policies as the board may establish.

Collective agreements

(6) An allocation under subsection (3) or (4) may be made despite any applicable conditions or restrictions in a collective agreement.

Calculation

(7) The calculation required by subsection (2) shall be based on all of the board's classroom teachers in secondary schools and their assignments to provide instruction or supervision or to perform duties in eligible programs, on a regular timetable, during the school year.

Part-time employees

(8) For the purposes of subsection (2), the minimum time required in respect of each classroom teacher who is employed on a part-time basis by the board is correspondingly reduced.

Regulations

(9) The Lieutenant Governor in Council may make regulations,

(a) prescribing courses or programs, or portions of courses or programs, as credit-equivalent courses for the purposes of this section;
(b) prescribing courses or programs, or portions of courses or programs, as equivalent programs for the purposes of this section;
(c) prescribing programs, or portions of programs, as programs of special duties for the purposes of this section;
(d) respecting how to count credit courses for the purposes of this section;
(e) respecting how to count credit-equivalent courses for the purposes of this section;
(f) respecting how to count equivalent programs for the purposes of this section;
(g) authorizing boards, for the purposes of this section, to count equivalent programs differently than as provided under clause (f), subject to such conditions as are set out in the regulations;
(h) respecting how to count programs of special duties for the purposes of this section;
(i) respecting when a classroom teacher is considered to be assigned to provide instruction or supervision or to perform duties in an eligible program for the purposes of this section.

Same

(10) Without limiting the generality of subsection (9), a regulation made under that subsection may, for the purposes of the calculation required by subsection (2),

(a) set maximum average numbers for which specified types of eligible programs may be counted;
(b) set special rules for how to count specified type of eli-

gible programs, including but not limited to rules that provide that specified types of eligible programs shall be excluded from the calculation;

(c) set special rules for how to count eligible programs, or specified types of eligible programs, in specified kinds of circumstances, including but not limited to circumstances relating to,

    (i) pupil attendance levels,
    (ii) class size,
    (iii) patterns of teacher assignments.

General or particular

(11) A regulation made under this section may be general or particular in its application.

Plans, reports

(12) The Minister may require boards to,

(a) submit their plans for complying with this section in respect of any school year; and

(b) report on any matter related to compliance with this section.

Same

(13) A requirement under subsection (12) may apply to all boards or to specified boards and every board to which the requirement applies shall comply with it.

Same

(14) The Minister may give such directions as he or she considers appropriate respecting the form, content and deadline for submission of a plan or report required under subsection (12) and boards shall comply with those directions.

Alterations

(15) Where the Minister has concerns that plans submitted by a board under clause (12)(a) may not result in compliance with the requirements of this section and the regulations made under it, the Minister may direct the board to alter the plans, in the manner directed by the Minister, and the board shall make the alteration and implement the plan as altered.

Non-application of *Regulations Act*

(16) An act of the Minister under this section is not a regulation within the meaning of the *Regulations Act*.

Interpretation

(17) Nothing in this section or the regulations made under this section shall be construed as a limit on the amount of supervision or instruction in an eligible program to which a board may assign classroom teachers.

2000, c. 11, s. 6; 2001, c. 14, Sched. A, s. 4

Transitional Provisions

2000, c. 11, s. 6 amended the Act by adding s. 170.2.1.

2000, c. 11, subss. 22(4) and (5) provide as follows:

> 22. (4) Section 170.2.1 of the Act does not apply in respect of the 1999-2000 school year.
>
> (5) In this section,

"school year" has the same meaning as in the Act.
2000, c. 11, subss. 23(1), (2), (4) and (5) provide as follows:

> 23. (1) Subject to subsection (2), this section applies where the first collective agreement entered into after December 31, 1997 between a board and a designated bargaining agent,
>
> > (a) provided, at the time that it was first entered into, for a three year term of operation;

(b) *is in operation on the day this Act receives Royal Assent; and*

(c) *provides that it continues to operate until August 31, 2001.*

(2) *If any amendment is made to the collective agreement on or after May 10, 2000, this section does not apply, or ceases to apply, as the case may be.*

(4) *Section 170.2.1 of the Act does not apply in respect of the 2000-2001 school year.*

(5) *In this section,*

"board" has the same meaning as in the Act;

"designated bargaining agent" has the same meaning as in Part X.1 of the Act;

"school year" has the same meaning in the Act.

Definitions

170.2.2 (1) In this section,

"designated bargaining agent" has the same meaning as in Part X.1; *"agent négociateur désigné"*

"teachers' bargaining unit" has the same meaning as in Part X.1; *"unité de négociation d'enseignants"*

Application of section

(2) This section applies where a provision in a collective agreement that is in operation on May 10, 2000 between a board and a designated bargaining agent for a teachers' bargaining unit would, in the opinion of the board, require a board to employ more teaching staff than the board needs to meet its obligations under section 170.2.1.

Labour Relations Act, 1995, ss. 17, 86

(3) In the circumstances described in subsection (2), section 17 and subsection 86(1) of the *Labour Relations Act, 1995* do not apply to prevent the board from altering terms and conditions of employment, or rights, privileges or duties of the board, the designated bargaining agent, the teachers' bargaining unit or members of that unit, as the board sees fit to enable it to alter the level of teaching staff that it employs to a level that it considers appropriate, having regard to its obligations under section 170.2.1.

2000, c. 11, s. 6

Teachers' assistants, etc.

170.3 The Lieutenant Governor in Council may make regulations governing duties and minimum qualifications of persons who are assigned to assist teachers or to complement instruction by teachers in elementary or secondary schools.

1997, c. 31, s. 81

Powers of boards

171. (1) A board may,

1. **committees** — establish committees composed of members of the board to make recommendations to the board in respect of education, finance, personnel and property;

2. **idem** — establish committees that may include persons who are not members of the board in respect of matters other than those referred to in paragraph 1;

3. **appoint employees** — except as otherwise provided under this Act, appoint and remove such officers and servants and, appoint and remove such teachers, as it considers expedient, determine the terms on which such officers, servants and teachers are to be employed, prescribe their duties and fix their salaries, except that

in the case of a secretary of a board who is a member of the board, the board may pay only such compensation for his or her services as is approved by the electors at a meeting of the electors;

4. **voluntary assistants** — permit a principal to assign to a person who volunteers to serve without remuneration such duties in respect of the school as are approved by the board and to terminate such assignment;

5. **supervisors** — appoint supervisors of the teaching staff for positions that are provided for in any Act or regulation administered by the Minister and every appointee shall hold the qualifications and perform the duties required in the Act or regulations;

6. **psychiatrist or psychologist** — appoint one or more,
    i. psychiatrists who are on the register of specialists in psychiatry of The Royal College of Physicians and Surgeons of Canada or of the College of Physicians and Surgeons of Ontario,
    ii. psychologists who are legally qualified medical practitioners are members of the College of Psychologists of Ontario;

7. **schools and attendance areas** — determine the number and kind of schools to be established and maintained and the attendance area for each school, and close schools in accordance with policies established by the board from guidelines issued by the Minister;

8. **courses of study** — provide instruction in courses of study that are prescribed or approved by the Minister, developed from curriculum guidelines issued by the Minister or approved by the board where the Minister permits the board to approve courses of study;

9. **computer programming** — in lieu of purchasing a computer or system of computer programming, enter into an agreement for the use thereof by the board;

10. **playgrounds, parks, rinks** — operate the school ground as a park or playground and rink during the school year or in vacation or both, and provide and maintain such equipment as it considers advisable, and provide such supervision as it considers proper, provided the proper conduct of the school is not interfered with;

11. **gymnasiums** — organize and carry on gymnasium classes in school buildings for pupils or others during the school year or in vacation or both, and provide supervision and training for such classes, provided the proper conduct of the school is not interfered with;

12. **milk** — purchase milk to be consumed by the pupils in the schools under the jurisdiction of the board during school days in accordance with the terms and conditions prescribed by the regulations;

13. **provision of supplies, etc.** — provide school supplies, other than the textbooks that it is required to provide under paragraph 13 of section 170, for the use of pupils;

14. **libraries** — establish and maintain school libraries and resource centres;

15. **junior kindergartens** — operate junior kindergartens.

16. **signatures mechanically reproduced** — provide that the signature of the treasurer and of any other person authorized to sign cheques issued by the treasurer may be written or engraved, lithographed, printed or otherwise mechanically reproduced on cheques;

17. **membership fees and traveling expenses** — pay the traveling expenses and membership fees of any member of the board, or of any teacher or officer of the board, incurred in attending meetings of an educational association and may make grants and pay membership fees to any such organization;

18. **legal costs** — pay the costs, or any part thereof, incurred by any member of the board or by any teacher, officer or other employee of the board in successfully defending any legal proceeding brought against him or her,
    i. for libel or slander in respect of any statements relating to the employment, suspension or dismissal of any person by the board published at a meeting of the board or of a committee thereof, or
    ii. for assault in respect of disciplinary action taken in the course of duty;
19. [Repealed 1997, c. 31, s. 82.]
20. [Repealed 1997, c. 31, s. 82.]
21. [Repealed 1997, c. 31, s. 82.]
22. [Repealed 1997, c. 31, s. 82.]
23. **student fees** — subject to the provisions of this Act and the regulations, fix the fees to be paid by or on behalf of pupils, and the times of payment thereof, and when necessary enforce payment thereof by action in the Small Claims Court, and exclude any pupil by or on behalf of whom fees that are legally required to be paid are not paid after reasonable notice;
24. **permit use of school and school buses** — permit the school buildings and premises and school buses owned by the board to be used for any educational or other lawful purpose;
25. **surgical treatment** — provide for surgical treatment of children attending the school who suffer from minor physical defects, where in the opinion of the teacher and, where a school nurse and medical officer are employed, of the nurse and medical officer, the defect interferes with the proper education of the child, and includes in the estimates for the current year the funds necessary for cases where the parents are not able to

pay, provided that no such treatment shall be undertaken without the consent that complies with the *Health Care Consent Act*, 1996;

26. **cadet corps** — establish and maintain cadet corps;

27. **athletics** — provide for the promotion and encouragement of athletics and for the holding of school games;

28. **activities** — provide, during the school year or at other times, activities and programs on or off school premises, including field trips, and exercise jurisdiction over those persons participating therein;

29. **guidance** — appoint one or more teachers qualified in guidance according to the regulations to collect and distribute information regarding available occupations and employments, and to offer such counsel to the pupils as will enable them to plan intelligently for their educational and vocational advancement;

30. **public lectures** — conduct free lectures open to the public and include in the estimates for the current year the expenses thereof;

31. **continuing education** — establish continuing education courses and classes.

31.1 **deposit for continuing education textbooks** — require a pupil enrolled in a continuing education course or class that is eligible for credit towards a secondary school diploma to pay a nominal deposit for a textbook provided by the board that will be forfeited to the board in whole or in part if the textbook is not returned or is returned in a damaged condition;

32. **courses for teachers** — establish and conduct during the school year courses for teachers;

33. **evening classes** — establish evening classes;

34. **erect fences** — erect and maintain any wall or fence

considered necessary by the board for enclosure of the school premises;

35. **school fairs** — contribute toward the support of school fairs;

36. **student activities** — authorize such school activities as pertain to the welfare of the pupils and exercise jurisdiction in respect thereof;

37. **cafeteria** — operate a cafeteria for the use of the staff and pupils;

38. **records management** — institute a program of records management that will, subject to the regulations in respect of pupil records,

   i. provide for the archival retention by the board or the Archivist of Ontario of school registers, minute books of the board and its predecessors, documents pertaining to boundaries of school sections, separate school zones and secondary school districts, original assessment and taxation records in the possession of the board and other records considered by the board to have enduring value or to be of historical interest, and

   ii. establish, with the written approval of the auditor of the board, schedules for the retention, disposition and eventual destruction of records of the board and of the schools under its jurisdiction other than records retained for archival use;

39. **education of children in charitable organizations** — employ and pay teachers, when so requested in writing by a charitable organization having the charge of children of school age, for the education of such children, whether such children are being educated in premises within or beyond the limits of the jurisdiction of the board, and pay for and furnish school supplies for their use;

40. **programs in detention homes** — with the approval of the Minister, conduct an education program in a centre facility, home, hospital or institution that is approved, designated, established, licensed or registered under any Act and in which the Ministry does not conduct an education program, or in a demonstration school for exceptional pupils;

41. **maternity leave** — provide for maternity leave for a teacher, not exceeding two years for each pregnancy;

42. **assumption of treatment centres, etc.** — when requested by the board of a cerebral palsy treatment centre school, a crippled children's treatment centre school, a hospital school or a sanatorium school, and with the approval of the Minister, by agreement, assume the assets and liabilities of such board and continue to operate such a school, and, upon the effective date of the agreement between the two boards, the board making the request is dissolved;

43. [Repealed 1997, c. 31, s. 82(4).]

44. **agreement for provision and use of recreational facilities** — with the approval of the Minister, enter into an agreement with a university, college of a university, or the board of governors of a polytechnical institute or of a college of applied arts and technology, in respect of the provision, maintenance and use of educational or recreational facilities on the property of either of the parties to the agreement;

45. **election recounts** — pass a resolution referred to in subsection 57(1) of the *Municipal Elections Act* 1996.

46. **insurance** — provide for insurance against risks that may involve pecuniary loss or liability on the part of the board, and for paying premiums therefor;

47. [Repealed 1997, c. 31, s. 82(5).]

48. **Child care facilities** — construct and renovate child care facilities in any school.

49. **day nurseries** — establish, operate and maintain day nurseries within the meaning of the *Day Nurseries Act*, subject to that Act.

50. [Repealed 1996, c. 13, s. 6(2).]

Powers of boards re: days of work

(2) A board may require teachers to work during some or all of the five working days preceding the start of the school year.

Same

(3) A board may authorize the principal of a school to make determinations respecting the work to be done by teachers of the school during the working days referred to in subsection (2) and the principal shall exercise that discretion subject to the authority of the appropriate supervisory officer.

Same

(4) For the purposes of subsections (2) and (3), a working day is a day other than Saturday, Sunday or a holiday as defined in subsection 29(1) of the *Interpretation Act*.

Same

(5) Work that may be required under subsections (2) and (3) includes but is not limited to participation in professional development activities.
   1991, Vol. 2, c. 10, s. 5; 1992, c. 32 s. 9; 1993, c. 11, s. 31; 1993, c. 26, s. 44; 1994, c. 27, s. 108(5); 1996, c. 2, s. 65; 1996, c. 13, ss. 6, 12; 1996, c. 32, s. 70(4); 1997, c. 31, s. 82; 2001, c. 24, s. 3

. . .

Part X
Teachers, Pupil Records and Education Numbers
[Heading added 1997, c. 31, s. 115.]

. . .

Duties

Duties of teacher

264. (1) It is the duty of a teacher and a temporary teacher,

(a) **teach** — to teach diligently and faithfully the classes or subjects assigned to the teacher by the principal;

(b) **learning** — to encourage the pupils in the pursuit of learning;

(c) **religion and morals** — to inculcate by precept and example respect for religion and the principles of Judaeo-Christian morality and the highest regard for truth, justice, loyalty, love of country, humanity, benevolence, sobriety, industry, frugality, purity, temperance and all other virtues;

(d) **co-operation** — to assist in developing co-operation and co-ordination of effort among the members of the staff of the school;

(e) **discipline** — to maintain, under the direction of the principal, proper order and discipline in the teacher's classroom and while on duty in the school and on the school ground;

(f) **language of instruction** — in instruction and in all communications with the pupils in regard to discipline and the management of the school,

    (i) to use the English language, except where it is impractical to do so by reason of the pupil not understanding English, and except in respect of instruction in a language other than English when such other language is being taught as one of the subjects in the course of study, or

    (ii) to use the French language in schools or classes in

which French is the language of instruction except where it is impractical to do so by reason of the pupil not understanding French, and except in respect of instruction in a language other than French when such other language is being taught as one of the subjects in the course of study;

(g) **timetable** — to conduct the teacher's class in accordance with a timetable which shall be accessible to pupils and to the principal and supervisory officers;

(h) **professional activity days** — to participate in professional activity days as designated by the board under the regulations;

(i) **absence from school** — to notify such person as is designated by the board if the teacher is to be absent from school and the reason therefor;

(j) **school property** — to deliver the register, the school key and other school property in the teacher's possession to the board on demand, or when the teacher's agreement with the board has expired, or when for any reason the teacher's employment has ceased; and

(k) **textbooks** — to use and permit to be used as a textbook in a class that he or she teaches in an elementary or a secondary school,

(i) in a subject area for which textbooks are approved by the Minister, only textbooks that are approved by the Minister, and

(ii) in all subject areas, only textbooks that are approved by the board.

(l) **duties assigned** — to perform all duties assigned in accordance with this Act and the regulations.

Sign language

(1.1) Despite clause (1)(f), a teacher or temporary teacher may use American Sign Language or Quebec Sign Language in accordance with the regulations.

(1.2) [Repealed 2001, c. 14, Sched. A, s. 7.]

(1.3) [Repealed 2001, c. 14, Sched. A, s. 7.]

Refusal to give up school property

(2) A teacher who refuses, on demand or order of the board that operates the school concerned, to deliver to the board any school property in the teacher's possession forfeits any claim that the teacher may have against the board.

Teachers, conferences

(3) Teachers may organize themselves for the purpose of conducting professional development conferences and seminars.

1993, c. 11, s. 36; 2000, c. 11, s. 17; 2001, c. 14, Sched. A, s. 7; 2003, c. 2, s. 20(1)

Duties of principal

265. (1) It is the duty of a principal of a school, in addition to the principal's duties as a teacher,

- (a) **discipline** — to maintain proper order and discipline in the school;
- (b) **co-operation** — to develop co-operation and co-ordination of effort among the members of the staff of the school;
- (c) **register pupils and record attendance** — to register the pupils and to ensure that the attendance of pupils for every school day is recorded either in the register supplied by the Minister in accordance with the instructions contained therein or in such other manner as is approved by the Minister;
- (d) **pupil records** — in accordance with this Act, the regulations and the guidelines issued by the Minister, to collect information for inclusion in a record in respect of each pupil enrolled in the school and to establish, maintain, retain, transfer and dispose of the record;

(e) **timetable** — to prepare a timetable to conduct the school according to such timetable and the school year calendar or calendars applicable thereto, to make the calendar or calendars and the timetable accessible to the pupils, teachers and supervisory officers and to assign classes and subjects to the teachers;

(f) **examinations and reports** — to hold, subject to the approval of the appropriate supervisory officer, such examinations as the principal considers necessary for the promotion of pupils or for any other purpose and report as required by the board the progress of the pupil to his or her parent or guardian where the pupil is a minor and otherwise to the pupil;

(g) **promote pupils** — subject to revision by the appropriate supervisory officer, to promote such pupils as the principal considers proper and to issue to each such pupil a statement thereof;

(h) **textbooks** — to ensure that all textbooks used by pupils are those approved by the board and, in the case of subject areas for which the Minister approves textbooks, those approved by the Minister;

(i) **reports** — to furnish to the Ministry and to the appropriate supervisory officer any information that it may be in the principal's power to give respecting the condition of the school premises, the discipline of the school, the progress of the pupils and any other matter affecting the interests of the school, and to prepare such reports for the board as are required by the board;

(j) **care of pupils and property** — to give assiduous attention to the health and comfort of the pupils, to the cleanliness, temperature and ventilation of the school, to the care of all teaching materials and other school property, and to the condition and appearance of the school buildings and grounds;

(k) **report to M.O.H.** — to report promptly to the board and to the medical officer of health when the principal

has reason to suspect the existence of any communicable disease in the school, and of the unsanitary condition of any part of the school building or the school grounds;
(l) **persons with communicable diseases** — to refuse admission to the school of any person who the principal believes is infected with or exposed to communicable diseases requiring an order under section 22 of the *Health Protection and Promotion Act* until furnished with a certificate of a medical officer of health or of a legally qualified medical practitioner approved by the medical officer of health that all danger from exposure to contact with such person has passed;
(m) **access to school or class** — subject to an appeal to the board, to refuse to admit to the school or classroom a person whose presence in the school or classroom would in the principal's judgment be detrimental to the physical or mental well-being of the pupils; and
(n) **visitor's book** — to maintain a visitor's book in the school when so determined by the board.

Co-instructional activities

(2) In addition, it is the duty of a principal in accordance with the board plan to provide for co-instructional activities under subsection 170(1), to develop and implement a school plan providing for co-instructional activities.

School council

(3) The principal shall consult the school council at least once in each school year respecting the school plan providing for co-instructional activities.

(4) [Repealed 2001, c. 14, Sched. A, s. 8.]
1991, c. 10, s. 6; 2000, c. 11, s. 18; 2001, c. 14, Sched. A, s. 8

. . .

Part XIII
Behaviour, Discipline and Safety

Definition

300. (1) In this Part,

"school premises" means, with respect to a school, the school buildings and premises.

Interpretation

(2) In this Part, where reference is made to a regulation or to a matter prescribed by regulation, it means a regulation to be made by the Minister under this Part.

2000, c. 12, s. 3

Provincial code of conduct

301. (1) The Minister may establish a code of conduct governing the behaviour of all persons in schools.

Purposes

(2) The following are the purposes of the code of conduct:

1. To ensure that all members of the school community, especially people in positions of authority, are treated with respect and dignity.
2. To promote responsible citizenship by encouraging appropriate participation in the civic life of the school community.
3. To maintain an environment where conflict and difference can be addressed in a manner characterized by respect and civility.
4. To encourage the use of non-violent means to resolve conflict.
5. To promote the safety of people in the schools.
6. To discourage the use of alcohol and illegal drugs.

Notice

(3) Every board shall take such steps as the Minister directs to bring the code of conduct to the attention of pupils, parents and guardians of pupils and others who may be present in schools under the jurisdiction of the board.

Code is policy

(4) The code of conduct is a policy of the Minister.

Policies and guidelines governing conduct

(5) The Minister may establish additional policies and guidelines with respect to the conduct of persons in schools.

Same, governing discipline

(6) The Minister may establish policies and guidelines with respect to disciplining pupils, specifying, for example, the circumstances in which a pupil is subject to discipline and the forms and the extent of discipline that may be imposed in particular circumstances.

Same, promoting safety

(7) The Minister may establish policies and guidelines to promote the safety of pupils.

Different policies, etc.

(8) The Minister may establish different policies and guidelines under this section for different circumstances, for different locations and for different classes of persons.

Duty of boards

(9) The Minister may require boards to comply with policies and guidelines established under this section.

Not regulations

(10) Policies and guidelines established under this section are not regulations within the meaning of the *Regulations Act*.
2000, c. 12, s. 3

Boards' policies and guidelines governing conduct

302. (1) Every board shall establish policies and guidelines with respect to the conduct of persons in schools within the board's jurisdiction and the policies and guidelines must address such matters and include such requirements as the Minister may specify.

Same, governing discipline

(2) A board may establish policies and guidelines with respect to disciplining pupils, and the policies and guidelines must be consistent with this Part and with the policies and guidelines established by the Minister under section 301, and must address such matters and include such requirements as the Minister may specify.

Same, promoting safety

(3) If required to do so by the Minister, a board shall establish policies and guidelines to promote the safety of pupils, and the policies and guidelines must be consistent with those established by the Minister under section 301 and must address such matters and include such requirements as the Minister may specify.

Same, governing access to school premises

(4) A board may establish policies and guidelines governing access to school premises, and the policies and guidelines must be consistent with the regulations made under section 305 and must address such matters and include such requirements as the Minister may specify.

Same, governing appropriate dress

(5) If required to do so by the Minister, a board shall establish policies and guidelines respecting appropriate dress for pupils in schools within the board's jurisdiction, and the policies and guidelines must address such matters and include such requirements as the Minister may specify.

Same, procedural matters

(6) A board shall establish policies and guidelines governing a review or appeal of a decision to suspend a pupil and governing, with respect to expulsions, a prinicipal's inquiry, an expulsion hearing and an appeal of a decision to expel a pupil, and the policies and guidelines must address such matters and include such requirements as the Minister may specify.

Different policies, etc.

(7) A board may establish different policies and guidelines under this section for different circumstances, for different locations and for different classes of persons.

Role of school councils

(8) When establishing policies and guidelines under this section, a board shall consider the views of school councils with respect to the contents of the policies and guidelines.

Periodic review

(9) The board shall periodically review its policies and guidelines established under this section and shall solicit the views of pupils, teachers, staff, volunteers working in the schools, parents and guardians, school councils and the public.

Not regulations

(10) Policies and guidelines established under this section are not regulations within the meaning of the *Regulations Act*.

2000, c. 12, s. 3

Local codes of conduct

303. (1) A board may direct the principal of a school to establish a local code of conduct governing the behaviour of all persons in the school, and the local code must be consistent with the provincial code established under subsection 301(1) and must address such matters and include such requirements as the board may specify.

Same, mandatory

(2) A board shall direct a principal to establish a local code of conduct if the board is required to do so by the Minister, and the local code must address such matters and include such requirements as the Minister may specify.

Role of school council

(3) When establishing or reviewing a local code of conduct, the principal shall consider the views of the school council with respect to its contents.

Not regulation

(4) A local code of conduct is not a regulation within the meaning of the *Regulations Act*.

2000, c. 12, s. 3

Opening and closing exercises at schools

304. (1) Every board shall ensure that opening or closing exercises are held in each school under the board's jurisdiction, in accordance with the requirements set out in the regulations.

Same

(2) The opening or closing exercises must include the singing of *O Canada* and may include the recitation of a pledge of citizenship in the form set out in the regulations.

Exceptions

(3) A pupil is not required to participate in the opening or closing exercises in such circumstances as are prescribed by regulation.

2000, c. 12, s. 3

Access to school premises

305. (1) The Minister may make regulations governing access to school premises, specifying classes of persons who are permitted to be on school premises and specifying the days and times at which different classes of persons are prohibited from being on school premises.

Prohibition

(2) No person shall enter or remain on school premises unless he or she is authorized by regulation to be there on that day or at that time.

Same, board policy

(3) A person shall not enter or remain on school premises if he or she is prohibited under a board policy from being there on that day or at that time.

Direction to leave

(4) The principal of a school may direct a person to leave the school premises if the principal believes that the person is prohibited by regulation or under a board policy from being there.

Offence

(5) Every person who contravenes subsection (2) is guilty of an offence.

2000, c. 12, s. 3

Mandatory suspension of a pupil

306. (1) It is mandatory that a pupil be suspended from his or her school and from engaging in all school-related activities if the pupil commits any of the following infractions while he or she is at school or is engaged in a school-related activity:

1. Uttering a threat to inflict serious bodily harm on another person.
2. Possessing alcohol or illegal drugs.
3. Being under the influence of alcohol.
4. Swearing at a teacher or at another person in a position of authority.
5. Committing an act of vandalism that causes extensive damage to school property at the pupil's school or to property located on the premises of the pupil's school.
6. Engaging in another activity that, under a policy of the board, is one for which a suspension is mandatory.

Duration of mandatory suspension

(2) The minimum duration of a mandatory suspension is one school day and the maximum duration is 20 school days. The minimum and maximum duration may be varied by regulation, and different standards may be established for different circumstances or different classes of persons.

Duties of teachers

(3) If a teacher observes a pupil committing an infraction that requires a mandatory suspension, the teacher shall suspend the pupil or refer the matter to the prinicpal.

Duty to suspend, principal

(4) The principal has a duty to suspend a pupil who commits an infraction requiring a mandatory suspension, unless a teacher has already suspended the pupil for the infraction.

Mitigating factors

(5) Despite subsection (1), suspension of a pupil is not mandatory in such circumstances as may be prescribed by regulation.

Restriction on suspension by teacher

(6) A teacher cannot suspend a pupil under this section for a period longer than the minimum duration required by subsection (2).

Referral to principal

(7) If a teacher who suspends a pupil under this section is of the opinion that a longer suspension of the pupil is warranted, the teacher shall recommend to the principal that the suspension be extended.

Extension by principal

(8) Upon receiving a recommendation from a teacher to extend the suspension imposed on a pupil by the teacher, the principal may extend the suspension up to the maximum duration permitted by subsection (2).

Factors affecting duration of suspension

(9) In order to determine the duration of a mandatory suspension, the principal shall consider the pupil's history and such other factors as may be prescribed by regulation and the principal may consider such other matters as he or she considers appropriate.

Notice

(10) The teacher or principal who suspends a pupil under this section shall ensure that written notice of the mandatory suspension is given promptly to the pupil and, if the pupil is a minor, to the pupil's parent or guardian.

Policies and guidelines

(11) The Minister may issue policies and guidelines to boards to assist principals and teachers in interpreting and administering this section.

School-related activities

(12) A pupil who is suspended is not considered to be engaged in school-related activities by virtue of using services, taking a course or participating in a program to assist such pupils.

Definition

(13) In this section,

"mandatory suspension" means a suspension required by subsection (1).

Commencement

(14) This section comes into force on a day to be named by proclamation of the Lieutenant Governor.

2000, c. 12, s. 3

Discretionary suspension of a pupil

307. (1) A pupil may be suspended if he or she engages in an activity that, under a policy of the board, is an activity for which suspension is discretionary.

Same

(2) A pupil may be suspended,

(a) from his or her school and from engaging in all school-related activities; or
(b) from one or more classes or one or more school-related activities or both.

Duration of discretionary suspension

(3) The minimum duration of a discretionary suspension is as specified by the board policy that authorizes the suspension and the maximum duration is 20 school days. The maximum duration may be varied by regulation, and different standards may be established for different circumstances or different classes of persons.

Authority to suspend, principal

(4) The principal may suspend a pupil who engages in an activity for which suspension is discretionary.

Authority of teachers

(5) If a teacher observes a pupil engaging in an activity for which suspension is discretionary, the teacher may suspend the pupil or refer the matter to the principal.

Restriction on suspension by teacher

(6) A teacher cannot suspend a pupil under this section for a period longer than the minimum duration described in subsection (3).

Other matters

(7) Subsections 306(7) to (10) and 306(12) apply, with necessary modifications, with respect to a discretionary suspension under this section.

Definition

(8) In this section,

"**discretionary suspension**" means a suspension authorized by subsection (1).

Commencement

(9) This section comes into force on a day to be named by proclamation of the Lieutenant Governor.

2000, c. 12, s. 3

Review of suspension

308. (1) The following persons may request a review of a decision to suspend a pupil, other than a decision to suspend a pupil for one day or less:

1. If the pupil is a minor, his or her parent or guardian.
2. If the pupil is not a minor, the pupil.
3. Such other persons as may be specified in a policy of the board.

The review process

(2) The review shall be conducted in accordance with the requirements established by board policy.

Same

(3) The review shall be conducted by the person specified in the board policy and, for the purposes of the review, the person has the powers and duties set out in the policy.

Appeal of suspension

(4) Following a review, the following persons may appeal a decision to suspend a pupil, other than a decision to suspend a pupil for one day or less:

1. If the pupil is a minor, his or her parent or guardian.
2. If the pupil is not a minor, the pupil.
3. Such other persons as may be specified by board policy.

The appeal process

(5) An appeal under this section must be conducted in accordance with the requirements established by board policy.

Same

(6) The board shall hear and determine an appeal and, for that purpose, the board has the powers and duties set out in its policy. The decisions of the board are final.

Delegation by board

(7) The board may delegate its powers and duties under subsection (6) to a committee of the board, and may impose conditions and restrictions on the committee.

Commencement

(8) This section comes into force on a day to be named by proclamation of the Lieutenant Governor.

2000, c. 12, s. 3

Mandatory expulsion of a student

309. (1) It is mandatory that a pupil be expelled if the pupil commits any of the following infractions while he or she is at school or is engaged in a school-related activity:
 1. Possessing a weapon, including possessing a firearm.
 2. Using a weapon to cause or to threaten bodily harm to another person.
 3. Committing physical assault on another person that causes bodily harm requiring treatment by a medical practitioner.
 4. Committing sexual assault.
 5. Trafficking in weapons or in illegal drugs.
 6. Committing robbery.
 7. Giving alcohol to a minor.
 8. Engaging in another activity that, under a policy of the board, is one for which expulsion is mandatory.

Duty to suspend pending expulsion, principal

(2) The principal shall suspend a pupil who the principal believes may have committed an infraction for which expulsion is mandatory.

Mitigating factors

(3) Despite subsection (1), expulsion of a pupil is not mandatory in such circumstances as may be prescribed by regulation.

Action following suspension

(4) If the principal suspends a pupil under subsection (2), the principal shall promptly refer the matter to the board or conduct an inquiry to determine whether the pupil has committed an infraction for which expulsion is mandatory.

Notice of suspension

(5) The principal shall ensure that written notice of the suspension under subsection (2) is given promptly to the pupil and, if the pupil is a minor, to the pupil's parent or guardian.

Conduct of inquiry

(6) The principal's inquiry shall be conducted in accordance with the requirements established by a policy of the board and the powers and duties of the principal are as specified by board policy.

Action following inquiry

(7) If, after the inquiry, the principal is satisfied that the pupil committed an infraction for which expulsion is mandatory, the principal shall,

  (a) impose a limited expulsion as described in subsection (14) on the pupil; or
  (b) refer the matter to the board for its determination.

Restriction on expulsion by principal

(8) The principal cannot expel a pupil if more than 20 school days have expired since the principal suspended the student under subsection (2), unless the parties to the inquiry agree upon a later deadline.

Hearing by board

(9) When a matter is referred to the board under subsection (4) or clause (7)(b), the board shall hold an expulsion hearing and, for that purpose, the board has the powers and duties specified by board policy.

Conduct of hearing

(10) The expulsion hearing shall be conducted in accordance with the requirements established by board policy.

Duty to expel, board

(11) If, after the expulsion hearing, the board is satisfied that the pupil committed an infraction for which expulsion is mandatory, the board shall impose a limited expulsion as described in subsection (14) or a full expulsion as described in subsection (16) on the pupil.

Restriction on expulsion by board

(12) The board cannot expel a pupil if more than 20 school days have expired since the principal suspended the pupil under subsection (2), unless the parties to the expulsion hearing agree upon a later deadline.

Delegation

(13) The board may delegate its duty to hold an expulsion hearing and its powers and duties under subsection (11) to a committee of the board, and may impose conditions and restrictions on the committee.

Limited expulsion

(14) A pupil who is subject to a limited expulsion is not entitled to attend the school the pupil was attending when he or she committed the infraction and is not entitled to engage in school-related activities of that school until the later of,

> (a) the date specified by the principal or the board when expelling the pupil, which date cannot be more than one year after the date on which the principal suspended the pupil under subsection (2); and
> (b) the date on which the pupil meets such requirements as may be established by the board for returning to school after being expelled.

Same

(15) A regulation may vary the limit described in clause (14)(a) and may specify a different limit for different circumstances or different classes of persons.

Full expulsion

(16) A pupil who is subject to a full expulsion is not entitled to attend any school in the province or to engage in school-related activities of any school in the province until he or she meets such requirements as may be established by regulation for returning to school after being expelled.

Effect on other rights

(17) A pupil's rights under sections 33, 36, 42 and 43 are inoperative during a full expulsion.

Minimum duration of mandatory expulsion

(18) The minimum duration of a mandatory expulsion is 21 school days and, for the purposes of this subsection, the period of a pupil's suspension under subsection (2) shall be deemed to be a period of expulsion. The minimum duration

may be varied by regulation, and a different standard may be established for different circumstances or different classes of persons.

Factors affecting type and duration of expulsion

(19) When considering the type and duration of expulsion that may be appropriate in particular circumstances, the principal or board shall consider the pupil's history and such other factors as may be prescribed by regulation and may consider such other matters as he, she or it considers appropriate.

Notice

(20) The prinicipal or board that expels a pupil under this section shall ensure that written notice of the mandatory expulsion is given promptly to the pupil and, if the pupil is a minor, to the pupil's parent or guardian.

Policies and guidelines

(21) The Minister may issue policies and guidelines to boards to assist boards and principals in interpreting and administering this section.

School-related activities

(22) A pupil who is expelled is not considered to be engaged in school-related activities by virtue of using services to assist such pupils or taking a course or participating in a program that prepares the pupil to return to school.

Commencement

(23) This section comes into force on a day to be named by proclamation of the Lieutenant Governor.

2000, c. 12, s. 3

Discretionary expulsion of a pupil

310. (1) A pupil may be expelled if the pupil engages in an activity that, under a policy of the board, is one for which expulsion is discretionary.

Suspension pending expulsion, principal

(2) If the principal believes a pupil may have engaged in an activity for which expulsion is discretionary, the principal may suspend the pupil.

Other matters

(3) If the principal suspends a pupil under subsection (2), subsections 309(4) to (20) and 309(22) apply, with necessary modifications, with respect to an expulsion authorized by this section.

Commencement

(4) This section comes into force on a day to be named by proclamation of the Lieutenant Governor.

2000, c. 12, s. 3

Appeal of expulsion

311. (1) The following persons may appeal a decision to expel a pupil, including a decision under section 310 respecting the type and duration of the expulsion:

1. If the pupil is a minor, his or her parent or guardian.
2. If the pupil is not a minor, the pupil.
3. Such other persons as may be specified by a policy of the board.

The appeal process

(2) An appeal under this section must be conducted in accordance with the requirements established by board policy.

Same, expulsion by principal

(3) The board shall hear and determine an appeal from a decision of a principal to expel a pupil and, for that purpose, the board has the powers and duties set out in its policy. The decisions of the board are final.

Delegation by board

(4) The board may delegate its powers and duties under subsection (3) to a committee of the board, and may impose conditions and restrictions on the committee.

The appeal process, expulsion by board

(5) A person or entity designated by regulation shall hear and determine an appeal from a decision of a board to expel a pupil, and, for that purpose, the person or entity has the powers and duties set out in the regulations. The decisions of the person or entity are final.

Same

(6) For the purposes of subsection (5), the Minister may by regulation establish an entity to exercise the powers and perform the duties referred to in that subsection, and the Minister may determine the composition and the other powers and duties of the entity.

Commencement

(7) This section comes into force on a day to be named by proclamation of the Lieutenant Governor and different subsections may be proclaimed into force as of different dates.

2000, c. 12, s. 3

Programs, etc., for suspended pupils

312. (1) The Minister may require boards to establish and maintain specified programs, courses and services for pupils who are suspended, and may impose different requirements

for different circumstances, different locations or different classes of pupils.

Same, expelled pupils

(2) The Minister may require boards to establish and maintain specified programs, courses and services for pupils who are expelled and may authorize boards,

(a) to enter into agreements with other boards for the provision of the programs, courses and services;
(b) to retain others to provide the programs, courses and services; or
(c) to establish one or more corporations to provide the programs, courses and services.

Authorization

(3) The Minister may impose conditions and restrictions when authorizing a board to engage in an activity described in subsection (2).

Programs for expelled pupils

(4) The Minister may establish one or more programs for expelled pupils to prepare the pupils to return to school and may require boards to give specified information about the programs to expelled pupils.

Same

(5) The Minister may establish policies and guidelines respecting pupils' eligibility to participate in a program established under subsection (2) or (4) and respecting the criteria to be met for successful completion of the program.

2000, c. 12, s. 3

Transition, suspension of a pupil

313. (1) This section applies with respect to a pupil who engages in an activity before section 306 comes into force that

may result in his or her suspension under section 23 as it reads on the day the pupil engages in the activity.

Same

(2) Section 23, as it reads on the day the pupil engages in the activity, continues to apply after section 306 comes into force for the purpose of determining whether, and for how long, the pupil is to be suspended and for the purpose of determining any appeal relating to the suspension of the pupil.

2000, c. 12, s. 3

Transition, expulsion of a pupil

314. (1) This section applies with respect to a pupil who engages in an activity before section 309 comes into force that may result in his or her expulsion under section 23 as it reads on the day the pupil engages in the activity.

Same

(2) Section 23, as it reads on the day the pupil engages in the activity, continues to apply after section 309 comes into force for the purpose of determining whether, from where and for how long the pupil is to be expelled and determining the criteria for the pupil's return to school.

2000, c. 12, s. 3

Collection of personal information

315. (1) The Minister may collect and may by regulation require boards to collect such personal information as is specified by regulation from, or about, the classes of persons specified by regulation for the following purposes, and the Minister may specify or restrict the manner in which the information is to be collected:

1. To ensure the safety of pupils.
2. To administer programs, courses and services to pupils who are suspended or expelled and to determine

whether an expelled pupil has successfully completed a program, course or service and as a result is eligible to return to school.

Disclosure

(2) A board or other person is authorized to disclose the personal information collected under subsection (1) to the Minister for the purposes described in that subsection, and the Minister may disclose it to such persons or entities as may be prescribed by regulation for those purposes.

Definition

(3) In this section,

"personal information" has the same meaning as in section 38 of the *Freedom of Information and Protection of Privacy Act* and section 28 of the *Municipal Freedom of Information and Protection of Privacy Act*.

2000, c. 12, s. 3

Regulations

316. (1) The Minister may make regulations,

(a) prescribing such matters as are required, or permitted, under this Part to be prescribed or to be done by regulation;

(b) specifying when, during a school day, a suspension of a pupil is permitted to begin and to end.

Classes

(2) A regulation under subsection (1) may impose different requirements on different classes of person, place or thing or in different circumstances.

Exceptions

(3) A regulation under subsection (1) may provide that one or more provisions of this Part or of the regulation does not apply to specified persons or in specified circumstances.

2000, c. 12, s. 3

. . .

Ontario Regulation 298 — Operation of Schools — General
made under the *Education Act*

R.R.O. 1990, Reg. 298 as am. O. Reg. 339/91 (Fr.); 242/92; 95/96; 425/98; 436/00; 613/00; 492/01; 209/03; 191/04; 132/05

1. In this Regulation,

"business studies" means the courses prescribed or developed under subsection 8(1) of the Act and described in,

(a) the document entitled "Business Studies—The Ontario Curriculum, Grades 9 and 10—1999", available on the Ministry of Education web site at *www.edu.gov.on.ca*, and

(b) the document entitled "Business Studies—The Ontario Curriculum, Grades 11 and 12—2000", available on the Ministry of Education web site at *www.edu.gov.on.ca*; "enseignement commercial"

"certificate of qualification" means a certificate of qualification granted under Ontario Regulation 184/97 made under the *Ontario College of Teachers Act, 1996*; "certificat de compétence"

"division" means the primary division, the junior division, the intermediate division or the senior division; "cycle"

"French as a second language" includes programs for English speaking pupils in which French is the language of instruction; "français langue seconde"

"general studies" means the courses prescribed or developed for the intermediate and senior divisions under subsection 8(1) of the Act and described in the secondary curriculum documents available on the Ministry of Education web site at *www.edu.gov.on.ca*, excluding the courses described in,

(a) the document entitled "Technological Education—The Ontario Curriculum, Grades 9 and 10—1999", other than the sections relating to Computer and Information Science, Grade 10, Open and Computer Engineering Technology, Grade 10, Open, and

(b) the document entitled "Technological Education—The Ontario Curriculum, Grades 11 and 12—2000", other than Part B: Computer Studies; "enseignement général"

"OSIS" [Revoked O. Reg. 191/04, s. 1(4).]

"parent" includes guardian; "père ou mère"

"technological studies" means the courses prescribed or developed under subsection 8(1) of the Act and described in,

(a) the document entitled "Technological Education—The Ontario Curriculum, Grades 9 and 10—1999", other than the sections relating to Computer and Information Science, Grade 10, Open and Computer Engineering Technology, Grade 10, Open, available on the Ministry of Education web site at *www.edu.gov.on.ca*, and

(b) the document entitled "Technological Education—The Ontario Curriculum, Grades 11 and 12—2000", other than Part B: Computer Studies, available on the Ministry of Education web site at *www.edu.gov.on.ca*. "études technologiques"

O. Reg. 191/04, s. 1

Accommodation

2. (1) A board shall file with the Ministry plans for the erection of, addition to, or alteration of a school building together with details of the site thereof.

(2) It is a condition of the payment of a legislative grant in respect of capital cost that the plans and details referred to in subsection (1) be approved by the Minister.

Daily Sessions

3. (1) The length of the instructional program of each school day for pupils of compulsory school age shall be not less than five hours a day excluding recesses or scheduled intervals between classes.

(2) The instructional program on a school day shall begin not earlier than 8 a.m. and end not later than 5 p.m. except with the approval of the Minister.

(3) Despite subsection (1), a board may reduce the length of the instructional program on each school day to less than five hours a day for an exceptional pupil in a special education program.

(4) Every board may establish the length of the instructional program on each school day for pupils in junior kindergarten and kindergarten.

(5) Each pupil and each teacher shall have a scheduled interval for a lunch break.

(5.1) A pupil's interval for a lunch break shall be not less than forty consecutive minutes and need not coincide with the scheduled interval for the lunch break of any other pupil or any teacher.

(5.2) A teacher's interval for a lunch break shall be not less than forty consecutive minutes and need not coincide with the scheduled interval for the lunch break of any other teacher or any pupil.

(6) In the intermediate division and the senior division, a principal may, subject to the approval of the board, provide for recesses or intervals for pupils between periods.

(7) Every board shall determine the period of time during each school day when its school buildings and playgrounds shall be open to its pupils, but in every case the buildings and the playgrounds shall be open to pupils during the period

beginning fifteen minutes before classes begin for the day and ending fifteen minutes after classes end for the day.

(8) There shall be a morning recess and an afternoon recess, each of which shall be not less than ten minutes and not more than fifteen minutes in length, for pupils in the primary and junior divisions.

O. Reg. 492/01, s. 1

Opening or Closing Exercises

4. (1) This section applies with respect to opening and closing exercises in public elementary schools and in public secondary schools.

(2) The opening or closing exercises may include the singing of *God Save the Queen* and may also include the following types of readings that impart social, moral or spiritual values and that are representative of Ontario's multicultural society:

1. Scriptural writings including prayers.
2. Secular writings.

(3) The opening or closing exercises may include a period of silence.

(4) In the following circumstances, a pupil is not required to participate in the opening or closing exercises described in this section:

1. In the case of a pupil who is less than 18 years old, if the pupil's parent or guardian applies to the principal of the school for an exemption from the exercises.
2. In the case of a pupil who is at least 18 years old, if the pupil applies to the principal for an exemption from the exercises.

O. Reg. 436/00, s. 1

Flag

5. (1) Every school shall fly both the National Flag of Canada and the Provincial Flag of Ontario on such occasions as the board directs.

(2) Every school shall display in the school the National Flag of Canada and the Provincial Flag of Ontario.

Emergency Procedures

6. (1) In addition to the drills established under the fire safety plan required under *Regulation 454* of the *Revised Regulations of Ontario, 1990* (*Fire Code*), every board may provide for the holding of drills in respect of emergencies other than those occasioned by fire.

(2) Every principal, including the principal of an evening class or classes or of a class or classes conducted outside the school year, shall hold at least one emergency drill in the period during which the instruction is given.

(3) When a fire or emergency drill is held in a school building, every person in the building shall take part in the fire or emergency drill.

Textbooks

7. (1) The principal of a school, in consultation with the teachers concerned, shall select from the list of the textbooks approved by the Minister the textbooks for the use of pupils of the school, and the selection shall be subject to the approval of the board.

(2) Where no textbook for a course of study is included in the list of the textbooks approved by the Minister the principal of a school, in consultation with the teachers concerned, shall, where they consider a textbook to be required, select a suitable textbook and, subject to the approval of the board, such textbook may be introduced for use in the school.

(3) In the selection of textbooks under subsection (2), preference shall be given to books that have been written by Canadian authors and edited, printed and bound in Canada.

(4) Every board shall provide without charge for the use of each pupil enrolled in a day school operated by the board such textbooks selected under subsections (1) and (2) as relate to the courses in which the pupil is enrolled.

Elementary School Boards

8. (1) Where the area of jurisdiction of a district school area board, a Roman Catholic school authority, or a Protestant separate school board is not within a secondary school district, the board shall provide instruction that would enable its resident pupils to obtain sixteen credits towards a secondary school graduation diploma or an Ontario secondary school diploma.

(2) A board referred to in subsection (1) that offers courses of instruction during July or August or both in any year may provide instruction that would enable its resident pupils to obtain two credits in addition to the sixteen credits referred to in subsection (1).

(3) Where a board referred to in subsection (1) provides,

(a) daily transportation for its resident pupils; or
(b) reimbursement for board and lodging and for transportation once a week to and from the places of residence of its resident pupils,

that it considers necessary to enable its resident pupils to attend a school operated by another board, the other board may provide such instruction as would enable such resident pupils to obtain the number of credits referred to in subsections (1) and (2).

(4) A Roman Catholic school authority, or a Protestant separate school board that has jurisdiction in a secondary school district may provide instruction for its resident pupils

that would enable the pupils to obtain up to eighteen credits towards a secondary school graduation diploma or an Ontario secondary school diploma.

O. Reg. 191/04, s. 2

Qualifications for Principals and Vice-Principals

9. (1) The principal and vice-principal of a school having an enrolment greater than 125 shall each be a teacher who,

(a) holds or is deemed to hold, under Ontario Regulation 184/97, made under the *Ontario College of Teachers Act, 1996*, principal's qualifications; or

(b) holds a principal's certificate that is a qualification to be principal or vice-principal, as the case may be, in the type of school identified on the certificate, or is deemed under section 50 of Ontario Regulation 184/97, made under the *Ontario College of Teachers Act, 1996* to hold such a certificate,

and, in the case of a school,

(c) in which English is the language of instruction; or

(d) that is established under Part XII of the Act and in which French is the language of instruction,

shall each be a person who is eligible to teach in such school under subsection 19(11), (12) or (13), as the case may be.

(2) Despite subsection (1), where a teacher who does not hold the degree of Bachelor of Arts or Bachelor of Science from an Ontario university or a degree that the Minister considers equivalent thereto was, prior to the 1st day of September, 1961, employed by a board as principal or vice-principal of an elementary school that had an enrolment of 300 or more pupils, the teacher shall be deemed to be qualified as principal or vice-principal, as the case may be, of any elementary school operated by that board or its successor board.

(3) Despite subsection (1), where a teacher who does not hold the qualifications referred to in subsection (1),

(a) was employed by a board prior to the 1st day of September, 1972 as principal of an elementary school that had an enrolment of 300 or more pupils and is employed by such board as principal of an elementary school on the 8th day of September, 1978;
(b) was employed by a board on the 1st day of September, 1978 as vice-principal of an elementary school that had an enrolment on the last school day in April, 1978 of 300 or more pupils; or
(c) was employed by a board on the 1st day of September, 1978 as principal or vice-principal of an elementary school that had an enrolment on the last school day in April, 1978 that was greater than 125 and less than 300,

such teacher shall be deemed to be qualified as principal or vice-principal, as the case may be, of any elementary school operated by that board or its successor board.

(4) A board may appoint a person who holds the qualifications required by subsection (1) as a supervising principal to supervise the administration of two or more elementary schools operated by the board and such person shall be subject to the authority of the appropriate supervisory officer.

(5) A supervising principal may be principal of only one school.

(6) Despite subsection (1), a teacher who, before the 1st day of September, 1970, held the necessary qualifications as principal of a secondary school continues to be qualified as principal or vice-principal of a secondary school.

O. Reg. 191/04, s. 3

10. [Revoked O. Reg. 191/04, s. 4.]

Duties of Principals

11. (1) The principal of a school, subject to the authority of the appropriate supervisory officer, is in charge of,

(a) the instruction and the discipline of pupils in the school; and
(b) the organization and management of the school.

(2) Where two or more schools operated by a board jointly occupy or use in common a school building or school grounds, the board shall designate which principal has authority over those parts of the building or grounds that the schools occupy or use in common.

(3) In addition to the duties under the Act and those assigned by the board, the principal of a school shall, except where the principal has arranged otherwise under subsection 26(3),

(a) supervise the instruction in the school and advise and assist any teacher in co-operation with the teacher in charge of an organizational unit or program;
(b) assign duties to vice-principals and to teachers in charge of organizational units or programs;
(c) retain on file up-to-date copies of outlines of all courses of study that are taught in the school;
(d) upon request, make outlines of courses of study available for examination to a resident pupil of the board and to the parent of the pupil, where the pupil is a minor;
(e) provide for the supervision of pupils during the period of time during each school day when the school buildings and playgrounds are open to pupils;
(f) provide for the supervision of and the conducting of any school activity authorized by the board;
(g) where performance appraisals of members of the teaching staff are required under a collective agreement or a policy of the board, despite anything to the contrary in such collective agreement or board policy, conduct performance appraisals of members of the teaching staff;
(h) subject to the provisions of the policy of the board or the provisions of a collective agreement, as the case may

be, in respect of reporting requirements for performance appraisals, report thereon in writing to the board or to the supervisory officer on request and give to each teacher so appraised a copy of the performance appraisal of the teacher;
(i) where the performance appraisals of members of the teaching staff are not required by board policy or under a collective agreement, report to the board or to the supervisory officer in writing on request on the effectiveness of members of the teaching staff and give to a teacher referred to in any such report a copy of the portion of the report that refers to the teacher;
(j) make recommendations to the board with respect to,

(i) the appointment and promotion of teachers, and
(ii) the demotion or dismissal of teachers whose work or attitude is unsatisfactory;

(k) provide for instruction of pupils in the care of the school premises;
(l) inspect the school premises at least weekly and report forthwith to the board,

(i) any repairs to the school that are required, in the opinion of the principal,
(ii) any lack of attention on the part of the building maintenance staff of the school, and
(iii) where a parent of a pupil has been requested to compensate the board for damage to or destruction, loss or misappropriation of school property by the pupil and the parent has not done so, that the parent of the pupil has not compensated the board;

(m) where it is proposed to administer a test of intelligence or personality to a pupil, inform the pupil and the parent of the pupil of the test and obtain the prior written permission for the test from the pupil or from the parent of the pupil, where the pupil is a minor;

(n) report promptly any neglect of duty or infraction of the school rules by a pupil to the parent or guardian of the pupil;

(o) promote and maintain close co-operation with residents, industry, business and other groups and agencies of the community;

(p) provide to the Minister or to a person designated by the Minister any information that may be required concerning the instructional program, operation or administration of the school and inform the appropriate supervisory officer of the request;

(q) assign suitable quarters for pupils to eat lunch.

(4) A principal shall only make a recommendation to the board under subclause (3)(j)(ii) after warning the teacher in writing, giving the teacher assistance and allowing the teacher a reasonable time to improve.

(5) A principal of a school,

(a) in which there is a French-language instructional unit as defined in subsection 1(1) of the Act, who does not hold qualifications to teach in the French language as required by subsection 19(12) or is qualified to teach in such unit only under subsection 19(13); or

(b) in which pupils receive instruction in the English language under subsection 290(5) or 291(4) of the Act, who does not hold qualifications to teach in the English language as required by subsection 19(11) or is qualified to teach in each unit only under subsection 19(13),

shall notify the appropriate supervisory officer in writing of the impracticability of the duty placed on the principal, having regard to the qualifications of the principal, to supervise the instruction, to conduct performance appraisals and to assist and advise the teachers referred to in the notice.

(6) Where arrangements are made under subsection 26(3), the principal is relieved from compliance with clauses (3)(a),

(g), (h) and (i) to the extent that such duties are performed by another qualified person or persons.

(7) The other qualified person or persons who perform the duties shall be responsible to the board for the performance of such duties.

(8) The outlines of the courses of study mentioned in clause (3)(c) shall be written and provided,

> (a) in the French language in the case of courses of study provided in a French-language instructional unit operated under Part XII of the Act; and
> (b) in both the English and French languages in the case of a course of study in a program established in the school under paragraph 25 of subsection 8(1) of the Act.

(9) Where, after reasonable notice by the principal, a pupil who is an adult, or the parent of a pupil who is a minor, fails to provide the supplies required by the pupil for a course of study, the principal shall promptly notify the board.

(10) A principal shall transmit reports and recommendations to the board through the appropriate supervisory officer.

(11) A principal, subject to the approval of the appropriate supervisory officer, may arrange for home instruction to be provided for a pupil where,

> (a) medical evidence that the pupil cannot attend school is provided to the principal; and
> (b) the principal is satisfied that home instruction is required.

(12) The principal of a school shall provide for the prompt distribution to each member of the school council of any materials received by the principal from the Ministry that are identified by the Ministry as being for distribution to the members of school councils.

(12.1) The principal shall post any materials distributed to members of the school council under subsection (12) in the school in a location that is accessible to parents.

(13) In each school year, the principal of a school shall make the names of the members of the school council known to the parents of the pupils enrolled in the school, by publishing those names in a school newsletter or by such other means as is likely to bring the names to the attention of the parents.

(14) The principal shall meet the requirements of subsection (13) in each school year not later than 30 days following the election of parent members of the school council.

(15) The principal of a school shall promptly provide the names of the members of the school council to a supporter of the board that governs the school or to a parent of a pupil enrolled in the school, on the request of the supporter or the parent.

(16) The principal of a school shall attend every meeting of the school council, unless he or she is unable to do so by reason of illness or other cause beyond his or her control.

(17) The principal of a school shall act as a resource person to the school council and shall assist the council in obtaining information relevant to the functions of the council, including information relating to relevant legislation, regulations and policies.

(18) The principal of a school shall consider each recommendation made to the principal by the school council and shall advise the council of the action taken in response to the recommendation.

(19) In addition to his or her other obligations to solicit the views of the school council under the Act and the regulations, the principal of a school shall solicit the views of the school council with respect to the following matters:

1. The establishment or amendment of school policies and

guidelines that relate to pupil achievement or to the accountability of the education system to parents, including,

   i. a local code of conduct established under subsection 303(1) or (2) of the Act governing the behaviour of all persons in the school, and
   ii. school policies or guidelines related to policies and guidelines established by the board under subsection 302(5) of the Act respecting appropriate dress for pupils in schools within the board's jurisdiction.

2. The development of implementation plans for new education initiatives that relate to pupil achievement or to the accountability of the education system to parents, including,

   i. implementation plans for a local code of conduct established under subsection 303(1) or (2) of the Act governing the behaviour of all persons in the school, and
   ii. implementation plans for school policies or guidelines related to policies and guidelines established by the board under subsection 302(5) of the Act respecting appropriate dress for pupils in schools within the board's jurisdiction.

3. School action plans for improvement, based on the Education Quality and Accountability Office's reports on the results of tests of pupils, and the communication of those plans to the public.

(20) Subsection (19) does not limit the matters on which the principal of a school may solicit the views of the school council.

O. Reg. 425/98, s. 1; 613/00, s. 1; 191/04, s. 5

Vice-Principals

12. (1) A board may appoint one or more vice-principals for a school.

(2) A vice-principal shall perform such duties as are assigned to the vice-principal by the principal.

(3) In the absence of the principal of a school, a vice-principal, where a vice-principal has been appointed for the school, shall be in charge of the school and shall perform the duties of the principal.

Principals, Vice-Principals and Teachers in Charge of Schools and Classes Established Under Part XII of the Act

13. (1) Where, under section 290 of the Act, more than two classes where French is the language of instruction are established in an elementary school that is not a French-language elementary school, the board that operates the school shall appoint one of the teachers of such classes or a teacher who holds the qualifications required to teach such classes to be responsible to the principal for the program of education in such classes.

(2) Where the enrolment in classes established under section 291 of the Act in a secondary school that is not a French-language secondary school is more than seventy-five but not more than 200 pupils, the board that operates the school shall appoint one of the teachers of such classes or a teacher who holds the qualifications required to teach such classes to be responsible to the principal for the program of education in such classes.

(3) Where, in a secondary school, the enrolment in the classes referred to in subsection (2) is more than 200 pupils, the board shall appoint for such school a vice-principal who is qualified to teach in such classes and who shall be responsible to the principal for the program of education in such classes.

(4) Despite subsections (1), (2) and (3), where a teacher who does not hold the qualifications referred to in such subsections was, on the 8th day of September, 1978, employed by the board as a teacher or vice-principal, as the case may be, to carry out the responsibility referred to in such subsections, the teacher shall be deemed to be qualified for such position in any elementary or secondary school, as the case may be, operated by that board or its successor board.

(5) Subsections (1) to (4) apply with necessary modifications to schools or classes for English-speaking pupils established under sections 290 and 291 of the Act.

O. Reg. 191/04, s. 6

Teachers in Charge of Organizational Units

14. (1) The organization of a secondary school may be by departments or other organizational units.

(2) The organization of an elementary school may be by divisions or other organizational units.

(3) A board may appoint for each organizational unit of an elementary or secondary school a teacher to direct and supervise, subject to the authority of the principal of the school, such organizational unit.

(4) A teacher appointed under subsection (3) may be appointed to direct and supervise more than one organizational unit.

O. Reg. 95/96, s. 1

15. [Revoked O. Reg. 95/96, s. 1.]

16. [Revoked O. Reg. 95/96, s. 1.]

Subject and Program Supervision and Co-Ordination

17. (1) A board may, in respect of one or more subjects or programs in the schools under its jurisdiction, appoint a teacher to supervise or co-ordinate the subjects or programs

or to act as a consultant for the teachers of the subjects or programs.

(2) A teacher appointed under subsection (1) shall hold specialist or honour specialist qualifications, if such are available, in one or more of the subjects or programs in respect of which the teacher is appointed.

(3) Despite subsection (1), a teacher who, on the 8th day of September, 1978, was employed by a board to supervise or co-ordinate a subject or program in its schools or to act as a consultant shall be deemed to be qualified for such position in the schools operated by that board or its successor board.

18. (1) Subject to the authority of the appropriate supervisory officer, a teacher appointed in a subject or program under section 17 shall assist teachers in that subject or program in maintaining proper standards and improving methods of instruction.

(2) A teacher appointed under section 17 in performing duties in a school is subject to the authority of the principal of that school.

Qualifications of Teachers

19. (1) Subject to subsection (3), no person shall be a teacher in a school unless he or she,

(a) holds or is deemed to hold a certificate of qualification of any kind or class provided for in Ontario Regulation 184/97 made under the *Ontario College of Teachers Act, 1996*; and

(b) subject to subsections (4), (5), (11) and (12), is assigned or appointed to teach according to a qualification recorded on the certificate of qualification.

(2) [Revoked O. Reg. 132/05, s. 1.]

(3) A person who does not have any of the qualifications referred to in subsection (2) but who holds a letter of eligibility

referred to in section 14 of Ontario Regulation 184/97 made under the *Ontario College of Teachers Act, 1996* may be employed by a board as an occasional teacher,

    (a) in classes where English is the language of instruction if the letter of eligibility is in Form 5 of Regulation 297 of the Revised Regulations of Ontario, 1990 as that regulation read immediately before it was revoked; or

    (b) in classes where French is the language of instruction if the letter of eligibility is in Form 5a of Regulation 297 of the Revised Regulations of Ontario, 1990 as that regulation read immediately before it was revoked.

(4) Subject to subsections (6), (11), (12), (14) and (15), and with due regard for the safety and welfare of the pupils and the provision of the best possible program, a teacher whose certificate of qualification, indicates qualification in the primary division, the junior division, the intermediate division in general studies or the senior division in general studies may, by mutual agreement of the teacher and the principal of a school and with the approval of the appropriate supervisory officer, be assigned or appointed to teach in a division or a subject in general studies for which no qualification is recorded on the teacher's certificate of qualification.

(5) Subject to subsections (11), (12) and (15), and with due regard for the safety and welfare of the pupils and the provision of the best possible program, a teacher whose certificate of qualification, has entries indicating qualifications in technological studies may by mutual agreement of the teacher and the principal of a school, with the approval of the appropriate supervisory officer, be assigned or appointed to teach a subject in technological studies for which no qualification is recorded on the certificate of qualification.

(6) Subject to subsections (7), (8), (9) and (10), a teacher who does not hold an acceptable post-secondary degree as defined in subsection 1(1) of Ontario Regulation 184/97 made under the *Ontario College of Teachers Act, 1996* shall not be

assigned or appointed to teach general studies in a secondary school, except that where the teacher is qualified to teach in the primary division, the junior division and the intermediate division of an elementary school and,

- (a) on the 30th day of June, 1981 was teaching in a secondary school; or
- (b) on or before the 2nd day of October, 1981 was assigned or appointed to teach general studies in a secondary school, and on the 30th day of June, 1982 was teaching in a secondary school,

the teacher may be assigned or appointed to teach general studies to pupils enrolled in a modified or basic level course by that board or its successor board.

(7) Despite subsection (1), a teacher who holds,

- (a) a commercial-vocational qualification; or
- (b) technological studies qualifications in any one or more of clerical practice, merchandising or warehousing,

may be assigned or appointed to teach the courses in business studies equivalent to the courses in business studies shown on the teacher's certificate of qualification.

(8) A teacher who holds qualifications in technological studies in sewing and dressmaking, or textiles and clothing, or home economics may be assigned or appointed to teach in a secondary school the clothing portion of the family studies course.

(9) A teacher who holds qualifications in technological studies in food and nutrition or home economics may be assigned or appointed to teach in a secondary school the food and nutrition portion of the family studies course.

(10) A teacher who holds qualifications in technological studies in vocational art, instrumental music or vocal music may be assigned or appointed to teach art, instrumental music

or vocal music, as the case may be, in general studies in a secondary school.

(11) A teacher who has not received basic teacher education in the English language or who is not otherwise qualified under the regulations for such assignment or appointment shall not be assigned or appointed to teach in classes where English is the language of instruction.

(12) A teacher who has not received basic teacher education in the French language or who is not otherwise qualified under the regulations for such assignment or appointment shall not be assigned or appointed to teach in schools or classes established under Part XII of the Act where French is the language of instruction.

(13) Despite subsections (11) and (12), a teacher who holds qualifications to teach in the intermediate division and the senior division may be assigned or appointed to teach in either or both of such divisions in classes where English or French is the language of instruction.

(14) No teacher shall,

(a) be assigned, or appointed to teach, in any of grades 9, 10, 11 and 12 in any one school year for more than the time required for two courses that are recognized for credit in art, business studies, guidance including counselling, family studies, instrumental music, vocal music or physical education; or

(b) be placed in charge of,

    (i) a school library program,
    (ii) a guidance program, or
    (iii) special education; or

(c) be assigned or appointed to teach,

    (i) French as a second language,
    (ii) English as a second language,
    (iii) design and technology,

(iv) subject to subsections (5) and (15), technological studies,
(v) in a special education class,
(vi) in a class for deaf, hard of hearing, blind or limited vision pupils, or
(vii) as a resource or withdrawal teacher in special education programs, unless,

(d) the teacher's certificate of qualification indicates qualifications in the subject or program to which the teacher is to be assigned or appointed or placed in charge; or
(e) the teacher is qualified for such assignment, appointment or placement under subsection (2) or (16) or deemed to be qualified therefor under subsection (17).

(15) On or after the 1st day of September, 1982, no teacher shall be assigned or appointed to teach courses in the senior division in technological studies at the General or Advanced levels unless the teacher's certificate of qualification indicates advanced level qualifications in the area of technological studies to which the teacher is to be assigned or appointed.

(16) [Revoked O. Reg. 191/04, s. 7(9).]

(17) A teacher who, on the 8th day of September, 1978, was employed by a board to teach,

(a) French as a second language or English as a second language in an elementary school or a secondary school; or
(b) industrial arts in an elementary school,

and is not qualified for such position under subsection (14), shall be deemed to be qualified for such position in the elementary schools or the secondary schools, as the case may be, that are operated by that board or its successor board.

(18) Where a teacher's certificate of qualification has entries indicating qualifications both in technological studies and in guidance, the teacher may be assigned or appointed to teach

guidance and counselling in general studies in a secondary school.

(19) The provision of subsection (14) that no teacher shall be assigned or appointed to teach in a special education class or program unless the teacher holds qualifications in special education does not apply to the teaching of classes in general studies or technological studies in what was formerly designated a special vocational or occupational program until the 1st day of September, 1985.

(20) A teacher may be assigned or appointed to teach those courses that are equivalent to those courses that appear on the teacher's certificate of qualification.
O. Reg. 242/92, s. 1; 191/04, s. 7; 132/05, s. 1

Duties of Teachers

20. In addition to the duties assigned to the teacher under the Act and by the board, a teacher shall,

(a) be responsible for effective instruction, training and evaluation of the progress of pupils in the subjects assigned to the teacher and for the management of the class or classes, and report to the principal on the progress of pupils on request;

(b) carry out the supervisory duties and instructional program assigned to the teacher by the principal and supply such information related thereto as the principal may require;

(c) where the board has appointed teachers under section 14 or 17, co-operate fully with such teachers and with the principal in all matters related to the instruction of pupils;

(d) unless otherwise assigned by the principal, be present in the classroom or teaching area and ensure that the classroom or teaching area is ready for the reception of pupils at least fifteen minutes before the commencement of classes in the school in the morning and, where applicable, five minutes before the commencement of classes in the school in the afternoon;

(e) assist the principal in maintaining close co-operation with the community;

(f) prepare for use in the teacher's class or classes such teaching plans and outlines as are required by the principal and the appropriate supervisory officer and submit the plans and outlines to the principal or the appropriate supervisory officer, as the case may be, on request;

(g) ensure that all reasonable safety procedures are carried out in courses and activities for which the teacher is responsible;

(h) co-operate with the principal and other teachers to establish and maintain consistent disciplinary practices in the school;

(i) ensure that report cards are fully and properly completed and processed in accordance with the guides known in English as Guide to the Provincial Report Card, Grades 1–8 and Guide to the Provincial Report Card, Grades 9–12, and in French as Guide d'utilisation du bulletin scolaire de l'Ontario de la 1ère à la 8e année and Guide du bulletin scolaire de l'Ontario de la 9e à la 12e année, as the case may be, both available electronically through a link in the document known in English as Ontario School Record (OSR) Guideline, 2000 and in French as Dossier scolaire de l'Ontario: Guide, 2000, online at *www.edu.gov.on.ca/eng/document/curricul/osr/osr.html* or *www.edu.gov.on.ca/fre/document/curricul/osr/osrf.html*;

(j) co-operate and assist in the administration of tests under the *Education Quality and Accountability Office Act, 1996*;

(k) participate in regular meetings with pupils' parents or guardians;

(l) perform duties as assigned by the principal in relation to co-operative placements of pupils; and
(m) perform duties normally associated with the graduation of pupils.

O. Reg. 209/03, s. 1

Appointment to Teach in the Case of an Emergency

21. (1) Where no teacher is available, a board may appoint, subject to section 22, a person who is not a teacher or a temporary teacher.

(2) A person appointed under subsection (1) shall be eighteen years of age or older and the holder of an Ontario secondary school diploma, a secondary school graduation diploma or a secondary school honour graduation diploma.

(3) An appointment under this section is valid for ten school days commencing with the day on which the person is appointed.

Cancelled and Suspended Certificates

22. (1) A board shall not appoint a person whose teaching certificate is cancelled or under suspension to teach under section 21 or in accordance with a Letter of Permission.

(2) A person whose teaching certificate is cancelled or under suspension ceases to hold teacher's qualifications during the period of cancellation or suspension and shall not be appointed as a teacher.

Requirements for Pupils

23. (1) A pupil shall,

(a) be diligent in attempting to master such studies as are part of the program in which the pupil is enrolled;
(b) exercise self-discipline;
(c) accept such discipline as would be exercised by a kind, firm and judicious parent;

(d) attend classes punctually and regularly;
(e) be courteous to fellow pupils and obedient and courteous to teachers;
(f) be clean in person and habits;
(g) take such tests and examinations as are required by or under the Act or as may be directed by the Minister; and
(h) show respect for school property.

(2) When a pupil returns to school after an absence, a parent of the pupil, or the pupil where the pupil is an adult, shall give the reason for the absence orally or in writing as the principal requires.

(3) A pupil may be excused by the principal from attendance at school temporarily at any time at the written request of a parent of the pupil or the pupil where the pupil is an adult.

(4) Every pupil is responsible for his or her conduct to the principal of the school that the pupil attends,

(a) on the school premises;
(b) on out-of-school activities that are part of the school program; and
(c) while travelling on a school bus that is owned by a board or on a bus or school bus that is under contract to a board.

Advertisements and Announcements

24. (1) No advertisement or announcement shall be placed in a school or on school property or distributed or announced to the pupils on school property without the consent of the board that operates the school except announcements of school activities.

(2) Subsection (1) does not apply to anything posted in the school in accordance with the regulations.

O. Reg. 613/00, s. 2

Canvassing and Fund-Raising

25. (1) It is the duty of a pupil to ensure that any canvassing or fund-raising activity on school property by the pupil is carried on only with the consent of the board that operates the school.

(2) No principal, vice-principal or teacher, without the prior approval of the board that operates the school at which they are employed, shall authorize any canvassing or fund-raising activity that involves the participation of one or more pupils attending the school.

Supervision

26. (1) The appropriate supervisory officer, in addition to the duties under the Act, may, during a visit to a school, assume any of the authority and responsibility of the principal of the school.

(2) Psychiatrists, psychologists, social workers and other professional support staff employed by a board shall perform, under the administrative supervision of the appropriate supervisory officer, such duties as are determined by the board and, where such persons are performing their duties in a school, they shall be subject to the administrative authority of the principal of that school.

(3) A supervisory officer who is notified under subsection 11(5) shall forthwith notify the French-language education council or section, English-language education council or section or majority language section of the board, as the case requires, and arrange for,

    (a) the provision of supervision of instruction;
    (b) assistance and advice to the teachers in respect of whom the supervisory officer was given notice under subsection 11(5); and
    (c) the conducting of performance appraisals, where ap-

propriate, of the teachers in respect of whom the supervisory officer was given notice under subsection 11(5),

in the language in which the instruction is provided.

Religion in Schools

27. Sections 28 and 29 do not apply to a Roman Catholic board or to a Protestant separate school board.

O. Reg. 191/04, s. 8

28. (1) A board may provide in grades one to eight and in its secondary schools an optional program of education about religion.

(2) A program of education about religion shall,

(a) promote respect for the freedom of conscience and religion guaranteed by the *Canadian Charter of Rights and Freedoms*; and
(b) provide for the study of different religions and religious beliefs in Canada and the world, without giving primacy to, and without indoctrination in, any particular religion or religious belief.

(3) A program of education about religion shall not exceed sixty minutes of instruction per week in an elementary school.

29. (1) Subject to subsections (2) and (3), a board shall not permit any person to conduct religious exercises or to provide instruction that includes indoctrination in a particular religion or religious belief in a school.

(2) A board may enter into an agreement with a Roman Catholic board that permits the Roman Catholic board to use space and facilities to conduct religious exercises or provide religious instruction for the purposes of the Roman Catholic board.

(3) A board may permit a person to conduct religious exercises or to provide instruction that includes indoctrination in a particular religion or religious belief in a school if,

(a) the exercises are not conducted or the instruction is not provided by or under the auspices of the board;
(b) the exercises are conducted or the instruction is provided on a school day at a time that is before or after the school's instructional program, or on a day that is not a school day;
(c) no person is required by the board to attend the exercises or instruction; and
(d) the board provides space for the exercises or instruction on the same basis as it provides space for other community activities.

(4) A board that permits religious exercises or instruction under subsection (3) shall consider on an equitable basis all requests to conduct religious exercises or to provide instruction under subsection (3).

O. Reg. 191/04, s. 9

Special Education Programs and Services

30. A hearing-handicapped child who has attained the age of two years may be admitted to a special education program for the hearing-handicapped.

31. The maximum enrolment in a special education class shall depend upon the extent of the exceptionalities of the pupils in the class and the special education services that are available to the teacher, but in no case shall the enrolment in a self-contained class exceed,

(a) in a class for pupils who are emotionally disturbed or socially maladjusted, for pupils who have severe learning disabilities, or for pupils who are younger than compulsory school age and have impaired hearing, eight pupils;
(b) in a class for pupils who are blind, for pupils who are deaf, for pupils who have developmental disabilities, or for pupils with speech and language disorders, ten pupils;

(c) in a class for pupils who are hard of hearing, for pupils with limited vision, or for pupils with orthopaedic or other physical handicaps, twelve pupils;

(d) in a class for pupils who have mild intellectual disabilities, twelve pupils in the primary division and sixteen pupils in the junior and intermediate divisions;

(e) in an elementary school class for pupils who are gifted, twenty-five pupils;

(f) in a class for aphasic or autistic pupils, or for pupils with multiple handicaps for whom no one handicap is dominant, six pupils; and

(g) on and after the 1st day of September, 1982, in a class for exceptional pupils consisting of pupils with different exceptionalities, sixteen pupils.

O. Reg. 191/04, s. 10

Family Law Act

R.S.O. 1990, c. F.3 as am. S.O. 1992, c. 32, s. 12; 1993, c. 27, Sched.; 1997, c. 20; 1997, c. 25, Sched. E, s. 1; 1998, c. 26, s. 102; 1999, c. 6, s. 25; 2000, c. 4, s. 12; 2000, c. 33, s. 22 [Not in force at date of publication.]; 2002, c. 17, Sched. F, s. 1; 2002, c. 24, Sched. B, ss. 25, item 9, 37; 2004, c. 31, Sched. 38, s. 2 [Not in force at date of publication.]; 2005, c. 5, s. 27(1), (2) (Fr.), (3)–(5), (6) (Fr.), (7)–(28)

. . .

Definitions

1. (1) In this Act,

"**child**" includes a person whom a parent has demonstrated a settled intention to treat as a child of his or her family, except under an arrangement where the child is placed for valuable consideration in a foster home by a person having lawful custody;

"**child support guidelines**" means the guidelines established by the regulations made under subsections 69(2) and (3);

"**cohabit**" means to live together in a conjugal relationship, whether within or outside marriage;

"**court**" means the Ontario Court (Provincial Division), the Unified Family Court or the Ontario Court (General Division);

"**domestic contract**" means a domestic contract as defined in Part IV (Domestic Contracts);

"**parent**" includes a person who has demonstrated a settled intention to treat a child as a child of his or her family, except under an arrangement where the child is placed for valuable consideration in a foster home by a person having lawful custody;

"**paternity agreement**" means a paternity agreement as defined in Part IV (Domestic Contracts);

"**spouse**" means either of two persons who,

(a) are married to each other, or

(b) have together entered into a marriage that is voidable or void, in good faith on the part of a person relying on this clause to assert any right.

Polygamous marriages

(2) In the definition of "spouse", a reference to marriage includes a marriage that is actually or potentially polygamous, if it was celebrated in a jurisdiction whose system of law recognizes it as valid.

1997, c. 20, s. 1; 1999, c. 6, s. 25(1); 2005, c. 5, s. 27(1)

. . .

Part III
Support Obligations

Definitions

29. In this Part,

"**dependant**" means a person to whom another has an obligation to provide support under this Part;

"**same-sex partner**" [Repealed 2005, c. 5, s. 27(4).]

"**spouse**" means a spouse as defined in subsection 1 (1), and in addition includes either of two persons who are not married to each other and have cohabited,

(a) continuously for a period of not less than three years, or

(b) in a relationship of some permanence, if they are the natural or adoptive parents of a child.

1999, c. 6, s. 25(2); 2005, c. 5, s. 27(4), (5)

Obligation of spouses for support

30. Every spouse has an obligation to provide support for himself or herself and for the other spouse, in accordance with need, to the extent that he or she is capable of doing so.

1999, c. 6, s. 25(3); 2005, c. 5, s. 27(7)

Obligation of parent to support child

31. (1) Every parent has an obligation to provide support for his or her unmarried child who is a minor or is enrolled in a full time program of education, to the extent that the parent is capable of doing so.

Idem

(2) The obligation under subsection (1) does not extend to a child who is sixteen years of age or older and has withdrawn from parental control.

1997, c. 20, s. 2

Obligation of child to support parent

32. Every child who is not a minor has an obligation to provide support, in accordance with need, for his or her parent who has cared for or provided support for the child, to the extent that the child is capable of doing so.

Order for support

33. (1) A court may, on application, order a person to provide support for his or her dependants and determine the amount of support.

Applicants

(2) An application for an order for the support of a dependant may be made by the dependant or the dependant's parent.

Same

(2.1) The *Limitations Act, 2002* applies to an application made by the dependant's parent or by an agency referred to in subsection (3) as if it were made by the dependant himself or herself.

Same

(3) An application for an order for the support of a dependant who is the respondent's spouse or child may also be made by one of the following agencies,

(a) the Ministry of Community and Social Services in the name of the Minister;

(b) a municipality, excluding a lower-tier municipality in a regional municipality;

(c) a district social services administration board under the *District Social Services Administration Boards Act*;

(d) a band approved under section 15 of the *General Welfare Assistance Act*; or

(e) a delivery agent under the *Ontario Works Act, 1997*,

if the agency is providing or has provided a benefit under the *Family Benefits Act*, assistance under the *General Welfare Assistance Act* or the *Ontario Works Act, 1997* or income support under the *Ontario Disability Support Program Act, 1997* in respect of the dependant's support, or if an application for such a benefit or assistance has been made to the agency by or on behalf of the dependant.

Setting aside domestic contract

(4) The court may set aside a provision for support or a waiver of the right to support in a domestic contract or paternity agreement and may determine and order support in an application under subsection (1) although the contract or agreement contains an express provision excluding the application of this section,

(a) if the provision for support or the waiver of the right to support results in unconscionable circumstances;
(b) if the provision for support is in favour of or the waiver is by or on behalf of a dependant who qualifies for an allowance for support out of public money; or
(c) if there is default in the payment of support under the contract or agreement at the time the application is made.

Adding party

(5) In an application the court may, on a respondent's motion, add as a party another person who may have an obligation to provide support to the same dependant.

Idem

(6) In an action in the Ontario Court (General Division), the defendant may add as a third party another person who may have an obligation to provide support to the same dependant.

Purposes of order for support of child

(7) An order for the support of a child should,

(a) recognize that each parent has an obligation to provide support for the child;
(b) apportion the obligation according to the child support guidelines.

Purposes of order for support of spouse

(8) An order for the support of a spouse should,

(a) recognize the spouse's contribution to the relationship and the economic consequences of the relationship for the spouse;
(b) share the economic burden of child support equitably;
(c) make fair provision to assist the spouse to become able to contribute to his or her own support; and

(d) relieve financial hardship, if this has not been done by orders under Parts I (Family Property) and II (Matrimonial Home).

Determination of amount

(9) In determining the amount and duration, if any, of support for a spouse or parent in relation to need, the court shall consider all the circumstances of the parties, including,

(a) the dependant's and respondent's current assets and means;

(b) the assets and means that the dependant and respondent are likely to have in the future;

(c) the dependant's capacity to contribute to his or her own support;

(d) the respondent's capacity to provide support;

(e) the dependant's and respondent's age and physical and mental health;

(f) the dependant's needs, in determining which the court shall have regard to the accustomed standard of living while the parties resided together;

(g) the measures available for the dependant to become able to provide for his or her own support and the length of time and cost involved to enable the dependant to take those measures;

(h) any legal obligation of the respondent or dependant to provide support for another person;

(i) the desirability of the dependant or respondent remaining at home to care for a child;

(j) a contribution by the dependant to the realization of the respondent's career potential;

(k) [Repealed 1997, c. 20, s. 3(3).]

(l) if the dependant is a spouse,

(i) the length of time the dependant and respondent cohabited,

(ii) the effect on the spouse's earning capacity of the responsibilities assumed during cohabitation,
(iii) whether the spouse has undertaken the care of a child who is of the age of eighteen years or over and unable by reason of illness, disability or other cause to withdraw from the charge of his or her parents,
(iv) whether the spouse has undertaken to assist in the continuation of a program of education for a child eighteen years of age or over who is unable for that reason to withdraw from the charge of his or her parents,
(v) any housekeeping, child care or other domestic service performed by the spouse for the family, as if the spouse were devoting the time spent in performing that service in remunerative employment and were contributing the earnings to the family's support,
(v.1) [Repealed 2005, c. 5, s. 27(12).]
(vi) the effect on the spouse's earnings and career development of the responsibility of caring for a child; and

(m) any other legal right of the dependant to support, other than out of public money.

Conduct

(10) The obligation to provide support for a spouse exists without regard to the conduct of either spouse, but the court may in determining the amount of support have regard to a course of conduct that is so unconscionable as to constitute an obvious and gross repudiation of the relationship.

Application of child support guidelines

(11) A court making an order for the support of a child shall do so in accordance with the child support guidelines.

Exception: special provisions

(12) Despite subsection (11), a court may award an amount that is different from the amount that would be determined in accordance with the child support guidelines if the court is satisfied,

(a) that special provisions in an order or a written agreement respecting the financial obligations of the parents, or the division or transfer of their property, directly or indirectly benefit a child, or that special provisions have otherwise been made for the benefit of a child; and

(b) that the application of the child support guidelines would result in an amount of child support that is inequitable given those special provisions.

Reasons

(13) Where the court awards, under subsection (12), an amount that is different from the amount that would be determined in accordance with the child support guidelines, the court shall record its reasons for doing so.

Exception: consent orders

(14) Despite subsection (11), a court may award an amount that is different from the amount that would be determined in accordance with the child support guidelines on the consent of both parents if the court is satisfied that,

(a) reasonable arrangements have been made for the support of the child to whom the order relates; and

(b) where support for the child is payable out of public money, the arrangements do not provide for an amount less than the amount that would be determined in accordance with the child support guidelines.

Reasonable arrangements

(15) For the purposes of clause (14)(a), in determining whether reasonable arrangements have been made for the support of a child,

- (a) the court shall have regard to the child support guidelines; and
- (b) the court shall not consider the arrangements to be unreasonable solely because the amount of support agreed to is not the same as the amount that would otherwise have been determined in accordance with the child support guidelines.

1997, c. 20, s. 3; 1997, c. 25, Sched. E, s. 1; 1999, c. 6, s. 25(4)–(10); 2002, c. 17, Sched. F, s. 1; 2002, c. 24, Sched. B, s. 37; 2005, c. 5, s. 27(8)–(14)

Powers of court

34. (1) In an application under section 33, the court may make an interim or final order,

- (a) requiring that an amount be paid periodically, whether annually or otherwise and whether for an indefinite or limited period, or until the happening of a specified event;
- (b) requiring that a lump sum be paid or held in trust;
- (c) requiring that property be transferred to or in trust for or vested in the dependant, whether absolutely, for life or for a term of years;
- (d) respecting any matter authorized to be ordered under clause 24 (1) (a), (b), (c), (d) or (e) (matrimonial home);
- (e) requiring that some or all of the money payable under the order be paid into court or to another appropriate person or agency for the dependant's benefit;
- (f) requiring that support be paid in respect of any period before the date of the order;
- (g) requiring payment to an agency referred to in subsection 33 (3) of an amount in reimbursement for a benefit

or assistance referred to in that subsection, including a benefit or assistance provided before the date of the order;

(h) requiring payment of expenses in respect of a child's prenatal care and birth;

(i) requiring that a spouse who has a policy of life insurance as defined in the *Insurance Act* designate the other spouse or a child as the beneficiary irrevocably;

> **Proposed Amendment — 34(1)(i)**
>
> (i) requiring that a spouse or same-sex partner who has a policy of life insurance as defined under the *Insurance Act* designate the other spouse or same-sex partner or a child as the beneficiary irrevocably;
>
> 2004, c. 31, Sched. 38, s. 2(3) [Not in force at date of publication.]

(j) requiring that a spouse who has an interest in a pension plan or other benefit plan designate the other spouse or a child as beneficiary under the plan and not change that designation; and

(k) requiring the securing of payment under the order, by a charge on property or otherwise.

Limitation on jurisdiction of Ontario Court (Provincial Division)

(2) The Ontario Court (Provincial Division) shall not make an order under clause (1) (b), (c), (i), (j) or (k) except for the provision of necessities or to prevent the dependant from becoming or continuing to be a public charge, and shall not make an order under clause (d).

Assignment of support

(3) An order for support may be assigned to an agency referred to in subsection 33 (3).

Same

(3.1) An agency referred to in subsection 33(3) to whom an order for support is assigned is entitled to the payments due under the order and has the same right to be notified of and to participate in proceedings under this Act to vary, rescind, suspend or enforce the order as the person who would otherwise be entitled to the payments.

Support order binds estate

(4) An order for support binds the estate of the person having the support obligation unless the order provides otherwise.

Indexing of support payments

(5) In an order made under clause (1) (a), other than an order for the support of a child, the court may provide that the amount payable shall be increased annually on the order's anniversary date by the indexing factor, as defined in subsection (6), for November of the previous year.

Definition

(6) The indexing factor for a given month is the percentage change in the Consumer Price Index for Canada for prices of all items since the same month of the previous year, as published by Statistics Canada.

1997, c. 20, s. 4; 1999, c. 6, s. 25(11); 2005, c. 5, s. 27(15)

. . .

Order restraining harassment

46. (1) On application, a court may make an interim or final order restraining the applicant's spouse or former spouse from molesting, annoying or harassing the applicant or children in the applicant's lawful custody, or from communicating with the applicant or children, except as the order provides,

and may require the applicant's spouse or former spouse to enter into the recognizance that the court considers appropriate.

Offence

(2) A person who contravenes a restraining order is guilty of an offence and upon conviction is liable,

(a) in the case of a first offence, to a fine of not more than $5,000 or to imprisonment for a term of not more than three months, or to both; and

(b) in the case of a second or subsequent offence, to a fine of not more than $10,000 or to imprisonment for a term of not more than two years, or to both.

Proposed Repeal — 46(2)

(2) [Repealed 2000, c. 33, s. 22(1). Not in force at date of publication.]

[Editor's Note: Section 23 of S.O. 2000, c. 33 provides that on a day to be named by proclamation of the Lieutenant Governor, subsection 46(2) of the Family Law Act, R.S.O. 1990, c. F.3 is repealed by subsection 22(1) of S.O. 2000, c. 33. Subsection 22(3) of S.O. 2000, c. 33 provides, however, that despite the repeal of subs. 46(2) of the Family Law Act, any prosecution begun under that subsection before its repeal shall continue as if that subsection were still in force.]

Arrest without warrant

(3) A police officer may arrest without warrant a person the police officer believes on reasonable and probable grounds to have contravened a restraining order.

Existing orders

(4) Subsections (2) and (3) also apply in respect of contraventions, committed, on or after the 1st day of March, 1986, of

restraining orders made under Part II of the *Family Law Reform Act*, being chapter 152 of the Revised Statutes of Ontario, 1980.

Proposed Repeal—46

46. [Repealed 2000, c. 33, s. 22(2). Not in force at date of publication.]

[Editor's Note: Section 23 of S.O. 2000, c. 33 provides that on a day to be named by proclamation of the Lieutenant Governor, s. 46 of the Family Law Act, R.S.O. 1990, c. F.3 is repealed by subsection 22(2) of S.O. 2000, c. 33. Subsection 22(4) of S.O. 2000, c. 33 provides, however, that despite the repeal of s. 46 of the Family Law Act, any prosecution begun under that section before its repeal shall continue as if that subsection were still in force.]

1999, c. 6, s. 25(20); 2005, c. 5, s. 27(23)

. . .

Ontario Regulation 391/97 — Child Support Guidelines made under the *Family Law Act*

O. Reg. 391/97 as am. O. Reg. 26/00 [Amended O. Reg. 126/00.]; 446/01

Objectives

1. The objectives of these guidelines are,

(a) to establish a fair standard of support for children that ensures that they benefit from the financial means of their parents and, in the case of divorce, from the financial means of both spouses after separation;

(b) to reduce conflict and tension between parents or spouses by making the calculation of child support more objective;

(c) to improve the efficiency of the legal process by giving courts, and parents and spouses, guidance in setting the levels of child support and encouraging settlement; and

(d) to ensure consistent treatment of parents or spouses and their children who are in similar circumstances.

Interpretation

Definitions

2. (1) The definitions in this subsection apply in these guidelines.

"child" means,

(a) a child who is a dependant under the Act, or

(b) in cases where the *Divorce Act* (Canada) applies, a child of the marriage under that Act; ("enfant")

"income" means the annual income determined under sections 15 to 20; ("revenu")

"order assignee" means,

(a) an agency to whom an order is assigned under subsection 34(3) of the Act, or

(b) a minister, member or agency referred to in subsection 20.1(1) of the *Divorce Act* (Canada) to whom an order or the support of a child is assigned in accordance with hat subsection; ("cessionnaire de la créance alimentaire")

"parent", in a case to which the Act applies, means a parent to whom section 31 of the Act applies; ("pére ou mére")

"spouse", in a case to which the *Divorce Act* (Canada) applies, has the meaning assigned by subsection 2 of that Act, and includes a former spouse; ("époux")

"table" means,

(a) if the parent or spouse against whom an order is sought ordinarily resides in Ontario at the time of the application, the Child Support Table for Ontario set out in Schedule I to this Regulation,

(b) if the parent or spouse against whom an order is sought ordinarily resides elsewhere in Canada, the table set out in the Federal Child Support Guidelines for the province or territory in which the parent or spouse ordinarily resides at the time of the application,

(c) if the court is satisfied that the province or territory in which the parent or spouse against whom an order is sought ordinarily resides has changed since the time of the application, the table set out in the Federal Child Support Guidelines for the province or territory in which the parent or spouse ordinarily resides at the time the amount of support is determined,

(d) if the court is satisfied that the parent or spouse against whom an order is sought will, in the near future after the amount of support is determined, ordinarily reside in another province or territory than the one in which he or she ordinarily resides at the time the amount of support is determined, the table set out in the Federal

Child Support Guidelines for that other province or territory,

(e) if the parent or spouse against whom an order is sought ordinarily resides outside of Canada or if the ordinary residence of the parent or spouse is unknown,

  (i) the Child support Table for Ontario set out in Schedule I to this Regulation if the other parent or spouse applying for the order resides in Ontario, or

  (ii) the table set out in the Federal Child Support Guidelines for the province or territory in which the parent or spouse applying for the order ordinarily resides. ("table")

Income Tax Act **(Canada)**

(2) Words and expressions that are used in sections 15 to 21 and that are not defined in this section have the meanings assigned to them under the *Income Tax Act* (Canada).

Most current information

(3) Where, for the purposes of these guideline, any amount is determined on the basis of specified information, the most current information must be used.

Application of guidelines

(4) In addition to their application to orders for support of a child, these guidelines apply, with such modifications as the circumstances require, to

(a) interim orders under subsection 34 (1) of the Act or subsections 15.1 (2) and 19 (9) of the *Divorce Act* (Canada);

(b) orders varying a child support order; and

(c) orders referred to in subsection 19 (7) of the *Divorce Act* (Canada).

O. Reg. 446/01, s. 1

Amount of Child Support

Presumptive rule

3. (1) Unless otherwise provided under these guidelines, the amount of an order for the support of a child for children under the age of majority is,

(a) the amount set out in the applicable table, according to the number of children under the age of majority to whom the order relates and the income of the parent or spouse against whom the order is sought; and

(b) the amount, if any, determined under section 7.

Child the age of majority or over

(2) Unless otherwise provided under these guidelines, where a child to whom an order for the support of a child relates is the age of majority or over, the amount of an order for the support of a child is,

(a) the amount determined by applying these guidelines as if the child were under the age of majority; or

(b) if the court considers that approach to be inappropriate, the amount that it considers appropriate, having regard to the condition, means, needs and other circumstances of the child and the financial ability of each parent or spouse to contribute to the support of the child.

Incomes over $150,000

4. Where the income of the parent or spouse against whom an order for the support of a child is sought is over $150,000, the amount of an order for the support of a child is,

(a) the amount determined under section 3; or

(b) if the court considers that amount to be inappropriate,

(i) in respect of the first $150,000 of the parent's or spouse's income, the amount set out in the table for the number of children under the age of majority to whom the order relates,

(ii) in respect of the balance of the parent's or spouse's income, the amount that the court considers appropriate, having regard to the condition, means, needs and other circumstances of the children who are entitled to support and the financial ability of each parent or spouse to contribute to the support of the children, and

(iii) the amount, if any, determined under section 7.

Spouse in place of a parent

5. Where the spouse against whom an order for the support of a child is sought stands in the place of a parent for a child or the parent is not a natural or adoptive parent of the child, the amount of the order is, in respect of that parent or spouse, such amount as the court considers appropriate, having regard to these guidelines and any other parent's legal duty to support the child.

Medical and dental insurance

6. In making an order for the support of a child, where medical or dental insurance coverage for the child is available to either parent or spouse through his or her employer or otherwise at a reasonable rate, the court may order that coverage be acquired or continued.

Special or extraordinary expenses

7. (1) In an order for the support of a child, the court may, on the request of either parent or spouse or of an applicant under section 33 of the Act, provide for an amount to cover all or any portion of the following expenses, which expenses may be estimated, taking into account the necessity of the expense in relation to the child's best interests and the reasonableness of the expense in relation to the means of the parents or spouses

and those of the child and to the spending pattern of the parents or spouses in respect of the child during cohabitation:

   (a) child care expenses incurred as a result of the custodial parent's employment, illness, disability or education or training for employment;

   (b) that portion of the medical and dental insurance premiums attributable to the child;

   (c) health-related expenses that exceed insurance reimbursement by at least $100 annually, including orthodontic treatment, professional counselling provided by a psychologist, social worker, psychiatrist or any other person, physiotherapy, occupational therapy, speech therapy, prescription drugs, hearing aids, glasses and contact lenses;

   (d) extraordinary expenses for primary or secondary school education or for any educational programs that meet the child's particular needs;

   (e) expenses for post-secondary education; and

   (f) extraordinary expenses for extracurricular activities.

Sharing of expense

(2) The guiding principle in determining the amount of an expense referred to in subsection (1) is that the expense is shared by the parents or spouses in proportion to their respective incomes after deducting from the expense, the contribution, if any, from the child.

Subsidies, tax deductions, etc.

(3) In determining the amount of an expense referred to in subsection (1), the court must take into account any subsidies, benefits or income tax deductions or credits relating to the expense, and any eligibility to claim a subsidy, benefit or income tax deduction or credit relating to the expense.

O. Reg. 446/01, s. 2

Split custody

8. Where each parent or spouse has custody of one or more children, the amount of an order for the support of a child is the difference between the amount that each parent or spouse would otherwise pay if such an order were sought against each of the parents or spouses.

Shared custody

9. Where a parent or spouse exercises a right of access to, or has physical custody of, a child for not less than 40 per cent of the time over the course of a year, the amount of the order for the support of a child must be determined by taking into account

(a) the amounts set out in the applicable tables for each of the parents or spouses;
(b) the increased costs of shared custody arrangements; and
(c) the condition, means, needs and other circumstances of each parent or spouse and of any child for whom support is sought.

Undue hardship

10. (1) On the application of either spouse or an applicant under section 33 of the Act, a court may award an amount of child support that is different from the amount determined under any of sections 3 to 5, 8 or 9 if the court finds that the parent or spouse making the request, or a child in respect of whom the request is made, would otherwise suffer undue hardship.

Circumstances that may cause undue hardship

(2) Circumstances that may cause a parent, spouse or child to suffer undue hardship include,

(a) the parent or spouse has responsibility for an unusually

high level of debts reasonably incurred to support the parents or spouses and their children during cohabitation or to earn a living;
(b) the parent or spouse has unusually high expenses in relation to exercising access to a child;
(c) the parent or spouse has a legal duty under a judgment, order or written separation agreement to support any person;
(d) the spouse has a legal duty to support a child, other than a child of the marriage, who is

   (i) under the age of majority, or
   (ii) the age of majority or over but is unable, by reason of illness, disability or other cause, to obtain the necessaries of life;

(e) the parent has a legal duty to support a child, other than the child who is the subject of this application, who is under the age of majority or who is enrolled in a full time course of education;
(f) the parent or spouse has a legal duty to support any person who is unable to obtain the necessaries of life due to an illness or disability.

Standards of living must be considered

(3) Despite a determination of undue hardship under subsection (1), an application under that subsection must be denied by the court if it is of the opinion that the household of the parent or spouse who claims undue hardship would, after determining the amount of child support under any of sections 3 to 8, 8 or 9 have a higher standard of living than the household of the other parent or spouse.

Standards of living test

(4) In comparing standards of living for the purpose of subsection (3), the court may use the comparison of household standards of living test set out in Schedule II.

Reasonable time

(5) Where the court awards a different amount of child support under subsection (1), it may specify, in the order for child support, a reasonable time for the satisfaction of any obligation arising from circumstances that cause undue hardship and the amount payable at the end of that time.

Reasons

(6) Where the court makes an order for the support of a child in a different amount under this section, it must record its reason for doing so.

Elements of an Order for the Support of a Child

Form of payments

11. Where these guidelines apply to orders made under the *Divorce Act* (Canada) section 34 of the Act applies.

Security

12. The court may require in the order for the support of a child that the amount payable under the order be paid or secured, or paid and secured, in the manner specified in the order.

Information to be specified in order

13. An order for the support of a child must include,
  (a) the name and birth date of each child to whom the order relates;
  (b) the income of any parent or spouse whose income is used to determine the amount of the order;
  (c) The amount determined under clause 3 (1) (a) for the number of children to whom the order relates;
  (d) The amount determined under clause 3 (2) (b) for a child the age of majority or over;
  (e) The particulars of any expense described in subsection

7 (1), the child to whom the expense relates and the amount of the expense or, where that amount cannot be determined, the proportion to be paid in relation to the expense; and
(f) The date on which the lump sum or first payment is payable and the day of the month or other time period on which all subsequent payments are to be made.

Variation of Orders for the Support of a Child

Circumstances for variation

14. For the purposes of subsection 37(2.2) of the Act and subsection 17(4) of the *Divorce Act* (Canada), any one of the following constitutes a change of circumstances that gives rise to the making of a variation order:

1. In the case where the amount of child support includes a determination made in accordance with the table, any change in circumstances that would result in a different order for the support of a child or any provision thereof.
2. In the case where the amount of child support does not include a determination made in accordance with a table, any change in the condition, means, needs or other circumstances of either parent or spouse or of any child who is entitled to support.
3. In the case of an order made under the *Divorce Act* (Canada) before May 1, 1997, the coming into force of section 15.1 of that Act, enacted by section 2 of chapter 1 of the Statutes of Canada, (1997).
4. In the case of an order made under the Act, the coming into force of subsection 33 (11) of the Act.

O. Reg. 446/01, s. 3

Income

Determination of annual income

15. (1) Subject to subsection (2), a parent's or spouse's annual income is determined by the court in accordance with sections 16 to 20.

Agreement

(2) Where both parents or spouses agree in writing on the annual income of a parent or spouse, the court may consider that amount to be the parent's or spouse's income for the purposes of these guidelines if the court thinks that the amount is reasonable having regard to the income information provided under section 21.

Calculation of annual income

16. Subject to sections 17 to 20, a parent's or spouse's annual income is determined using the sources of income set out under the heading "Total income" in the T1 General form issued by the Canada Customs and Revenue Agency and is adjusted in accordance with Schedule III.

O. Reg. 446/01, s. 4

Pattern of income

17. (1) If the court is of the opinion that the determination of a parent's or spouse's annual income under section 16 would not be the fairest determination of that income, the court may have regard to the parent's or spouse's income over the last three years and determine an amount that is fair and reasonable in light of any pattern of income, fluctuation in income or receipt of a non-recurring amount during those years.

Non-recurring losses

(2) Where a parent or spouse has incurred a non-recurring capital or business investment loss, the court may, if it is of the

opinion that the determination of the parent's or spouse's annual income under section 16 would not provide the fairest determination of the annual income, choose not to apply sections 6 and 7 of Schedule III, and adjust the amount of the loss, including related expenses and carrying charges and interest expenses, to arrive at such amount as the court considers appropriate.

O. Reg. 446/01, s. 5

Shareholder, director or officer

18. (1) Where a parent or spouse is a shareholder, director or officer of a corporation and the court is of the opinion that the amount of the parent's or spouse's annual income as determined under section 16 does not fairly reflect all the money available to the parent or spouse for the payment of child support, the court may consider the situations described in section 17 and determine the parent's or spouse's annual income to include,

(a) all or part of the pre-tax income of the corporation, and of any corporation that is related to that corporation, for the most recent taxation year; or

(b) an amount commensurate with the services that the parent or spouse provides the corporation, provided that the amount does not exceed the corporation's pre-tax income.

Adjustment to corporation's pre-tax income

(2) In determining the pre-tax income of a corporation for the purposes of subsection (1), all amounts paid by the corporation as salaries, wages or management fees, or other payments or benefits, to or on behalf of person with whom the corporation does not deal at arm's length must be added to the pre-tax income, unless the parent or spouse establishes that the payments were reasonable in the circumstances.

Imputing income

19. (1) The court may impute such amount of income to a parent or spouse as it considers appropriate in the circumstances, which circumstances include,

- (a) the parent or spouse is intentionally under-employed or unemployed, other than where the under- employment or unemployment is required by the needs of any child or by the reasonable educational or health needs of the parent or spouse;
- (b) the parent or spouse is exempt from paying federal or provincial income tax;
- (c) the parent or spouse lives in a country that has effective rates of income tax that are significantly lower than those in Canada;
- (d) it appears that income has been diverted which would affect the level of child support to be determined under these guidelines;
- (e) the parent's or spouse's property is not reasonably utilized to generate income;
- (f) the parent or spouse has failed to provide income information when under a legal obligation to do so;
- (g) the parent or spouse unreasonably deducts expenses from income;
- (h) the parent or spouse derives a significant portion of income from dividends, capital gains or other sources that are taxed at a lower rate than employment or business income or that are exempt from tax; and
- (i) the parent or spouse is a beneficiary under a trust and is or will be in receipt of income or other benefits from the trust.

Reasonableness of expenses

(2) For the purpose of clause (1) (g), the reasonableness of an expense deduction is not solely governed by whether the deduction is permitted under the *Income Tax Act* (Canada).

O. Reg. 446/01, s. 6

Non-resident

20. Where a parent or spouse is a non-resident of Canada, the parent's or spouse's annual income is determined s though the parent or spouse were a resident of Canada.

Income Information

Obligation of applicant

21. (1) A parent or spouse who is applying for an order for the support of a child and whose income information is necessary to determine the amount of the order must include with the application,

(a) a copy of every personal income tax return filed by the parent or spouse for each of the three most recent taxation years;

(b) a copy of every notice of assessment and reassessment issued to the parent or spouse for each of the three most recent taxation years;

(c) where the parent or spouse is an employee, the most recent statement of earnings indicating the total earnings paid in the year to date, including overtime, or, where such a statement is not provided by the employer, a letter from the parent's or spouse's employer setting out that information including the parent's or spouse's rate of annual salary or remuneration;

(d) where the parent or spouse is self-employed, for the three most recent taxation years,

(i) the financial statements of the parent's or spouse's business or professional practice, other than a partnership, and

(ii) a statement showing a breakdown of all salaries, wages, management fees or other payments or benefit paid to, or on behalf of, persons or corporations with whom the parent or spouse does not deal at arm's length;

(e) where the parent or spouse is a partner in partnership, confirmation of the parent's or spouse's income and draw from, and capital in, the partnership for its three most recent taxation years;

(f) where the parent or spouse controls a corporation, for its three most recent taxation years,

   (i) the financial statements of the corporation and its subsidiaries, and
   (ii) a statement showing a breakdown of all salaries, wages, management fees or other payments or benefits paid to, or on behalf of, persons or corporations with whom the corporation, and every related corporation, does not deal at arm's length;

(g) where the parent or spouse is a beneficiary under a trust, a copy of the trust settlement agreement and copies of the trust's three most recent financial statements; and

(h) in addition to any information that must be included under clauses (c) to (g), where the parent or spouse receives income from employment insurance, social assistance, a pension, workers compensation, disability payments or any other source, the most recent statement of income indicating the total amount of income from the applicable source during the current year or, if such a statement is not provided, a letter from the appropriate authority stating the required information.

Obligation of respondent

(2) A parent or spouse who is served with an application for an order for the support of a child and whose income information is necessary to determine the amount of the order, must, within 30 days after the application is served if the parent or spouse resides in Canada or the United States or within 60

days if the parent or spouse resides elsewhere, or such other time limit as the court specifies, provide the court, as well as the other spouse, an applicant under section 33 of the Act or the order assignee with the documents referred to in subsection (1).

Special expenses or undue hardship

(3) Where, in the course of proceedings in respect of an application for an order for the support of a child, a parent or spouse requests an amount to cover expenses referred to in subsection 7 (1) or pleads undue hardship, the parent or spouse who would be receiving the amount of child support must, within 30 days after the amount is sought or undue hardship is pleaded if the parent or spouse resides in Canada or the United States or within 60 days if the parent or spouse resides elsewhere, or such other time limit as the court specifies, provide the court and the other parent or spouse with the documents referred to in subsection (1).

Income over $150,000

(4) Where, in the course of proceedings in respect of an application for an order for the support of a child, it is established that the income of the parent or spouse who would be paying the amount of child support is greater than $150,000, the other parent or spouse must, within 30 days after the income is established to be greater than $150,000 if the other parent or spouse resides in Canada or the United States or within 60 days if the other parent or spouse resides elsewhere, or such other time limit as the court specifies, provide the court and the other parent or spouse with the documents referred to in subsection (1).

O. Reg. 446/01, s. 7

. . .

Constitution Act, 1982

R.S.C. 1985, Appendix II, No. 44

En. Canada Act 1982 (U.K.), c. 11 as am. Constitution Amendment Proclamation, 1983, SI/93-54, Schedule, SI/84-102, Schedule B **Constitution Act, 1982**

Part I — Canadian Charter of Rights and Freedoms

Whereas Canada is founded upon principles that recognize the supremacy of God and the rule of law:

Guarantee of Rights and Freedoms

Rights and freedoms in Canada

1. The *Canadian Charter of Rights and Freedoms* guarantees the rights and freedoms set out in it subject only to such reasonable limits prescribed by law as can be demonstrably justified in a free and democratic society.

Fundamental Freedoms

Fundamental freedoms

2. Everyone has the following fundamental freedoms:
   (a) freedom of conscience and religion;
   (b) freedom of thought, belief, opinion and expression, including freedom of the press and other media of communication;
   (c) freedom of peaceful assembly; and
   (d) freedom of association.

Democratic Rights

Democratic rights of citizens

3. Every citizen of Canada has the right to vote in an election of members of the House of Commons or of a legislative assembly and to be qualified for membership therein.

Maximum duration of legislative bodies

4. (1) No House of Commons and no legislative assembly shall continue for longer than five years from the date fixed for the return of the writs at a general election of its members.

Continuation in special circumstances

(2) In time of real or apprehended war, invasion or insurrection, a House of Commons may be continued by Parliament and a legislative assembly may be continued by the legislature beyond five years if such continuation is not opposed by the votes of more than one-third of the members of the House of Commons or the legislative assembly, as the case may be.

Annual sitting of legislative bodies

5. There shall be a sitting of Parliament and of each legislature at least once every twelve months.

Mobility Rights

Mobility of citizens

6. (1) Every citizen of Canada has the right to enter, remain in and leave Canada.

Rights to move and gain livelihood

(2) Every citizen of Canada and every person who has the status of a permanent resident of Canada has the right

  (a) to move to and take up residence in any province; and
  (b) to pursue the gaining of a livelihood in any province.

Limitation

(3) The rights specified in subsection (2) are subject to

  (a) any laws or practices of general application in force in a province other than those that discriminate among persons primarily on the basis of province of present or previous residence; and

(b) any laws providing for reasonable residency requirements as a qualification for the receipt of publicly provided social services.

Affirmative action programs

(4) Subsections (2) and (3) do not preclude any law, program or activity that has as its object the amelioration in a province of conditions of individuals in that province who are socially or economically disadvantaged if the rate of employment in that province is below the rate of employment in Canada.

Legal Rights

Life, liberty and security of person

7. Everyone has the right to life, liberty and security of the person and the right not to be deprived thereof except in accordance with the principles of fundamental justice.

Search or seizure

8. Everyone has the right to be secure against unreasonable search or seizure.

Detention or imprisonment

9. Everyone has the right not to be arbitrarily detained or imprisoned.

Arrest or detention

10. Everyone has the right on arrest or detention

   (a) to be informed promptly of the reasons therefor;
   (b) to retain and instruct counsel without delay and to be informed of that right; and
   (c) to have the validity of the detention determined by way

of *habeas corpus* and to be released if the detention is not lawful.

Proceedings in criminal and penal matters

11. Any person charged with an offence has the right

(a) to be informed without unreasonable delay of the specific offence;

(b) to be tried within a reasonable time;

(c) not to be compelled to be a witness in proceedings against that person in respect of the offence;

(d) to be presumed innocent until proven guilty according to law in a fair and public hearing by an independent and impartial tribunal;

(e) not to be denied reasonable bail without just cause;

(f) except in the case of an offence under military law tried before a military tribunal, to the benefit of trial by jury where the maximum punishment for the offence is imprisonment for five years or a more severe punishment;

(g) not to be found guilty on account of any act or omission unless, at the time of the act or omission, it constituted an offence under Canadian or international law or was criminal according to the general principles of law recognized by the community of nations;

(h) if finally acquitted of the offence, not to be tried for it again and, if finally found guilty and punished for the offence, not to be tried or punished for it again; and

(i) if found guilty of the offence and if the punishment for the offence has been varied between the time of commission and the time of sentencing, to the benefit of the lesser punishment.

Treatment or punishment

12. Everyone has the right not to be subjected to any cruel and unusual treatment or punishment.

Self-crimination

13. A witness who testifies in any proceedings has the right not to have any incriminating evidence so given used to incriminate that witness in any other proceedings, except in a prosecution for perjury or for the giving of contradictory evidence.

Interpreter

14. A party or witness in any proceedings who does not understand or speak the language in which the proceedings are conducted or who is deaf has the right to the assistance of an interpreter.

Equality Rights

Equality before and under law and equal protection and benefit of law

15. (1) Every individual is equal before and under the law and has the right to the equal protection and equal benefit of the law without discrimination and, in particular, without discrimination based on race, national or ethnic origin, colour, religion, sex, age or mental or physical disability.

Affirmative action programs

(2) Subsection (1) does not preclude any law, program or activity that has as its object the amelioration of conditions of disadvantaged individuals or groups including those that are disadvantaged because of race, national or ethnic origin, colour, religion, sex, age or mental or physical disability.

Official Languages of Canada

Official languages of Canada

16. (1) English and French are the official languages of Canada and have equality of status and equal rights and priv-

ileges as to their use in all institutions of the Parliament and government of Canada.

Official languages of New Brunswick

(2) English and French are the official languages of New Brunswick and have equality of status and equal rights and privileges as to their use in all institutions of the legislature and government of New Brunswick.

Advancement of status and use

(3) Nothing in this Charter limits the authority of Parliament or a legislature to advance the equality of status or use of English and French.

English and French linguistic communities in New Brunswick

16.1 (1) The English linguistic community and the French linguistic community in New Brunswick have equality status and equal rights and privileges, including the right to distinct educational institutions and such distinct cultural institiutions as are necessary for the preservation and promotion of those communities.

Role of the legislature and government of New Brunswick

(2) The role of the legislature and government of New Brunswick to preserve and promote the status, rights and privileges referred to in subsection (1) is affirmed.

SI/93-54, Sched., s. 1

Proceedings of Parliament

17. (1) Everyone has the right to use English or French in any debates and other proceedings of Parliament.

Proceedings of New Brunswick legislature

(2) Everyone has the right to use English or French in any debates and other proceedings of the legislature of New Brunswick.

Parliamentary statutes and records

18. (1) The statutes, records and journals of Parliament shall be printed and published in English and French and both language versions are equally authoritative.

New Brunswick statutes and records

(2) The statutes, records and journals of the legislature of New Brunswick shall be printed and published in English and French and both language versions are equally authoritative.

Proceedings in courts established by Parliament

19. (1) Either English or French may be used by any person in, or in any pleading in or process issuing from, any court established by Parliament.

Proceedings in New Brunswick courts

(2) Either English or French may be used by any person in, or in any pleading in or process issuing from, any court of New Brunswick.

Communications by public with federal institutions

20. (1) Any member of the public in Canada has the right to communicate with, and to receive available services from, any head or central office of an institution of the Parliament or government of Canada in English or French, and has the same right with respect to any other office of any such institution where

>   (a) there is a significant demand for communications with and services from that office in such language; or

(b) due to the nature of the office, it is reasonable that communications with and services from that office be available in both English and French.

Communications by public with New Brunswick institutions

(2) Any member of the public in New Brunswick has the right to communicate with, and to receive available services from, any office of an institution of the legislature or government of New Brunswick in English or French.

Continuation of existing Constitutional provisions

21. Nothing in sections 16 to 20 abrogates or derogates from any right, privilege or obligation with respect to the English and French languages, or either of them, that exists or is continued by virtue of any other provision of the Constitution of Canada.

Rights and privileges preserved

22. Nothing in sections 16 to 20 abrogates or derogates from any legal or customary right or privilege acquired or enjoyed either before or after the coming into force of this Charter with respect to any language that is not English or French.

Minority Language Educational Rights

Language of instruction

23. (1) Citizens of Canada

(a) whose first language learned and still understood is that of the English or French linguistic minority population of the province in which they reside, or
(b) who have received their primary school instruction in Canada in English or French and reside in a province where the language in which they received that instruc-

tion is the language of the English or French linguistic minority population of the province,
have the right to have their children receive primary and secondary school instruction in that language in that province.

Continuity of language instruction

(2) Citizens of Canada of whom any child has received or is receiving primary or secondary school instruction in English or French in Canada, have the right to have all their children receive primary and secondary school instruction in the same language.

Application where numbers warrant

(3) The right of citizens of Canada under subsections (1) and (2) to have their children receive primary and secondary school instruction in the language of the English or French linguistic minority population of a province

- (a) applies wherever in the province the number of children of citizens who have such a right is sufficient to warrant the provision to them out of public funds of minority language instruction; and
- (b) includes, where the number of those children so warrants, the right to have them receive that instruction in minority language educational facilities provided out of public funds.

Enforcement

Enforcement of guaranteed rights and freedoms

24. (1) Anyone whose rights or freedoms, as guaranteed by this Charter, have been infringed or denied may apply to a court of competent jurisdiction to obtain such remedy as the court considers appropriate and just in the circumstances.

Exclusion of evidence bringing administration of justice into disrepute

(2) Where, in proceedings under subsection (1), a court concludes that evidence was obtained in a manner that infringed or denied any rights or freedoms guaranteed by this Charter, the evidence shall be excluded if it is established that, having regard to all the circumstances, the admission of it in the proceedings would bring the administration of justice into disrepute.

General

Aboriginal rights and freedoms not affected by Charter

25. The guarantee in this Charter of certain rights and freedoms shall not be construed so as to abrogate or derogate from any aboriginal treaty or other rights or freedoms that pertain to the aboriginal peoples of Canada including

(a) any rights or freedoms that have been recognized by the Royal Proclamation of October 7, 1763; and
(b) any rights or freedoms that now exist by way of land claims agreements or may be so acquired.

SI/84–102, Schedule.

Other rights and freedoms not affected by Charter

26. The guarantee in this Charter of certain rights and freedoms shall not be construed as denying the existence of any other rights or freedoms that exist in Canada.

Multicultural heritage

27. This Charter shall be interpreted in a manner consistent with the preservation and enhancement of the multicultural heritage of Canadians.

Rights guaranteed equally to both sexes

28. Notwithstanding anything in this Charter, the rights and freedoms referred to in it are guaranteed equally to male and female persons.

Rights respecting certain schools preserved

29. Nothing in this Charter abrogates or derogates from any rights or privileges guaranteed by or under the Constitution of Canada in respect of denominational, separate or dissentient schools.

Application to Territories and territorial authorities

30. A reference in this Charter to a province or to the legislative assembly or legislature of a province shall be deemed to include a reference to the Yukon Territory and the Northwest Territories, or to the appropriate legislative authority thereof, as the case may be.

Legislative powers not extended

31. Nothing in this Charter extends the legislative powers of any body or authority.

Application of Charter

Application of Charter

32. (1) This Charter applies

(a) to the Parliament and government of Canada in respect of all matters within the authority of Parliament including all matters relating to the Yukon Territory and Northwest Territories; and

(b) to the legislature and government of each province in respect of all matters within the authority of the legislature of each province.

Exception

(2) Notwithstanding subsection (1), section 15 shall not have effect until three years after this section comes into force.

Exception where express declaration

33. (1) Parliament or the legislature of a province may expressly declare in an Act of Parliament or of the legislature, as the case may be, that the Act or a provision thereof shall operate notwithstanding a provision included in section 2 or sections 7 to 15 of this Charter.

Operation of exception

(2) An Act or a provision of an Act in respect of which a declaration made under this section is in effect shall have such operation as it would have but for the provision of this Charter referred to in the declaration.

Five year limitation

(3) A declaration made under subsection (1) shall cease to have effect five years after it comes into force or on such earlier date as may be specified in the declaration.

Re-enactment

(4) Parliament or a legislature of a province may re-enact a declaration made under subsection (1).

Five year limitation

(5) Subsection (3) applies in respect of a re-enactment made under subsection (4).

Citation

Citation

34. This Part may be cited as the *Canadian Charter of Rights and Freedoms.*

. . .

VII General

Primacy of Constitution of Canada

52. (1) The Constitution of Canada is the supreme law of Canada, and any law that is inconsistent with the provisions of the Constitution is, to the extent of the inconsistency, of no force or effect.

Constitution of Canada

(2) The Constitution of Canada includes

(a) the *Canada Act 1982*, including this Act;
(b) the Acts and orders referred to in the schedule; and
(c) any amendment to any Act or order referred to in paragraph (a) or (b).

Amendments to the Constitution of Canada

(3) Amendments to the Constitution of Canada shall be made only in accordance with the authority contained in the Constitution of Canada.

. . .

Divorce Act

R.S.C. 1985, c. 3 (2nd Supp.) as am. R.S.C. 1985, c. 27 (2nd Supp.), s. 10; S.C. 1990, c. 18, ss. 1, 2; 1992, c. 51, s. 46; 1993, c. 8, ss. 1–5; 1993, c. 28, s. 78 (Sched. III, items 41–43) [Amended 1998, c. 15, ss. 22, 23; 1999, c. 3, s. 12 (Sched., item 11).]; 1997, c. 1, ss. 1–15; 1998, c. 30, ss. 13(f) (Fr.), 15(f); 1999, c. 3, s. 61; 1999, c. 31, s. 74 (Fr.); 2002, c. 7, ss. 158–160; 2002, c. 8, s. 183(1)(i)

Short Title

Short title

1. This Act may be cited as the *Divorce Act*.

Interpretation

Definitions

2. (1) In this Act,

"age of majority", in respect of a child, means the age of majority as determined by the laws of the province where the child ordinarily resides, or, if the child ordinarily resides outside of Canada, eighteen years of age;

"appellate court", in respect of an appeal from a court, means the court exercising appellate jurisdiction with respect to that appeal;

"applicable guidelines", means

(a) where both spouses or former spouses are ordinarily resident in the same province at the time an application for a child support order or a variation order in respect of a child support order is made, or the amount of a child support order is to be recalculated pursuant to section 25.1, and that province has been designated by an order made under subsection (5), the laws of the province specified in the order, and

(b) in any other case, the Federal Child Support Guidelines;

"child of the marriage" means a child of two spouses or former spouses who, at the material time,

(a) is under the age of majority and who has not withdrawn from their charge, or

(b) is the age of majority or over and under their charge but unable, by reason of illness, disability or other cause, to withdraw from their charge or to obtain the necessaries of life;

"child support order", means an order made under subsection 15.1(1);

"corollary relief proceeding" means a proceeding in a court in which either or both former spouses seek a child support order, a spousal support order or a custody order;

"court", in respect of a province, means

(a) for the Province of Ontario, the Superior Court of Justice,

(a.1) for the Province of Prince Edward Island or Newfoundland, the trial division of the Supreme Court of the Province,

(b) for the Province of Quebec, the Superior Court,

(c) for the Province of Nova Scotia and British Columbia, the Supreme Court of the Province,

(d) for the Province of New Brunswick, Manitoba, Saskatchewan or Alberta, the Court of Queen's Bench for the Province, and

(e) for Yukon or the Northwest Territories, the Supreme Court, and in Nunavut, the Nunavut Court of Justice,

and includes such other court in the province the judges of which are appointed by the Governor General as is designated by the Lieutenant Governor in Council of the province as a court for the purposes of this Act;

"custody" includes care, upbringing and any other incident of custody;

"custody order" means an order made under subsection 16(1);

"divorce proceeding" means a proceeding in a court in which either or both spouses seek a divorce alone or together with a child support order, a spousal support order or a custody order;

"Federal Child Support Guidelines" means the guidelines made under section 26.1;

"provincial child support service" means any service, agency or body designated in an agreement with a province under subsection 25.1(1);

"spousal support order" means an order made under subsection 15.2(1);

"spouse" means either of a man or woman who are married to each other;

"support order" means a child support order or a spousal support order;

"variation order" means an order made under subsection 17(1);

"variation proceeding" means a proceeding in a court in which either or both former spouses seek a variation order.

Child of the marriage

(2) For the purposes of the definition "child of the marriage" in subsection (1), a child of two spouses or former spouses includes

(a) any child for whom they both stand in the place of parents; and
(b) any child of whom one is the parent and for whom the other stands in the place of a parent.

Term not restrictive

(3) The use of the term "application" to describe a proceeding under this Act in a court shall not be construed as limiting the name under which and the form and manner in which that proceeding may be taken in that court, and the name, manner and form of the proceeding in that court shall be such as is provided for by the rules regulating the practice and procedure in that court.

Idem

(4) The use in section 21.1 of the terms "affidavit" and "pleadings" to describe documents shall not be construed as limiting the name that may be used to refer to those documents in a court and the form of those documents, and the name and form of the documents shall be such as is provided for by the rules regulating the practice and procedure in that court.

Provincial child support guidelines

(5) The Governor in Council may, by order, designate a province for the purposes of the definition "applicable guidelines" in subsection (1) if the laws of the province establish comprehensive guidelines for the determination of child support that deal with the matters referred to in section 26.1. The order shall specify the laws of the province that constitute the guidelines of the province.

Amendments included

(6) The guidelines of a province referred to in subsection (5) include any amendments made to them from time to time.
R.S.C. 1985, c. 27 (2nd Supp.), s. 10 (Sched., item 7(1), (2)); 1990, c. 18, s. 1; 1992, c. 51, s. 46; 1993, c. 28, s. 78 (Sched. III, item 41) [Repealed 1999, c. 3, s. 12 (Sched., item 11).]; 1997, c. 1, s. 1; 1998, c. 30, s. 15(f); 1999, c. 3, s. 61; 2002, c. 7, s. 158

. . .

Divorce

Divorce

8. (1) A court of competent jurisdiction may, on application by either or both spouses, grant a divorce to the spouse or spouses on the ground that there has been a breakdown of their marriage.

Breakdown of marriage

(2) Breakdown of a marriage is established only if

(a) the spouses have lived separate and apart for at least one year immediately preceding the determination of the divorce proceeding and were living separate and apart at the commencement of the proceeding; or
(b) the spouse against whom the divorce proceeding is brought has, since celebration of the marriage,

  (i) committed adultery, or
  (ii) treated the other spouse with physical or mental cruelty of such a kind as to render intolerable the continued cohabitation of the spouses.

Calculation of period of separation

(3) For the purposes of paragraph (2)(a),

(a) spouses shall be deemed to have lived separate and apart for any period during which they lived apart and either of them had the intention to live separate and apart from the other; and
(b) a period during which spouses have lived separate and apart shall not be considered to have been interrupted or terminated

  (i) by reason only that either spouse has become incapable of forming or having an intention to continue to live separate and apart or of continuing to live separate and apart of the spouse's own volition, if it appears to the court that the separation would probably have continued if the spouse had not become so incapable, or

(ii) by reason only that the spouses have resumed cohabitation during a period of, or periods totalling, not more than ninety days with reconciliation as its primary purpose.

. . .

**Corollary Relief
Interpretation**

Definition of "spouse"

15. In section 15.1 to 16, **"spouse"** has the meaning assigned by subsection 2(1), and includes a former spouse.

1997, c. 1, s. 2

. . .

Custody Orders

Order for custody

16. (1) A court of competent jurisdiction may, on application by either or both spouses or by any other person, make an order respecting the custody of or the access to, or the custody of and access to, any or all children of the marriage.

Interim order for custody

(2) Where an application is made under subsection (1), the court may, on application by either or both spouses or by any other person, make an interim order respecting the custody of or the access to, or the custody of and access to, any or all children of the marriage pending determination of the application under subsection (1).

Application by other person

(3) A person, other than a spouse, may not make an application under subsection (1) or (2) without leave of the court.

Joint custody or access

(4) The court may make an order under this section granting custody of, or access to, any or all children of the marriage to any one or more persons.

Access

(5) Unless the court orders otherwise, a spouse who is granted access to a child of the marriage has the right to make inquiries, and to be given information, as to the health, education and welfare of the child.

Terms and conditions

(6) The court may make an order under this section for a definite or indefinite period or until the happening of a specified event and may impose such other terms, conditions or restrictions in connection therewith as it thinks fit and just.

Order respecting change of residence

(7) Without limiting the generality of subsection (6), the court may include in an order under this section a term requiring any person who has custody of a child of the marriage and who intends to change the place of residence of that child to notify, at least thirty days before the change or within such other period before the change as the court may specify, any person who is granted access to that child of the change, the time at which the change will be made and the new place of residence of the child.

Factors

(8) In making an order under this section, the court shall take into consideration only the best interests of the child of

the marriage as determined by reference to the condition, means, needs and other circumstances of the child.

Past conduct

(9) In making an order under this section, the court shall not take into consideration the past conduct of any person unless the conduct is relevant to the ability of that person to act as a parent of a child.

Maximum contact

(10) In making an order under this section, the court shall give effect to the principle that a child of the marriage should have as much contact with each spouse as is consistent with the best interests of the child and, for that purpose, shall take into consideration the willingness of the person for whom custody is sought to facilitate such contact.

. . .

Youth Criminal Justice Act

An Act in respect of criminal justice for young persons and to amend and repeal other Acts

S.C. 2002, c. 1 as am. S.C. 2002, c. 7, s. 274; 2002, c. 13, s. 91; 2004, c. 11, ss. 48, 49; 2005, c. 22, s. 63

. . .

Short Title

Short title

1. This Act may be cited as the *Youth Criminal Justice Act*.

Interpretation

Definitions

2. (1) The definitions in this subsection apply in this Act.

"adult" means a person who is neither a young person nor a child. "adulte"

"adult sentence", in the case of a young person who is found guilty of an offence, means any sentence that could be imposed on an adult who has been convicted of the same offence. "peine applicable aux adultes"

"Attorney General" means the Attorney General as defined in section 2 of the *Criminal Code*, read as if the reference in that definition to "proceedings" were a reference to "proceedings or extrajudicial measures", and includes an agent or delegate of the Attorney General. "procureur général"

"child" means a person who is or, in the absence of evidence to the contrary, appears to be less than twelve years old. "enfant"

"conference" means a group of persons who are convened to give advice in accordance with section 19. "groupe consultatif" "**confirmed delivery service**" means certified or registered mail or any other method of service that provides proof of delivery. "service de messagerie"

"**custodial portion**", with respect to a youth sentence imposed on a young person under paragraph 42(2)(n), (o), (q) or (r), means the period of time, or the portion of the young person's youth sentence, that must be served in custody before he or she begins to serve the remainder under supervision in the community subject to conditions under paragraph 42(2)(n) or under conditional supervision under paragraph 42(2)(o), (q) or (r). "période de garde"

"**disclosure**" means the communication of information other than by way of publication. "communication"

"**extrajudicial measures**" means measures other than judicial proceedings under this Act used to deal with a young person alleged to have committed an offence and includes extrajudicial sanctions. "mesures extrajudiciaires"

"**extrajudicial sanction**" means a sanction that is part of a program referred to in section 10. "sanction extrajudiciaire"

"**offence**" means an offence created by an Act of Parliament or by any regulation, rule, order, by-law or ordinance made under an Act of Parliament other than an ordinance of the Northwest Territories or a law of the Legislature of Yukon or the Legislature for Nunavut. "infraction"

"**parent**" includes, in respect of a young person, any person who is under a legal duty to provide for the young person or any person who has, in law or in fact, the custody or control of the young person, but does not include a person who has the custody or control of the young person by reason only of proceedings under this Act. "père ou mère" ou "père et mère"

"**pre-sentence report**" means a report on the personal and family history and present environment of a young person made in accordance with section 40. "rapport prédécisionnel"

"presumptive offence" means

(a) an offence committed, or alleged to have been committed, by a young person who has attained the age of fourteen years, or, in a province where the lieutenant governor in council has fixed an age greater than fourteen years under section 61, the age so fixed, under one of the following provisions of the *Criminal Code*:

   (i) section 231 or 235 (first degree murder or second degree murder within the meaning of section 231),
   (ii) section 239 (attempt to commit murder),
   (iii) section 232, 234 or 236 (manslaughter), or
   (iv) section 273 (aggravated sexual assault); or

(b) a serious violent offence for which an adult is liable to imprisonment for a term of more than two years committed, or alleged to have been committed, by a young person after the coming into force of section 62 (adult sentence) and after the young person has attained the age of fourteen years, or, in a province where the lieutenant governor in council has fixed an age greater than fourteen years under section 61, the age so fixed, if at the time of the commission or alleged commission of the offence at least two judicial determinations have been made under subsection 42(9), at different proceedings, that the young person has committed a serious violent offence. "infraction désignée"

"provincial director" means a person, a group or class of persons or a body appointed or designated by or under an Act of the legislature of a province or by the lieutenant governor in council of a province or his or her delegate to perform in that province, either generally or in a specific case, any of the duties or functions of a provincial director under this Act. "directeur provincial" ou "directeur" "**publication**" means the communication of information by making it known or accessible to the general public through any means, including print, radio or television broadcast, telecommunication or electronic means. "publication"

"**record**" includes any thing containing information, regardless of its physical form or characteristics, including microform, sound recording, videotape, machine-readable record, and any copy of any of those things, that is created or kept for the purposes of this Act or for the investigation of an offence that is or could be prosecuted under this Act. "dossier"

"**review board**" means a review board referred to in subsection 87(2). "commission d'examen"

"**serious violent offence**" means an offence in the commission of which a young person causes or attempts to cause serious bodily harm. "infraction grave avec violence"

"**young person**" means a person who is or, in the absence of evidence to the contrary, appears to be twelve years old or older, but less than eighteen years old and, if the context requires, includes any person who is charged under this Act with having committed an offence while he or she was a young person or who is found guilty of an offence under this Act. "adolescent"

"**youth custody facility**" means a facility designated under subsection 85(2) for the placement of young persons and, if so designated, includes a facility for the secure restraint of young persons, a community residential centre, a group home, a child care institution and a forest or wilderness camp. "lieu de garde"

"**youth justice court**" means a youth justice court referred to in section 13. "tribunal pour adolescents"

"**youth justice court judge**" means a youth justice court judge referred to in section 13. "juge du tribunal pour adolescents"

"**youth sentence**" means a sentence imposed under section 42, 51 or 59 or any of sections 94 to 96 and includes a confirmation or a variation of that sentence. *"peine spécifique"*
"**youth worker**" means any person appointed or designated, whether by title of youth worker or probation officer or by any other title, by or under an Act of the legislature of a province or by the lieutenant governor in council of a province or his or her delegate to perform in that province, either generally or in a specific case, any of the duties or functions of a youth worker under this Act. *"délégué à la jeunesse"*

Words and expressions

(2) Unless otherwise provided, words and expressions used in this Act have the same meaning as in the *Criminal Code*.

Descriptive cross-references

(3) If, in any provision of this Act, a reference to another provision of this Act or a provision of any other Act is followed by words in parentheses that are or purport to be descriptive of the subject-matter of the provision referred to, those words form no part of the provision in which they occur but are inserted for convenience of reference only.

2002, c. 7, s. 274

Declaration of Principle

Policy for Canada with respect to young persons

3. (1) The following principles apply in this Act:

(a) the youth criminal justice system is intended to

　(i) prevent crime by addressing the circumstances underlying a young person's offending behaviour,

　(ii) rehabilitate young persons who commit offences and reintegrate them into society, and

　(iii) ensure that a young person is subject to meaningful consequences for his or her offence in order to promote the long-term protection of the public;

(b) the criminal justice system for young persons must be separate from that of adults and emphasize the following:

    (i) rehabilitation and reintegration,

    (ii) fair and proportionate accountability that is consistent with the greater dependency of young persons and their reduced level of maturity,

    (iii) enhanced procedural protection to ensure that young persons are treated fairly and that their rights, including their right to privacy, are protected,

    (iv) timely intervention that reinforces the link between the offending behaviour and its consequences, and

    (v) the promptness and speed with which persons responsible for enforcing this Act must act, given young persons' perception of time;

(c) within the limits of fair and proportionate accountability, the measures taken against young persons who commit offences should

    (i) reinforce respect for societal values,

    (ii) encourage the repair of harm done to victims and the community,

    (iii) be meaningful for the individual young person given his or her needs and level of development and, where appropriate, involve the parents, the extended family, the community and social or other agencies in the young person's rehabilitation and reintegration, and

    (iv) respect gender, ethnic, cultural and linguistic differences and respond to the needs of aboriginal young persons and of young persons with special requirements; and

(d) special considerations apply in respect of proceedings against young persons and, in particular,
- (i) young persons have rights and freedoms in their own right, such as a right to be heard in the course of and to participate in the processes, other than the decision to prosecute, that lead to decisions that affect them, and young persons have special guarantees of their rights and freedoms,
- (ii) victims should be treated with courtesy, compassion and respect for their dignity and privacy and should suffer the minimum degree of inconvenience as a result of their involvement with the youth criminal justice system,
- (iii) victims should be provided with information about the proceedings and given an opportunity to participate and be heard, and
- (iv) parents should be informed of measures or proceedings involving their children and encouraged to support them in addressing their offending behaviour.

Act to be liberally construed

(2) This Act shall be liberally construed so as to ensure that young persons are dealt with in accordance with the principles set out in subsection (1).

Part 1 — Extrajudicial Measures

Principles and Objectives

Declaration of principles

4. The following principles apply in this Part in addition to the principles set out in section 3:
- (a) extrajudicial measures are often the most appropriate and effective way to address youth crime;
- (b) extrajudicial measures allow for effective and timely

interventions focused on correcting offending behaviour;

(c) extrajudicial measures are presumed to be adequate to hold a young person accountable for his or her offending behaviour if the young person has committed a nonviolent offence and has not previously been found guilty of an offence; and

(d) extrajudicial measures should be used if they are adequate to hold a young person accountable for his or her offending behaviour and, if the use of extrajudicial measures is consistent with the principles set out in this section, nothing in this Act precludes their use in respect of a young person who

(i) has previously been dealt with by the use of extrajudicial measures, or

(ii) has previously been found guilty of an offence.

Objectives

5. Extrajudicial measures should be designed to

(a) provide an effective and timely response to offending behaviour outside the bounds of judicial measures;

(b) encourage young persons to acknowledge and repair the harm caused to the victim and the community;

(c) encourage families of young persons—including extended families where appropriate—and the community to become involved in the design and implementation of those measures;

(d) provide an opportunity for victims to participate in decisions related to the measures selected and to receive reparation; and

(e) respect the rights and freedoms of young persons and be proportionate to the seriousness of the offence.

Warnings, Cautions and Referrals

Warnings, cautions and referrals

6. (1) A police officer shall, before starting judicial proceedings or taking any other measures under this Act against a young person alleged to have committed an offence, consider whether it would be sufficient, having regard to the principles set out in section 4, to take no further action, warn the young person, administer a caution, if a program has been established under section 7, or, with the consent of the young person, refer the young person to a program or agency in the community that may assist the young person not to commit offences.

Saving

(2) The failure of a police officer to consider the options set out in subsection (1) does not invalidate any subsequent charges against the young person for the offence.

Police cautions

7. The Attorney General, or any other minister designated by the lieutenant governor of a province, may establish a program authorizing the police to administer cautions to young persons instead of starting judicial proceedings under this Act.

Crown cautions

8. The Attorney General may establish a program authorizing prosecutors to administer cautions to young persons instead of starting or continuing judicial proceedings under this Act.

Evidence of measures is inadmissible

9. Evidence that a young person has received a warning, caution or referral mentioned in section 6, 7 or 8 or that a police officer has taken no further action in respect of an offence, and evidence of the offence, is inadmissible for the purpose of

proving prior offending behaviour in any proceedings before a youth justice court in respect of the young person.

Extrajudicial Sanctions

Extrajudicial sanctions

10. (1) An extrajudicial sanction may be used to deal with a young person alleged to have committed an offence only if the young person cannot be adequately dealt with by a warning, caution or referral mentioned in section 6, 7 or 8 because of the seriousness of the offence, the nature and number of previous offences committed by the young person or any other aggravating circumstances.

Conditions

(2) An extrajudicial sanction may be used only if

(a) it is part of a program of sanctions that may be authorized by the Attorney General or authorized by a person, or a member of a class of persons, designated by the lieutenant governor in council of the province;

(b) the person who is considering whether to use the extrajudicial sanction is satisfied that it would be appropriate, having regard to the needs of the young person and the interests of society;

(c) the young person, having been informed of the extrajudicial sanction, fully and freely consents to be subject to it;

(d) the young person has, before consenting to be subject to the extrajudicial sanction, been advised of his or her right to be represented by counsel and been given a reasonable opportunity to consult with counsel;

(e) the young person accepts responsibility for the act or omission that forms the basis of the offence that he or she is alleged to have committed;

(f) there is, in the opinion of the Attorney General, sufficient evidence to proceed with the prosecution of the offence; and

(g) the prosecution of the offence is not in any way barred at law.

Restriction on use

(3) An extrajudicial sanction may not be used in respect of a young person who

(a) denies participation or involvement in the commission of the offence; or
(b) expresses the wish to have the charge dealt with by a youth justice court.

Admissions not admissible in evidence

(4) Any admission, confession or statement accepting responsibility for a given act or omission that is made by a young person as a condition of being dealt with by extrajudicial measures is inadmissible in evidence against any young person in civil or criminal proceedings.

No bar to judicial proceedings

(5) The use of an extrajudicial sanction in respect of a young person alleged to have committed an offence is not a bar to judicial proceedings under this Act, but if a charge is laid against the young person in respect of the offence,

(a) the youth justice court shall dismiss the charge if it is satisfied on a balance of probabilities that the young person has totally complied with the terms and conditions of the extrajudicial sanction; and
(b) the youth justice court may dismiss the charge if it is satisfied on a balance of probabilities that the young person has partially complied with the terms and conditions of the extrajudicial sanction and if, in the opinion of the court, prosecution of the charge would be unfair having regard to the circumstances and the

young person's performance with respect to the extrajudicial sanction.

Laying of information, etc.

(6) Subject to subsection (5) and section 24 (private prosecutions only with consent of Attorney General), nothing in this section shall be construed as preventing any person from laying an information or indictment, obtaining the issue or confirmation of any process or proceeding with the prosecution of any offence in accordance with law.

Notice to parent

11. If a young person is dealt with by an extrajudicial sanction, the person who administers the program under which the sanction is used shall inform a parent of the young person of the sanction.

Victim's right to information

12. If a young person is dealt with by an extrajudicial sanction, a police officer, the Attorney General, the provincial director or any organization established by a province to provide assistance to victims shall, on request, inform the victim of the identity of the young person and how the offence has been dealt with.

Part 2 — Organization of Youth Criminal Justice System

Youth Justice Court

Designation of youth justice court

13. (1) A youth justice court is any court that may be established or designated by or under an Act of the legislature of a province, or designated by the Governor in Council or the lieutenant governor in council of a province, as a youth justice court for the purposes of this Act, and a youth justice court judge is a person who may be appointed or designated as a

judge of the youth justice court or a judge sitting in a court established or designated as a youth justice court.

Deemed youth justice court

(2) When a young person elects to be tried by a judge without a jury, the judge shall be a judge as defined in section 552 of the *Criminal Code*, or if it is an offence set out in section 469 of that Act, the judge shall be a judge of the superior court of criminal jurisdiction in the province in which the election is made. In either case, the judge is deemed to be a youth justice court judge and the court is deemed to be a youth justice court for the purpose of the proceeding.

Deemed youth justice court

(3) When a young person elects or is deemed to have elected to be tried by a court composed of a judge and jury, the superior court of criminal jurisdiction in the province in which the election is made or deemed to have been made is deemed to be a youth justice court for the purpose of the proceeding, and the superior court judge is deemed to be a youth justice court judge.

Court of record

(4) A youth justice court is a court of record.

. . .

Part 6 — Publication, Records and Information

. . .

Disclosure of Information in a Record

Disclosure by peace officer during investigation

125. (1) A peace officer may disclose to any person any information in a record kept under section 114 (court records)

or 115 (police records) that it is necessary to disclose in the conduct of the investigation of an offence.

Disclosure by Attorney General

(2) The Attorney General may, in the course of a proceeding under this Act or any other Act of Parliament, disclose the following information in a record kept under section 114 (court reports) or 115 (police records):

(a) to a person who is a co-accused with the young person in respect of the offence for which the record is kept, any information contained in the record; and

(b) to an accused in a proceeding, if the record is in respect of a witness in the proceeding, information that identifies the witness as a young person who has been dealt with under this Act.

Information that may be disclosed to a foreign state

(3) The Attorney General or a peace officer may disclose to the Minister of Justice of Canada information in a record that is kept under section 114 (court records) or 115 (police records) to the extent that it is necessary to deal with a request to or by a foreign state under the *Mutual Legal Assistance in Criminal Matters Act*, or for the purposes of any extradition matter under the *Extradition Act*. The Minister of Justice of Canada may disclose the information to the foreign state in respect of which the request was made, or to which the extradition matter relates, as the case may be.

Disclosure to insurance company

(4) A peace officer may disclose to an insurance company information in a record that is kept under section 114 (court records) or 115 (police records) for the purpose of investigating a claim arising out of an offence committed or alleged to have been committed by the young person to whom the record relates.

Preparation of reports

(5) The provincial director or a youth worker may disclose information contained in a record if the disclosure is necessary for procuring information that relates to the preparation of a report required by this Act.

Schools and others

(6) The provincial director, a youth worker, the Attorney General, a peace officer or any other person engaged in the provision of services to young persons may disclose to any professional or other person engaged in the supervision or care of a young person – including a representative of any school board or school or any other educational or training institution – any information contained in a record kept under sections 114 to 116 if the disclosure is necessary

- (a) to ensure compliance by the young person with an authorization under section 91 or an order of the youth justice court;
- (b) to ensure the safety of staff, students or other persons; or
- (c) to facilitate the rehabilitation of the young person.

Information to be kept separate

(7) A person to whom information is disclosed under subsection (6) shall

- (a) keep the information separate from any other record of the young person to whom the information relates;
- (b) ensure that no other person has access to the information except if authorized under this Act, or if necessary for the purposes of subsection (6); and
- (c) destroy their copy of the record when the information is no longer required for the purpose for which it was disclosed.

Time limit

(8) No information may be disclosed under this section after the end of the applicable period set out in subsection 119(2) (period of access to records).

. . .

INDEX

ABDUCTION OF CHILD
extradition as remedy, 159-160
Hague Convention as remedy, 156-158
parental
   Criminal Code sanctions, 158-159
   preventing child from returning to Canada, 157-158
   where permission initially granted, 157
safeguards against, 158

ABUSE, *see also* **DISCIPLINE OF CHILDREN**
child-rearing practices affecting understanding of, 20-22
physical discipline, boundaries of, 21
reporting, *see also* REPORTING OBLIGATIONS
   analysis of report, 37
   legislative amendments, 15
   obligation generally, 13-14, 48-52
   penalty for failure to report, 15, 52-56
student by employee of school board, 267-269

ACCESS
decision-making during, 154-155
defined, 149-150
rights of access parent, 113, 150-151
   lack of decision-making power, 152
   limitation upon, 131
   make inquiries, 150
   maximum contact principle, 151
   notice of change in residence, 150
   visit with child, 151
supervised access, 155-156

ADD-ONS, *see* **CHILD SUPPORT GUIDELINES**

ADULT CHILDREN
entitlement to child support, 293, 295

AGE OF MAJORITY
capacity to enter contract, 8
citizenship rights, 8
incorporation of company, rights, 9
restricted movies, 9

ALCOHOLIC BEVERAGES
right to consume, 10

APPRENTICE HUNTER SAFETY CARD
child over age 12, 4

ASSESSMENT REPORT
content, 321
court-ordered, 323
   child protection proceedings, 323-324
   custody proceedings, 324-326
   weight in court proceeding, 321-322
parenting ability, 323-324
process of preparing, 321, 322
purpose, 321, 322

BEST INTERESTS OF CHILD
Charter and, 91
child protection proceedings
   application to, 29-31
   definition for purposes of, 33
custody disputes, factors
   Children's Law Reform Act, 125
   Divorce Act, 125
   domestic violence, history of, 127-128

past conduct, 127-129
"primary parent" approach, 137-139
status quo, 137-139, *see also* STATUS QUO
historical development of concept
child's preference for one parent, 119
gender vs. ability to parent, 121
maternal preference by court, 120
paternal viewpoint, 117-118
tender years approach, 118-119
legislative directions regarding, 121
comparison between legislation, 124-129
test for custody, as, 114, 115
discretion in applying, 126
objective application of, 126

BULLYING
cyber-bullying, 277
anti-bullying websites, 278
defined, 278
interventions, effective, 278-279
legal constraints, 278
victims redress
civil lawsuits, 279
human rights complaints, 279-281

CHARTER OF RIGHTS AND FREEDOMS
balancing mechanisms within, 86
child abuse and, 99-104
best interests and, 99-100
principles of fundamental justice, and, 99
sexual abuse, 100-101
school context, 102-103
child protection and, 95-99
legislative amendments reflecting, 96

parental rights, 92-95, 96, 98
procedural rights of children, 96-98
controversy over, 86
discipline of children and, 223-230
family and, 88-95
access and religious expression, 89-91
best interests test and, 91
child protection and parents' "security of the person", 92-95
infringement of individual rights, 87
limitation of rights within, 86
patriation of constitution and, 85
schools and, 238-240
shifting power to courts, 85-86
unborn children and, 104-108, *see also* UNBORN CHILDREN
wardship proceedings
issues raised by, 32

CHILD, *see also* **CHILDREN**
age 7 and over, 2
age 12 and under, 3
age 15, 6
age 16, 6-8
age 17, 8
age 18, 8-9
age 19, 9-10
apprenticeship, 7, 8
capacity to enter contract, 8
defined generally, 1-2
child protection purposes, 34-35
context-specific, 10
driving licence, 7
employment of, 7
under age 10, 2
over age 12, 3-4
over age 14, 5
under age 21, 10-11
withdrawal from parental control, 6

CHILD AND FAMILY SERVICES ACT
abuse, reporting obligations, 14-16
age 16, effect upon child protection, 6
apprehension of "child in need of protection", 3
code for protecting children, as, 24
consent of child to adoption, 2
provisions related to children over 12, 4
purpose, 24-25
withdrawal from parental control, 6

CHILD PROTECTION
applications
    adjournment, 41
        care of child during, 41-42
        least disruptive order, 42
    apprehension of child, 40
    commencement of, 39-40
    first appearance in court, 40
    hearing, 41, 43
    plan of care by Society, 45-46
    potential orders, 43-45
    status review application, 46-47
"child in need of protection"
    defined, 17-23
    cultural differences affecting, 20
    emotional harm, 20
    legislative provisions, 17-19
    physical harm, 19-20
    subjective values regarding, 17, 19
    value differences respecting, 20-21
constitutional responsibility for, 14
disposition where finding made
    balancing of values, 31
    best interests of child, role of, 29-31
    Crown wardship, 47-48
    factors considered by court, 28-29, 44-45
    potential orders, 43-45
distinguished from criminal law, 33-34
distinguished from custody, 26-27, 114-117
from person having charge of child, 35-36
investigative tools for assessment, 23
legislation
    amendments regarding child abuse reporting, 15
    defined, 14
    timelines and limitation periods, 46-48
legal representation of child, 329-330
minimum standard of care vs. best interests, 30
parental rights and, 32
"security of the person" *Charter* challenges, 92-95
    to choose or refuse medical treatment, 92-94
school boards, statutory duties regarding, 254-258
self-represented parents in proceedings, 16
voluntary intervention to protect, 37-38

CHILD PROTECTION AGENCY
abuse report, analysis of, 37
agent of state, as, 32
Children's Aid Societies, 26
Crown wards, obligation to secure adoption, 48
investigative tools of assessment, 23
limits upon, 23
plan for child's care, 45-46
powers under CFSA, 23, 25
right to documents in possession of third party, 318-320

service provider, as, 37-38
voluntary intervention by, 37-38
youth court, involvement in, 188

CHILDREN, *see also* CHILD;
   STUDENTS
affected by changes, 112
born within or outside marriage
   no distinction, 110
discipline, *see* DISCIPLINE OF
   CHILDREN
evidence of, *see* EVIDENCE
legal and social rights, 110
raising
   biological parents, by, 110
   cultural differences in, 110
   traditional family unit, by, 110
representation, *see*
   REPRESENTATION OF
   CHILDREN
school attendance, *see* SCHOOLS
unborn, *see* UNBORN CHILDREN
vulnerability of, 110

CHILDREN'S LAW REFORM ACT
application of, 121-122
custody, standing to apply, 124, 143-145
   grandparents, 143
   strangers, 143

CHILD SUPPORT
absolute nature of obligation, 287
amount, determination of, *see*
   CHILD SUPPORT GUIDELINES
child support guidelines, *see* CHILD
   SUPPORT GUIDELINES
enforcement
   Family Responsibility Office, 305
   operation of system, 305
   penalties for failure to pay, 306
   statute governing, 305
   support deduction orders, 305

entitlement
   adult children, 293, 295
   "child of the marriage" under
      Divorce Act, 292-293
   "child" under *Family Law Act*,
      293
   child withdrawn from parental
      control, 293, 294
   legislative authority for, 288-289, 290
   tax consequences, 290-291

CHILD SUPPORT GUIDELINES
add-ons
   benefit of child, for, 302
   expenses amounting to, 300
   related to individual child, 299
   shared in proportion to parents'
      incomes, 300-301
adult children
   discretion to depart from table
      amount, 295
basis for, 291, 294
extraordinary expenses, *see* add-ons
financial disclosure
   imputing income, where no
      disclosure, 301
   obligation of both parents, 301-302
objective or rationale, 291-292, 296-297
payor parent earning in excess of
   $150,000
   benefit to other parent rather
      than child, 296
   discretion to depart from table
      amount, 295-296
   presumption favouring table
      amount, 296-297
predictability engendered by, 304
presumptive rule generally, 294-295
shared custody
   defined, 303

INDEX ♦ 545

discretion to depart from table amount, 303
split custody
set off of two parents, 302
tax changes coinciding with, 304
undue hardship claims
circumstances causing hardship, 298
payor parent with low income, 297
standards of living of parents considered, 298-299
test for, 297-299

COMMUNITY COLLEGES
admission ages, 10

CRIMINAL CODE
application to children over 14, 5
parental child abduction provisions, 158-159
use of force against children, limits upon, 216-223

CROWN WARDSHIP
access by parents after, 47
considerations before ordering, 47
obligations of Society, 48
when permitted, 47

CUSTODY
case by case consideration, 109
child protection, distinguished from, 26-27, 114-117
courts, choice of 123
decision-making vs. time spent with child, 152
de facto custody, 145
discretion, 109, 126
defined, 113, 114, 129-130, 131
equal entitlement of parents, 140
enforcement, international, 156-157, *see also* HAGUE CONVENTION

incidents of
defined, 136-137
generally, 115
joint custody, 131-134, *see also* JOINT CUSTODY
legal representation of child, 331-332
legislation, *see* CHILDREN'S LAW REFORM ACT; DIVORCE ACT
orders
interim, 146-147
final, 147
variation, 148-149
rights and responsibilities of custodian, 144
separation agreements, 146
standing to apply for, 124
test for, 114, *see also* BEST INTERESTS OF CHILD
time-sharing, 153
variation, 148-149

DAYCARE PROVIDERS, *see also* **REPORTING OBLIGATIONS**
impermissible disciplinary measures, 230-233
observations during family break-up, 113, 143
witness, as, 113
reporting suspected abuse or neglect
consequences for failure to report, 52-56
obligation, 14-16, 48-52
relationship to children's aid society after reporting, 41
what and when to report, 19-23

DAY NURSERIES ACT
children applicable to, 2

DISCIPLINE OF CHILDREN
Criminal Code provisions, 216-223
balancing protection of child and caregivers, 216

Charter challenges to, 223-230
general principles, 217
history, 218-223
interpretation by Supreme Court of Canada, 230-233
justification for use of force, 217
reasonableness of use of force, 217-218
expulsion from school, 271-277
impermissible disciplinary measures, 230-233
need for boundaries generally, 215-216

DISCLOSURE OF INFORMATION
requests of professionals for information, 307-308
health information, 308
privacy laws and protocols for releasing, 308
suspected child abuse, 307

DIVORCE
history of, in Canada, 111

DIVORCE ACT
application of, 121-122
custody, standing to apply, 124
paramount over provincial legislation, 123

DOMESTIC VIOLENCE
custody factor, as, 127-128

EDUCATION, *see* **DISCIPLINE; SCHOOLS; SCHOOL BOARDS; TEACHERS**

EDUCATION ACT
truancy under, 3

EVIDENCE
Charter challenges to, 57

children
ability to swear oath, 62-63, 64
credibility, assessment of, 67-69, 80, 81-82
cross-examination, 79-80
general approach, 59-60
hearsay evidence of
admissibility, 69-72
caution with respect to, 73-74
child's wishes in custody dispute, 82-83
necessity and reliability test, 69-72
weight, 72-74
promise to tell truth, 65-67
testimonial competence, 63-65
trial judge's role, 67
unsworn testimony, 65-67
videotaped evidence, 74-79
voir dire, 77-79
discretion to exclude, 58
family law, 58-59, 60
material evidence, 60
relevance as primary rule, 57, 58, 60
rules governed by common law, 57
statutes governing, 61

EXTRADITION
remedy for child abduction, as, 159-160

EXTRA-JUDICIAL MEASURES, *see* **YOUTH CRIMINAL JUSTICE ACT**

FAMILY
break-up
affect upon children, 112-113
lack of agreement among adults, 113
changes in nature of, 87, 110-111

INDEX ♦ 547

Charter and, 88-95, *see also* CHARTER
   OF RIGHTS AND FREEDOMS
traditional family unit
   changes to, 87-88, 111
   family laws protecting, 88
   raising children, 110

FAMILY LAW ACT
withdrawal from parental control, 6

**FAMILY RESPONSIBILITY
   OFFICE**
enforcement of child support, 305

FORCE, USE OF, *see* **DISCIPLINE
   OF CHILDREN**

GRANDPARENTS
application for custody, access, 143-144

GUILY PLEA
youth court, in, 183-184

HAGUE CONVENTION
applicability of, 157-158
defined, 156
enforcement of custody, as, 156-157
objectives, 157
scope, 157

HUMAN RIGHTS LEGISLATION
redress for bullying, use as, 279-281
schools, application to, 240-241

INTERNATION ABDUCTION, *see*
   ABDUCTION OF CHILD

JOINT CUSTODY
conditions necessary for, 132-133
defined, 131
distinguished from sole custody, 132-134

"forced" joint custody, 133, 135
legislative authority for, 132
nature of arrangements, 133-134
parallel parenting as form of, 134, *see
   also* PARALLEL PARENTING

JUSTICE OF THE PEACE, 177

MARRIAGE
changes in concept of, 111
same-sex marriage
   recognition of, 112

**MATERIAL CHANGE IN
   CIRCUMSTANCES**
change in custody, as ground for, 148-149
defined, 148
potential changes, 149

*OCCUPATIONAL HEALTH AND
   SAFETY ACT*
application to children over 14, 5

**OFFICE OF THE CHILDREN'S
   LAWYER**
representation of children, 327

PARALLEL PARENTING
benefit to children, 135
communication book, use of, 134
defined, 134
detailed residential arrangements, 134
when appropriate, 134, 135-136

PARENTAL ABDUCTION, *see*
   ABDUCTION OF CHILD

PRIVACY PROTECTION
youth records under YCJA, 209-213
   non-disclosure exceptions, 210-212

PROVINCIAL OFFENCES ACT
no conviction under age 12, 3

RECORDS IN POSSESSION OF THIRD PARTIES
civil matters, obtaining
  children's aid society, right to, 318-320
  court-ordered access, 319-320
  pre-trial disclosure of documents, 318-320
criminal matters, obtaining
  application, steps in determining, 312-315
  balancing interests of accused person and victim, 312
  hearing, 315-316
  notice to parties affected, 314
  O'Connor application generally, 311-317
  reasons for obtaining, 311
  release of records to accused person, 317
  relevancy of documents, 313-314
  review by court to determine relevancy, 316-317
student
  school board duties, 258-260

REPORTING OBLIGATIONS
child abuse or neglect, 48-52, 307
  amendments to legislation, 52
  civil liability for failure to report, 55
  contents of guidance sessions, 103
  penalties for failure to report, 54-56
  police officers, 52-53
  professionals generally, 48-56
  psychiatrists, 53-54
  sexual abuse in school context, 102-103

REPRESENTATION OF CHILDREN
age of child, effect upon, 328
child protection proceedings, 329-330
custody proceedings, 331-332
Office of the Children's Lawyer, 327
role of child's lawyer, 327, 328-329

SCHOOL BOARDS
abuse of student by employee, legal liability, 267-269
  sexual assault by school janitor, 267-268
administration, 252-253
bullying, *see* BULLYING
common law obligations, 261
  abuse by employee, 267-269
  duty of care beyond classroom, 264-267
  duty to protect student from harm, 262-263, 267-269
  presumption of position of trust and authority, 265
  vicarious liability for actions of employees, 263, 267-269
defined, 247-248
discipline of students, 271-277
duties, 246-247
  curriculum content, 248-249
  instruction, providing, 248
  principals, teachers, hiring of, 249
employees, statutory duties of, 253-254
expulsion of students, 271-277
health and safety responsibilities, 269-270
in loco parentis to students, 261
powers, 270
special education, 249-252
  autistic children, 251-252
  funding controversy, 251-252

identification of students in
    need, 250-251
  process leading to, 250-252
  types of exceptional students,
    249-250
statutory duties
  child protection, 254-258
  employees, 253-254
  student records, 258-260

SCHOOLS
attendance
  enforcing, 244-245
  mandatory, 242
  right, 242-244
boards, duties, 246-247
bullying, 277-281, see also BULLYING
Charter application to, 238-240
defined, 235
denominational, 236
duties of educational institutions,
    245-246
human rights legislation, application
    to, 240-241
laws governing, 236-237
minority language education rights,
    236-237
parental rights, 284-285
role, 236
trespassing on school property,
    preventing, 281-284

SEPARATION AGREEMENTS
custody provisions, 146

SHARED CUSTODY
Child Support Guidelines purposes
  effect upon child support, 303

SPLIT CUSTODY
Child Support Guidelines purposes
  effect upon child support, 302

STATUS QUO
as factor in custody disputes
  advantages, 141
  deference to by courts, 140
  determining, 142-143
  generally, 137-139
  legislation governing, 139-141
  power struggle between parents,
    exacerbating, 141
changes to, 144-145
de facto custody, creation by, 145

STUDENTS
abuse by employee of school board,
    267-279
bullying, 277-281, see also BULLYING
expulsion from school, 271-277
records, duties of board, 258-260
school attendance, 242-245
special education, 249-252
truancy, 3

SUBPOENA, *see* **SUMMONS**

SUMMONS
defined, 308, 309
failure to obey, 310-311
obligation to attend, 310
purpose, 308
records in possession of third
  parties, 314
service, 309-310
types of proceedings, 309

SUPERVISED ACCESS, 155-156

SUPPORT DEDUCTION ORDERS
as method of support enforcement,
    305

TAX CONSEQUENCES
Child Support guidelines, coinciding
  with, 304

child support, prior to guidelines, 290-291

TEACHERS, *see also* **SCHOOLS**
common law duties, *see* SCHOOL BOARDS
impermissible disciplinary measures, 230-233
observations during family break-up, 113
off-duty conduct, 266-267
reporting suspected abuse or neglect, *see also* REPORTING OBLIGATIONS
    consequences for failure to report, 52-56
    obligation, 14-16, 48-52, 307
    relationship to children's aid society after reporting, 41
    what and when to report, 19-23
standards of behaviour expected, 265-266
witness, as, 113, 143

THEATRES ACT
application to children over 14, 5

TIME-SHARING
custody and access, as feature of, 153
formula for, 153

UNBORN CHILDREN
Charter rights
    abortion, 104-105
    defining personhood, 104, 105-106
    fetus, legal status of, 104-106
    in vitro embryo, 108
    parens patriae jurisdiction of court, 107-108
    pregnant woman, right to control body, 104
    primacy of mother's rights, 107
    suit for pre-natal injuries, 106
        against own mother, 106-107
        against third party, 106
Child and Family Services Act, under 6
Family Law Act, under, 6

UNDUE HARDSHIP
as ground for reduction of child support, 297-299

YOUTH COURT
child welfare agencies, involvement, 188
contrasted with adult court, 174-175
court clerk, role of, 178
judicial measures
    counsel, right to, 179
    first court appearance, 182
    guilty pleas, 183-184
    medical or psychological evaluation, 185-188
    non-disclosure of identity of young person, 180
        exceptions, 180-181
    presumptive offences, 183
    pre-trial detention, 181
    proceeding to trial, 188
    procedural protections, 179-180
    release from custody, 184-185
jurisdiction, 175
    age unknown at time of alleged offence, 176
justice of the peace, role of, 177
    bail hearings, 177
offences drawn from other statutes, 176
powers, 175-176
procedure, 176, *see also* judicial measures
sentencing, 190-213, *see also* YOUTH SENTENCING
trial
    mode of, 188-189

proceeding to, 188
rules for conduct of, 189-190

YOUTH CRIMINAL JUSTICE ACT,
see also **YOUTH COURT; YOUTH SENTENCING**
application, 162
conferences, 174
contrasted with former *YOA*, 162-165
Criminal Code, application to, 162
extra-judicial measures, 167-172
  advantages, 169
  aim, 168-169
  criteria for use, 168
  defined, 167-168
  police decision to use, 169
  role in youth criminal justice, 172
  success of, 172
extra-judicial sanctions
  admissions inadmissible as evidence, 171
  criminal charges in addition to, 171
  defined, 170
  when invoked, 170-171
guiding principles, 165-166
history
  Juvenile Delinquents Act, 161
  Young Offenders Act, 161-162
organization of legislation, 166-167
records, protection of privacy, 209-213
significance of age 12 under, 3
significance of age 14 under, 5
youth justice committees, 172-174

YOUTH SENTENCING
adult sentences
  criteria for imposing, 204, 206-207
  custody, 208-209
  factors relevant to, 207
  length, 208
  murder and related crimes, 205
  "non-presumptive offences", for, 206
  principles considered, 206-207
  process, 205-206
  publication ban not applicable to, 208
  serious violent offences, 205-206
alternatives to, 200-203
conditional sentences, 196-197
custodial sentences
  generally, 208-209
  length of, 199
external input
  conference recommendations, 196
  generally, 193-194
  medical or psychological report, 195
  parents, 196
  pre-sentence report, 194-195
  records, documents, 198
factors considered, 192-193
general principles, 192
purpose, 191
"reasonable alternative to custody", 198